P9-DTK-651

Know Your Antiques®

By the same authors

DICTIONARY OF MARKS—POTTERY AND PORCELAIN
A DIRECTORY OF AMERICAN SILVER, PEWTER AND SILVER PLATE
AMERICAN COUNTRY FURNITURE 1780–1875

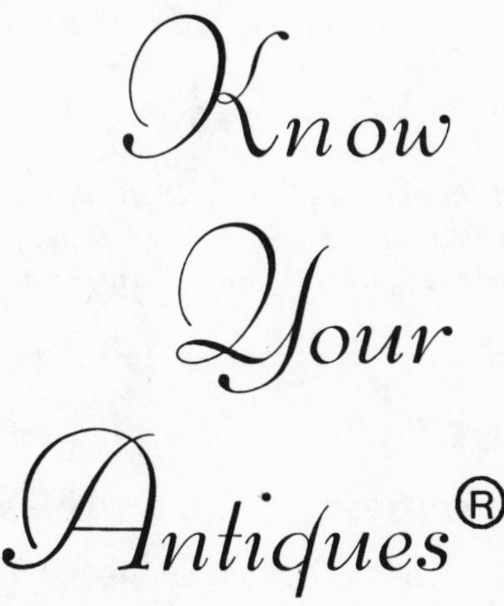

Know Your Antiques®

Revised

HOW TO RECOGNIZE AND EVALUATE ANY ANTIQUE—LARGE OR SMALL—LIKE AN EXPERT

by Ralph and Terry Kovel

CROWN PUBLISHERS, INC., NEW YORK

Special thanks are given to Dr. William Macey, who took all photographs in this book that are not credited to a specific collection; to Joyce Enterline, who helped with the manuscript, and to Lawrence J. Ungar, who did the drawings.

BELATED DEDICATION – SEVERAL BOOKS LATER

Writers are made—not born—and can never exist without encouragement. Thus:

To Anne and Bob Levine and Anne Udin, who were the first to think we had a book;

To Bob Simon and Herbert Michelman of Crown Publishers, Inc., who knew we had a book;

To Louis B. Seltzer and Thomas Boardman of the *Cleveland Press,* who thought we had a newspaper column;

To Henry Martin, Bruce Horton, Frank Clark, and Phillip Reed of Register and Tribune Syndicate, who made the column a national feature

this book is dedicated

and

to Lee and Kim, who suffer with us through every word we write

LIBRARY OF CONGRESS CATALOG CARD NUMBER: 67–17713
ISBN: 0-517-513218
PRINTED IN THE UNITED STATES OF AMERICA
Fifteenth Printing, April, 1978

Contents

Acknowledgments vi
Introduction vii
1. Pottery and Porcelain 1
2. Glass 55
3. Bottles 100
4. Furniture and Furniture Construction 117
5. Lighting Devices 147
6. Silver 162
7. Pewter 190
8. Tinware and Toleware 197
9. Clocks 202
10. Needlework 208
11. Jewelry 235
12. Prints, Paintings, Pictures to Hang 240
13. Paper Antiques 276
14. Store Stuff 279
15. Books 290
16. Music 293
17. Toys 298
18. Other Collectible Items 320
19. Price Guides 321
20. Antique Publications 330
21. Bibliography of General Books About Antiques 332
22. Collectors Groups 335
Index 344

Acknowledgments

ILLUSTRATIONS AND INFORMATION have come from many sources during the twelve years we have been writing our syndicated newspaper column "Know Your Antiques." The information was collected, filed, and considered when this manuscript was begun. A few of the museums, historical societies, antique dealers, and collectors who helped us in the search are listed below:

Arnold Bakers, Inc.; Harry M. Buten, Buten Museum of Wedgwood; Association for Preservation of Virginia Antiquities; Baltimore Museum of Art; The Art Institute of Chicago; Carol Hortense Macht, Cincinnati Art Museum; Dr. Harold Collins; The Corning Museum of Glass; Christian Rohlfing, Administrator, The Cooper Union for the Advancement of Science and Art; Dedham Historical Society; J. P. Spang III, Associate Curator, Heritage Foundation of Deerfield, Massachusetts; Eleutherian Mills–Hagley Foundation Incorporated; Dean A. Fales, Jr., Director, Essex Institute; Mr. and Mrs. Paul Greaser; James E. Jones, Henry Ford Museum and Greenfield Village; The Home Insurance Company; The Index of American Design; The Smithsonian Institution; The International Silver Company; Miss Mildred Goosman, Joslyn Art Museum; Edgar deN. Mayhew, Lyman Allyn Museum; The Metropolitan Museum of Art; The Minneapolis Institute of Arts; William Rockhill Nelson Gallery of Art; Charles Terwilliger, President, National Association of Watch and Clock Collectors; J. J. Heslin, Director, The New-York Historical Society; Ohio Historical Society; Eric de Jonge, Chief, Decorative Arts and Crafts, William Penn Memorial Museum; Dorothy D. Merrick, Director, Pilgrim Society of Plymouth, Massachusetts; Bill Rusterholtz; Seattle Art Museum; Sterling D. Emerson, Director, Shelburne Museum, Inc.; *Spinning Wheel* magazine; A. Christian Revi; Alexander J. Wall, Old Sturbridge Village; J. Walter Thompson Company; The Toledo Museum of Art; Bob Muckleston of the Ontario Department of Tourism and Information; Towle Manufacturing Company; The Victoria and Albert Museum; The Western Reserve Historical Society; Colonial Williamsburg; and The Henry Francis du Pont Winterthur Museum.

Introduction

Books about antiques have almost always been written for the collector or for persons with a basic knowledge of the subject. Everyone seems to ignore the beginner, who might be an expert in fourteenth-century armor but a neophyte concerning eighteenth-century glass. It is possible for an expert in silver to be a beginner in collecting furniture, and for the most learned pewter expert to know little about early advertising signs. Every expert has some clever little tricks that quickly help him to determine the good from the bad. A few minutes with a shelf full of old dishes is all that is needed by the knowledgeable. He can spot the "Instant Expert" clues, and immediately determine which of the dishes should be examined further. The truly gifted collector will say, "It shouted at me from across the room at the antique show." Beginners often wonder how, with thousands of antiques on display, the collector can frequently find the one really fine example.

This is what it is to "know your antiques." It is that almost sixth sense that develops because the obvious signs are recognized and considered. Most of this book has been devoted to these Instant Expert tips; but this introduction is concerned with the other parts of antique collecting, such as how to price an antique and how to research an antique once you have decided it is worth your time. Many of these suggestions are quite apparent, and you may wonder why they are included; but it is often the very obvious that escapes us.

How to look up that mysterious antique

It is hardly necessary to say this, but LOOK IN THE OBVIOUS PLACE FIRST. Try a good general encyclopedia. These volumes are filled with very important information. For example, an encyclopedia is the best place to learn about old sewing machines. Call or visit your local library, and ask for help. Surprising amounts of information may be gained by telephone; but if your research problem is a complex one, a trip to the library may be necessary. Most libraries have large collections of books about antiques. We suggest that if the item you are interested in is a signed or marked piece of silver, pewter, china, or glass, start with the books devoted to marks. Results are quicker if the mark can be located and then the history of the antique researched by the factory name. Even if you do not recognize the crescent-moon mark in blue on your cup, you can find it in a book of porcelain marks. (This was a mark of the Worcester factory in England during the Dr. Wall period.) Further research about Worcester will show the type of patterns and cup shapes used. Our tip to look for the green porcelain may be the final proof. (See Chapter 1, "Pottery and Porcelain.")

Magazine articles are always a good source of information about antiques. The *Readers' Guide* can be found in any library with an index to most magazines of importance. Unfortunately, several of the magazines that are devoted exclusively to antiques are not listed in *Readers' Guide*. (See Chapter 20, "Antique Publications.") Those that are not listed in *Readers' Guide* have their own index guide, which appears in a separate publication or in one issue each year.

Another aid to research, if it appears on your antique, is the patent date. The patent-record rooms of any large city library can help you find a specific patent, and discover more about the original invention. One word of caution: Patents for inventions and patents for designs are listed separately, and must be looked up accordingly.

Related fields

One of the best resources for the collector is information on similar subjects already in print. Look at the lists of silver-plate makers to find pewter makers, because one man often worked in both fields. China dolls can be traced in books devoted to pottery and porcelain. Because many silversmiths founded firms that eventually became jewelry stores, the missing clue to a signed lamp may be the record of a grandfather who worked as a silversmith. Clues will lead to the city and city directories, and local histories will help from that point.

Though other types of research clues are important, they require only plain common sense. One old bottle bore a paper label that mentioned the vitamins contained in the oil inside in terms of government standard units. Because these government units were not established until the twentieth century, the bottle could not be as old as it first appeared to be. Company names, particularly those of firms that still exist, can often be a help in dating. There have been slight changes in the wordings of the names for many companies, and the Business Information section of a library can usually help you find when the name was actually in use.

If you think your antique has come from the immediate area, your local historical society may be able to help. Local catalogs and newspapers of the past will also prove useful to your search.

Another source in the library is general books about antiques. Odd, unrelated subjects, such as horse brasses, loving cups, nutmeg graters, or any one of a hundred-odd items, may be mentioned in a single chapter of a general book. Such objects are difficult to locate, and the only method is a search through the table of contents or the index of each book on the shelf. Such a procedure may be slow, but it can often be most rewarding. Many books tell the source of their pictures. A letter to a collector or to a curator of a museum that owns a similar item may be of additional help. Enclose postage as a courtesy gesture, and send as clear a picture as possible, preferably one that need not be returned.

How to buy or sell an antique

Because any dealer who sells antiques must also buy antiques for stock, all the rules on how to buy are just the reverse of those on how to sell. This book has been written for the collector, the about-to-be collector, and the acquisitive person who is interested in owning more valuable antiques. Obviously, the more you know about antiques, the easier it is to find what you want. If you are not sure of your abilities, go to a good antique dealer. The extra money you pay for an antique may be regarded as tuition for your education, too, and is a sum well spent. Look in the yellow pages of the phone book, and visit all the local shops. Ads in newspapers and in publications about antiques will list the antique shows. The shows attract many out-of-town dealers with unfamiliar merchandise. If you collect in a limited field, such as playing cards, lithographs of chickens, or pressed glass of a special pattern, tell your local dealers as well as the show dealers. They will make notes, and try to find your special pieces. You are under no obligation if the antique found is not exactly what you want.

After you have learned about specific antiques by practice, study, and by visits to museums and shops, you may try the local resale or junk stores. A surprising number of antiques go unrecognized in such places. The prices are low, but the gamble is yours. House sales are another place to find good antiques, and only the limitations of your knowledge would cause you to overlook some of the antiques priced for a quick sale. The collector of the "not yet" antique (such as old eggbeaters, and so on) will find the house sale an excellent source.

Local auctions are a good place to search, but be sure to arrive early and check the condition of the items offered for sale. The auctioneer often knows only that it is "an old dish." He will try to mention any chips or cracks, but it is possible that they may be overlooked in the haste of the bidding. Any reputable auction will refund your money if a piece is found to be less than perfect and if the auctioneer did not mention it at the time of the bidding.

Mail-order antiques have become a big business, and are 99 percent honest. The large New York auction houses will send you illustrated catalogues, and accept your bids by mail.

Antique publications will not accept ads from anyone who is not honest, and refunds are made quickly if the articles purchased are not as expected. Check the ads in papers and magazines, and either call or send an air mail letter for what might be a very choice addition to your collection. It is surprising how often someone else will get there first, and all you will get back is your money. Send your check with a clearly written order, and enclose a stamped envelope. Keep a carbon copy of the letter or the ad so that you can refer to it if the antique is not what you expected. Misinformation is frequent because some of the mail-order dealers do not know the history of all types of antiques, and often they too are fooled. If a dealer sells you an antique and you wish to return it, mail it back, insured, within a week. Usually the dealer will refund your money; but if any problem should arise, get in touch with the publication that carried the ad, and they may be able to help you.

Sometimes it is necessary for you to place an ad asking for specific antiques. The local newspaper is good; local weekly suburban papers are better; and the antique trade papers are best. The ads are inexpensive; but unless you want hundreds of campaign tokens or one expensive piece of furniture, it is not the most economical method of buying.

To match china or glass patterns, write to the dealers who specialize in such items and who are listed in the publications devoted to antiques.

Don't forget to tell your friends about what you want, and have them tell their friends too, because often one man's junk is another man's treasure. The inherited belongings of your friend's Great-Aunt May may be of no value to the friend, who probably doesn't even know the best way to sell them. In exchange for your advice and help in settling his problems, you may get a few bargains or even a gift.

Appraisals

If you own many antiques, you may at some time need an appraisal. This can be a very expensive process, and we do not recommend it unless your antiques are numerous or exceptionally rare. Any large collection should be insured, and the insurance company will require a current appraisal. Most local antique dealers do some appraising, or a professional appraiser specializing in antiques could be hired. (There is a national association of appraisers of antiques: Appraisers Association of America, 510 Madison Avenue, New York, New York 10022.)

Most serious collectors can give a fairly accurate appraisal of antiques. A record of the date and price of purchase of each antique should always be kept. When an appraisal is necessary, use of the original records, plus verification in a recent value book, should be enough to convince an insurance company.

1

Pottery and Porcelain

EVERY HOME HAS DISHES that are old, new, in sets, or just some odd plates that Grandmother owned. Most of the assortment of dishes, figurines, and vases are not antiques or even old. The easiest way to determine the china that is antique is to look first for the newest, and by a process of elimination discover those that might be valuable items. It is much easier to determine whether a dish is new than it is to be sure that it is old. Judging a painting is much the same, for it is often easier to tell that a painting is *not* a work of art.

Our system is based on the theory that common pieces are plentiful. If you can identify the common items, you will recognize the rarer ones because they are different. The Instant Expert way to study a dish is to use the most obvious clues first. Turn the dish over. There may be a mark on the bottom. IF THE NAME OF THE COUNTRY OF ORIGIN IS ON THE BOTTOM, THE DISH WAS PROBABLY MADE AFTER 1890, when the United States Government passed a law requiring that the name of the country of origin appear in writing on each piece of pottery or porcelain imported into the United States. If the name "England" (or that of some other country) appears, the dish was made after 1891, but it may have been made as early as 1887. THE WORDS "MADE IN ENGLAND" (OR SOME OTHER COUNTRY) INDICATE THE PIECE WAS MADE AFTER 1914. (Exception: a few pieces were marked with paper labels which may have been removed.)

If no country name appears, examine the mark. The more elaborate the mark used by the factory, the newer the piece. Initials or short names usually appeared on the better pieces. Fancy trademarks were used during the last half of the nineteenth century. THE WORD "TRADEMARK" WAS USED ON ENGLISH WARES AFTER 1855, but most of the pieces with the letters "LTD." were made after 1880.

ENGLISH REGISTRY MARKS

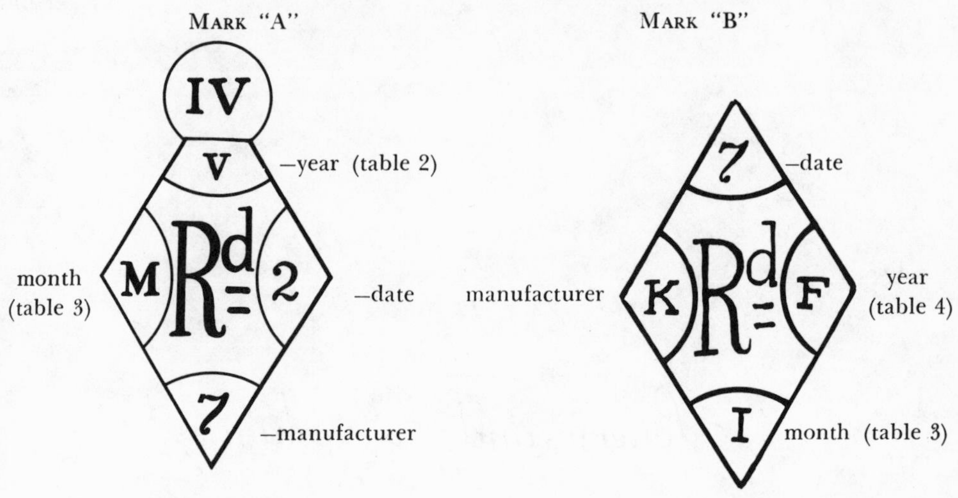

TABLE 1

I – metal	III – glass
II – wood	IV – earthenware

TABLE 3

Month of the Year of Manufacture

C – January	I – July
G – February	R – August
W – March	D – September
H – April	B – October
E – May	K – November
M – June	A – December

TABLE 2

Year of Manufacture

X – 1842	P – 1851	Z – 1860
H – 1843	D – 1852	R – 1861
C – 1844	Y – 1853	O – 1862
A – 1845	J – 1854	G – 1863
I – 1846	E – 1855	N – 1864
F – 1847	L – 1856	W – 1865
U – 1848	K – 1857	Q – 1866
S – 1849	B – 1858	T – 1867
V – 1850	M – 1859	

TABLE 4

Year of Manufacture

X – 1868	U – 1874	Y – 1879
H – 1869	S – 1875	J – 1880
C – 1870	V – 1876	E – 1881
A – 1871	P – 1877	L – 1882
I – 1872	D – 1878	K – 1883
F – 1873		

"RD" is the abbreviation for the word "Registered." Each pattern of English china was registered with the government Patent Office after 1885. THE LETTERS "RD" IN THE CENTER OF A DIAMOND MEAN THE DISH WAS DESIGNED FROM 1842 TO 1883. IF THERE IS A LETTER AT THE TOP INSIDE THE DIAMOND, THE DISH WAS DESIGNED FROM 1842 TO 1867 (MARK "A"). IF A NUMBER FROM 1 TO 31 APPEARS INSIDE THE TOP OF THE MARK, THE PIECE WAS DESIGNED FROM 1868 TO 1883 (MARK "B"). If the registry number is over 360,000, the dish was made after 1900. The approximate YEAR OF MANUFACTURE IS THE REGISTRY NUMBER DIVIDED BY 10,000 AND ADDED TO 1885. For example, if the number is 140,000, the piece was designed in 14 plus 1885 or 1899. To get the exact date, send 50 cents and the number to The Registry Patent Office Design, 25 Southampton Building, London W.C. 2, England.

Other date systems

There may be several small impressed numbers on the bottom of the dish. Several factories had a date-number system that appeared on dishes, and if your dish is Wedgwood, Rookwood, a Mettlach stein, or any of several other nineteenth- or twentieth-century English firms, you will find the key to the numbering system later in this chapter. Some of the small impressed numbers are just model numbers from the factory, and will give no help in dating the dish.

If your dish just has a pattern or factory name but no country name, it is still relatively easy to judge the age of the dish. Many books have been written that are devoted to the listing of pottery and porcelain marks. If you know nothing about the plate, use a book, such as *Dictionary of Marks—Pottery and Porcelain* by Ralph and Terry Kovel, that has the marks listed by their shape. If you are sure that the dish is English, German, or French, look in any of the special books listed at the end of this chapter. Almost every English mark can be traced, but for those of us who can do research in only one language, it is more difficult to trace French, German, Russian, or Danish pieces. The research books exist, but they are written in other languages.

The shape tells the tale

If there is no mark on a dish, it is still possible to determine the age from Instant Expert clues. EARLIER WARES ARE HEAVIER THAN LATER ONES OF THE SAME TYPE. The change in weight has been due to improved methods of manufacturing. EARLY PLATES OFTEN HAVE NO RIM ON THE BOTTOM. The foot rim is found on nineteenth-century wares. PLATES MADE PRIOR TO 1850 OFTEN HAVE AN UNGLAZED FOOT. Some early plates show three small marks on the face of the plate where the "spur" rubbed. The spur is a three-pronged piece that separated the plates during the baking. Although spurs were not used extensively after 1825, the spur, or stilt, mark can still be found on some inexpensive pieces of pottery.

Sometimes the plate will be slightly uneven. Old dishes should show some signs of wear, even if it is only a scratch in the glaze from years of use.

Teacup shapes have changed through the years. The earliest tea sets were copies of Oriental ones; and since the Chinese drank only lukewarm tea, the cup could be gripped, and no handle was necessary. In the early sets the teacup was often without a handle; only the coffee cups and chocolate cups had handles. As a general rule, CUPS WITHOUT HANDLES ARE USUALLY OLDER THAN THOSE WITH HANDLES. By the nineteenth century, most cups had handles. Cups with no handles were made during the first quarter of the nineteenth century for saucering the tea or coffee. The beverage was poured into a saucer to cool, and was sipped from the saucer. When "saucering" went out of style, all cups were made with handles.

The giant-sized coffee cups that many believe are a new idea were first made as early as 1820. The large cup held two regular-sized cups of coffee.

The teapot shape in silver, pewter, pottery, or porcelain went through the same series of changes. (See Chapter 6, "Silver.") Early teapots were much smaller because tea was an expensive beverage during the eighteenth century. And since small cups were used, only a small one- or two-cup teapot was necessary.

There are several other Instant Expert tips that can help in judging the age of a teapot. Look at the holes inside the pot that lead to the spout. THE EARLIER POTS (EIGHTEENTH CENTURY) HAD FEWER HOLES (AS FEW AS THREE) THAN THE LATER POTS, The holes are often jagged and uneven. The lid was usually held onto an eighteenth-century pot by means of a deep rim. Because the Chinese were able to make the teapot and lid, and then glaze and fire the entire piece, there is no shiny glaze where the lid rests. The English and Europeans were not so skilled as the Orientals, and they had to make the lid and pot separately, glazing each alone. If the top rim of a non-Oriental teapot is examined, it can be noted that the glaze covers all of it.

Decorations can help

A piece of pottery or porcelain will tell not only its age but also the country where it was made; however, long study and training are required to tell the differences.

The type of decoration can give a general hint about the age of a dish. Blue or black transfer designs (they look like prints) were first used at the end of the eighteenth century. Green, pink, or brown transfer designs were used about 1820 (see the section "Staffordshire"). Hand-painted plates were popular from 1870 to 1900. Decal designs indicate that the piece is a twentieth-century edition. Some gold-bordered plates marked "22 carat" are mid-twentieth century.

It's all called china but . . . .

Pottery, porcelain, bone china, ironstone, majolica, stoneware, and dozens of other kinds of dishes have been made through the centuries. *But* there is a difference that is important to the collector as well as to the housewife because each type has its advantages and disadvantages.

POTTERY IS OPAQUE. You can't see through it. PORCELAIN IS TRANSLUCENT. When a porcelain dish is held in front of a strong light, it is possible to see the light through the dish. If a piece of pottery is held in one hand and porcelain in the other, the piece of porcelain will be colder to the touch. If a dish is broken, a porcelain dish will chip with small shell-like breaks, while pottery cracks on a line. Pottery is softer, and easier to break, and it will stain more easily because it is more porous. Porcelain is thinner, lighter, more durable, and more expensive.

This early delft pitcher was made in Holland. It has blue-and-white decorations, although some delft was decorated with other colors.

Delft

Delft is a special type of pottery that has been popular through the years. Many makers learned to make decorations that suited the heavy texture of the tin-glazed pottery. Delft is still being made, but the early delft was made in Holland and England during the seventeenth century. It was usually decorated with blue on a white surface; but some delft, called "polychrome," was decorated with green, yellow, and other colors. Most delftware has been known as "useful" ware, and they were the dishes needed for everyday living. Delft figures were made from about 1750 to 1800, and are very rare. The potters copied some of the designs of the Meissen potters of Germany.

With some study, it is possible to tell the old delft from the new. Delft is a ware that crumbles and chips easily, and the old dishes or tiles should show some signs of wear. The blue decorations on the old delft are slightly darker, and the old wares are much thicker and heavier than the new ones. The best way to be sure your delft is old or new is to compare it with a new fresh-from-a-gift-shop piece of delft. IF THE WORD "HOLLAND" APPEARS, IT WAS MADE AFTER 1891.

Majolica

The general term "majolica" means any pottery glazed with an opaque tin enamel that conceals the color of the clay body. This would include delft, faience, and the more familiar majolicas of England, Spain, Germany, and Italy.

Although majolica was made during the fourteenth century, the average collector will never find a piece older than the late eighteenth century.

During the sixteenth century the

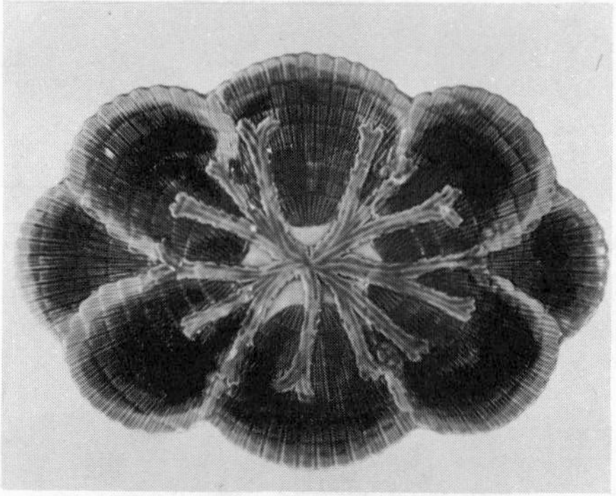

Etruscan majolica was made in Pennsylvania about 1881–1892. This platter is typical of the American majolica. (Henry Ford Museum, Dearborn, Michigan)

famous and eccentric Bernard Palissy made his unusual majolica wares in France. He used natural designs, but the most famous of his wares were his plaques of fish, snails, lizards, and snakes. The inspiration for later wares, they have been copied in every century and almost every country.

The Wheildon factory of England, which was the forerunner of the famous Wedgwood factory, made a type of majolica about 1740 that was inspired by the works of Palissy (see the section "Wedgwood"). The ware was popular until the early nineteenth century, when it lost its appeal for about fifty years. The real majolica craze hit Europe and North America about 1850, and the ware was made in quantity by English, Dutch, Italian, French, and United States factories. Victorian majolica ware is the type found by most collectors.

The same rule applies in identifying nineteenth-century majolica as identifying all other pottery—LOOK FOR THE MARK. Unfortunately, much of it was not marked, and it is almost impossible to identify the maker or even the country of origin; it is only possible to determine the date.

The words "Etruscan Majolica" or the letters "GSH" appear on the most famous of the American majolicas, the works of GRIFFIN, SMITH AND HILL OF PHOENIXVILLE, PENNSYLVANIA, a firm working during the 1880's. The firm also had another marking system that can help today's collector. A letter appeared that gave the general shape of the dish, and a number told of the decoration style. Each dish was marked with a number-letter combination; so if you own a piece of majolica marked with a letter and a number, and if the letter corresponds to the shape listed below, it is a piece of Griffin, Smith and Hill majolica:

SHAPE-LETTER MARKS FOR GRIFFIN, SMITH AND HILL MAJOLICA

A–Butterplates–round, leaf, or flower shape
B–Pickle dish
C–Cake dish of leaf or flower shape
D–Plate–round, leaf, or shell shape
E–Coffee, teapot, syrup jug, sugar, soup bowl, pitchers
F–Cuspidors, jardinieres
G–Cake basket
H–Candy dish
I–Covered box
J–Compote on stand
K–Paperweight, small trays, jars, cheese dishes
L–Salt shakers and pepper shakers, trays, compotes with dolphin feet, mugs, vases
M–Bowls, covered jars, dishes
O–Cups and saucers

One sleeps while the other preaches in this satirical Staffordshire figure of "The Vicar and Moses." This is one of many figures made by Ralph Wood. (Colonial Williamsburg, Williamsburg, Virginia)

Staffordshire

Staffordshire is a district in England where hundreds of pottery factories have made many types of wares since the mid-eighteenth century. Pottery such as the flowing blue, the transfer-printed dishes, the Woods-type figures, historical blues, and others were made in that district.

When the collector of eighteenth- or early-nineteenth-century pottery refers to "Staffordshire" wares, he usually means a ware similar to one made by the Wood family.

Ralph Wood (1715–1772) and possibly his brother Aaron (1717–1785) worked together, making many rustic figures. Ralph made the famous Staffordshire groupings such as "The Vicar and Moses" or "The Tithe Pig." They were satiric commentaries on the politics of the day. (Copies of the figures were made during the late 1880's.) The pottery made by Ralph and his cousin, Enoch Wood (1748–1795), has become one of the most famous Staffordshire wares. The firm was called Enoch Wood and Company in 1790. The name was changed to Wood and Caldwell, and in 1818 to Enoch Wood and Sons. The factory was closed in 1846, but it is obvious that each change of name tells of a change in partners.

The Wood potteries made all sorts of Staffordshire wares, including blue-printed earthenwares; they also made black basalts, jasper wares, and Toby jugs.

Other Staffordshire makers produced small figures of the same general type as the Woods figures. Neale and Company of Hanley, John Walton of Burslem, and Ralph Salt of Hanley all made figures that were sometimes marked with their name.

The Victorian Staffordshire figures are easier to find and are less expensive than those of the early nineteenth century. Many American collectors mistakenly believe that "Staffordshire ware" is represented only by the usually large fireplace mantel figures of royalty and important personages, dogs, and other animals.

Benjamin Franklin is looking sad because he has been named "Washington" by an English potter. This figure was made in the Staffordshire district before 1840, and is a famous "antique mistake." (Henry Ford Museum, Dearborn, Michigan)

Expert advice to collectors of the late Staffordshire figures is: BUY ONLY FIGURES REPRESENTING KNOWN PERSONS OR PLACES THAT CAN BE DATED. They will have not only the potter's art but also a place in history, with each piece having a double meaning. The Victorian figures are different from the earlier Staffordshire figures in many ways. The clay is whiter; the parts are molded and not handmade; and more gold was used in the decorations. The figures made after about 1850 do not try to imitate the earlier porcelain figures, but were designed to be made from pottery.

The first of the Victorian Staffordshire portrait figures were representations of Queen Victoria and Prince Albert. They were married in February of 1840, so any of the figures depicting their lives can easily be dated. Their children were shown later. Through the years wares of other political figures, murderers, murders' homes, actors, and other famous people were made.

Most of these figures were not marked by the maker; but during a recent study the works were divided into two groups, which were probably produced by two large factories, the Alpha and the Tallis.

The Alpha pieces were made from 1845 to 1851, and were made with the front and back modeled and painted, and each piece required three or more molds to manufacture. The Tallis factory made a series of seven Shakespearean figures based on engravings by Tallis in 1852–1853. Other pieces were made by the Tallis factory; the latest to be dated with certainty was made in 1884. Their figures had hard, heavy bodies, and were modeled and painted front and back. (Other firms made "flatbacks," as the figures were placed against a wall and it was necessary only to finish the front.) The base of the figure was colored with green, brown, and orange in a streaky design. The figures had no underglaze coloring, although the Alpha pieces were usually decorated with a blue underglaze. The titles were never in raised capital letters or gilt script.

A third famous factory making the figures was Sampson Smith, a maker who sometimes marked his figures. He worked from 1846 to 1878; but his molds have survived, and from 1948 to 1962 new figures have been made from the old molds. His firm made dogs, cottages, and historical figures in great quantity, and many of the still-unidentified pieces were probably from his factory.

Other factories in England, Scotland, and Wales made similar Staffordshire portrait figures from 1840 to 1900. Many STAFFORDSHIRE FIGURES HAVE BEEN REPRODUCED. The old glazes are not as perfect as today's, and the finish on the early figures tends to craze or crack in a fine network of lines. A comparison of a known old and new piece will also show a difference in the colors.

Many collect the animals made at the same time by Staffordshire potters. The spaniel is a strange-looking dog called a "comforter," and is no longer bred. These dogs, as well as poodles, sporting dogs, and domestic animals and zoo animals, were made in quantity.

Printed Staffordshire

To a large group of antique collectors, the word "Staffordshire" means printed dishes that were often blue and white. If you go to your library and obtain a book about Staffordshire ware, about half of the books with that title will discuss the printed plates; one-fourth will discuss the Victorian portrait figures; and one-fourth the early English wares made in eighteenth-century Staffordshire.

Most of the old blue or historic blue Staffordshire plates were made in England from about 1818 to 1848, but copies have been, and still are being, made. Each English maker had his own characteristic border design (see list), while the center designs were often copied. The views were transfer pattern pictures of actual events or cities on a white china. THE BLUE PATTERNS WERE THE EARLIEST, WITH BOTH BLACK AND BLUE TRANSFER DESIGNS USED DURING THE EIGHTEENTH CENTURY. PINK, GREEN, OR BROWN TRANSFER DESIGNS WERE USED ABOUT 1820, AND THE COMBINATION OF SEVERAL COLORS BEGAN ABOUT 1820.

American historical views on china bring higher prices than the European scenes, although the same factories made the wares at the same time. Historical china was made from 1800 to 1900 in varying qualities. Most of the desirable American scenes were made from 1820 to 1840.

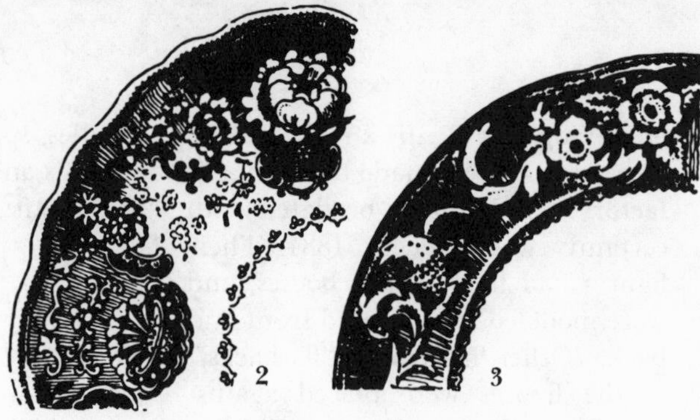

List of borders

For a more complete listing of borders and sketches on plates, check the book *American Historical Views on Staffordshire China,* by Ellouise Baker Larsen. (It is now out of print, but it can be found in many libraries.)

Border	Maker
1–Acorns and oak leaves	Ralph Stevenson and Williams
2–Baskets of roses and fan-shaped medallions	W. Adams and Sons
Diamond-shaped design, stenciled	Thomas Green
3–Eagles, scrolls, and flowers	Joseph Stubbs
4–Floral	J. and J. Jackson
Floral	John Rogers and Son
5–Flowers and fruit	Enoch Wood and Sons
6–Flowers and scrolls	A. Stevenson
Flowers (large) in wreath	Enoch Wood and Sons
7–Flowers, mixed	A. Stevenson
Lace	Ralph Stevenson
Lace, narrow	William Ridgway and Company
8–Leaves and vines	Ralph Stevenson
Medallions, arms of states	Mellow Venables and Company
Medallions, roses and animals	William Adams and Sons
9–Medallions, rose and leaf	J. and W. Ridgway
Medallions of urns and	James and Thomas Edwards
Medallions of turns and flowers	Enoch Wood
Moss, sprays	William Ridgway and Company
Moss sprays and tiny flowers	Charles Meigh
10–Roses, birds, and scrolls	James and Ralph Clews
Roses, large	A. Stevenson
Scrolls, flowers, and urns	R. Stevenson and Williams
11 & 12–Shells	Enoch Wood and Sons
Stars, large and small	John Ridgway
Trees with foliage	S. Tams and Company
13–Trumpet flower and vine	Thomas Mayer

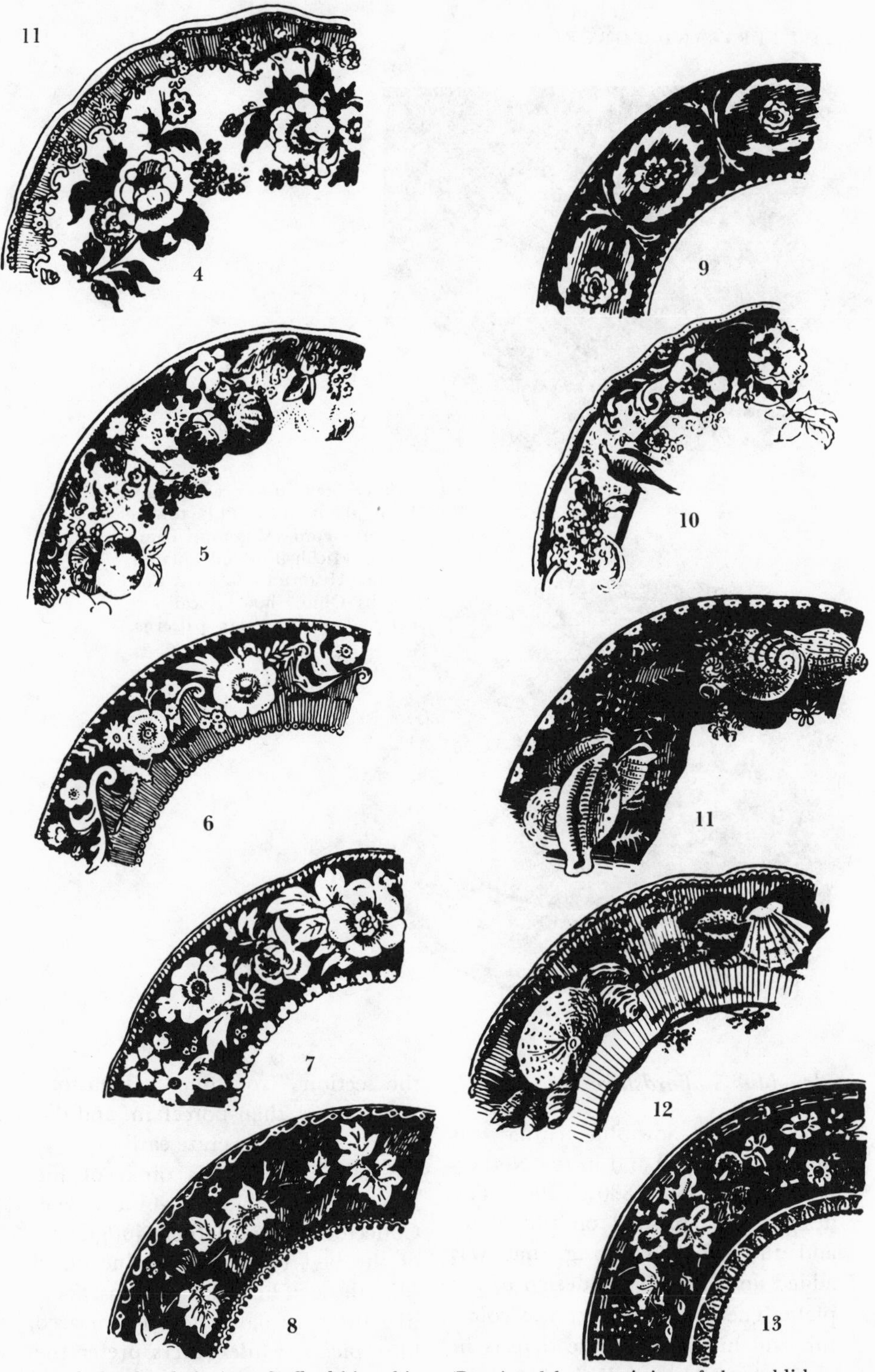

Sample border designs on Staffordshire china. (Reprinted by permission of the publisher Doubleday and Co., Inc., from *American Historical Views on Staffordshire China* by Ellouise Baker Larsen; copyright 1939.)

Printed Staffordshire wares date from about 1818. This tureen (Henry Ford Museum, Dearborn, Michigan) and platter (Ohio Historical Society, Columbus, Ohio) show typical border and center design patterns.

Flow-blue Staffordshire

The famous flow-blue china was made in England and in the Netherlands from about 1830 to 1900. The designs were printed on the plates and the cobalt coloring that was added flowed from the design to the plate. The smeared effect was colorful, and hid most of the defects in the pottery. Almost all the flow blue was printed on ironstone china. (See the section "Ironstone.") Ironstone was cheaper than porcelain, and did not chip, stain, or craze easily.

Historical china is often of the flow-blue or "bleeding-blue" type. Collectors differ in their judgments of the best type of flow blue other than those of historical designs. Some like the very dark, heavily smeared blue pieces, while others prefer the lighter blue with more legible designs.

Ironstone

Ironstone china is a product of the nineteenth century, even though it was first made by Miles Mason, an English potter who began making ceramics about 1780. Mr. Mason sold Chinese export ware in England, and was unable to get replacements for broken dishes. Rather than have his customers complain, he decided to make a ware that could be used with export ware. Charles James Mason, the son of Miles, patented ironstone china in 1813. All large pieces were marked to "prevent imposition." The marks used were blue underglaze with the name "Mason" appearing on most of them.

Mason's ironstone was made from ironstone slag, flint, Cornish stone, clay, and blue oxide of cobalt. Some experts believe the name "ironstone" came from the slag, while others believe it derived from the fact that it had a clear ring when struck and that the ware was as hard as iron. It may also have been named for a true ironware made in the eighteenth century. The name "ironstone" was used by Mason; and the other firms that copied the popular tableware called their products by names such as "white granite," "Parisian granite," "stone china," "granite ware," "opaque porcelain," "semi-china," and, later, "semi-porcelain."

Marks on Mason's ironstone

Miles Mason	1780 – 1800	not ironstone
M. Mason	1780 – 1800	
G. M. & C. J. Mason	before 1829	
G. & C. J. M.	circa 1825	
Fenton Stone Works		
Mason's Patent Ironstone China	1813	
Real Ironstone China	1851	
Ashworth's (printed in a banner)	1860 – (Later marks included the words England or Made in England)	

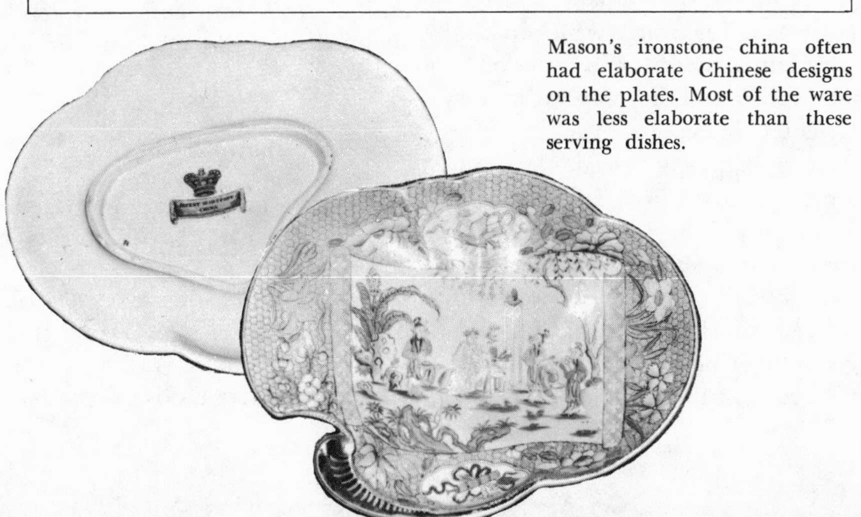

Mason's ironstone china often had elaborate Chinese designs on the plates. Most of the ware was less elaborate than these serving dishes.

Ironstone patterns

Ironstone was used as the base for the flow-blue and the historic-blue plates. About 1855 a type of "gaudy ironstone" was decorated with orange and blue imari (Japanese-inspired) type designs. Many of the pieces were marked with the maker's name. Do not confuse Gaudy ironstone with Gaudy Dutch, which was a soft paste made about 1820, or Gaudy Welsh, which was a slightly later version of the imari-patterned English ware with some gold decoration.

Mason and other English firms made ironstone to resemble the porcelain patterns that were in use.

It is not difficult to distinguish ironstone from porcelain. Go to the china department of any department store and ask to see a piece of each. The characteristics have not changed in the past hundred years. IRONSTONE IS HEAVY AND THICK AND NOT TRANSLUCENT.

Dating ironstone

USE THE TYPE OF DECORATION AND THE COLORING OF THE IRONSTONE DESIGN TO DATE IT IF A MAKER'S MARK IS MISSING. The wares were copies of porcelain patterns of the period to about 1830, and they were either very Oriental in appearance, or blue. Blue, pink, purple, green, black, and sepia were used from about 1830 to 1845. Purple, black, and light blue were used to about 1850, when flow blue became very popular. Light-colored transfer prints of the pink, green, light blue, or puce color were favored until about 1860. Gaudy ironstone was in vogue from 1855 to 1865, with bright colors, luster, or gold included in the decoration. Luster-decorated ironstone, featuring tea-leaf or Chelsea-grape type decorations, was not made until after 1850, and mainly in the 1870–1880 period. Plain white ironstone with raised decorations was most popular about 1875 and after.

The shape of the plate helps with the dating. THE PLATES HAD SIMPLE PLAIN CURVES BEFORE 1820. ABOUT 1820 TO 1830, SLIGHT INDENTATIONS APPEARED IN THE RIM. THERE WAS VERY LITTLE RAISED DECORATION. THE MAKERS BEGAN MAKING SCALLOPED RIMS FROM 1830 TO 1840; AND BY 1840 TO 1860, GEOMETRIC SHAPES, OCTAGONAL, AND OTHERS WERE INTRODUCED. ROUND PLATES CAME BACK INTO FAVOR FROM 1860 TO 1880, BUT THE PLATES WERE FLATTER THAN THE EARLIER ONES, AND OFTEN HAD A RAISED DESIGN AS THE BORDER. THE ELABORATELY ROCOCO SHAPES WITH EMBOSSED DESIGNS WERE FURTHER DECORATED WITH PRINTED DESIGNS AFTER 1880.

Ironstone wares are still being made in many of the early shapes; but fortunately most of these new wares are not attempts to fool the antique collector, and are plainly stamped with a modern maker's mark.

American ironstone

Many firms made ironstone ware in the United States. Taylor, Goodwin and Company of Trenton, New Jersey, was one of the first of these American factories, working from 1819 to 1870. John Wyllie of Pittsburgh, Pennsylvania, is said to have been the first potter to manufacture ironstone west of the Allegheny Mountains. He worked in 1874.

American ironstone manufacturers felt their product would sell better if the label hinted that the piece was of English origin. Many manufacturers adopted the seals of the United States or Great Britain for their factory marks. The lion and the unicorn holding a shield were used in many ways, which often misled the public. The English-looking marks were used until 1891, when the word "England" was required to appear by law; most of the firms then immediately stopped trying to fool the public.

Most of the English and American makers' marks are listed in books, and a marked piece of ironstone can easily be traced.

Tea-leaf ironstone

The tea-leaf pattern, which pictured a luster tea leaf on a white ironstone dish, was made by at least twelve English factories after about 1850. The idea of a tea leaf painted at the bottom of a cup was a natural one. There was a superstition that it was lucky if a whole tea leaf unfolded in your cup. The brown tea-leaf pattern became quite popular during the 1870's.

White ironstone patterns

The white ironstone became popular about 1875, but it was first made after 1855. Wheat-pattern ironstone was made by several English firms from 1855 to 1865. Other patterns pictured grapes, other types of fruit, ivy (late patterns have buds), flowers, and all sorts of geometric shapes with border designs.

Tea-leaf ironstone was a popular pattern about 1850. The leaf was pictured in a copper luster glaze.

Luster

Luster has been used on porcelain for centuries. Sixteenth-century Spain produced some of the finest early luster decorations. About ninety-four out of every one hundred early pottery dishes broke during the firing, and those difficulties should explain the reason for the high cost and rarity of early luster.

There are many colors of luster. The fifteenth and sixteenth centuries had blue, reddish-gold, copper, or green luster decorations, while the seventeenth-century luster included bright-red copper and golden yellow. The very metallic gold, silver, copper, and pink lusters were made during the late eighteenth century. A pearly luster was used during the nineteenth century.

Lusterwares were popular in England and America in the early nineteenth century. These silver luster pitchers were made about 1810. (Ohio Historical Society, Columbus, Ohio)

The luster glaze was made from a mixture of platinum, copper, or gold salts. (For example, the gold made pink, purple, or copper luster.)

Most of the English luster was made in the Staffordshire district, and was at the height of its popularity from 1775 to 1830. It is still being made, and has remained popular.

OLD LUSTER IS HEAVIER. THE POTTING RIM AT THE BASE OF THE NEW WARE IS SMOOTHER AND SHALLOWER. Some experts can recognize a new piece from the color. IT IS BRIGHTER.

Many of the luster pieces of the eighteenth and nineteenth centuries were almost entirely covered with metallic glaze. The silver-coated pieces were made in shapes to resemble the solid silver or silver plate. Copper luster pitchers were very popular.

Solid luster pieces were decorated with bands of colored flowers or figures about 1830. By 1850, plain luster pieces imitating metal were discontinued. The cheaper process of electroplating metal had been discovered, and the plated metal was inexpensive and unbreakable.

EARLY LUSTER PIECES HAD THE SAME GLAZE ON THE INSIDE AS ON THE OUTSIDE. MOST NINETEENTH-CENTURY PIECES HAD LUSTER ON THE OUTSIDE AND WHITE ON THE INSIDE.

Several English factories made copper, silver, and gold luster during the Victorian era. Many of the late-nineteenth-century pieces, especially the copper luster pitchers, can still be found.

A luster was developed in 1860 that had the appearance of an iridescent mother-of-pearl. Though it was attractive, it washed off after a few years.

Pink Luster

Pink luster is a special decorative glaze that appears metallic and glossy. The Leeds, Newcastle, and Sunderland pottery factories in England made pink luster. The most famous wares were made by Sunderland, and the name Sunderland was often incorrectly given to any pink luster piece.

Two general types of pink lusterware were made. Some had luster lines or leaves painted into the design for added glimmer, but the most spectacular pieces were made with

The lopsided lion is roaming on white hills against a silver background. The silver resist platter was made by the Leeds pottery factory of England about 1812. This is an excellent example of silver luster pottery. (Nelson Gallery-Atkins Museum, Nelson Fund, Kansas City, Missouri)

The tea-leaf pattern often found on ironstone ware is another example of luster-decorated ware (see the section "Ironstone"). Transfer printed wares in brown, black, lilac, pink, or green were sometimes decorated with luster (see the section "Staffordshire").

Care

Lusterware requires special handling because it can wear away if it is improperly washed. The ware should be washed in warm water with a mild soap or detergent. Do not rub too hard, or you will remove the luster glaze.

wide bands of bubble pink luster. Large bowls and porcelain-framed pitchers were often made this way. Poorly colored black transfer patterns of sailors, ships, bridges, drinking scenes, sporting events, and so on, were made during the mid-nineteenth century. Some pieces were made with verses and political slogans that help to date the lusterware.

The famous Chelsea-grape pattern of dishes is typical of the patterns made with small luster designs. A small bunch of grapes was made in a raised design on a white plate. The grapes were colored lavender, blue, or purple luster. Most of the Chelsea-grape pattern is unmarked, and was probably made by the Coalport factory in England before 1840. It was *never* made by the Chelsea factory of England. The pattern is also called Aynsely or Grandmother.

Pink luster was used by the Sunderland Company on many of its wares. This pitcher features a caricature by George Cruikshank. (Collection of Dr. Harold Collins, Brockport, New York)

China trade and Chinese export porcelain, and the name game with Lowestoft

The Chinese potter made a fine, restrained, well-designed pottery or porcelain for his own country. Chinese porcelain was considered a rarity worth more than gold when the first few pieces were brought back to Europe by Marco Polo. The Europeans were not able to make porcelain until the eighteenth century, when the secret was discovered at Meissen, Germany. The search for the secret of the porcelain was one of the great projects for the kings of Europe.

During the eighteenth century, when trading with the Orient became more common, the ships of England and Holland brought back dishes that we now call Chinese export porcelain. The wares in demand by the Europeans were very different from those made in the Orient for the Oriental. The porcelain was not so fine in quality, and the design was distinctly European. Family coats of arms, figures dressed in European clothes, Stars and Stripes, Biblical scenes, and other local mottoes and symbols were ordered.

Lowestoft is a town in England where pottery and porcelain were made during the eighteenth century. A well-known nineteenth-century author of books about antique porcelain wrote that all eighteenth-century Chinese export porcelain was Lowestoft. His misnaming of the

There is no doubt that this piece of Chinese export porcelain was made for the American market. "Rebellion to tyrants, is obedience to God" was part of the design made about 1790. This jug was given to John Adams by Thomas Jefferson. (Cincinnati Art Museum, Cincinnati, Ohio)

porcelain has led to years of confusion.

Some Chinese porcelain was decorated in Lowestoft, England, but it is also possible that some English wares were sent to China for decorating. Only a few pieces of true English Lowestoft ware are known to exist. Most of the so-called Lowestoft is really of Chinese origin. It is for these reasons that the collector refers to it as "Chinese export porcelain" or "China trade porcelain."

More silly names

There are even some collectors and authors who have referred to "American Lowestoft" or "Spanish Lowestoft," which are completely confusing names. Chinese export porcelain was made for many markets, and each country had special designs they favored; so the name "American Lowestoft" refers to any of the many pieces of the China-trade porcelain made in the American taste. Americans had no coats of arms, so similar designs or eagles were pictured in the center of the plate. The border was frequently made of blue with gold stars or another motif inspired by the flag.

Italians liked the black-and-white or Jesuit designs. Biblical scenes were painted on some of the plates. The Dutch ordered porcelains with designs that resembled the designs on delft. The French liked pieces decorated with flowers and scrolls that resembled the Sèvres patterns. The English ordered dinnerwares with the family coat of arms emblazoned in the center of each plate.

The English-designed wares were made with a coat of arms or crest, and are called "armorial" china. They were made to order in China, and sent by boat to England. The English porcelain factories of Worcester, Spode, Wedgwood, and Leeds also made armorial porcelains as replacements for broken pieces. CHINESE EXPORT PORCELAIN HAD A GRAYISH-COLORED BODY. The English firms made their ware to match the Chinese sets.

Export porcelain is very popular with collectors; and since the ware is very expensive, study is required to distinguish the good from the bad. Several very fine books have been written about this subject (see the bibliography at the end of this chapter), and many color pictures are available.

The term "China-trade porcelain" means not only the misnamed Lowestoft but also some of the later china products. Canton ware, a blue-and-white china, was made at potteries near Canton or north of Canton, China. Much of the decorating was done by families living in the city of Canton. The earliest Canton ware was made about 1785. Dishes were decorated with blue pictures of the willow pattern, with a teahouse, bridge, willow trees, and birds. True Canton ware never pictured a person on the bridge. The ware made before 1890 is of collectible quality. Much of the later work is very inferior.

Nanking china is a blue-and-white porcelain ware made and exported from China during the eighteenth century.

Willow pattern was popular at many factories. Left to right: bowl from the Coalport factory of England c. 1850; cup and saucer from Caughley factory, England c. 1800; bowl from Buffalo factory, Buffalo, New York, c. 1904.

Willow pattern

The willow pattern that pictures a bridge, three figures, birds, trees, and a Chinese landscape was first introduced to England by Thomas Turner in 1780 at the Caughley Pottery Works. It was inspired by a similar Chinese design without figures on the bridge. (Early English versions show two or three figures, while some of the late-nineteenth-century versions often show no people.) Original pieces were hand painted, while transfer designs were used on the later ones. There is no pattern that has been copied so often as Willow. Minton, Spode, Wedgwood, Adams, Davenport, and other English factories, as well as German, Japanese, and United States factories, have made it, and still are making it.

The legend connected with willow ware was invented long after the pattern first arrived in England, because no Chinese folklore was translated into English until after 1800. While the scene is Oriental in origin, the legend of a romantic pair fleeing from a cruel father is not Chinese in thought. China was a land of arranged marriages, and not one of romantic love. The Chinese version did not picture the lovers, so the story could not have applied.

The English version claims the figures on the bridge were fleeing from a cruel father who wanted to stop their marriage. The gods took pity on the lovers, and changed them into birds so they could escape.

There is one Chinese legend that may be the true story of the willow pattern. A political group that tried to overthrow the government circulated the dishes to remind the people of their aims. The three figures represented three Buddhas, past, present, and future. The doves were the souls of those slain in battle, and the pagoda was a symbol of shelter for escaping monks. There are no early Chinese examples of the design with the figures, but the legend claims they were all destroyed by the government.

The willow design has been and is still being made by so many firms it is virtually impossible to distinguish the old from the new without checking the marks on the bottom of a piece. (See the earlier section on marks on pottery and porcelain.) It was made in porcelain and pottery dishwares. The general rule is: THE OLDER THE WILLOW PATTERN, THE GREATER THE VALUE.

For some unexplained reason there has been a rumor that the number of apples on the tree determines the value of the willow dish. There are no apples on a willow tree, so the rumor must have really referred to the round leaves seen on some of the other trees. This is a splendid idea, but there is not one shred of evidence that older or newer plates had more or less of the "apples."

Wedgwood

The Wedgwood factory of England has been one of the most famous and important of all pottery factories. Josiah Wedgwood came from a family of potters, but his brother did not want him in the family business. Josiah went into partnership with several other men after 1752, and invented many types of pottery and glaze. He became the head of his own firm in 1759, and continued with his experimentation and work. Wedgwood's early work in partnership with Thomas Whieldon resulted in several types of earthenware, agateware, white stoneware, and marbleized wares. He discovered a green glaze at his own plant that made it possible to make earthenware pieces resembling cauliflowers, pineapples, and other natural fruits. The cauliflower ware was made about 1750 to 1770, and was copied by European majolica makers during the last half of the nineteenth century. It was also made in the United States. (See the section "Majolica.")

By 1765, Josiah Wedgwood developed a cream-colored pottery that was used by the queen, and consequently "queensware" came into fashion.

The Wedgwood factory made many kinds of pottery, such as black basalt, redware, and caneware, and in later years they made lusterware, majolica, bone china, and porcelain (1811–1816).

The most famous of all the Wedgwood products was jasper ware. It was a blue, lavender, green, or some other colored hard, nonporous pottery. The decorations were of a raised material that was usually white. The most famous piece of jasper ware was the Portland vase, which was a copy of an early Roman glass vase. Jasper ware was so popular it has been copied by many factories, but mainly by the late-nineteenth-century German firms.

WEDGWOOD IS ALMOST ALWAYS CLEARLY MARKED. The quality of Wedgwood products is so obvious that it takes only a short time to recognize the less-expensive copies. The Instant Expert system is still to use the marks as a quick reference and then study further if the mark is not there. One word of warning: The word "Wedgewood" is found on china that was *not* made by the famous factory of Josiah Wedgwood. William Smith and Company of Stockton on Tees, England, made a cream-colored ware marked "Wedgewood" from 1826 to 1848. The mark was a deliberate attempt to mislead the public and to misrepresent the china as that of the more famous factory.

The English courts agreed that there was an infringement of rights, and forced the company to stop using the mark. Other firms run by relatives of Josiah Wedgwood have used the name in their marks but they can be quickly identified by looking at the list of Josiah Wedgwood marks.

Wedgwood Marks	
Wedgwood (impressed)	1759 – 1769, 1780 – 1795 On bone china 1812 – 1815 On queensware (impressed or printed) 1769 to the present
Wedgwood, England	After 1891
Wedgwood and Bentley (in circle or plain)	1769 – 1780
Wedgwood & Sons	(rare) 1790
Josiah Wedgwood Feb. 2, 1805	(rare) 1805
Wedgwood Etruria	1840 –
Wedgwood (printed under a picture of the Portland vase)	1878 – present (on bone china)
Wedgwood, Bone China	– present
Made in England (printed under a picture of the Portland vase)	
Wedgwood of Etruria & Barlaston, Made in England	1940 – present (printed in color on queensware)
Date-Letter System	1860 –

The Wedgwood factory made many types of wares. The Portland vase (opposite) is probably the most famous design made by the Wedgwood works. Jasper ware was a great commercial success. This teaset (above) was made about 1790. Creamware or queensware was another popular type of dish. The two covered soup tureens, c. 1800, have a hand-painted border of strawberry leaves and lines. (Buten Museum of Wedgwood, Merion, Pennsylvania)

DATE-LETTER SYSTEM

There are three capital letters, with the first representing the month, the second the potter, and the third the year the piece was made:

1860 – 1864	Monthly marks			1864 – 1907	Monthly marks		
J	January	V	July	J	January	L	July
F	February	W	August	F	February	W	August
M	March	S	September	R	March	S	September
A	April	O	October	A	April	O	October
Y	May	N	November	M	May	N	November
T	June	D	December	T	June	D	December

YEAR MARKS 1860 – 1930

Cycle I		Cycle II		Cycle III		Cycle I	Cycle II		Cycle III	
1860	O	1872	A	1898	A		1885	N	1911	N
1861	P	1873	B	1899	B		1886	O	1912	O
1862	Q	1874	C	1900	C		1887	P	1913	P
1863	R	1875	D	1901	D		1888	Q	1914	Q
1864	S	1876	E	1902	E		1889	R	1915	R
1865	T	1877	F	1903	F		1890	S	1916	S
1866	U	1878	G	1904	G		1891	T	1917	T
1867	V	1879	H	1905	H		1892	U	1918	U
1868	W	1880	I	1906	I		1893	V	1919	V
1869	X	1881	J	1907	J		1894	W	1920	W
1870	Y	1882	K	1908	K		1895	X	1921	X
1871	Z	1883	L	1909	L		1896	Y	1922	Y
		1884	M	1910	M		1897	Z	1923	Z

In 1907 the month mark changed to "3" for every month.

Thus the letters "LBS" on a piece could mean July 1864, or July, 1890.

The letter code "3B S" means 1916.

After 1930 another code was used. The months were given by the numbers 1 to 12, the potter by letter, the year by the last two digits. Thus the mark "6 P 50" means June, 1950.

The English registry marks were also used. (See Introduction to this chapter.)

The famous Meissen factory of Germany made the equally famous Swan dinner service about 1740. This sauceboat modeled by J. J. Kaendler was part of the set. (Seattle Art Museum, Seattle, Washington

Meissen

The term "Meissen" is frequently misused. Meissen is a town in Germany where a porcelain factory was built about 1710. The Meissen factory was located in several countries, although the factory didn't move. Boundaries were changed by numerous wars; so the factory was located first in Saxony, then in Prussia, and finally in Germany.

The word "Meissen" should mean any ware, regardless of whether it is a porcelain or stoneware, that was made at the Meissen factory from 1710 to the present time. The English refer to Meissen as "Dresden," while the French use the word "Saxe." Many people refer to Meissen porcelain as "Dresden" because the factory was located near Dresden, Germany.

French, Italian, English, and other factories copied Meissen china. These pieces are Meissen or Dresden type.

True Meissen china may be unmarked or may have one of several marks, such as the famous crossed lines or crossed swords, imitation Chinese letters, the "KPM" or "MPM" marks, or even the letters "AR" or "KHC" or some other letter combination. The word "Meissen" appears as a mark on porcelain made by another factory in Meissen, Germany that was founded in 1864 by C. Teichert.

Old Meissen may be differentiated from the new by careful study. Many of the eighteenth-century figures were reproduced during the nineteenth and even twentieth centuries. OLD MEISSEN WAS CAREFULLY DECORATED. IT IS HEAVIER THAN NEW MEISSEN. The colors used in the decorating can be of help in determining the age. MAROON AND YELLOWISH CHROME GREEN WERE NEVER USED DURING THE EIGHTEENTH CENTURY. ALMOST ALL THE EIGHTEENTH-CENTURY FIGURES HAD BROWN EYES. Blue or brown eyes appeared during the nineteenth and twentieth centuries. EARLY MEISSEN HAS A SLIGHTLY GREEN COLOR, while the later porcelains were dead white.

The crossed-swords mark was first used by the Meissen factory about

1716, and variations of the mark have been used ever since. The mark "KPM" stands for Königliche Porzellan Manufaktur, or Royal Porcelain Manufacture. "KPF" is the mark for Königliche Porzellan Fabrik, or Royal Porcelain Factory. Both marks were used on the royal porcelain made at the Meissen factory beginning about 1723. "MPM" is the mark that represents the Meissener Porzellan Manufaktur, or the Meissen Porcelain Manufacture, and was first used about 1723. ALL THESE MARKS WERE USED DURING THE NINETEENTH CENTURY. If these letters appear either alone or with some symbol, look the mark up in a book explaining porcelain marks.

Blue onion pattern

The blue-and-white "onion" Meissen has been made since the eighteenth century. There has been little change in the pattern, which was first made in 1732. The design is Chinese in origin, and pictures peaches and pomegranates. The fruit on the border pointed toward the center of the plate only before 1800, while the later patterns used fruit that alternately pointed in and out. Twentieth-century pieces have the fruit pointing either way. The design has been simplified, and fewer of the "onions" or pomegranates are shown in the plate border. The early plates were gray-blue in color, with the design in a clear blue. A stronger and darker cobalt blue was used for the decorations on a dead-white plate about 1820. Occasionally, a pink version of the onion pattern has been found that would date from the mid-nineteenth century. "Red Bud Onion" was also made, which was the blue onion pattern with gold and red overglaze decoration added.

Blue onion pattern is still made today. This plate is in the pattern of about 1840.

"Onion Meissen" was made by many German, French, English, and Japanese factories. It is still being made.

Mettlach steins

The stoneware steins of Germany have been popular with collectors for years. The most famous steins came from the pottery factory of Villeroy and Boch, located in the city of Mettlach, Germany. The factory was founded in 1841 by Jean François Boch and Nicholas Villeroy. It was a merger of three pottery factories at Wallerfangen, Septfontaines, and Mettlach. The factory was in an old abbey that had been restored and pictured as part of the "castle mark." The firm made stoneware from 1842.

Several types of improvements were developed at the new factory.

Another Mettlach factory mark used about 1880.

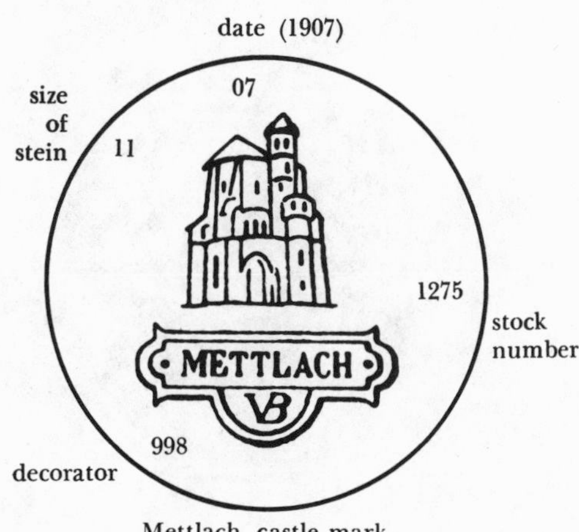

Mettlach castle mark.

They had a process for making inlaid stoneware, mosaic ware or chromolith ware, in which colored clay was inlaid into a body clay to form designs. It was expensive at first, but the method gradually improved, and the price was reduced. The ware was popular in America, and won awards at the great fairs in 1876, 1893, and 1904.

Fine Mettlach steins can be recognized by the workmanship. They are not all marked, although many of the collectors prefer only the marked examples. The mark is an easily read date-letter system. (See picture.)

The factory "castle" and the name Mettlach are in the center, and the other numbers tell the date, size of stein, decoration number, and stock number.

ENGLISH WARES FOR THE AMERICAN MARKET

Mocha ware

Mocha ware was a popular English-made product that was sold in America during the 1800's. It was a special type of heavy pottery with colored decorations. Once you have seen several pieces of mocha ware you will find it easy to identify and date. The name "mocha" comes from the color of the pottery, which was a light shade of "coffee-with-cream." The body was decorated, but the handles were always a light coffee color, and were applied to the main piece.

Ten different groupings of the design were made, including plain banded, specked, checkered, combed, scrambled, variegated, cat's-eye, tree, and miscellaneous. The tree design is the most desired pattern. Blue, brown, green, gray, buff, orange, black, and white were the only colors used on the mocha design.

Mocha ware was not really "discovered" until 1945 when an article on banded creamware was published in *Antiques* magazine. Since that time the interest and the prices have risen.

Mocha ware was made in England for the American market. This pitcher was made about 1800. (Old Sturbridge Village, Sturbridge, Massachusetts)

Mocha ware was sold in the United States and Canada from 1800 to about 1850, and was rarely marked. A few pieces with the name Adams or Leeds have been found. THE OLDER THE MOCHA THE LIGHTER THE COLOR. The almost yellow-colored kitchen bowls of Victorian times were the last of the ware.

Spatterware or sponged ware

Spatterware is an inexpensive ceramic ware that was made in England to be used as "everyday" dishes, primarily for the Pennsylvania Ger-

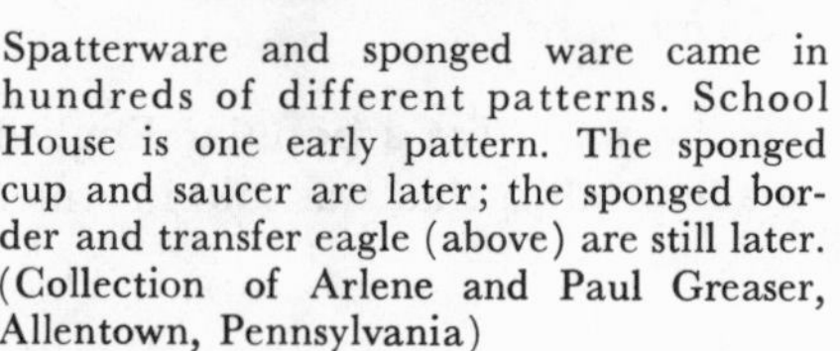

Spatterware and sponged ware came in hundreds of different patterns. School House is one early pattern. The sponged cup and saucer are later; the sponged border and transfer eagle (above) are still later. (Collection of Arlene and Paul Greaser, Allentown, Pennsylvania)

man market. The spatterware, or sponged ware, was an earthenware. Many plates, cups, and other useful pieces were decorated in bright colors with a stipple design. The design was made by spattering or daubing the plate with a paint-covered sponge. Colors such as green, red, blue, yellow, brown, and black were used. Most of the ware had a border of the color. The center of the plate had designs that were popular with the Pennsylvania German settlers, such as tulip, eagle, flower, peacock, schoolhouse, star, and others. Some of the later examples of spatterware had transfer designs of the Staffordshire-ware factories, since many of the dishes were made at the Staffordshire potteries.

Spatterware is sometimes called Pennsylvania Dutch ware, but that is not the correct name.

Studies have shown that some of the creamware or soft paste bodies decorated with spatter designs date from the late 1700's, but most of the spatterware found today was made in the 1800–1850 period. YELLOW IS THE RAREST COLOR IN SPATTERWARE, BUT GREEN IS ALSO UNUSUAL. OLD SPATTER SHOULD HAVE THREE ROUGH SPOTS OR KILN MARKS ON THE BOTTOM OF THE DISH. MOST REPRODUCTIONS OF THE EARLY PATTERNS ARE MISSING THOSE SPOTS.

Portneuf

A special type of spatterware was made for the Canadian market and it is called Portneuf. It was originally believed that the crude earthenware was made at Portneuf, Quebec, but studies have proved that it was probably made at Staffordshire for sale in Canada. Portneuf is very similar to the spatterware that was made for sale in Pennsylvania and

Portneuf is a special type of spatterware made for the Canadian market. (Upper Canada Village Collection, Ontario Department of Tourism and Information, Toronto, Canada)

"Carnation" pattern was one of many designs of Gaudy Dutch ware. (Teapot, Henry Ford Museum, Dearborn, Michigan; others, Ohio Historical Society, Columbus, Ohio)

New England. It is a thick pottery and was decorated with elk, deer, robins, wild flowers, ferns, leaves, or stylized designs and it often had spatter or sponged decorations. The ware was usually decorated in green, blue, or other muted tones.

Gaudy Dutch, Gaudy Welsh, and others

Gaudy Dutch pottery was made in England, and exported to the United States about 1810 to 1820. It was sold in quantity in Pennsylvania, Ohio, New Jersey, and Maryland. The English Staffordshire potters made the ware for the American market. It is a white earthenware with Japanese imari-style decorations of bold designs in rusty red, blue, green, yellow, and black.

It has been said that the pottery was made only for the German settlements of Pennsylvania, but that is probably not true. The surplus of the unpopular English ware was "dumped" on the American public, and it became a success.

A few pieces were marked with factory names, such as Riley (1802–1827), E. Woods and Sons, Burslem (before 1814), and Rogers (1815–1842).

Gaudy Welsh is a similar but later pottery that was also copied from the imari patterns. It was made in England after 1820, but the china is heavier and the coloring cruder than the Gaudy Dutch.

Some of the wares had impressed borders, but most of them had dark-blue scalloped borders with large flowers or leaves in blue, red, green, or gold. The tulip–and–vine and wheel patterns were most popular.

Each pattern of Gaudy Dutch and Gaudy Welsh pottery has been named today. King's Rose, Sunflower, War Bonnet, and other such names are modern, and were not used when the ware was first sold.

Gaudy Dutch and Gaudy Welsh wares are easy to identify once they have been seen. Almost no copies of these wares have been made that could even confuse the inexperienced collector.

Made in America

"Made in the USA" was not used as a mark on porcelain until the twentieth century. One of the first men who could have used that mark on porcelain was Thomas Ellis Tucker. The Philadelphia, Pennsylvania, firm operated by Tucker has been credited with making one of the earliest porcelains in the United States. The clear white porcelain was decorated with colors and gold in a French manner.

The firm worked from 1825 to 1838, and made wares that were as fine as any made in Europe. Attempts to make porcelain in the United States had been made as early as 1770. White wares and red pottery were made by 1760.

The Smith Fife and Company was established about 1830, and made a porcelain that was almost identical to that of Tucker. The molds of some of the marked pieces are the same, and the decorating is similar, but the quality is a bit inferior. A few marked pieces of Smith Fife and Company marked in red still exist, but the factory was in business for only a few years.

Tucker was rarely marked and was so similar to the French porcelain of the same period that even some museums have had cases of mistaken identity. This is a place for an expert of long experience, and there are no instant tips that can be of help. The early-American porcelains are so very rare that the average collector will never find one.

Horses and riders gallop around this white pitcher made by Thomas Tucker c. 1825–1838. (Henry Ford Museum, Dearborn, Michigan)

Bennington

The Bennington pottery made at Bennington, Vermont, is the most famous American ware. Two factories were in the town, and neither company was named Bennington. Lyman and Fenton, Norton, and later The United States Pottery Company were the names used by the firms whose products are now referred to as Bennington pottery. All the pottery firms working in Bennington stopped producing pottery by 1896.

Amateur antique collectors have hundreds of untrue tips about Bennington ware. It requires long study to understand the works of the factories, and even many experts connected with museums with collections of Bennington ware will admit that there is much still to learn. MOST BENNINGTON WARE IS UNMARKED. It is almost impossible to say that a piece is Bennington if it has no mark. Only exact duplicates of marked pieces could be considered Bennington.

The brown-and-yellow glazed pottery made by the factory was very similar to the brown wares made in many Ohio and Pennsylvania factories. Bennington ware was not only brown ware but also Parian, scroddle (a marbleized-type glaze), stoneware, graniteware, yellowware, Staffordshire type vases, and others.

There were so many types of Bennington ware made that we have made no attempt to tell how to identify special pieces. That has already been done in a small book listed in the bibliography. Two favorite tips are given as a sample:

1. THERE IS AN EASY METHOD TO TELL A BENNINGTON HOUND HANDLE PITCHER FROM AN OHIO BROWN HOUND HANDLE PITCHER. PUT YOUR HAND UNDER THE DOG'S HEAD. IF THERE IS ROOM BETWEEN THE DOG'S HEAD AND THE BODY OF THE PITCHER, YOU MIGHT OWN A PIECE OF BENNINGTON WARE. THE HOUND HANDLE PITCHER BY BENNINGTON HAS A DOG THAT WEARS A CHAIN. THE DOG'S BELLY IS NOT FLAT OR VERY ROUND. YOUR FINGER SHOULD FIT UNDER THE DOG'S HEAD AND REST ON HIS PAWS.

2. A BENNINGTON COW CREAMER OF YELLOW OR GRANITEWARE SHOULD HAVE THE EYES OF THE COW OPEN AND WELL DEFINED, THE NOSTRILS CRESCENT-SHAPED, AND THE RIBS AND THE FOLDS OF THE NECK WELL DEFINED.

The "Rebecca at the Well" teapot is another famous piece. Everyone likes to talk about the Bennington Rebecca teapot, but there seems to be no evidence that the design was ever made at the Vermont factory. It was first made by Edwin and William Bennett of Baltimore, Maryland, who in 1851 copied the design from an English pot made by Samuel Alcock and Company. Many other English and American firms also made this style of teapot.

AMERICAN ART POTTERY

There were many types of American art pottery made in the United States from about 1850. The firms worked in many cities and in all parts of the country, and are just being identified. Any of the art potteries will gain in value over the

The term "Bennington ware" means any of many types of ware made in Bennington, Vt., in the nineteenth century. (Dog and lion, Metropolitan Museum of Art, New York City; pitchers, Ohio Historical Society, Columbus, Ohio. Left: East Liverpool, Ohio. Right: Burlington, Vt.)

years as more of their history is known to collectors.

Rookwood

The Rookwood Pottery Company of Cincinnati, Ohio, made a fine quality of pottery after 1880. The monogram "R P" with the "R" reversed was first used in 1886. Each year after that, a flame was added to the mark. By 1900 there were 14 flames, and

Rookwood marks 1886 and 1901.

These two vases were made by the Rookwood factory of Cincinnati, Ohio. The vase with the birds is dated 1887.

The Dedham Pottery Company of Dedham, Massachusetts, started in 1866. Several of the designs made were "grape," "swan," and "rabbit." (Dedham Historical Society, Dedham, Massachusetts)

after that a Roman numeral was added that indicated the year. For example, "XV" was used in 1915. The earliest pieces of Rookwood were signed with the year. Other letters impressed into the bottom of a Rookwood vase explain the size or the color of the clay. Many artists signed their works, and it is possible to find the full list of decorators and identify the artist.

Dedham pottery

The Dedham Pottery Company of Dedham, Massachusetts, worked during the nineteenth century. Designs such as Rabbit, Iris, Turkey, or other plants and animals were featured on full sets of crackleware dishes. The firm started in 1866, and made several kinds of pottery, including red bisque, gray earthenware, oxblood, and several other attractive colors. In July of 1891 the firm was reorganized as the Chelsea Pottery U.S., and it was not until 1895 that the name was changed to Dedham Pottery.

Several marks are used by the firm.

C
The monogram K A for Chelsea
W
Keramic Art Works, or the name "Chelsea Keramic Art Works, Robertson & Sons," was used from 1875 to 1889. A cloverleaf with the initials "CPUS" was used in 1891–1892, and a rabbit after 1893.

Dedham pottery marks.

The Buffalo Pottery Company was known for several types of pottery, the most famous the Deldare ware (center). The pitchers are examples of cream-colored Buffalo pottery.

Buffalo ware

The Buffalo Pottery Company of Buffalo, New York, was another turn-of-the-century firm (1901) making pottery that is now in demand. The Deldare ware made by the company has a dark khaki-brown background with English hunting scenes, and was first made about 1908. The factory also made cream-colored pitchers with colored decorations and many types of commemorative plates and semivitreous china dinner sets. The firm used a picture of a buffalo and the date as part of its mark, so it is easy to identify.

Weller Pottery of Fultonham, Ohio, made a pottery resembling Rookwood and this Louwelsa ware (left) and Sicard (right).

Weller

The Weller pottery worked in Fultonham, Ohio, from 1873 to 1900. Samuel Weller made stoneware and artware that resembled Rookwood. Lonhuda and Louwelsa are names for potteries put out by this firm. A gold metallic luster pottery by Sicard has been a sought-after product of the Weller firm.

Most Weller is marked with the name of the company.

Lotus ware

The Knowles, Taylor, and Knowles factory of East Liverpool, Ohio, was established in 1854 by Isaac W. Knowles and Isaac A. Harvey. John Taylor and Homer Knowles joined the firm in 1870, and made many types of pottery and porcelain. The most famous and expensive of their products is a velvety glazed bone china called "lotus ware." It was made from 1890 to 1900 and is marked "KTK" or with a special mark including the words "lotus ware."

Stockton

The Stockton Terra Cotta Company was founded in Stockton, California, in 1891. They made several types of art pottery. The name was changed to the Stockton Art Pottery Company by 1897. Many of their pieces are marked "Rekston," which was the factory's trade name for a mottled pottery. The firm was never financially successful, and went out of business in 1902 after a fire.

Others

Pewabic Pottery was made in Detroit about 1905. Harker Pottery Company worked in East Liverpool, Ohio, after 1840. Pauline Pottery was made in Edgerton, Wis., and Chicago, Ill., after 1888. Roseville Pottery Company began in 1891 in Zanesville, Ohio. Other art potteries just now being rediscovered by the antique collectors are Newcomb Art Pottery of New Orleans, Louisiana (established 1896); Van Briggle Pottery, Colorado Springs, Colorado (established 1901); Gates Pottery, Terre Haute, Indiana; Poillon Pottery, Woodbridge, New Jersey; Grueby Faience Company, Boston, Massachusetts (established 1897); Moravian Pottery and Tile Works, Doylestown, Pennsylvania (established 1890); and Merrimac Ceramic Company, Newburyport, Massachusetts (established 1897).

Belleek

The glaze on Belleek closely resembles a piece of polished mother-of-pearl. It is creamy yellow. Occasionally, pieces are decorated with gold or very pale colors.

The open basketwork designs are, perhaps, the most famous. Dishes made to resemble shells or flowers are among the most beautiful. A few pieces were made of Belleek with a Parian figure incorporated into the design so that the texture of the two

Belleek marks. Willett's Manufacturing Co., Trenton, New Jersey (left). Irish mark (right).

Belleek marks. Lenox Company, Trenton, New Jersey.

types of china added to the beauty of the finished pieces.

Irish Belleek is almost always marked, although a few unmarked pieces have been identified. The mark is an Irish wolfhound, a harp, a round tower, and a shamrock with the name Belleek imprinted on it. This mark can be green, brown, black, red, or blue. The words "Belleek-Fermanagh" were also used.

Brianchon of France developed a glaze for a lustrous pearl-like ware that he patented in 1857. He called this ware "Nacre," and it is very much like the Irish Belleek glaze.

Ott and Brewer of Trenton, New Jersey, hired William Bromley to make Belleek ware. The ware was very successfully made about 1880.

The Knowles, Taylor and Knowles Company made Belleek and another porcelain similar to Belleek called "lotus ware."

Willett's Manufacturing Company and the Ceramic Art Pottery, both of Trenton, New Jersey, made Belleek (1879). Walter Scott Lenox learned about Belleek as an apprentice in the Ott and Brewer factory and later at the Willett's factory. He organized the Lenox Company in 1906 and made a ware similar to Belleek, but more translucent, and warmer in color.

Other United States factories used the name Belleek, but produced ware that is easily distinguished from the Irish product.

Haviland

Haviland china was the "company" dish set of grandmother's day. Many complete sets of Haviland can still be found and many are still in use.

Haviland has been made at Limoges, France, since the 1840's. David and Daniel Haviland of New York City went to France to search for French porcelain. It was to be decorated in the English manner for their American customers.

They started a factory in Limoges, France, in 1842. The dishes made by Haviland were popular because of their beauty, quality and low price.

Some Haviland china was decorated in the United States by the twentieth century. The name Haviland appeared in many marks on porcelain made by the several branches of the family.

There is unnecessary confusion about the marks used by the Haviland family.

Family

Haviland Brothers and Company (1852)
Haviland and Company (1866)
La Porcelaine Théodore Haviland (1892)

H&Co.
DEPOSE

HAVILAND, France. Whiteware. Painted green. 1876–1886.

H&Co.
L

HAVILAND, France. Painted red, black, blue, or green on decorated ware; painted green on whiteware. 1876.

H&Co.

HAVILAND, France. Whiteware. Painted green. Circa 1880.

H&Co.
L
FRANCE

HAVILAND, France. Whiteware. Painted green. 1891.

HAVILAND & CO.

HAVILAND, France. Decorated ware. Painted red, green, black, blue. 1876.

HAVILAND, France. Red. 1890–1926.

Haviland's
Chantilly

HAVILAND, France. Decorated ware. Painted red and green. 1948–1953.

Other Branches

Charles Field Haviland & Company (1876)

G. D. A. Limoges China
or
Charles Field Haviland
Limoges China.

(Now marked on Decorated in Red.)

GDA
LIMOGES

(On Rich Decorated; Gold Letters in Green Wreath.)

(White Ware.)

Prior to 1868, Æ

1868 *to* 1882, CFH

1882 *to* 1891, CFH / GDM

1891 *to* 1897, CFH / GDM / FRANCE

1897 *to present,* GDA / FRANCE

(Decorated Ware.)

Prior to 1897.

La Porcelaine Théodore Haviland (1892)

Aout 1892 TH

1892

1893 Theo Haviland
Limoges
FRANCE

1936 to 1945

1894 Porcelaine Mousseline
TH
Limoges FRANCE

1893 Haviland
France

1894 Porcelaine Mousseline
T H
Limoges FRANCE

1958 HAVILAND
LIMOGES
FRANCE

1903 Theodore Haviland
Limoges
FRANCE

1895 Porcelaine
Theo. Haviland
Limoges FRANCE

1925 Théodore Haviland
Limoges
FRANCE

1895 Porcelaine
Theo. Haviland
Limoges FRANCE

1920 à 1936 THEODORE HAVILAND
FRANCE

1903 Théodore Haviland
Limoges
FRANCE

OTHER FACTORIES WORKING IN LIMOGES, FRANCE

C. AHRENFELDT.
LIMOGES
FRANCE.

Charles Ahrenfeldt and Son.

P. H. Leonard.

BASSETT LIMOGES.

George F. Bassett
and Co.

A. Lanternier.

A. K. Limoges.

(*Underglaze in Blue.*)

R. Delinieres & Cie
Limoges

R. Delinieres & Cie.

A H & Co
V
FRANCE

A. Hache & Co.
Vierzon.

Alfred Hache & Co.
Vierzon, France.

L. BERNARDAUD & CIE, LIMOGES.
(*In Red.*)

L. Bernardaud & Cie.

Ch. Martin &
Neveu.

Wm GUERIN & Co
Limoges
FRANCE.

William
Guerin & Co.

L. W. Levy and Co.

Elite China, 1894–1900.

Elite China, after 1900.

Redon China.

Hinrichs & Co.

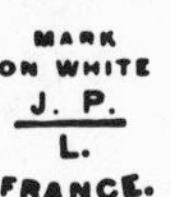

Pouyat China.

Royal China Decorating Co. New York.

Lazarus, Rosenfeld & Lehmann.

L. Straus & Sons.

NOT A GLOSSARY, NOT A DICTIONARY—JUST AN ALPHABETICAL LISTING OF SOME TERMS AND INSTANT EXPERT TIPS THAT MAY BE OF SOME HELP

Alphabet plates—see *Children's alphabet plates*

Biscuit ware

Bisque, or biscuit, porcelain has been made for many years. Any piece of unglazed porcelain is bisque. It gained popularity during the late Victorian era until the bisque figures

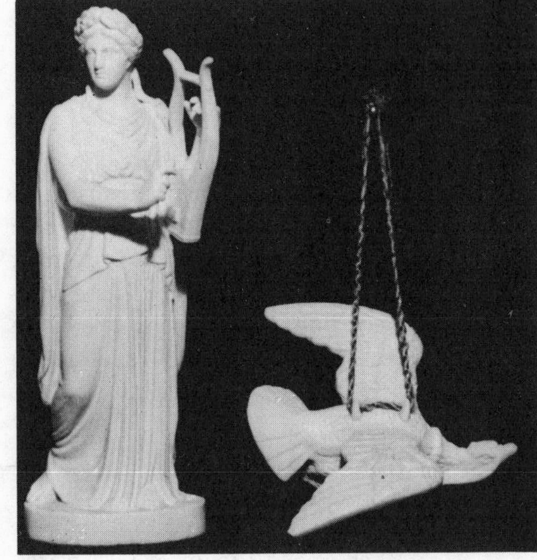

Biscuit ware pieces, (left) Royal Copenhagen figure, (right) bird which hangs on window-shade pull probably made by a Bennington factory.

were finally mass-produced by the millions.

During the Victorian period many people claimed the best bisque was made in Austria. Excellent bisque was made before the late nineteenth century by English, French, and other factories. There is no doubt that the finest bisque was made in Europe before the 1850's.

Bone china

Almost every type of animal bone can be satisfactorily burned and the ashes used in the manufacturing of bone china. The Spode Museum in England has a punch bowl that was made from bones that were left after a banquet. When the guests at the party finished eating, the bones remaining on their plates were collected and burned to ashes, and added to the clay that made the bone china punch bowl. It was a silly stunt, but it proved that finished bone china was hard and white. Bone china was developed about 1800.

Bone dishes

During the late Victorian era, fishbones were placed in small dishes at the dinner table. Hotels often gave the dishes to the diners as souvenirs. Most bone dishes were crescent-shaped, but some were shaped like a fish. BONE DISHES WERE USED DURING THE LATE 1890'S AND EARLY 1900'S.

Butter pats

Small dishes that held butter were another of the Victorian tablewares. BUTTER CHIPS WERE USED ONLY DURING THE LATE-NINETEENTH AND EARLY-TWENTIETH CENTURIES.

Calendar plates

CALENDAR PLATES WERE MADE FROM 1906 TO 1929. A calendar and the name of the store were printed on the plate. A few of the plates were made in England before 1906, but NO AMERICAN CALENDAR PLATES DATE BEFORE 1906.

Children's alphabet plates

MOST OF THE ABC PLATES WERE MADE FROM 1780 TO 1860. They were made as teaching aids for the young child who was learning to read. The outside border had the letters of the alphabet with appropriate pictures of a hero, famous landmark, Aesop's fables, or storybook characters decorating the center of the plate. The plates were made of glass, tin, pottery, pewter, or silver plate. Most of them were made in England. Some of the unusual examples include the alphabet in Braille or in sign language for the deaf.

Bone dish.

DENMARK.

Royal Copenhagen marks.

Christmas plates

The Danish Christmas plates were first made in 1895 by the Bing and Grondahl factory, and in 1908 by the Royal Copenhagen factory. A limited number of plates with a new design are made every year, and the molds destroyed, which assures a limited edition. Each plate has a scene in the center, the date, and usually the word "Jule." All the plates have been made with a blue-and-white glaze.

Coal-scuttle mugs

The coal-scuttle mug was given its name because of its peculiar shape. The small "pocket" that protruded in front held a shaving brush. The first of these mugs was made as a soap package. THE COAL-SCUTTLE MUG WAS A TYPE USED FROM 1870 TO 1900.

Coffee can

The term "coffee can" is English, and refers to what Americans call a "mug." It was a popular china form in the eighteenth century. Most of the English potters made the coffee cans as well as cups and saucers, and sold them as parts of dinner sets. A STRAIGHT-SIDED CAN WAS 2½ INCHES HIGH AND 2½ INCHES IN DIAMETER. ANY OTHER SIZE, EVEN THOSE WITH ONE-HALF INCH DIFFERENCE, IS A COLLECTOR'S RARITY.

Coronation cups

Most of the souvenir coronation cups have been made since the 1800's. Pictures of the English kings appear on some earlier pieces of pottery. Any of the many porcelain or pottery pieces made as souvenirs for the coronations is a coronation piece.

Coronation cup.

Fairings

Souvenirs have always been sold at fairs. Small china boxes, or "fairings" were popular during the nineteenth century. Hundreds of designs were made during the 1855 to 1870 period, when they were in great demand for pins, matches, and so on. The work was crude, but the designs were amusing and the boxes colorful. Most of them were made in the Staffordshire district in England or in Germany. (See bibliography at end of chapter for book about "fairings.")

Fish and game plates

A game plate is any type of plate decorated with pictures of birds or wild game. Most fish and game plates came in sets of twelve plus a serving platter. Most of the game plates were made in Germany, Bavaria, and France during the 1880's.

Fish plate, made by the Wedgwood factory of England.

Hot-water dish, export porcelain c. 1820.

Hot-water dish

The hot-water dish looks like a covered soup bowl with a lower section that can be filled with water. Hot water was poured inside, and it kept the upper plate warm and the food hot. It was popular after 1830.

Leeds

Leeds was a popular English factory during the eighteenth and early nineteenth centuries. Leeds ware has several characteristics that are easy to recognize. THE HANDLES WERE USUALLY MADE OF TWISTED, ENTWINED STRIPS OF CLAY. THE RIM WAS OFTEN BEADED. CREAMWARE WAS USUALLY TINGED GREEN AT THE RIM. Best of all for positive identification, if everything else checks, it is nice to find the word "Leeds" impressed on the bottom—a rarity but a possibility.

Lithopane

A lithopane is a transparent panel of biscuit porcelain. The design was made by varying the thickness of the panel. When a lithopane was held to the light, the thick parts appeared dark and the thinner ones light.

The process for making lithopanes was developed in 1827 by Baron de Bourgoing of Paris. They were made in Berlin and in Meissen, Germany, and in Holland, France, Denmark, and England.

LITHOPANES WERE POPULAR FROM 1834 TO 1860. They were hung in windows, mounted in lampshades, placed on candlestands, and even used at the bottom of children's milk glasses or adults' beer mugs. Most of them were white, but a few colored ones were made. The process was very difficult, and forgeries are rare. A few new lithopanes were made in 1965.

Moss rose china

The moss rose was a very popular flower during the early nineteenth century. Gardeners prized the fuzzy flower, and because of its popularity it was often pictured on china and glassware. The earliest Moss Rose china was made about 1808. The fad was over by the late 1890's, and the pattern was discontinued.

Because the moss rose is being grown again, and sold in many parts of the United States and Canada, dishes picturing the flower have become popular with the collectors.

Moustache cup

The flowing moustache became the feature of many men's faces after the Mexican War. Proper care of a moustache included curlers, oil, dye, brushes, combs, and even nets that held it curled at night. After all his care of his moustache, no man wanted to dip it in hot coffee and spoil his appearance. The moustache cup was a large coffee cup with a porcelain ledge near the rim. The curled moustache could rest on the ledge, safe from the dangers of hot drinks.

Victorian moustache cup.

The first factory to make a moustache cup was Harvey Adams and Company of Longton, Staffordshire, England, about 1850. THE CUPS AND MOUSTACHES WENT OUT OF STYLE ABOUT 1900.

Moustache cups were made by most of the famous factories, from demitasse size to quart size. They are made of silver, pottery, or porcelain, and were usually made to order for the individual.

In Victoria's day it was considered good taste to give a moustache cup inscribed, "To Pop," "Forget Me Not," "Love the Giver," "Birthday Greetings," "Present," or "Remember Me."

Left-handed moustache cups were made, but they are a rarity.

Parian ware

Parian ware is an unglazed white porcelain resembling Parian marble. It was first made by the English Spode factory about 1842. Many other firms manufactured Parian ware after that date. Some of it was colored.

Pâté sur pâté

Pâté sur pâté was a special type of porcelain. The word is French, and when translated means "paste on paste." Thin layers of white creamy slip were applied to an unfired clay vase. The slip, or thin clay, formed a raised decoration on the finished piece.

Marc Louis Solon tried to copy an early Chinese vase. His mistakes and efforts developed the skills that were used in making pâté sur pâté. He worked at the Sèvres factory in France until 1870, when he moved to the Minton firm in England.

Pâté sur pâté ware is beautiful and expensive. It required many time-consuming applications of the slip. The ware was in great demand, and Solon trained Birks, Hollins, Mellor, Morgan, Rhead, Rice, Sanders, and Toft. All these men made and signed work for Minton.

The demand continued, and many other European potteries began making pâté sur pâté. Many of the factories, such as Sèvres and Worcester, had several artists who signed the ware.

Pâté sur pâté was out of production by most firms by 1890. It was still in demand but slow and expensive to manufacture and not a profitable ware.

Photograph plates

A PROCESS WAS DEVELOPED IN THE 1860'S THAT MADE IT POSSIBLE TO REPRODUCE A PHOTOGRAPH ON A PIECE OF PORCELAIN. A few porcelain firms used the system, but most of the plates were made with photographs by individual photographers interested in experimenting. The picture was sealed under a glaze and baked on the plate.

Pot lids

The Pratt factory was the most famous of the English firms that made multicolored pot lids. These were china tops that were used on commercial soap, cosmetics, and moustache wax boxes. The lids became very popular with collectors, and are often framed and hung as a group.

F. and R. Pratt Company made the lids in Fenton, England, during the late 1840's. THE FIRST POT LID WITH A COLORED TRANSFER PRINT WAS MADE IN 1846, and was called "Polar Bears." Hundreds of different lids were made during the next forty years. Pratt also made dishes and small porcelain objects. (See bibliography for book with complete listing.)

Do not confuse Pratt ware with the earlier Staffordshire pottery made by Felix Pratt during the late eighteenth century. It was a cream-colored earthenware that had decorations painted in orange, blue, and green.

Puzzle jug. (Colonial Williamsburg, Williamsburg, Virginia)

Puzzle jug

There are several types of puzzle jugs made by the practical jokers of their generation.

One jug, the simplest of the puzzles, has a frog on the bottom. When the unwary tippler drank his grog, the frog appeared—a startling, lifelike visitor. Many hard drinkers must have had a real fright from this jug.

Another type of jug had holes under the handle at the neck of the jug. It was the original "dribble glass," for the contents of the jug spilled all over the drinker.

If you knew it was a puzzle jug, you could safely drink from it by covering all but one of the holes with your fingers.

Stirrup cups are not true puzzles, but are often collected with puzzle jugs. They were shaped like the heads of animals, such as a fox or a dog, and were made during the eighteenth and nineteenth centuries. The cup could not be put down until it was empty because there was no flat bottom surface.

There was another puzzle jug copied after an earlier Oriental design. It is probably the most famous. The Cadogan pot was made at Nottingham, England, and was named after the Earl of Cadogan. This pot has no lid. It was shaped like a peach, with trailing vinelike designs twined about it. There was a hole in the bottom of the pot, but no other opening except the end of the spout. It is hard to believe, but if you filled the pot from the bottom and turned it over, no water would spill, though water would pour from the spout.

Quintal

A five-finger posy vase is a quintal. The design started in Holland but was also made in England.

Saltglaze

Legend says a farm girl was pickling pork in a salt-water brine and the brine boiled over onto a hot earthenware pot. When the pot cooled, it had a bright hard glaze. It's a nice story, but we doubt if it really ever happened that way. Saltglaze was made by throwing salt into the kiln

Saltglaze. (Colonial Williamsburg, Williamsburg, Virginia)

while the pottery was being fired. It was a late-seventeenth-century method.

Shaving mugs (See Coal-scuttle mug)

Occupational shaving mugs pictured fire engines, milk wagons, or other easily identifiable trade items. The shaving mug was kept in a mug case at the local barbershop. THEY WERE USED FROM 1860 TO 1900, AND LATER.

Tapestry china

"Tapestry china" is a name that was developed during the 1950's, and refers to a type of porcelain made about 1890. The porcelain was covered with a tightly stretched piece of fabric; then it was decorated and glazed. The finished piece had a rough texture that was similar to a piece of tapestry. Many of the tapestry china pieces were labeled "Royal Bayreuth," a late-nineteenth-century German mark.

Tiles

TILES WITH RAISED RELIEF DECORATIONS WERE NOT MADE UNTIL AFTER THE CENTENNIAL EXPOSITION IN 1876.

Toby jugs

The Toby jug was named for Toby Philpot, a notorious drinker in a song written in 1761. The jug was shaped to resemble a seated person. MOST TOBY JUGS WERE MADE FROM 1776 TO 1825.

Worcester

This is too good a tip to omit even though it is about an eighteenth-

Shaving mug. (Collection of A. Christian Revi)

century English porcelain. HOLD THE DISH IN FRONT OF A BRIGHT LIGHT. THE BODY OF THE PORCELAIN WILL APPEAR TO BE GREEN IF THE PIECE IS DR. WALL WORCESTER, an eighteenth-century English ware. Most porcelain when held to a bright light appears to be white, blue-white, or pink.

And a word about some special marks

Spode, the English factory, dates from 1754. The name is often on the wares, and some have pattern numbers. THE LOW NUMBERS ARE ON THE EARLIER PIECES, BUT OVER 5,000 PATTERN NUMBERS WERE USED BY 1833.

Mettlach beer steins are clearly marked with numbers. The firm worked from 1809, and is still operating. The famed steins were made during the nineteenth century. Each stein was numbered, lettered, and had a picture of the abbey and the word "Mettlach" on it after 1874. (See picture in section about Mettlach.)

Nippon

Nippon is found on Japanese wares made after 1891. Noritake is a Japanese ware made in 1904 by Nippon Toki Kaisha. It is still being made.

Royal Doulton

The word, "Royal" was used after 1901. Before that it was just "Doulton."

Marks to watch out for

The gold anchor mark attributed to Chelsea.

The crossed swords of Meissen.

The "N" and crown of Capo di Monte.

The crowned circle of Hoechst.

These are all marks that have been forged thousands of times—*so beware!*

Hints on care of pottery and porcelain

Wash antique dishes in the same manner as you would any fine modern china dishes. A dishwasher can handle anything that is not crazed or does not have gold decorations. These dishes must be washed by hand. Badly stained dishes can be soaked overnight in laundry bleach.

Pottery and Porcelain: Bibliography

Marks

Chaffers, William. *Marks and Monograms on European and Oriental Pottery and Porcelain.* Los Angeles, California: Borden, 1946.
This is the fourteenth edition of the famous book first written in 1863. It contains thousands of marks and explanations of the factories and makers. Though it is a difficult book to use, it is worth the effort.

Godden, Geoffrey A. *Encyclopedia of British Pottery and Porcelain Marks.* New York: Crown, 1964.
An excellent, all-inclusive listing of the marks used on British ceramics. Over 4000 marks, arranged alphabetically.

Haggar, Reginald G. *The Concise Encyclopedia of Continental Pottery and Porcelain.* New York: Hawthorn, 1960.
An encyclopedia of information about ceramics other than American and English, with many color plates, copies of marks, and other illustrations.

Kovel, Ralph and Terry. *Dictionary of Marks—Pottery and Porcelain.* New York: Crown, 1953.
The simplest listing of marks available, arranged by the shape of the mark.

Mankowitz, Wolf, and Reginald G. Haggar. *The Concise Encyclopedia of English Pottery and Porcelain.* New York: Hawthorn, n.d.
This volume of a set of two is concerned with English ceramics. Color plates, reproductions of marks, and much information are included.

General

Cox, Warren. *The Book of Pottery and Porcelain.* New York: Crown, 1949.
Two-volume book about ceramics from prehistoric to modern.

Litchfield, Frederick. *Pottery and Porcelain.* New York: Barrows, 1951.
General book about ceramics of Europe from medieval times.

Delft

de Jonge, C. H. *Delft Ceramics.* New York: Praeger, 1970. A history of delft from all parts of Europe. Interesting choice of illustrations.

———. *Dutch Tiles.* New York: Praeger, 1971.
The definitive work on Dutch tiles of the seventeenth and eighteenth centuries.

Moore, N. Hudson. *Delftware, Dutch and English.* New York: Stokes, 1908.
A small book concerned with the finest delftwares; includes a listing of marks.

Majolica

Rickerson, Wildey C. *Majolica, It's Fun to Collect.* Privately printed. (Order from author, P. O. Box 110, Deep River, Conn.)
A paper pamphlet which gives the history of many American and European Majolica manufacturers. Sketches of marks and photographs.

Staffordshire

Balston, Thomas. *Staffordshire Portrait Figures of the Victorian Age.* Newton 59, Mass.: Branford, 1958.
An illustrated listing and history of the Victorian Staffordshire figures. A very valuable book for the collector of this type of ware.

Pugh, P. D. Gordon. *Staffordshire Portrait Figures.* New York: Praeger, 1971.
A very comprehensive picture listing of 1500 Victorian Staffordshire figures. Values and reproductions are discussed.

Rackham, Bernard. *Early Staffordshire Pottery.* New York: Pitman, n.d.
Pottery of the Staffordshire district from 1660 to 1800 is photographed and discussed.

Stanley, Louis T. *Collecting Staffordshire Pottery.* New York: Doubleday, 1963.
An illustrated book about the origins and development of Staffordshire figures of the eighteenth and nineteenth centuries. The author has included his opinion of the market and future values.

Printed Staffordshire

Laidacker, Sam. *Anglo-American China,* Parts I and II. Bristol, Pennsylvania: Laidacker, 1951.
Book One pictures and prices the American views, and Book Two the other views shown on the many pieces of blue-and-white transfer pottery made in the Staffordshire district in the mid-nineteenth century.

Larsen, Ellouise Baker. *American Historical Views on Staffordshire China.* New York: Doubleday, Doran, 1939.
The definitive work on this subject, a collection of photographs and a history of the American market views on china of the Staffordshire district in England. Of special value is the information about border designs, facts that aid in the identification of other types of blue-and-white transfer china.

Little, W. L. *Staffordshire Blue.* New York: Crown, 1969.
An alphabetic listing of the Staffordshire potters who made blue transfer wares. History, marks, and photographs are included.

Williams, Petra. *Flow Blue China, An Aid to Identification.* Jeffersontown, Kentucky: Fountain House East, P.O. Box 99298, 1971.
Blue transfer decorated plates are alphabetically listed and pictured. Marks and pattern variations are indicated. England, France, Germany and other countries are included.

Ironstone

Freeman, Larry. *Ironstone China, China Classics IV.* Watkins Glen, New York: Century, 1954.
This book is a listing of makers and pattern names, and contains a little history of ironstoneware. The section on white ironstone is excellent.

Shull, Thelma. *Victorian Antiques.* Rutland, Vermont: Tuttle, 1963.
Two chapters in this general book discuss white ironstone and tea-leaf ironstone.

Luster

John, W. D., and Warren Baker. *Old English Lustre Pottery.* Newport Mon, England: The Ceramic Book Company, 1962.
Limited edition of English book about the history of English luster. American historical subjects, Wedgwood, Spode, Leeds, and other classifications are included. A well-illustrated book with both black and white and color photographs.

Chinese Export Porcelain

Beurdeley, Michel. *Chinese Trade Porcelain.* Rutland, Vermont: Tuttle, 1962.
An excellent, very important book about the many types of Chinese trade porcelains, this is a valuable reference work for anyone interested in the subject. Many black-and-white and color photographs.

Hyde, J. A. Lloyd. *Oriental Lowestoft.* New York: Charles Scribner's Sons, 1936.
An important book for the collector of export porcelains, with a special section about the wares made for the American market.

Mudge, Jean McClure. *Chinese Export Porcelain for the American Trade 1785–1835.* Newark, Delaware: University of Delaware Press, 1962.
A well-documented book with excellent photographs and an extensive bibliography, this is a useful research tool.

Wilson. Jane. *Canton China.* Essex, Connecticut: Riverside Press, 1961.
This small pamphlet features photographs of most of the shapes of blue-and-white Canton china of the export types.

Wedgwood

Buten, Harry M. *Wedgwood ABC but Not Middle E.* Merion, Pennsylvania: Buten Museum of Wedgwood, 1964.
An interesting general book about the works of the Wedgwood factory.

———. *Wedgwood Chronology.* Merion, Pennsylvania: Buten Museum of Wedgwood, n.d.
A very useful mimeographed dating guide.

Graham, John M., and Hensleigh C. Wedgwood. *Wedgwood.* Brooklyn, New York: Brooklyn Museum, Brooklyn Institute of Arts and Sciences, 1948.
A well-illustrated general book about Wedgwood wares.

Honey, W. B. *Wedgwood Ware.* New York: Van Nostrand, 1949.
This book has about 100 pieces of Wedgwood pictured, and tells a general history of the factory.

Mankowitz, Wolf. *Wedgwood.* New York: Dutton, 1953.
This is the most important book available about the general subject of Wedgwood wares; well illustrated.

Meissen

Charles, Rollo. *Continental Porcelain of the Eighteenth Century.* London: University of Toronto Press, 1964.
This is a beautiful book about European porcelains, with five chapters about the important Meissen periods.

Honey, W. B. *Dresden China.* New York: Tudor, 1946.

A good general study of Meissen, with 175 pieces illustrated.

Morley-Fletcher, Hugo. *Antique Porcelain in Color: Meissen.* New York: Doubleday, 1971.
A color picture listing of the history of the Meissen factory from 1710. The book has more color pictures than information.

Spatterware

Greaser, Arlene and Paul H. *Homespun Ceramics.* Allentown, Pennsylvania: Privately printed, 1965. (Order from author, Hess Department Store, Allentown, Pa.)
An excellent listing of types of spatterware, with limited commentary.

Made in America

Tucker China 1825–1835. Philadelphia: Philadelphia Museum of Art, 1957.
This pamphlet lists 488 pieces of Tucker china, and has many color pictures.

Barret, Richard Carter. *Bennington Pottery and Porcelain.* New York: Crown, 1958.
The definitive work on the subject of Bennington pottery and porcelain.

Schwartz, Marvin D., and Richard Wolfe. *A History of American Art Porcelain.* New York: Renaissance Editions, 1967.
Short illustrated book of American porcelain.

American Pottery

Altman, Seymour and Violet. *The Book of Buffalo Pottery.* New York: Crown, 1969.
Detailed history of the Buffalo Pottery plant and its wares. Over 400 pieces are illustrated.

Barret, Richard Carter. *A Color Guide to Bennington Pottery.* Privately printed, 1966. (Order from Forward's Color Productions, Inc., Manchester, Vermont.)
In this pamphlet, 193 pieces of Bennington ware are pictured in color.

Crawford, Jean. *Jugtown Pottery History and Design.* Winston-Salem, North Carolina: John F. Blair, 1964.
The story of the Jugtown, North Carolina, pottery from 1915.

Menzke, Lucile. *American Art Pottery.* Camden, New Jersey: Thomas Nelson, 1970.
General book about American pottery of the late nineteenth and early twentieth centuries.

Peck, Herbert. *The Book of Rookwood Pottery.* New York: Crown, 1968.
Detailed history of Rookwood pottery. Over 250 pieces are illustrated.

Ramsay, John. *American Potters and Pottery.* New York: Tudor, 1947.
An excellent general book about the pottery of the nineteenth century in the United States. Bibliography included.

Spargo, John. *Early American Pottery and China.* Garden City, New York: Garden City Publishing, 1926.
An excellent general book about potters in America from pre-revolutionary days to the end of the nineteenth century.

Haviland China

Schleiger, Arlene. *Two Hundred Patterns of Haviland China* (I–IV). Privately printed, 1950–

1959. (Order from author, 4039 Mary, Omaha 12, Nebraska.)

These four books list the patterns of Haviland china, and are used to identify patterns by the matching services and antique shops.

Wood, Serry. *Haviland-Limoges, China Classics II.* Watkins Glen, New York: Century, 1951.

A small book that is a compilation of earlier catalogs, with some additional information about the china of the Victorian period in Limoges, France.

Miscellaneous

Bristowe, W. S. *Victorian China Fairings.* New York: Taplinger, 1965.

This well-illustrated book tells the story of the small figurines and trinket boxes sold at fairs in the nineteenth century.

Clarke, Harold George. *Underglaze Colour Picture Prints on Staffordshire Pottery* (*The Pictorial Pot Lid Book*). London: Courier Press, 1960.

The English printed pot lids are listed and illustrated in this comprehensive book.

Eyles, Desmond. *Royal Doulton, 1815–1965.* London: Hutchinson, 1965.

This book is an informative, attractive history of the famous Doulton factory and its wares. It has many pictures.

Fisher, Stanley. *English Blue and White Porcelain of the Eighteenth Century.* London: Batsford, 1947.

The early blue and white wares are discussed with authority; factories such as Worcester, Liverpool, Bristol, Chelsea, and others are included.

Godden, Geoffrey. *Caughley & Worcester Porcelains 1775–1800.* New York: Praeger, 1969.

An unusual comparison of two English factories from 1775 to 1800. This book clarifies the confusion between Caughley and Worcester caused by earlier writers.

———. *An Illustrated Encyclopedia of British Pottery and Porcelain.* New York: Crown, 1966.

An excellent, very complete study of British porcelain from 1700 to 1900. Over 650 photographs of specimens.

———. *The Illustrated Guide to Mason's Patent Ironstone China.* New York: Praeger, 1971.

The definitive book about Mason's Ironstone China. A thoroughly documented and well-illustrated study.

Hammond, Dorothy. *Mustache Cups: History and Marks.* Des Moines, Iowa: Wallace-Homestead, 1972.

Over 800 mustache cups are pictured in color in this book.

Stringer, George Eyre. *New Hall Porcelain.* London: Salisbury Square, 1949.

This definitive work on the New Hall factory includes useful information about marks and pattern numbers.

Whiter, Leonard. *Spode.* New York: Praeger, 1970.

Beautifully illustrated history of the Spode factory from 1733 to 1833. Detailed information is given about patterns and marks.

2

Glass

Introduction

ALMOST EVERYONE HAS A PIECE of old glass that has been in the family for years, and every piece seems to have a glamorous history behind it. It is often a story that can never be substantiated. There were stories in our own family about six green glasses that had belonged to our grandfather. Each grandchild was given one of the priceless green glasses, with an appropriate story regarding its rarity. When we began studying antiques, we never looked up the priceless green glasses because they were too rare to be the subject of an article about popular glass. It can now be told: The green pressed glass with its gold decorations was a pattern called "Four Petal," and was made for the Atlantic and Pacific Tea Company about 1890 and *given away free* with the purchase of coffee. We still display Grandpa's green glasses in a special place, and fondly recall the fantastic stories of the rare green glass. Our priceless heirloom was just another piece of ordinary glass that has now become old enough to be considered an antique.

More than any other type of antique, glassware is haunted by the problem of mistaken identity. It is the late-Victorian glass or early-twentieth-century glass that is selling for thousands of dollars, and not the mid-Victorian or earlier glassware. Some of the rarest eighteenth-century American glasswares are being sold for astronomical sums, but they are so rare and hard to identify only a true expert could ever hope to recognize one. The average collector who goes to antique shows, house sales, or inherits Great Aunt Hattie's house full of assorted bric-a-brac, antiques, and monstrosities might find the expensive Victorian art glass, but not the eighteenth-century rarities.

The fastest, easiest Instant Expert way to learn about glass is to study the newest glass first. Most amateurs will treasure a piece of green glass like Grandpa's, and they will completely miss a newer, more valuable, piece of iridescent glass made in the 1920's. Glassware is different from many other types of antiques because of the various fads promoted by some collectors. Carnival glass, which was a cheap giveaway product of the early 1900's, has become the darling of many collectors, and the prices have risen far beyond the artistic worth of the ware. (Although, what is to determine worth better than supply and demand?) The study of glass requires time and effort, but you can learn how and where to start.

The most important Instant Expert tip on glass is: COLORED GLASS WAS NOT POPULAR UNTIL AFTER THE CIVIL WAR. Of course, some of the colored glass was made earlier, and many eighteenth-century pieces were produced from blue, purple, or bottle green; but the efforts of the glassmakers were directed to making glass as clear as possible until about 1860. After that time, many new types of colored glass were developed. There is one sad word of wisdom that you must heed: ALMOST EVERY KNOWN TYPE OF GLASSWARE—pressed, blown, colored, clear—HAS BEEN REPRODUCED DURING THE PAST FIFTY YEARS. The reproductions were often made from original molds, which makes identification more difficult but not impossible. We shall first start with definitions, and then give the story of the many types of glass, starting with the twentieth-century wares, and dating back to some of the rarities that can seldom be found.

Definitions

To understand glass, it is important to understand the basic methods of manufacture. Therefore it is necessary to learn a few of the technical terms. The basic materials that are used to make glass, such as sand and various alkalis, are mixed together to form a BATCH. The batch is melted together to get molten glass, or METAL. The metal is blown through a blowpipe or formed in another manner. The piece of hot glass that is formed is called a GATHER. The gather is held on a PONTIL, or PUNTY ROD, during the blowing of the glass. The rough spot often found on the bottom of a piece of glass is called the PONTIL MARK. It is left on the glass when the pontil is removed from the formed piece of glass.

There are many ways to shape glass. The earliest method was to blow the glass. A gather of glass was placed at the end of a pontil and then blown by air to the desired shape. FREEBLOWN or OFFHAND BLOWN means the same as BLOWN. The second method of forming glasswares was PATTERN MOLDED or BLOWN MOLDED GLASS. The gather of metal (molten glass) was blown into a mold similar to a waffle-iron grid. The glass was removed heated, and blown offhand. The finished piece would have geometric swirls or designs. The swirls were larger at one end of the piece because the blowing process "stretched" the glass and the design. If a design is drawn on a toy rubber balloon before it is blown up, it will distort in much the same manner as the swirls of blown molded glass.

BLOWN THREE MOLD glass was made during the 1820's and 1830's. The glass was blown into a full-size mold. The glass touched the edges of the mold; and since a mold was made in several parts, the seams could be seen on the finished piece. Many bottles were made by this method. Illogically there may be two, three, or four seams, but they are all called "three-mold glass."

PRESSED GLASS was made by placing the glass in a mold and pressing it with a weight. There is no blowing involved.

Decoration

There are many ways to decorate glass and there are hundreds of names for the glass decorations, but only a few are important. THREADING, LILYPAD, PRUNTS, and several other terms refer to added "blobs" of glass applied to a shaped piece. It was a popular eighteenth-century method of decoration in America, and it was also found on many late-nineteenth-century wares. If the glass was bent after it was shaped, the decoration was called CRIMPING. Every housewife knows how to crimp the edge of a pie shell, and this is exactly the same in glass.

It is possible to add colored designs to glassware while it is hot. Colored rods of glass (like strips of spaghetti) are worked into the gather before the piece is shaped. The LOOPINGS and SWIRLS made by the colored glass are typical of Nailsea and other glassware. There is another type of decoration with colored pieces of glass that is seen in paperweights. Accurately enough, it was named PAPERWEIGHT decoration. This technique is explained with the other material in the section devoted to paperweights.

ENGRAVED glass is cut with a copper wheel or a diamond point. A bit of glass is actually removed when glass is engraved. ETCHING is an acid process used to frost an area. It was popular in the late 1800's. TO TEST THE AGE OF ENGRAVING ON GLASS, PLACE A WHITE HANDKERCHIEF ON THE INSIDE. IF THE ENGRAVING IS OLD, THE LINES WILL USUALLY SHOW UP DARKER THAN THE REST OF THE GLASS. NEW ENGRAVING HAS A BRIGHT POWDERLIKE SURFACE.

CUT GLASS was made by literally cutting away some of the glass. Sections of a heavy, usually clear glass were removed with a cutting wheel. Simple cutting was used during the eighteenth century, but most of the brilliant cut glass was made in the 1880's.

Glass could be painted with a design, and heated so that the color was permanent. This was called ENAMELING.

TYPES OF GLASS

The easiest glassware to identify is the iridescent glass made in the 1894 to 1935 period. It is attractive, unusual, and in great demand. The father of iridescent glass was Louis Comfort Tiffany, a glassmaker with great skill, an artist of great renown, and a businessman who made a highly profitable product that was never inexpensive.

Mr. Tiffany first saw iridescent glass in Europe, and began making the ware in his factory at Corona, Long Island, in 1894, and continued until 1920. His glassmakers all came from Europe. MR. TIFFANY USUALLY SIGNED THE GLASS WITH THE NAME "TIFFANY," THE INITIALS "L. C. T.," OR "L. C. TIFFANY," OR THE WORD

Mr. Tiffany made many unusual colors and shapes of iridescent glass. The vase is orange and violet cased glass marked "Favrile"; the goblet is white, green, and pink; the bowl is also Favrile glass. (Toledo Museum of Art, Toledo, Ohio)

"FAVRILE." When the signature is missing, iridescent Tiffany glass can be identified only by an expert. There was only a small percentage of glass made without a signature. Iridescent glass was made in various shades of gold, green, blue, and other colors.

Iridescent glass by Tiffany was so successful that many other factories tried to copy the work. Quezal glass was made from 1901 to 1920 by Martin Bach, Sr., who had previously worked for Tiffany. It is said that ALL QUEZAL GLASS WAS MARKED. Some pieces of quezal were overlay glass, which is one layer of opaque white or colored glass over another layer of glass.

Durand glass was made by Victor Durand from 1897 to 1935. Some of his pieces were marked Durand with a large "V.," but most of them were not marked.

Aurene is the trade name of the glass made by Frederick Carder about 1904. Later, the mark "Steuben" was also used. Most of the Carder glass was marked either "Aurene" or "Steuben." A few pieces were also signed by Mr. Carder.

Kew Blas was the name used by the Union Glass Company at Somerville, Massachusetts. They made golden iridescent glass from the 1890's to 1924.

There is a subtle difference in the coloring of the iridescent glass of

The golden iridescent glass is often difficult to identify. This unmarked piece appears to be typical of the Loetz factory of Austria.

many factories; and only familiarity with the various glasses makes it possible to determine the difference. The Carder golden iridescent is sharper and harsher than most of the other wares. Aurene was a golden shade with a rosy tint around the edges.

The Imperial Glass Company of Bellaire, Ohio, and the Fenton Art Glass Company of Williamstown, West Virginia, made iridescent glass. Most of them were marked with paper stickers that washed off. The Loetz factory of Austria also made a similar type of iridescent glass.

Any of the iridescent glasswares are examples of Victorian art glass, even though many pieces were made during the twentieth century. All these factories made other types of glass, as well as iridescent.

To summarize the problem of markings on iridescent glasswares: ALMOST ALL THE IMPORTANT ART-GLASS PIECES MADE BY THE TIFFANY FACTORY OR MR. CARDER AT THE STEUBEN FACTORY WERE MARKED WITH ONE OF SEVERAL DIFFERENT MARKS USED BY THE MAKERS. The unmarked iridescent glasswares were usually the works of a minor American factory or one of the European factories, such as Loetz. The quality of the glassware will indicate its true importance; but for the beginner, it is safest to assume that if it is unmarked it is not Tiffany or Steuben.

Carnival glass

Carnival glass was a cheap pressed glass made by the carload to be given away at carnivals or sold in the five-and-ten-cent stores. The carnival, or taffeta, glass was made as a cheap version of the expensive Tiffany-type iridescent glassware. Carnival was made in dark purple, blue-green, orange, iridescent white, or red. It was made from about 1900 to 1920, and has recently been reproduced in huge quantities; but the new glass is much brighter, and can be distinguished from the old carnival with a little practice. Most of the carnival glass was made by the Northwood Glass Company of Martin's Ferry, Ohio, from 1910, the Imperial Glass Company of Bellaire, Ohio, from 1910 to 1920, and the Fenton Art Glass Company of Williamstown, West Virginia, from 1905 to 1930. Other firms also made the carnival glass, but only a few pieces are marked with an impressed mark that was molded into the glass. Carnival glass is a type of pressed glass

Carnival glass came in many patterns. This is the famous peacock pattern.

with many indentations and bumps, but the true golden iridescent Tiffany type of glassware was blown, and not molded in a machine.

The carnival glass marks most often found are the overlapping "I" and "G" of the Imperial Glass Company, and the letter "N" or "N" in a circle used by the Northwood Glass Company of Martin's Ferry, Ohio.

Over two hundred patterns of carnival glass are now listed in books, and more are appearing each year.

SATIN GLASS

There is one whole branch of the glass family tree that can be called satin glass. Satin glass is any opaque glass that was given a characteristic dull finish by means of hydrofluoric acid vapor treatment. All the satin glass has a velvety finish, and most of the colored pieces have a white lining.

Many English and American companies produced satin glass during the 1880's. Vases, rose bowls, fruit bowls, baskets, lamps, pickle jars, and other types of decorative pieces were made. The satin glass vase may have been left undecorated, but applied glass flowers were frequently added.

Several types of special ornamentation have been given names such as Mother-of-Pearl or Coralene. Special color effects have been named, but all the dull, satiny finished glasswares are satin glass, regardless of their age, color, or decoration.

Mother-of-pearl or pearl satin glass

A patent was given to an English firm in 1858 and to the Mt. Washington Glass Company of New Bedford, Massachusetts, after 1851 to make pearl satin ware or mother-of-pearl glass. It was a special type of blown

Satin glass was made in many colors and with many types of decoration. Left, a piece of Coralene glass decorated, in typical fashion, with tiny glass beads arranged in designs; center, satin glass bowl, probably English, with applied decorations; right, English satin-glass bowl in silver-plated holder. (Corning Museum of Glass, Corning, New York)

molded satin glass that is in great demand. It was made with indentations to trap air bubbles or with ridges that gave the same pearly effect, and it must be seen to be recognized.

A similar type of mother-of-pearl was made by other factories in the United States, England, Bohemia, and France, and was decorated in many different ways, including enamel, applied glass decorations, gold leaf, threading, and cameo technique.

Rainbow satin glass

Any of the many-colored pastel glasses with a satin-like finish. A very few pieces of this glass were made in the 1880's.

Coralene

Coralene was made at the Mt. Washington Glass Works in New Bedford, Massachusetts, during the 1880's. It was probably made at other American factories, in England, and on the Continent. The glass was decorated with an enamel paint; tiny glass beads were applied to the paint, and the entire piece was heated to set the enamel and fix the beads. One design resembled coral branches. Many imitations of the glass were made by painting old glass and gluing small beads to the paint.

The glass of the coralene vase was plain satin glass, mother-of-pearl satin glass, or a glossy finished glassware.

Crown Milano

A less well-known satin glass, made by Frederick Shirley, was Crown Milano; it had a pale biscuit color with a satin finish. The glass was decorated with flowers, and usually had gold scrolls. The decorations are easy to recognize, and any collector can learn to identify most pieces of Crown Milano glass.

Crown Milano is a pale-colored satin glass with gold or colored decorations. This cracker jar was made at the Mt. Washington Glass Co., New Bedford, Massachusetts, about 1890. (Corning Museum of Glass, Corning, New York)

Royal Flemish

The least popular of the satin-glass types was made by the Mt. Washington factory. It was a colored satin glass decorated with heavy gold designs and often dark colors. The Royal Flemish patterns were somewhat gaudy, and not so successful as the other satin-glass wares of the Mt. Washington works.

Burmese

After the first two colored glasses were introduced, other glass manufacturers decided to try something similar. Frederick Shirley developed a special type of shaded glass that was opaque, and shaded from salmon pink to lemon yellow. He called it "Burmese," and registered the new two-toned glass in December of 1885. The coloring on several pieces of Burmese may be slightly different, but if it shades from peach to yellow it should be Burmese, and was made only at the Mt. Washington Glass Works. Some Burmese is shiny on the outside surface (not satin-glass finish), but most of it has a slightly rough satin finish. A few pieces are pattern molded with diamond quilting, but most are plain. Some of the rarer examples of Burmese glass are decorated with pictures of ducks, flowers, ships, or Egyptian scenes. The rarest Burmese had applied leaves and flowers that were also made from the colored Burmese glass.

Royal Flemish was a satin glass in dark brown, tan, and maroon, with gold decorations. This vase with a metal cover was made at the Mt. Washington glass works about 1889. (Corning Museum of Glass, Corning, New York)

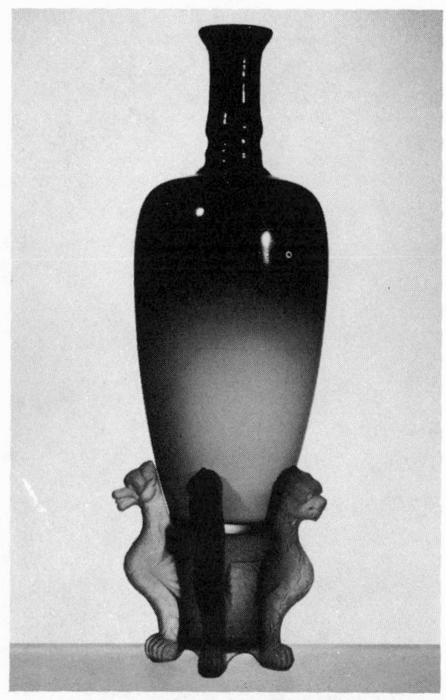

The most famous piece of peachblow glass was the "Morgan vase" design inspired by the sale of the Morgan collection of Chinese porcelain in 1886. The glassmakers liked the name "peachblow," and used it with great commercial success. The Mary Morgan peachbloom vase was the model for this vase in a stand, all made of glass. (Corning Museum of Glass, Corning, New York)

Peachblow

Peachblow is a colored glass originally developed by Hobbs, Brockunier & Company of Wheeling, West Virginia. It was probably made in 1883, soon after Amberina, which was the first of the bicolored glasswares, became popular. Though Hobbs's peachblow has the coloring of Amberina (see next section), it is two-layered or lined. The Wheeling peachblow is almost always made with a white lining, and most of the pieces have a glossy finish, but many had the typical satin finish. Peachblow was red at one end, and shaded to a deep yellow.

The New England Glass Works made a similar ware that was patented as "Wild Rose" in 1886, and is now called "New England peachblow" by most collectors. It has one layer of glass within a casing or lining shading from rose-red to white. Most of the New England peachblow had the satin finish, but some was glossy. A similar shaded glass was made in France about 1916.

Gundersen peachblow is a new ware made by the Gunderson-Pairpont Works of New Bedford, Massachusetts, from 1952 to 1957. The Gundersen peachblow shaded from

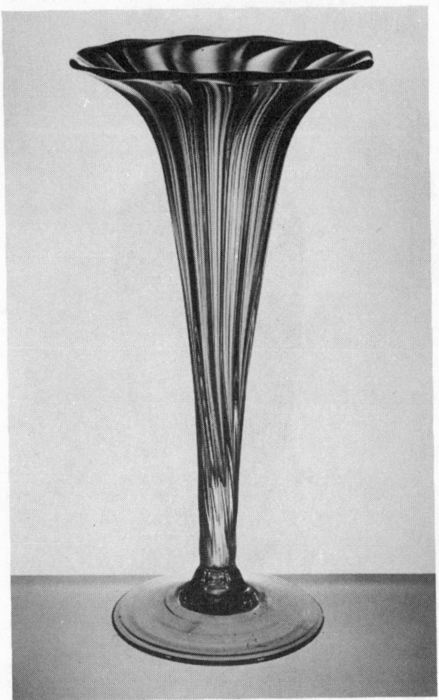

Amberina is the two-colored glass that shades from red to amber. This vase was made at the Libbey Glass Co. in Toledo, Ohio, about 1888–1900. (Corning Museum of Glass, Corning, New York)

white to a deep rose, and is heavier and thicker than the earlier wares. The shapes of the new ware are not the same as the old ones. The pontil marks are often large and unfrosted, and the ware cracks easily.

The other type of peachblow was made by the Mt. Washington Glass Company in small quantities, and is very rare. The color ranges from pink to blue, and the glass has a satin finish.

There are some bowls, called "rose bowls," that were made in colors ranging from a shaded pink and white to a pink and rose satin glass. It is not the true peachblow of any of the four types previously mentioned. The outer surface has a sheen that is not found in a true peachblow. Only the Wheeling peachblow was lined; and since most of the rose bowls were made with the two layers of glass, this glass cannot be any of the other peachblows.

Amberina

Amberina is a two-colored glass made from 1883 to about 1900. It was developed and patented by Joseph Locke, an Englishman working for the New England Glass Company. Amberina was the first of the two-colored clear glasswares that shaded from red to amber. When gold was added to amber glass, and heated, the glass became red. Mr. Locke discovered that if just a part of the piece was reheated, the glass would shade into the attractive two-colored Amberina.

Early Amberina is a purple-red, while the later pieces are more yellow-red. The earliest pieces were blown or pattern molded.

Most Amberina shades from red at the top to amber at the bottom, but the rarer pieces shading from amber to red are still Amberina. Because it was much easier to reheat the top of a piece than the bottom, most Amberina was red at the reheated top.

Rose amber

The Mt. Washington Glass Company of New Bedford, Massachusetts, which was involved in making every sort of popular colored glassware, made its own version of Amberina. The original ware was patented, and there was some difficulty, but it was finally resolved when the Mt. Washington Company agreed to call their version of Amberina by the name "Rose Amber." Theirs, too, shaded from yellow-amber to ruby and was made during the 1880's.

Collectors find it extremely difficult, if not impossible, to be sure whether a piece of the two-tone ware was made by the Mt. Washington Glass Company or by the New England Glass Company. Some experts claim the Mt. Washington ware was heavier and had a more purple shade of red, but this has been a standing argument for the advanced collector and not for those just interested in being an Instant Expert.

Ruby amber

Several Midwestern factories avoided the problems of patent infringement, and mass-produced pattern glass named "Ruby Amber Ware."

Many collectors simply add that ware to the other types of Amberina glass. "Watermelon" glass seems to be one of the new names given the many different factory types of glass that shaded from red to yellow.

Patterns of Amberina

Let us not forget that it was the color that gave the ware its name. Amberina also appeared in cut, pressed, and blown patterns. Pressed Amberina is a special type made by the New England Glass Company of Massachusetts, Hobbs, Brockunier & Company of Wheeling, West Virginia, Sowerby's Ellison Glass Works, Limited, of England, Critalleries de Baccarat of France, and others. It was *not* made by the Boston and Sandwich Glass works. (Instant Expert tip: ENGLISH AMBERINA IS OFTEN MARKED WITH THE PATENT RD NUMBER—see Chapter 1, "Pottery and Porcelain"—AND THE FRENCH GLASS IS OFTEN MARKED "DÉPOSE.")

Painted Amberina

A method was patented in 1895 by a Pittsburgh, Pennsylvania, man for making a shaded glassware by partially painting the glass. The painted glass was heated and reheated, and the color changed to shadings of red to yellow or even green. PAINTED AMBERINA CAN EASILY BE RECOGNIZED BECAUSE A PORTION OF THE PAINTED COLORING HAS USUALLY WORN OFF. IT ALSO HAS A MORE IRIDESCENT COLOR THAN TRUE AMBERINA.

Rubena Verde, Rubena Crystal, flashed glassware

The inside surface of a piece of glass was partly coated with glass of another color and the glass was heated. It made a "flashed" ware that had a variety of trade names, such as Rubena Verde, Rubena Crystal. THE FLASHED GLASS CAN BE RECOGNIZED BY THE RIM BECAUSE SEVERAL LAYERS OF GLASS WILL SHOW.

Plated Amberina

The queen of Amberina is the expensive and beautiful Plated Amberina. It ranges from red to yellow-shaded glass and was made by the New England Glass Works after 1886. TRUE PLATED AMBERINA ALWAYS

HAS CREAM-COLORED OR CHARTREUSE LINING, BUT NEVER WHITE. SMALL RIDGES, OR RIBS, WERE FORMED ON THE OUTSIDE.

Pomona

It is easy to recognize Pomona because it is unlike most of the other Victorian art glasswares. It is a clear glass with a very soft amber border decorated with very pale-blue or rose flowers or leaves. The colors are so pale they are often overlooked. The background is covered with a network of fine lines, and a diamond design is sometimes pattern-molded into the Pomona. The New England Glass Company made Pomona from 1885 to 1888.

A similar ware, with a light amber band and a frosted background, was made in the Midwest. TRUE POMONA HAS A STIPPLED OR FINE-LINE BACKGROUND.

The delicate flowers against the stippled background on the Pomona vase makes it easy to recognize. This vase was made by the New England Glass Co. about 1880–1900. (Corning Museum of Glass, Corning, New York)

Spangled, spattered Vasa Murrhina and End of Day tortoise

These are types of Victorian art glass where anyone can be an Instant Expert; it is all in the name. No one knows, or cares, who made which type of spangle or spatter glass. The color tells the tale. The name "End of Day" was first given to the variegated glassware that was made during the late nineteenth century. It was originally believed that the workers mixed their leftover glass bits at the end of the day and formed the ware, but it really was a deliberately manufactured product. Call your glass "spattered," because the name "End of Day" is going out of style.

Vasa Murrhina is the name of a company that made or distributed glass in the New England area. Experts do not use that name because they are not quite sure exactly what glass the firm sold.

SPATTER GLASS IS MULTICOLORED. SPANGLED GLASS IS SPATTER GLASS WITH METALLIC FLAKE INCLUDED. Spangle glass is usually a cased glass, with a thin layer of clear glass over the multicolored layer. Spatterware is not cased. Both types were made in many European countries, England, and the United States from about 1880 to 1900.

Many dealers and collectors argue endlessly about who made which piece of tortoiseshell glass. There is only one possible conclusion: No one seems to know. Tortoise glass was made to look like a tortoiseshell by using several shades of brown, yellow, or clear glass. Some was made in Germany during the 1880's, and it is possible that the United States Sandwich factory and many other places also made tortoise. Some of the tortoise was made in Europe during the 1930's. An expert on tortoiseshell glass knows one thing: IT IS A TYPE OF GLASS THAT LOOKS LIKE TORTOISESHELL.

Easiest to identify of the art-glass types is tortoiseshell glass. It looks like the true shell of the tortoise. Much of this glass was made at the Sandwich factory.

Agata

Agata glassware was made by the New England Glass Works for one year, 1887. The clever Joseph Locke, who had already developed Amberina, Wild Rose, Pomona, and other wares for his firm, discovered a way to make another new type of art glass. Agata is opaque, and ranged in color from pink to rose or from rose to white, and in some rare cases, green with a mottled band. The glass was mottled with spots resembling the Sunderland pottery lusterwares of an earlier era, but much less garish in color. Once you see Agata, you will always recognize it, so our tip is: GO TO A MUSEUM, COLLECTOR, OR ANTIQUE DEALER WHERE AGATA IS AVAILABLE, AND YOU WILL LEARN TO RECOGNIZE ITS UNIQUE APPEARANCE.

Cameo glass

What can be more annoying than to read a book that claims it can help you, and then discover that the book has really said nothing? A discussion of cameo glass in any volume about antiques should be long and technical because there is so much that must be learned about the artistic values and the difficult glassmaking techniques employed. A few short paragraphs will mislead the reader more than they will help him. Cameo glass is a specific type of glass made by a special method. If you know what a cameo looks like, you can recognize cameo glass. The glass was put together in layers, and part of the top layer was cut or carved away, leaving a raised portion, or the design. Some was white against dark glass, while other glass was mottled against another mottled colored glass; but if you run your fingers over the glass, you will find that the design is raised and irregular, carved by hand.

Cameo glass was made in England, France, and other parts of Europe, but rarely in the United States. True

Cameo glass was made in many countries, in many styles. This vase (left) made for Webb of England was made about 1910 of white to red glass on yellow. Emile Gallé made this vase (right) in France; notice the signature. (Cooper Union Museum, New York)

The finest cameo glass was made by Thomas Webb and Sons of England. George Woodall made this puce glass overlaid with white in the last decade of the eighteenth century.

cameo glass was made during the 1870's and afterward. The finest English pieces by Woodall or Northwood can cost thousands of dollars. French cameo glass by Gallé, Daum Brothers, and others is often in the *art nouveau* designs. Emile Gallé worked from 1879 to 1905, and EACH PIECE HE MADE WAS SIGNED WITH HIS NAME. AFTER 1905 THE NAME GALLÉ AND A STAR MARKED THE WARE.

Daum Nancy was the mark used by two brothers, Auguste and Antonin Daum, who worked after 1875.

American cameo glass was made by the Mt. Washington Glass Company, the Boston and Sandwich Glass Company, Bakewell, Pears and Company, Atterbury and Company, and the New England Glass Company after about 1885. None of the American cameo glass was of a top quality.

Mary Gregory

A woman named Mary Gregory decorated glass at the Sandwich Glass Works in Sandwich, Massachusetts. She painted white enamel figures on dark-colored Sandwich glass during the late 1880's.

The term "Mary Gregory" glass has come to mean the works of Miss

Mary Gregory glass was first made at Sandwich, Massachusetts, but many firms in many countries made it in the late 1880's. (Bill Rusterholtz, Erie, Pennsylvania)

Gregory and all the other glasswares that were made to resemble her work. It is more desirable to own a piece made at the Sandwich factory than one of the many European examples of the glass. The enameled Mary Gregory glassware was made from about 1870 to 1910. European reproductions, particularly of water sets, have been coming on the market.

The experts believe that TRUE SANDWICH MARY GREGORY GLASS WAS PAINTED WITH ALL-WHITE FIGURES. The examples with tinted faces and clothes were probably made in Europe, in Bohemia, France, Italy, Germany, Switzerland, and England. Another exception: European Mary Gregory glass was also made with plain white figures.

Crackle glass

Crackle glass was one of the early types of glasswares. The first crackle glass was Venetian, and was made during the sixteenth century.

The blown crackle glass was revived in the 1880's. The glass had small lines through it. Some of the Victorian art glasses, such as peachblow, were made with the crackle effect. Reproductions of the crackleware have been made. ONE COMMON REPRODUCTION IS OF A GLASS HAT, BUT THE NEW ONES DO NOT HAVE METAL RIMS.

Wavecrest, Kelva, and Nakara

The C. F. Monroe Company of Meriden, Connecticut, decorated a white glassware made by the Pairpont Manufacturing Company of New Bedford, Massachusetts. The glass was painted a pale pastel and was decorated with flowers, designs, or scenes. Three names were used on pieces of this glassware; Kelva was used about 1904, Wavecrest after 1898, and Nakara about the same time.

Most of the wares were made into ladies' dresser sets, jewel boxes, powder boxes, hair receivers, and other such wares. Many of the boxes were lined with gold, rose, or gray satin.

Very few pieces of Kelva, Nakara, or Wavecrest are labeled. The collector must learn to recognize the distinctive shape and decoration of the boxes.

A double wall of clear glass was formed; then the inside was filled with a silver solution to make mercury glass, a popular type about 1850. This Massachusetts piece was made about 1855. (Corning Museum of Glass, Corning, New York)

Findlay glass

Findlay silver deposit glass is very, very rare for several reasons. The glass was made in three layers by a very involved process, and the pieces often broke in the manufacturing process because the rate of contraction of the three layers differed. The breaking frequently continued; and without any apparent reason, a piece on a shelf will suddenly crack.

The pattern was made with silver, ruby, or black flowers, and was made in only one pattern by the Dalzell, Gilmore and Leighton Company of Findlay, Ohio.

COLORED GLASS OF THE 1850'S–1870'S

Mercury glass

Mercury, or silvered, glass became popular in the United States during the 1850's and again in the 1910's. It was first introduced in London, England, in the 1840's.

Silvered glass was made by an ingenious process wherein clear glass was blown with two walls separated by a small air space. The space was sucked clear of air and filled with a silver solution that was poured through a hole in the bottom. The hole was then closed with a metal stopper, and cemented. The silver clung to the sides of the glass. Gold glass was made by using the same technique; but instead of putting silver in clear glass, silver was used in amber glass.

The finished piece looks like metallic silver, and it never tarnishes. A good piece of mercury glass has no signs of worn silver.

Cranberry and ruby glass

The term "cranberry glass" refers to a color and not to a specific type of glassware. Most cranberry glass is almost transparent, although some of the hobnail glass is opaque (see the section on pressed glass).

Cranberry glass is yellowish-red, or much the same color as cranberry juice. Colored glass became popular after the Civil War, and cranberry glass was just one of the many colored wares to appear. Patterned glass was also made in the cranberry color. Plain, unpatterned lamps, cruets, sugar shakers, and many other such items were made in cranberry. Some of the cranberry was solid reddish-colored glass and some of it was overlay glass, made by applying one layer of glass over another layer. Most of the cranberry was flashed glass. A thin layer of color was applied over a clear or opaque glass. FLASHED GLASS SCRATCHES EASILY.

The cranberry-colored glass was made at the Boston and Sandwich Glass Company in Sandwich, Massachusetts, in other New England factories, and in Pittsburgh, Pennsylvania.

Ruby glass is the deep-red color of a gem ruby, and was made by many factories during the last part of the nineteenth century. True ruby glass is red because gold was added to the molten glass mixture.

Adding the gold was always a great event in the town of Sandwich, Massachusetts, home of the famous glass factory; the women of the town would take their children, and everyone went to see gold thrown into the glass.

Reproductions of both ruby and cranberry glass have been and are being made. The color and weight of the new wares are slightly different from those of the nineteenth-century pieces, but it requires expertise to differentiate the slight variations.

Vaseline glass

Some of the art and pressed-glass factories made a greenish-yellow glassware during the 1870's. The public called it Vaseline glass because of its color—Vaseline resembles the blue-yellow color typical of petroleum jelly. Many French factories also made the glass. The term "Vaseline" refers to color, and is no indication of age. Some dealers and collectors now call it "canary glass."

Uranium originally was used in Vaseline glass, and the old Vaseline can be identified by using the same technical equipment needed in locating traces of uranium. Uranium is not being used in the manufacture of all the reproductions.

FOOD-NAMED GLASSWARES

Clambroth and custard

The term "clambroth" refers to the color of a specific type of glassware that is grayish and semiopaque, like its namesake.

Custard glass is an opaque glass sometimes called "buttermilk glass." It is a yellowish-white opaque glassware. It was first made in 1886 at the La Belle Glass Works, Bridgeport, Ohio. Many of the pieces were decorated with gilt, especially on the feet.

Milk glass was at the height of its popularity in the United States about 1870–1880. These seven pieces are typical of the American-made glass. Left to right, top to bottom: a molded milk-glass plate showing the Wyoming monument made about 1903–1907; a syrup jug with a pewter top, palmette pattern, made about 1872; a covered canning jar shaped like an owl, with glass eyes and a tin cover, made about 1890; the pitcher has an applied photograph of William Jennings Bryan, c. 1900; molded opalescent milk-glass hat, c. 1880; compote with looped rim, possibly Sandwich Glass Co. or Atterbury Glass, Pittsburgh, Pennsylvania; covered dish shaped like Admiral Dewey, c. 1898. (Toledo Museum of Art, Toledo, Ohio)

To a collector, the best pieces are marked "N" on the bottom.

Camphor glass is a cloudy white glass that was blown, pressed, and even mold-blown. It was made by many Midwestern glass manufacturers during the mid-1800's. There were many factories making camphor glass in Pittsburgh, Pennsylvania, Wheeling, West Virginia, and southern Ohio.

Opal glass is a name that has changed through the years. The opaque white glass that we now refer to as "milk glass" originally was called "opal glass." For a short time some factories made a ware that had many colors, like a gemstone opal. The words "opal glass" now mean any dense white glass.

Milk glass (and slag, too)

The opaque white glass we now refer to as milk glass was made by the ancients; it was popular in England during the 1700's, but it seems to have reached its height during the 1870–1880 period in the United States. It was first named "milk glass" because it resembled milk, but now collectors refer to light- and dark-blue milk glass, green, amethyst, and black milk glass. Chocolate milk glass was never made.

Caramel slag and custard glass are other relatives of the original milk glass (see sections on slag and food-named glass wares). The factories making clear pressed glass also made the milk- and slag-glass pieces; thus, information about patterns will be the same for the various types (see the section "Pressed glass").

Milk glass, regardless of its age, is still milk glass. Though it is easy to recognize the glass, it can be difficult to determine its age.

MANY OLD MILK-GLASS PIECES HAVE A "C"-SHAPED ROUGH SPOT ON THE FOOT OF THE GLASS. The mark was formed in the molding, and cannot be found on the new pieces. OLD MILK GLASS HAS LESS BLUE IN IT. THE TEXTURE IS LESS OILY, AND THE GLASS IS HEAVIER.

You must become familiar with the old and the new wares because the differences are slight. Millions of new pieces of milk glass have been made from the old molds; look and compare, and buyer beware!

Slag

Picture a glassware streaked like a marble cake, and that is slag. Slag glass, or marble glass, was made at many American and English factories in the 1880's to 1900. Most of the American purple slag was made by a Pennsylvania firm.

Tan slag is called "caramel glass." Caramel glass (originally called "chocolate glass") was made at the Indiana Tumbler and Goblet Company of Greentown, Indiana, from November, 1900, to June, 1903. It looks like coffee streaked with cream, shading from tan to white. Some experts object to calling it a slag glass, but there is no doubt that it is related.

The short period of production meant that a small number of pieces were made and that the glassware is rare. It was not reproduced until the 1960's, when a line of small gift-shop items was made. They would not fool anyone familiar with the original color of caramel glass.

Blue slag is usually English in origin. It is often found with the English registry mark impressed on the bottom, or with a peacock, a trademark of the Sowerly Glass Works of England about 1880 to 1890.

Pink slag is one of the great mysteries of American Victorian glass. No one seems quite sure where it was made, but it is attractive, rare, and expensive. Only one pattern of pink slag is known. A poor imitation was made in the 1960's by an Indiana glass company.

Red slag has gained popularity, though it was ignored by many dealers until the very rare red Tiffany glass began bringing astronomical prices. As a result, all the other red glasswares made at the same time were sought by dealers and collectors.

There are several theories about the origin of red slag. The Northwood Company of carnival-glass fame and the Challinor Taylor Company of purple-slag fame both seem to have made a red slag. There are some who claim to own red slag made by Mr. Carder of the Steuben Glass Works.

Red slag can vary from a dark red to orange in a single piece. Other

Pressed-glass patterns are many and varied, differing in general style and shape in each period. The Lacy Sandwich glass cup plates went out of style in the nineteenth century when it was no longer proper to drink coffee from the saucer. (Joslyn Art Museum, Omaha, Nebraska) The lacy glass cake tray was also attributed to the Boston and Sandwich Glass Co., made about 1835. (Toledo Museum of Art, Toledo, Ohio)

colors of slag that are known are orange, green, butterscotch, and pieces that are a mixture of several colors.

PRESSED GLASS

It is necessary to go back to the beginnings of glass pressing to understand the many pressed-glass patterns. All glassware was made by free blowing or blowing it into a mold, until about 1820. The decorations were limited to applied pieces of glass, color, engraving, or etching, which removed part of the glass by a cutting method. The sparkling facet-cut crystal of Waterford was known throughout the world because of its design and beauty. Cut glass was expensive, and there was a need for a glassware available to the masses.

Pressed-glass machines were invented in the late 1820's. The molds were made in three or more pieces from brass, iron or other metal. If there was too much metal in the mold, all the glass could not be clearly impressed; if there was too little metal, the glass would be too thick. Early pressed-glass pieces, such as cup plates, sugars, and so on, were quite heavy, and had many bubbles and imperfections. The later pressed glass was almost perfect.

Pressed glass was designed to make the best possible use of a new technique of shaping glass. The early pieces had definite line designs with a granular texture that was caused by the mold. It was rough to touch on the pattern side, and smooth on the other side. The more facets the machine pressed into the glass, the more light reflections in the finished piece. "Lacy pressed glass" was an early attempt to get as many facets as possible into one piece of glass. Lacy glass was probably made first in France and then at the Boston and Sandwich glass works in Sandwich, Massachusetts. It was also made at the New England Glass Company, and in Pittsburgh, Pennsylvania, West Virginia, New Jersey, Mary-

Geometrics were popular in the pressed glass of the 1840's. This compote traveled to Nebraska in a covered wagon, one of the few possessions that could make the trip. (Joslyn Art Museum, Omaha, Nebraska)

land, and the Midwest. By the design of the glass, it is possible to determine the location of the factory. Coarser designs appeared in the Midwest than in the East. The early lacy pressed glass was mainly used for open salt dishes or cup plates. Any lacy pressed-glass piece that was made before 1840 is in great demand. While some of the cup plates have been reproduced, very few of the salts have been.

It is the later pattern glass that is of most interest to the casual collector. It could be a pattern such as Coin, which is expensive and of museum quality, or it could be a collected pattern of glass that can be used on a table. Hundreds of patterns of pressed glass were made in complete table settings, and they are still available. If you wish to look at many of the patterns, see the books written by Ruth Webb Lee or Minnie Watson Kamm that list and sketch the patterns, the history, and, in some cases, the prices. (See bibliography at the end of this chapter.)

It is necessary to have a feeling for the history of the designs used to date a piece of pressed glass. There are always exceptions to every rule, but patterns went in cycles, just as skirt lengths do. THE EARLY 1840's WERE THE TIME OF THE PRESSED-GLASS TABLE SETTINGS. THE EARLY PATTERNS WERE SIMPLE, WITH HEAVY LOOPS OR RIBBED EFFECTS. The glass itself was heavy. More elaborate geometrics appeared in the 1860's, and stylized flowers appeared. THE 1870's MEANT MORE ELABORATE NATURALISTIC PATTERNS. It was the time of Grape, Rose in Snow, Daisy, Thistle, and many other patterns. CLEAR AND FROSTED PATTERNS WITH FIGURES WERE IN STYLE DURING THE 1870's. Westward Ho, Lion, Three Face, and other combination patterns were made at that time. OVERALL PATTERNS THAT WERE SLIGHTLY GEOMETRIC IN FEELING WERE IN STYLE BY 1880, AND PATTERNS SUCH AS DAISY AND BUTTON AND HOBNAIL CAME INTO VOGUE. COLORED PRESSED-GLASS PATTERNS BECAME POPULAR AFTER THE CIVIL WAR.

There is no general book about antiques that can possibly tell everything about pressed glass. Although the Sandwich factory (1825–1888) was the most famous of the pressed-glass factories, there were also about sixteen other factories making pressed glass from 1830 to 1850, and still more from 1850 to 1900, when pressed glass reached its greatest popularity. The same pattern was made by several firms at the same time. Similar patterns were made, including many "variants" of such popular patterns as Daisy and Button.

It is of little use to write about the many factories and patterns. Look at the books listed in the bibliography at the end of the chapter; compare your pattern with those shown in some of the books, and you will be able to learn more about dating your pressed glass. Books have been written describing the copies of the early patterns and methods by which you can recognize the old from the new. Several of the magazines devoted to antiques print articles explaining how new reproductions differ from the original pressed glass. It is not easy to identify an unknown pattern of pressed glass; though a local collector or dealer may help you, what is really required is a determined search of the pressed-glass pattern books, page by page.

A few patterns of glass are described here because of pitfalls for inexperienced collectors who trust legend and hearsay more than research at a library.

The frosted-coin problem and others

Coin pattern is an expensive pattern of pressed glass, and most buyers know that it cannot be copied. The United States Government ordered the Central and Hobbs Glass companies to destroy their molds for the glass in 1892. The molds had been made from newly minted coins dated 1892, and the government declared that the glass was an illegal reproduction of money. Therefore the original pattern of coin glass was made for only a very short time (five months) before it was declared illegal. Some glass companies were quick to recognize that the pattern was quite salable, and they substituted Spanish coins for the illegal United States coins and called the pattern "Columbian Coin." It was, and still is, a popular pattern; but it is not so rare or expensive as the original United States frosted-coin glass.

A new pattern of coin glass was made to be sold as new glass to those who wanted a modern version of the nineteenth-century pattern glass during the 1960's. Because it bears no dates or names on the "coin-like" medallions, it is not an illegal reproduction of a coin. Nor is it an antique.

Many of the clear and frosted patterns have been reproduced because they are so desirable. The pattern Westward Ho, first made about 1879, features a wounded deer, bison, log cabin, pine trees, and an Indian, and has been reproduced several times. The clues for determining the old from the new describe such things as the size of the bison's leg or the clarity of the pine tree. Most of the reproductions have been discussed in detail in other books.

Frosted Lion, a pattern that was first made in 1876, is another of the patterns that has been reproduced. Unlike most of the earlier pieces, the frosting is rough on the new ware.

Many of the Hollywood movie stars have begun to collect Actress Glass; consequently, it is being reproduced. It was first made in 1879, and depicted the actors and actresses

Westward Ho was one of many plain and frosted patterns popular in the 1870's. These two covered compotes show deer, bison, and handles of seated Indians. (Toledo Museum of Art, Toledo, Ohio)

of the day. There were twenty-six different pieces of glass made. Fame is temporary. When an actress lost her popularity, her name was removed from the glass mold even though her picture remained. Early glass with the names intact is the type most often reproduced.

Daisy and Button

Daisy and button is probably one of the most well-known pressed-glass patterns. It was first made in 1876 for exhibition at the Philadelphia Centennial. Gillinder and Sons of Philadelphia made small novelties, umbrellas, canoes, and shoes in many colors, and they were sold in quantity as souvenirs at fairs.

About the same time, Hobbs, Brockunier & Company of Wheeling, West Virginia, made Daisy and Button pattern glass.

The famous Sandwich factory also made the pattern in many colors as well as in clear glass.

There are many variants of the design, such as Daisy and Button with Crossbar, Daisy and Button Oval Medallion, and about half a dozen others. There patterns were popular until about 1900.

The Daisy and Button glasswares have been made almost continually since they were first introduced in 1876. Many firms are still making inexpensive glasswares in the same pattern. A peanut-butter manufacturer sold his product in a Daisy and Button goblet in the late 1950's. There are literally hundreds of examples of twentieth-century Daisy and Button glass.

Bread trays

Glass bread trays have been made almost since the first pressed pattern glass was produced. Bread, the staff of life, has always played an important part in our diet, and the bread tray was used daily. Eighteenth-century examples of porcelain or metal trays are known, but the pressed-glass examples of the greatest interest date from the 1860's. The Lord's Supper tray was made about 1890 by the Model Flint Glass Company of Findlay, Ohio. The Liberty Bell platter was made in 1875. Hundreds of different patterns were made, many with the words "Give Us This Day Our Daily Bread."

Many of the trays were originally painted, and traces of the color and gilt still remain. Many of the trays are being reproduced.

The bread tray was made in many pressed-glass patterns that were not part of complete sets of tableware. Columbia Shield pictured Miss Columbia and the Stars and Stripes in glass; The Lord's Supper tray (right) was made about 1890, one of the most elaborate glass pressings made. (Arnold Bakers Collection)

Novelties

Pressed-glass novelties were made through most of the 1850–1900 period, and it is practically impossible to list the thousands of varieties and styles. Glass shoes, hats, animals, and so forth, were made to hold pins, toothpicks, salt and pepper, or just as decorations. Many of the styles of glass novelties are pictured in various books, and it is possible to learn more about your collection by research and study. (See the bibliography at the end of this chapter.) Many of the small items have been reproduced in both clear and colored glass. One particularly fine reproduction that is appearing in antique shops was originally made in the West for sale to gift shops. It was a complete line of small pressed-glass pieces, including an elephant head in milk glass or colors, open salts held by birds, shoes, hats, and several other animals in blue, yellow, clear, or milk glass.

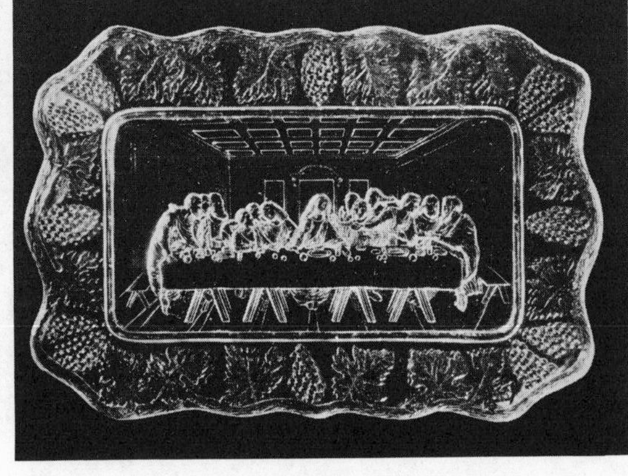

Canadian pressed glass

One of the neglected fields in collecting pressed glass is the work of the Canadian pressed-glass factories. Though several firms made pattern glass in Canada that was similar to the wares made by firms in the United States, the results are different enough to be identifiable. The Burlington Glass Works of Hamilton, Ontario (1875–1909), Napanee Glass House, Napanee, Ontario (1881–1883), the Sydenham Glass Company, Ltd., Wallaceburg, Ontario (1894–), the Excelsior Glass Company, St. Johns, Quebec (1878–1880), and Montreal, Quebec (1881–1885), Nova Scotia Glass Company, Trenton, Nova Scotia (1881–1892), Humphry Glass Works, Trenton, Nova Scotia (1890–1914), and other firms worked in Canada making pressed glass. Although a few of the patterns made by the firms are listed, much is still unknown, and any authenticated piece of Canadian pressed glass is always of interest. Of even greater interest and value today would be an old Canadian catalogue that pictured some of the patterns of pressed glass.

Holly Amber

One of the rare and very expensive pressed glasswares now grouped as part of the Victorian art glasswares is Holly Amber, or what was originally called Golden Agate. It is an amber-colored glass that was reheated to appear opalescent. A band of holly leaves made part of the pressed design.

This Holly Amber butter dish was made at the Indiana Tumbler Co. of Greentown, Indiana, about 1903. (Corning Museum of Glass, Corning, New York)

The glass was made by the Indiana Tumbler and Goblet Company for only a few months, from January 1, 1903, to June 13, 1903.

Star Holly

Star Holly was a glassware made to look like the jasper ware of the Wedgwood factory. It was a pressed milk glass that was made about 1951 by the Imperial Glass Company of Bellaire, Ohio. For many years it was thought that this glass was made much earlier. The glass was made with a border of holly leaves and a center medallion on the plate that was shaped like a star with seven holly leaves. It was made in blue, green, or rust so that the leaves appeared white against the colored border. The factory mark is an intwined "I G," and it appears in raised letters on the bottom of each piece. Because the coloring of the glass proved difficult and the process expensive, the Star Holly pattern was made for only a short time.

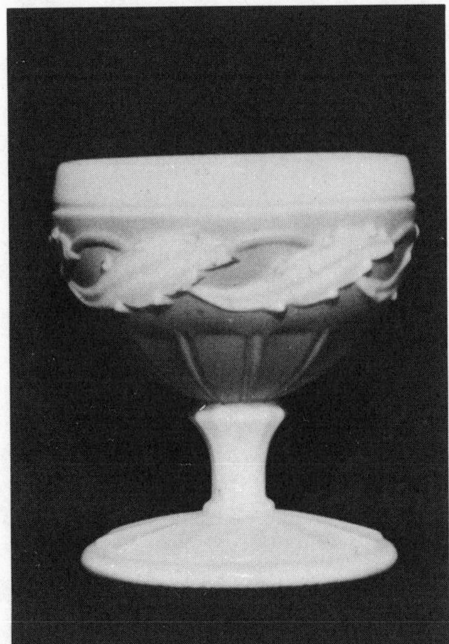

Star Holly was originally made to resemble the jasper wares made of pottery by Wedgwood. The glass Star Holly was made about 1951.

TRADE MARKS

The pressed-glass makers began to realize about 1905 that a trademark would be a valuable selling aid, and many began marking the glass. Collectors can now thank some of those factories for making twentieth-century pressed glass less of a puzzle.

MARKS ON PRESSED GLASS

Armstrong

C

Cambridge Glass Company
Cambridge, Ohio (before 1906)

NEAR-CUT

Cambridge Glass Company
Cambridge, Ohio (after 1906)

Diamond Glass Company, Indiana, Pennsylvania c. 1913–1931

(Dugan Glass Company, Indiana, Pennsylvania c. 1905?)

Fairmont Glass Works, c. 1889,
Pittsburgh, Pennsylvania

A. H. Heisey and Company, Newark, Ohio, 1902 (possibly in 1897)

J. B. Higbee, Bridgeville, Pennsylvania, c. 1900

Imperial Glass Company, Bellaire, Ohio, 1902

NU-CUT

Imperial Glass Company, Bellaire, Ohio, after 1900

Jefferson Glass Company, Follansbee, West Virginia, c. 1905

TRADE MARK

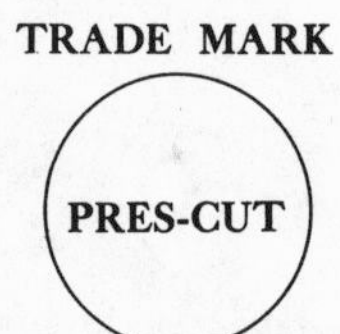

IN THE GLASS ON
EVERY PIECE

McKee Glass Company, Pittsburgh, Pennsylvania, before 1894

McKee Glass Company, Jeannette, Pennsylvania, 1903

McKee Glass Company, Jeannette, Pennsylvania, 1908

Northwood Glass Company

Ohio Flint Glass Company, Lancaster, Ohio, c. 1900

Seneca Glass Company, Fostoria, Ohio. 1891–

U.S. Glass Company, after 1914

Cut glass

The first problem for the beginning antique collector is to determine the difference between cut and pressed glass. There is a simple and almost too obvious difference, but it is necessary to learn this difference. A surprising number of people cannot tell cut glass from pressed glass if the pressed piece was made to resemble the brilliant cut glass of the late 1880's.

FEEL THE EDGES OF THE DESIGN OF THE GLASS. CUT GLASS HAS SHARP EDGES; PRESSED-GLASS DESIGNS WERE MOLDED INTO THE GLASS. The edges of the designs are rounded and feel dull to the touch. If this seems confusing, go to an antique shop or an antique show and ask a dealer to show you a piece of cut and a piece of pressed glass.

Cut glass will also "talk." Tap your finger against the edge of a piece of cut glass. CUT GLASS WILL RING WITH A CLEAR TONE. Try doing the same with a piece of pressed glass, and the tone will be dull and flat. There is an exception: If the piece of cut glass is cracked, it will also sound flat.

CUT GLASS IS HEAVY. Lift a piece of glass and compare it to a piece of pressed glass. CUT GLASS SPARKLES. A good piece of cut glass has many facets that will reflect the light and give it brilliance.

Cut glass has been known since ancient times. The famous Barberini vase copied by Josiah Wedgwood as the Portland vase is a form of cut glass called "cameo."

The English started cutting glass about 1715, and it began to gain fame; by 1760, England furnished cut glass to all of France and most of Europe. Ireland began making cut glass in 1750. It was so good that the English were forced to pass a tariff law in 1788 to keep it out of England. That was the period of the famous Waterford glass. Please try to sound like an expert, and never call a piece of glass "Waterford." It may be Waterford type, but there are few pieces that can positively be identified as coming from the Waterford factory. Waterford glass had a slightly blue cast, but that is not an infallible test.

Baron Stiegel is said to have made the first important glass in America in 1772. Several small factories were making bottle and window glass before that time. Next in importance came the Amelung factory, and by the early 1800's many American factories were making cut glasswares for table use.

Cut glass in America must be considered in three periods: Early (1771–1830), Middle (1830–1880), and Brilliant (1880–1905). Early glass was either a thin Bohemian glass or the heavier German flint glass. It had resonance (a note sounded when it was tapped) and a poor color, but it was suitable for engraving. Almost all the United States glass was lead glass by 1830. It was a clear crystal that was a bit gray in color. It was of good quality, but there were a few bubbles, and the glass had less luster than some of the other types.

The cut patterns resembled the English or Irish glass of the day, and there were few characteristic or geographic designs. The single star and

Cut glass was made in many styles. The first period of American cut glass resembled the earlier Irish and English pieces. This compote of clear glass, cut in flutes, strawberry diamonds, and scallops, was made by the New England Glass Co. of East Cambridge, Massachusetts, about 1872–1876. (Toledo Museum of Art, Toledo, Ohio)

panel curves were the most popular designs.

Early-period glass is rare and not often found by the casual collector. Middle-period glass featured four kinds of cut and engraved glass. Flute cutting was a popular design from 1830 to 1880. It was used earlier, but by 1830 the style had been perfected, and it gained in popularity.

Engraved decorations on glassware were another of the Middle-period techniques. The heavy lead glass was used, and the engraving or cutting was done with an elaborate copper wheel. Historical or mythological pictures were seen on many of the engraved glasswares. Colored glass was engraved late in the Middle period.

Fine-line cutting or crosshatch decoration was the third popular type of design, with flowers or bands of the cross-hatching incorporated into the design.

The most elegant cut glass of the Middle period was cased, or flashed, colored glass. The top layer of color was cut through, and the plain design could be seen. Ruby red and dark blue were popular colors.

Brilliant period

The cut glass known by most collectors is the elaborate cut ware of the 1880–1905 period. Cut glass became the rage after the Centennial Exhibition in Philadelphia, Pennsylvania, in 1876. Most brides were not given silver, but expensive, heavy cut-glass bowls and pitchers. The cutting was no longer the thin fine copper-wheel engraving; thick, heavy clear glass was cut with a deep miter cut, and large wedge-shaped pieces of the glass were removed to form the pattern. It was a costly glass when it was new, and is once again gaining favor. (New brilliant cut glass is being made in Europe.)

Cut glass was made in full sets for the table, including goblets, wineglasses, water tumblers, dishes, many serving pieces, and even knife rests shaped like barbells. The cut-glass pieces were used to serve any food that was not heated. NEVER PLACE ANYTHING HOT IN A CUT-GLASS BOWL. It was not made to withstand heat, and will crack.

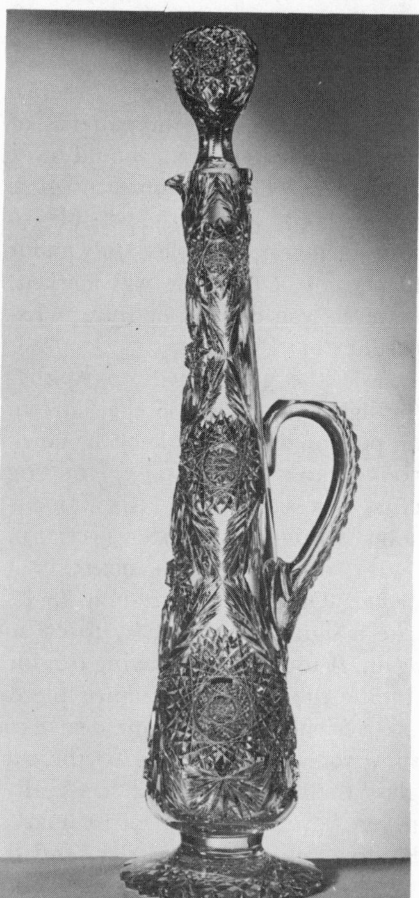

Brilliant cut glass of the late nineteenth and early twentieth centuries could be found in many objects. The floor lamp and decanter were made about 1904. The plate with the Libbey trademark cut into the center was made about 1892. (Toledo Museum of Art, Toledo, Ohio)

A listing of the hundreds of factories and thousands of patterns of cut glass that were made would be of little value. Though some cut glass was marked, and it is possible to read the marks, even then only about 10 percent of the glass was marked; however, you can be an Instant Expert for that 10 percent.

Hold the glass bowl up so that the light will reflect off the flat center portion on the inside of the bowl. LOOK ACROSS THE FLAT PART OF THE GLASS FOR SIGNS OF A FAINT TRADEMARK, WHICH WAS OFTEN WRITTEN IN SCRIPT, OR A PRINTED INSIGNIA IN A CIRCLE. Once you learn how to locate a signature, it is easy to do so again. If you continue having trouble finding the mark on a signed piece, ask a friend or an antique dealer to show you the mark. Most of the cut glass that is sold as old has really never been searched for a mark. Finding the mark is a trick, and it still is not well known. Signed cut glass is really no better than unsigned glass; but, like most antiques, collectors always place an extra value on a signed piece because it can be so completely identified and dated.

Two short hints about the care of cut glass. It should be washed in warm (NEVER HOT) water with pure soap. Do not use a detergent. Wipe the glass with tissue paper or newspaper to avoid any lint. Never put it in the refrigerator. After you wash the glass, a rinse in water with a little laundry blueing added will enhance the clear color. (If you own a piece of pale yellow cut glass, enjoy the rarity. It is called "Golden Glow," and was said to be made by the Sommerville Glass Works, Somerville, Mass.) If the glass is "sick," and has a white discoloration, wash it and apply a wax made for kitchen appliances.

MARKS ON CUT GLASS

Abraham & Straus, Inc.
Brooklyn, New York
Mark used after 1925.

AMERICAN WHOLESALE CORPORATION

American Wholesale Corporation
(Baltimore Bargain House)
Baltimore, Maryland
Mark used after 1922.

C. G. Alford & Company
New York, New York
Company worked 1872–1918.
Mark date unknown.

Bergen

J. D. Bergen Company
Meriden, Connecticut
Company worked 1885–1922.

George L. Borden & Company
(Krystal Krafters)
Trenton and Groveville,
New Jersey
Mark used after 1921.

George Borgfeldt & Company
New York, New York
Mark used after 1914.

Buffalo Cut Glass Company
Buffalo, New York
Company worked 1902–1920.
Mark date unknown.

Maple City Glass Company,
taken over by
T. B. Clark & Co., Inc.,
Honesdale, Pennsylvania
Mark used 1898.

TRADE
Clark
MARK

CLARK

T. B. Clark & Co., Inc.
Honesdale, Pennsylvania
Company worked 1886–1930.

Crystolene Cut Glass Company
Brooklyn, New York
Mark used 1919–1921.

Corona Cut Glass Company
Toledo, Ohio
Mark used after 1912.

SILVART

Deidrick Glass Company
Monaca, Pennsylvania
Mark used after 1916.

C. Dorflinger & Sons, Inc.
White Mills, Pennsylvania
Company worked 1881–1921.

O. F. Egginton Company
Corning, New York
Mark used after 1906.

Empire Cut Glass Co.
Flemington, New Jersey
Company worked c. 1895–1904.

H. C. Fry Glass Company
Rochester, Pennsylvania
Company worked 1901–1934.

J. Hoare & Company
Corning, New York
Company worked 1868–1921.
Mark used after 1895.

Mark used after 1890.

Hope Glass Works
Providence, Rhode Island
Company worked 1872–1951.

Mark used after 1903.

T. G. Hawkes & Co.
Corning, New York
Company worked 1880–1962.

Imperial Glass Co.
Bellaire, Ohio
Company working 1901 to present
(made pressed glass) .

PLUNGER

CUT

A. H. Heisey & Co., Inc.
Newark, Ohio
Company worked 1895–1958.
Mark used after 1906.

Irving Cut Glass Co., Inc.
Honesdale, Pennsylvania
Company worked 1900–c. 1933.

Hinsberger Cut Glass Company
New York, New York
Company worked 1895–1913.

Lansburgh & Bro.

Lansburgh & Brother, Inc.
Washington, D.C.
Mark used after 1922.

Mark used before 1896.

1896–1906 W. L. Libbey & Son 1906–
(Libbey Glass Company)
Toledo, Ohio

Lotus Cut Glass Company
Barnesville, Ohio
Mark used after 1911.

Lyons Cut Glass Company
Lyons, New York
Company worked 1903–1905.

McKanna Cut Glass Company
Honesdale, Pennsylvania
Company worked 1906–1930.

PRESCUT

McKee-Jeannette Glass Works
Jeannette, Pennsylvania
Mark used after 1904.

Meriden Cut Glass Company
Meriden, Connecticut
Company worked 1895–1923.

Mt. Washington Glass Company
(Pairpoint Corporation)
New Bedford, Massachusetts
Left, company working 1869–1894.
Right, mark used after 1883.

KOH-I-NOOR

Richard Murr
Chicago, Illinois
San Francisco, California
Mark used 1906–1928.

J. S. O'Connor
Hawley, Pennsylvania
Company worked from 1890–1913.

DIAMONKUT

Pope Cut Glass Company, Inc.
New York, New York
Mark used after 1922.

Quaker City Cut Glass Company
(Cut Glass Corporation of America)
Philadelphia, Pennsylvania
Company worked 1902–c. 1927.

SINCLAIRE
H. P. Sinclaire & Company
Corning, New York
Company worked 1905–1929.

L. Straus & Sons
(also I. Straus & Sons)
New York, New York
Mark used c. 1894–1917.

Standard Cut Glass Company
New York, New York
Mark used after 1895.

Steuben Glass Works
(Corning Glass Works)
Corning, New York
Mark used after 1903.

Taylor Brothers Company, Inc.
Philadelphia, Pennsylvania
Company worked 1902–1915.

Thatcher Brothers
Fairhaven, Massachusetts
Company worked 1894–1907.
Mark used after 1894.

Tuthill Cut Glass Company
Middletown, New York
Company worked 1902–1923.

Unger Brothers
Newark, New Jersey
Company worked 1901–1918.

Van Heusen, Charles, Company
Albany, New York
Company worked 1864–1893.

E. J. S. Van Houten
New York, New York
Mark used 1896–1919.

C. E. Wheelock & Company
Peoria, Illinois
Mark used after 1898.

Paperweights

It is hard to believe that paperweights, which are so valued as collectors' items, originated about 1820. It has been said that the first paperweights were made in Saint-Louis, France, and that other European glass factories copied their idea.

One of the famous legends of antique collectors is the story of a housewife in the 1930's who paid a trashman a quarter or two for some "colored globs" of glass that would be a collector's dream. If the trash heap was the best source of paperweights in the 1930's, that is certainly no longer true today. Collecting paperweights can be expensive or inexpensive, depending on your choice of weights.

One type of weight that should be explained is the millefiori paperweight, developed in the 1840's, and still being made. Picture a bunch of spaghetti strands, uncooked, stiff, and in bright colors. Cut across the strands to get small pieces with each piece colored on the edges but with the natural spaghetti beige on the inside where the dye could not reach. The small bits were arranged to form a pattern with the cut edge up. Millefiori paperweights were made the same way, but instead of spaghetti, thin colored rods of glass were made, cut, and arranged in the weights. Each rod of glass had a special design, such as a tiny horse or flower made to show as a silhouette on the edge of the cut rod. There are more millefiori weights with little value that are falsely considered to be old, rare, and priceless than practically any other type of antique. Weights from France and England, and some of the better American weights such as those made by Gillerland about 1850, are choice examples of millefiori weights. The canes are clear, separate pieces with sharply defined edges. The later copies of the weights, particularly the Chinese and those made in the twentieth century, have little value. A very good reproduction weight was made in Italy during the 1960's with the date 1856 worked into the canes.

Paperweights with large colored globs resembling abstract flowers were made in the United States and Europe during the late 1800's and early 1900's. Modern copies of these weights are being made. However, since very little has been written about such Midwestern paperweights, the demand for them has not been excessive, and they are still available to the ambitious collector.

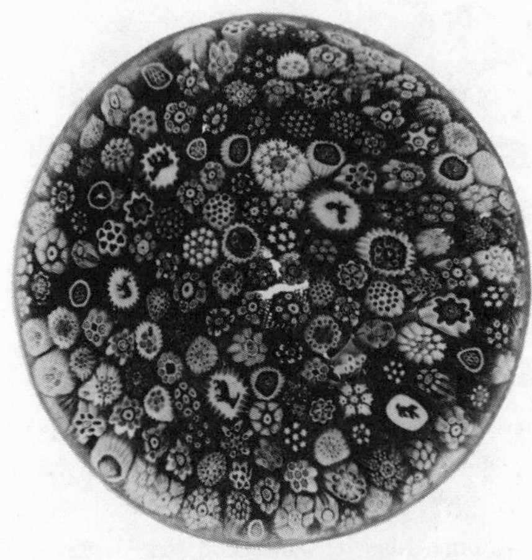

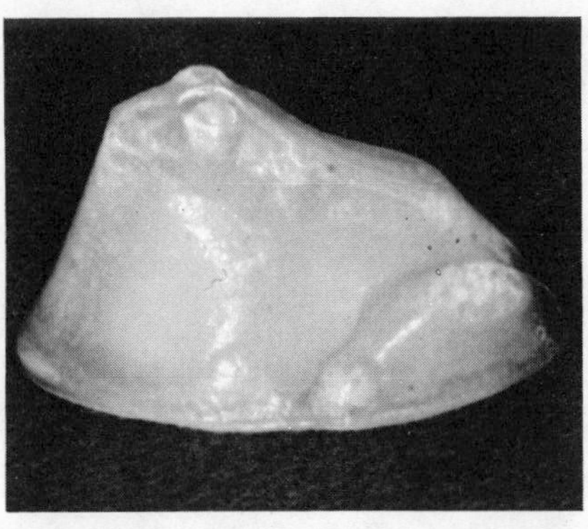

Paperweights take many shapes and sizes. Above right: the opalescent glass frog is of unknown American origin, probably late nineteenth century. (Kovel collection) Above left: The millefiori paperweight was made in France at the Baccarat factory. Notice the dated cane, 1848, to the right of center. (Corning Museum of Glass, Corning, New York) (Left) The Millville Rose was made in New Jersey. (New-York Historical Society)

Once any field of antiques has been researched and the results exposed, the price of such items rises on the open market. A book about any particular subject often doubles the price of the antique.

A popular paperweight that has been forged by dozens of firms is the so-called "Jersey Turtle." It is a green glass turtle made by roughly shaping the head, arms, and legs from a rounded piece of glass. They were first made during the Civil War by factories in Lancaster, Pennsylvania, New York, Cambridge and Sandwich, Massachusetts. Thousands were made during the 1860–1875 period. We suspect that some are still being made, because their availability seems endless, and great skill is not needed in production.

The Plymouth Rock weight is one of the easiest American weights to identify. It is a clear glass replica of the Rock with the numbers 1620 raised on one side and a poem about the Rock on the other side. It was made soon after 1876 by the Ink Stand Company of Providence, Rhode Island.

Sulfide paperweights were made during the early nineteenth century. A silvery-white figure was embedded in the center of the glass. The sulfide technique has also been used for door handles, portrait medallions, plates, and boys' marbles.

Overlay glass was used for some weights. It consisted of a layer of colored glass over clear glass, cut to expose the interior sections. The fine, carefully cut overlay weight, the glass weight with a carefully modeled animal, flower, or fruit inside, or the subtly colored glass pear or apple are among the finest of the paperweights. It takes much study to recognize a good weight from a fair one, but common sense can be a great help. The Instant Expert tips are few: DATED PAPERWEIGHTS ARE RARE, AND HAVE BEEN MADE SINCE 1830. LOOK FOR THE DATE IN THE CANE OF THE MILLEFIORI WEIGHTS. A GOOD WEIGHT WAS MADE FROM FINE, CLEAR GLASS. If the glass is yellow or uneven, it is not one of the best examples. BUBBLES ARE FLAWS, NOT SIGNS OF EXCELLENCE. Some designs incorporated either small bubbles that appear as dewdrops, or clear bubbles that were part of the design in the "glob flower" type of weight. The bubbles are intentional, but the small imperfection bubbles that are not part of the design indicate poor workmanship. AN OLD WEIGHT IS HEAVIER THAN A NEW ONE. If the glass was a good quality of lead glass, it was heavy. AN UNGROUND PONTIL IS THE SIGN OF A POOR PAPERWEIGHT. A FROSTED PONTIL IS THE SIGN OF A NEW PAPERWEIGHT. The pontil mark was always removed by a first-class glassmaker because it gave the weight a finished look. THE GRINDING WAS SLIGHTLY ROUNDED ON OLD PAPERWEIGHTS. NEW PAPERWEIGHTS ARE GROUND FLAT ON THE BOTTOM. Some of the finest French weights had elaborately cut bases shaped like a star.

Collectors have turned to the advertising weights of the Victorian era. The weights often had photographs or printed messages encased in the glass. Though they are of historic interest, they do not have the artistic value of the earlier and more colorful weights.

The "snow" weight is one type of weight that delights many collectors. Most of us can remember shaking the glass to see a "snowfall" inside a scenic paperweight. It was probably intended as a child's toy, but the adults were always captivated by its charm. The first of the snow weights was made in France about 1850. OLD SNOW WEIGHTS ARE MOUNTED ON CHINA OR MARBLE BASES. Today's versions are usually mounted on wood or plastic.

Sunglow Glass

Many collectors, particularly in the West, have tried to color glass by exposing it to the sun. Arizona, Oklahoma, and other dry, sunny states have the most favorable climates, but it is possible to color glass in any sunny state. A glass sample in Toledo, Ohio, was exposed to 158 hours of summer sunlight in one month, and noticeably changed color. Under favorable conditions glass will color to its darkest shade in about two years. In most cases the glass turns purple from the manganese in the glass. An experiment in 1881 showed that ten years of exposure to the sun would color any glass of the period. Today's glass is made with an inhibitor that slows the discoloration.

Most glass made between 1850 and 1910 has manganese in it; exposed to sun, it will probably turn purple. Glass made from 1910 to 1930 will probably color to an amber shade because it was made with selenium. The early clear glass may also change to brown, green, or yellow. Brown glass will turn purple; yellow glass turns green; and greenish glass becomes bluish-white. It is even possible to buy new glass that is guaranteed to become purple if left in bright sunlight.

Find a flat roof or patio and place the glass in the sun on a bed of sand. The sand will help to keep the temperature change from being too abrupt. Turn the glass occasionally to assure an even color.

SOME ODDS AND ENDS TOO GOOD TO OMIT

Crown glass and bull's-eye glass

Crown glass is frequently used in fine breakfronts. The absence of lead in the composition of the glass causes it to have excellent properties of reflection. The glass was blown into a bubble with a mark, the bull's-eye, left in the middle by the worker's rod. It is from this bubble that the small brilliant Crown glass is cut. The center "bull's-eye" was used above outside doorways, with the rough side out.

Bohemian glass

The glassmakers of Bohemia were well known during the early 1800's. They made a decorative glassware by fusing two layers of glass. The top layer, or overlay, was of a colored glass, while the bottom layer was clear. Into the colored layer designs were cut that allowed the clear glass to show.

Figures, animals, and flowers were popular motifs. The overlay glass could be of any color; however, red was the most popular. Some of the finished pieces were gilded.

"Bohemian glass"—glass of the same type as the early ware made in Bohemia—was made in many countries, and imported into the United States and Canada from the 1820's.

Jack-in-the-pulpit vase

The jack-in-the-pulpit vase is one of the unusual designs of the Victorian colored-glass period. One part of the top rim of the vase was curled down to look like the jack-in-the-pulpit flower. The vases were made of opaque glass and satin glass, and in practically every color. Because the curled edge, not the size, determines the name, all sizes of jack-in-the pulpit vases can be found.

Bride's basket

Glass baskets were made by the early Venetians. The Sandwich, Massachusetts, glass factory made baskets, usually one-of-a-kind novelties, by 1827. The bride's basket became a fad during the 1880's, when they were popular wedding gifts. Cut-glass baskets became the fad in the 1890's, but died out about 1905.

Witch ball

The superstition of the witch ball

began in England and spread to all parts of the United States and Canada from about 1820 to 1900. The ball was a glass globe that was usually placed in a vase-shaped stand or hung in a window to prevent disease or ward off evil spirits. The ball was wiped daily, and the wiping removed all the evil spirits.

The Irish kept the clear glass witch ball filled with bits of yarn, with a piece dangling from a small hole in the ball. The witch would pull out bits of yarn, and forget to harm the family.

Some experts believe that all the stories about witches' balls are just superstition, and they also believe that our forebears thought the same. Today, as yesterday, a witches' ball is kept for decoration.

Banana stands

A banana stand looks like a distorted cake stand. Instead of a flat dish on top of a tall stem, the banana stand has a dish that is curved up on two sides. From about 1865 to 1880, they were made from glass or ceramic to hold, we suppose, the obvious banana (first imported in 1804). They seemed most popular in the southern states.

Syrian temple shrine glassware

Syrian temple shrine glassware was made from 1893 to 1917. It pictures the shrine symbols, and in most cases the piece was dated.

Cruets

A cruet is any small bottle made to hold oil and vinegar for use at the table. Most of the cruets collected were made by art-glass manufacturers during the Victorian era. Early-nineteenth-century cruets are scarce. A GOOD ANTIQUE CRUET SHOULD BE IN PERFECT CONDITION, WITH NO CHIPS OR CRACKS. IT SHOULD BE MADE FROM AN UNUSUAL TYPE OF GLASS, AND THE STOPPER SHOULD BE ORIGINAL. All the information written about Victorian glass should help to explain the cruet to the collector.

Open salts and saltshakers

Open salts were popular on our grandparents' tables. The pressed-glass salts from the nineteenth century are among some of the glass rarities being collected.

Open salts were made during the eighteenth century by Baron Stiegel, and by many other American glass factories soon afterward. Salt dishes were pressed by the New England Glass Company, the Boston and Sandwich Glass Company, and others, by 1827. The best pressed-glass open salts were made from 1827 to 1850. The earliest salts were simple, but many were rectangular in shape, and footed. A column was at each corner, with baskets of flowers or roses impressed on the sides. Some of the later designs had cut diamonds, fans, stars, swags, and other such decorations. A few rare salts have historic designs picturing an eagle, Lafayette, or boats. Salts of the period are found in blue, green, purple, citron, and yellow, but most often in clear glass.

In the mid-nineteenth century, pressed pattern glass saw a change:

Glass salt dishes make an interesting collection. The two salts on the right were made by the Tiffany factory of iridescent gold glass; the hen is of milk glass; behind it is a flashed ruby glass master salt; the others are pressed glass of the 1890 period. (Collection of Kim Kovel)

open salts were designed as a part of the complete dinner service. By the 1850's, novelties in pressed glass were made, and the salts had become amusing animals, birds, or other objects to hold salt at the table.

The saltshaker had to await the development of a salt that was fine enough to pour through the holes. It also needed the invention of the screw-top jar, which was first developed in 1858 by John Mason. THE SALTSHAKER RAGE BEGAN ABOUT 1860, AND CONTINUED THROUGH THE NINETEENTH AND PRESENT CENTURIES. In 1871 a method was found that kept the salt free-flowing even in damp weather, and the saltshaker became a permanent table item, with the open salt no longer in popular use. Many of the saltshakers were part of cruet sets, but by 1884 the words "shaker salt" were used by various manufacturers to explain that it was not for the open dish but for the new type of shaker. Before the 1890's you might find the words "spice box," "condiment box," "dredging box," "sifter," or "duster" used to describe what we now call a saltshaker.

Glass saltshakers were in the greatest demand during the 1880's when the art-glass and colored pressed-glass wares were popular. Cut-glass shakers became popular a few years later.

Hints on care of glass

Wash glass with a mild soapless detergent and water. Use a soft brush or cloth. Bluing may be added to the rinse; it will add to the luster of the glass. Each type of stain requires special and different care. Information on care and cleaning of old glass can be found in many books on glass.

Glass: Bibliography

General

Belknap, E. M. *Milk Glass.* New York: Crown, 1959.
An excellent picture book about all kinds of milk glass and slag glass. Some history of the glass patterns is included.

Gardner, Paul V. *The Glass of Frederick Carder.* New York: Crown, 1971.
Twenty percent of this book gives a history of the works of Frederick Carder. The rest of the book is filled with catalog reprints and photographs of the glass pieces.

Grover, Ray and Lee. *Art Glass Nouveau.* Rutland, Vermont: Tuttle, 1967.
An attractive book filled with over 400 color pictures of art glass of all types.

———. *Carved & Decorated European Art Glass.* Rutland, Vermont: Tuttle, 1970.
Color pictures of each piece of glass discussed make this book of unusual interest to the collector. Cameo glass, *paté de verre* and other glassware from 1880 to 1930.

Hartung, Marion T. *Carnival Glass in Color.* Leon, Iowa: Mid-American Book Company, 1967.
Factory history and pattern information is included in this book. Line drawings and color pictures are included.

Herrick, Ruth. *Greentown Glass.* Privately printed, 1959. (Order from author, 908 East Main Street, Lowell, Michigan.)
A good short history of the Indiana Tumbler and Goblet Company and other firms making such well-known glass as Golden Agate, Holly Amber, and Chocolate.

Kamm, Minnie Watson. *Two Hundred Pattern Glass Pitchers* (1–6). Watkins Glen, New York: Century House, 1939–1952.
A well-written series of books listing patterns of pressed glass, known history of the pattern, facts about manufacturers, and other important information. Illustrated with line drawings and catalogue reprints.

Koch, Robert. *Louis C. Tiffany, Rebel in Glass.* New York: Crown, 1964.
The story of the man more than the glass, but an interesting biography of Mr. Tiffany and his works.

———. *Louis C. Tiffany's Glass, Bronzes, Lamps.* New York: Crown, 1971.
A continuation of the history of the Tiffany works including lamps and bronze wares.

Lee, Ruth Webb. *Antique Fakes and Reproductions.* Wellesley Hills, Massachusetts: Lee Publications, 1938, 1950.
An excellent discussion of known reproductions of blown, pressed, milk, Bohemian, and other glasswares.

———. *Early American Pressed Glass.* Wellesley Hills, Massachusetts: Lee Publications, 1931.
A line-drawing listing of the patterns of pressed glass, with some history.

———. *Nineteenth Century Art Glass.* New York: Barrows, 1952.
A good general history of American art glass, including satin glass, Amberina, peachblow, spangled, Mary Gregory, Tiffany and other irridescent, and some cameo glass.

———. *Sandwich Glass.* Wellesley Hills, Massachusetts: Lee Publications, 1947.
An excellent illustrated history of

the glass of the Sandwich factory, including cup plates and lamps.

———. *Victorian Glass.* Wellesley Hills, Massachusetts: Lee Publications, 1944.

The history of many types of glass, including pressed pattern glass, Victorian novelties, Sandwich glass and art glass. Black-and-white photographs.

McKearin, George S. and Helen. *American Glass.* New York: Crown, 1948.

The definitive work on the subject of American glass, with over 2,000 photographs. All the early glassworks are discussed, and other chapters include pressed glass, paperweights, cameo glass, bottles, and flasks.

———. *Two Hundred Years of American Blown Glass.* New York: Crown, 1950.

An important book for the collector of early glass, with color and black-and-white plates. A small section discusses the newer blown glass, including Tiffany, paperweights, and flasks.

Neal, L. W. and D. B. *Pressed Glass Salt Dishes of the Lacy Period 1825–1850.* Privately printed, 1962. (Order from author, 1712 Rittenhouse Square, Philadelphia, Pa.)

A very complete picturing of pressed-glass lacy salt dishes. The illustrations are absolutely exact drawings that make identification simple by measurement and comparison.

Peterson, Arthur G. *American Art Nouveau Glass.* New York: Nelson, 1968.

An illustrated history of late-nineteenth- and early-twentieth-century glass. Well researched and illustrated.

———. *Salt and Salt Shakers.* Washington, D.C.: Washington College Press, 1960.

A brief history of saltshakers, including patent information and pictures.

———. *333 Glass Salt Shakers.* Takoma Park, Maryland: Washington College Press, 1965.

Photographs of 333 glass saltshakers and a listing of 260 others.

Revi, Albert Christian. *American Pressed Glass and Figure Bottles.* New York: Nelson, 1964.

An illustrated history of many pressed-glass factories taken from patent records and other research. One chapter is about bottles. The book is well indexed to include pattern names, names of factories, and other information.

———. *Nineteenth Century Glass, Its Genesis and Development.* New York: Nelson, 1959.

An excellent book about art glass of all types. Each type of glass is illustrated with a full-page photograph, and a page or two of detailed information about the manufacturer is given.

Unitt, Doris and Peter. *American and Canadian Goblets.* Peterborough, Ontario, Canada: Clock House Publications (P.O. Box 103), 1970.

Black and white photographs of goblets and an abbreviated history of each pattern make this a good guide for goblet collectors. Lee, Metz, Revi and other reference sources are listed with each pattern.

———. *Treasury of Canadian Glass.* Peterborough, Ontario, Canada: Clock House Publications (P.O. Box 103), 1969.

The works of Canadian factories have often been confused with those from the United States. This book identifies Canadian patterns and includes detailed close-up pictures of finials, handles, and feet to aid in the identification.

Paperbound Picture Books

The books listed below are paperbound picture books. Each has many color pictures but no information. Because the color photograph is often important to the collector of glass, these books are included.

Barret, Richard Carter. *Blown and Pressed American Glass.* Privately printed, 1966. (Order from Forward's Color Productions, Inc., Manchester, Vermont.)

———. *Identification of American Art Glass.* Privately printed, 1964. (Order from Forward's Color Productions, Inc., Manchester, Vermont.)

———. *Popular American Ruby-Stained Pattern Glass.* New York: Crown, 1968.

Hand, Sherman. *Colors in Carnival Glass.* Privately printed, 1967. (Order from author, P.O. Box 4764, Rochester, New York 14612.)

———. *Colors in Carnival Glass, Book 2.* Privately printed, 1968. (Order from author.)

———. *Colors in Carnival Glass, Book 3.* Privately printed, 1970. (Order from author.)

Lagerberg, Ted and Vi. *A Color Picture Guide to Over 100 Types of Collectible Glass* (Books 1 and 2). Privately printed, 1966. Order from author, P.O. Box 636, New Port Richey, Florida.)

Mouser, William Ernest, Jr. *Cristal d'Émile Gallé.* Privately printed, 1966. (Order from Peggy Gurn, Box 7504, Amarillo, Texas 79109.)

Whitlow, Harry. *Art, Colored and Cameo Glass.* Privately printed, 1966. (Order from author, 17436 Poplar, Riverview, Michigan 48192.)

English Glass

Davis, Derek C. *English and Irish Antique Glass.* New York: Praeger, 1964.

Hughes, G. Bernard. *English, Scottish and Irish Table Glass.* New York: Bramhall House, 1956.

Both of these books are good general reference books about English glass of the past three hundred years.

Paperweights

Bergstrom, Evangeline. *Glass Paperweights of the Bergstrom Art Center.* New York: Crown, 1969.

Color illustrated book of importance to all serious collectors.

———. *Old Glass Paperweights.* New York: Crown, 1947.

A good general book about paperweights, with many black-and-white and color photographs.

Hollister, Paul, Jr. *The Encyclopedia of Glass Paperweights.* New York: Clarkson N. Potter, 1969.

A comprehensive study of paperweights including a glossary of terms, bibliography, lists of paperweight collections and factory histories. Illustrated in black and white and color.

Cut Glass

Pearson, J. Michael and Dorothy T. *American Cut Glass for the Discriminating Collector.* New York: Vantage, 1965.

Over 600 illustrations and photographs of cut glass, divided into chapters by pattern name.

Revi, Albert Christian. *American Cut and Engraved Glass.* New York: Nelson, 1965.

Authoritative book with over 500 illustrations divided into chapters by factory and history. Excellent.

3

Bottles

A GREAT many bottle collectors have become collectors by literally digging up an old bottle. Others have discovered old bottles while cleaning the attic, basement, under the back porch, or by just looking in the dump. (Most of us avoid visits to the city dumps, but some collectors have found dumps to be exciting spots. The casual bottle collector may have begun by paying cash to a dealer or friends for a "pretty" or "amusing" bottle. Owning a group of bottles does not make one a collector, for a true collector must study constantly so that he may gather all the information available on the subject. If you are just buying bottles for their decorative effect, this section is not for you; but if you have been bitten by the bottle bug, read on.

The best place to start is by sorting out your possessions into orderly categories and learning which bottle is old, new, rare, or even unique. But first you must have an understanding of the methods of manufacture of a glass bottle.

Making a bottle

The earliest bottles made were blown at the end of a punty rod (see Chapter 2, "Glass," for a more complete explanation). The free-blown bottles had a neck, a shaped body, a flattened base, and a mark on the bottom where the punty rod was removed. There may or may not have been decoration made by adding glass, painting, or engraving.

The free-blown bottle had no mold seams, but it did have many bubbles and imperfections. Hand- or free-blown bottles were never exactly the same. The lack of uniformity is one of the reasons the mold-blown bottle came into use. FREE-BLOWN BOTTLES HAVE BEEN MADE SINCE VERY ANCIENT TIMES. BLOWN-MOLD BOTTLES WERE MADE BY THE EARLY ROMANS, BUT WERE NOT COMMON IN AMERICA UNTIL THE EARLY 1800's. The mold-blown bottle that was first used in America for commercial bottles was made from a hollowed-out mold of wood or metal. Glass was blown into a mold, and could only take the shape of the inside of the mold.

THE MOLD-BLOWN BOTTLE HAS SEAMS ON THE SIDES BUT NOT ON THE NECK. The neck of the bottle was finished by hand, and the seams from the pieces of the open mold are not there. THREE-PIECE MOLDS WERE FIRST USED ABOUT 1809. THEY

WERE USED UNTIL THE 1880'S. LOOK FOR THE SEAM MARKS THAT SHOW A THREE-PIECE MOLD. Any three-mold glass, bottle, or dish is considered rare.

WOODEN MOLDS WERE USED FROM ABOUT 1820 TO 1860. THE "WHITTLE MARKS" CAN BE SEEN ON THE FINISHED BOTTLE. ANY BOTTLE WITH "WHITTLE MARKS" IS CONSIDERED GOOD. "Whittle" marks were not caused by the carving; they were caused by a cold mold and hot glass. This closed mold shaped the neck as well as the body of the bottle. THE MOLD MARKS COULD BE SEEN ON THE SIDE OF THE BOTTLE AND ON THE NECK.

Automatic bottling equipment was developed in 1903, and most bottles are now being made entirely by machine, and no handwork is necessary.

Examining Lips and Tops

It's the lip that tells

A search for mold or whittle marks can give the first clue to the age of the bottle. Next examine the top or lip of the bottle. To learn how to do so may take study, but it is time worth spending if you want to buy and collect bottles.

Whittle-marked bottle made on a wooden mold.

A molded bottle of the late nineteenth century, with an applied lip.

Name	*Date*	*Method*
Sheared lip	until 1840	Glass cut with shears (several varieties of lip finish)
Sheared lip, not fire-polished	until 1840	Rough broken edge
Sheared lip, fire-polished	until 1840	Broken lip put back into fire, melted slightly, smooth satiny lip (used on small-mouthed bottles)
Flared lip	before 1840	Hot rod rotated in neck opening to smooth and flare lip
Folded lip (also called "infold," "welted")	before 1840	Edge of neck heated, glass folded back into bottle; smooth lip, interior edge
Ground (also called "bust off" and "grind")	1800–1900	Used on wide-mouthed bottles. Top sheared, ground smooth on a grindstone
Applied lip (also called "laid-on ring") ; crude	after 1800; most often 1840–1860	Extra glass added to neck, reheated (often seen on crooked-necked bottles because process was poor)
Applied lip (also called "laid-on ring") ; smooth	1860–	Extra glass added to neck, reheated, appeared to be part of bottle (better fuels made finished bottle better than previous lip type)
Tooled lip	after 1820, most often 1850–1860	Neck reheated, glass applied, then tool-shaped, smooth neck, no mold seam at lip; sometimes circular marks left on neck
Screw threads outside	known in 1700's	Thread carved into mold by hand
Screw threads inside	1861	Glass added inside neck, thread shaped by special tool
Inside screw thread, late type	1890's	Tool, inserted in neck of bottle, rotated to make thread; used with rubber or porcelain stopper
Outside screw thread	1858–	Diagonal thread from below top around neck to end at shoulder (Mason jar), ZINC TOP
"Blob" top	1880's	Thick rounded lip on soda bottles
Crown top	1892	Top of neck shaped by tools to shape needed to hold crown top (metal crown top—like today's soft-drink bottles)

Stoppers and Closures

Cork	600 B.C.
Screw top with metal closure	Late 19th cent.
Mason-jar screw top with zinc lid or glass-lined lid	1858–
Glass ball inside bottle	1873–
Jar with metal or glass lid held by clamps and wire bail	1882–
"Hutchinson" stopper, wire loop holding rubber gasket inside bottle (the original "pop" bottle)	1879–
Metal cap with neckband over cork	1880's–
"Lightning" stopped, vulcanized rubber plug on bail, clamped on (used for beer)	1880's–
Crown top, metal cap with crimped edges	1891–

The fold-over lip and the pontil mark on his bottle show it was made about 1840.

The closing of this bottle is a metal overcap used at the beginning of the twentieth century.

A small glass ball was molded inside the bottle to slow the liquid when it was poured. This is a rare type of bottle of the 1890's.

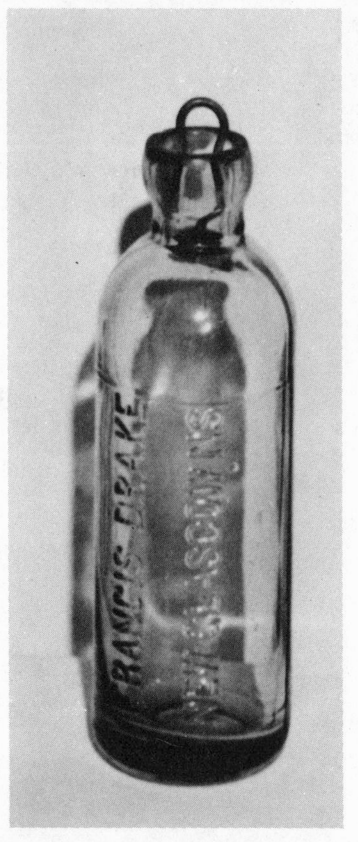

Soda water was put in many types of jars. This is the style of the original "pop" bottle; the stopper is the Hutchinson style.

Bottoms and Bases

Pontil mark	Prehistoric to 1860's	Rough scar
Graphite pontil	1850–1870	Smoother scar, with metallic iron-black deposit
Snap case	1850–1890	No scar
Wine bottle push-up base	before 1860	Push-up has pontil mark
Slight ring on base, molded in	after 1903	Mark left by automatic bottling machinery

A citrate-of-magnesia bottle of the 1890's, with a porcelain stopper.

Moxie, a soft drink, was bottled in this crown cap bottle about thirty years ago.

Instant Expert tip: EMBOSSED LETTERING OF THE TYPE USED ON BITTERS BOTTLES SEEN AFTER 1869.

How to judge the value of an unknown bottle

Bottle collecting has become a new part of antiquing. Early bottles (before 1800), historic flasks, free-blown bottles, or the early-nineteenth-century decorative decanters and tableware glasses can be judged by the same standards as any fine early glass. Age, rarity, quality, and appearance are the important factors. The commercial bottles of the nineteenth century or even the twentieth have become another problem, and what appears to be junk to the uninterested person can often be a rare and choice item. A basket of old bottles that may still be found in the barn could have great value, even if the bottles originally held pickles, catsup, or beer.

Color

Check on several points in judging old bottles. The COLOR, shape, and age as indicated by method of manufacture are all-important. GREEN IS COMMON; BROWNS, ODD SHADES OF GREENISH-YELLOW, LIGHT BLUE ARE GOOD; MILK GLASS AND DARK COBALT BLUE ARE BETTER; DARK PURPLE AND AMBER ARE THE BEST.

Shape

FIGURAL BOTTLES, THOSE SHAPED LIKE PEOPLE OR OBJECTS, ARE BEST. ANY ODD-SHAPED BOTTLE OR FLASK IS GOOD. COMMON SHAPES NEED SOME OTHER SPECIAL FEATURE TO BE DESIRABLE.

Age

MACHINE-MADE BOTTLES ARE COMMON AND NEW. TWO-PIECE MOLD BOTTLES WITH APPLIED TOPS ARE GOOD; THREE-MOLD BOTTLES ARE BETTER. FREE-BLOWN, PONTIL-MARKED, EARLY-NECKED BOTTLES ARE BEST.

Labels

PAPER LABELS ON MACHINE-MADE BOTTLES ARE COMMON. COMMON SHAPED BOTTLES WITH PAPER LABELS ARE GOOD; MOLDED BOTTLES WITH THE NAME IN RAISED LETTERS IN THE GLASS ARE BETTER; EARLY HAND-BLOWN LABELED BOTTLES ARE BEST.

ANY BOTTLE WITH ITS ORIGINAL BOX, INSTRUCTIONS, AND LABEL IS WORTH OWNING. ANY BOTTLE WITH A PONTIL MARK IS OLD ENOUGH TO SAVE.

FLASKS, OLD WHISKEY BOTTLES, FIGURAL BOTTLES, WATCH- OR CLOCK-SHAPED BOTTLES, BITTERS BOTTLES, SODA AND MINERAL-WATER BOTTLES, AND POISON BOTTLES ARE ALL COLLECTED BY SPECIALISTS. THEY HAVE ADDED VALUE BECAUSE OF THE ADDED DEMAND.

FUTURE COLLECTING

Much more should be said about the value of old bottles; but the research is just starting, and it will be years before the thousands of types of commercial bottles are identified and catalogued so that the average collector can learn the complete story.

After reading about bottles, it would seem that any old bottle is in demand by the collectors. This is almost true! Though bottle gathering is an important phase of collecting, almost indiscriminate buying of bottles is not a part of the pattern. If you want to collect bottles, and have plenty of space, buy any bottle made before the advent of the bottle-making machine, and it will probably increase in value each year. If space is a problem, collect examples of a special type, and try to acquire a complete collection that will show the gradual development of the bottle. If you find a group of old bottles, and you want to sell them, ask almost any friend or dealer. There is a ready market.

Antiques are fun to look for because so many of us seem to like different things, and bargains can be found because of one person's interest or another's lack of it. Bottle collectors get even greater bargains than other types of collectors because many of them quite literally go out in dumps and trash heaps and dig for old bottles. Bottle collecting is among the top three hobbies in the nation, and dozens of collectors' groups have been organized. Privately printed literature is available (see bibliography at the end of this chapter), and the study of bottles has become a new and growing field. Perhaps it is because there is so little known about bottles that the collector can become excited at most kinds or shapes.

Digging for bottles in a ghost-town dump or, if you are a city dweller, behind the bulldozer that is working on the new freeway can be fun. The excitement of a discovery, plus the outdoor activity and love of a beautiful bottle, all add to the many joys of bottle collecting.

A noncollector may find it hard to believe that ANY OLD BOTTLE IS A GOOD BOTTLE. There is no other field of collecting where there is so little quality differentiation. The best bottles are the oldest, rarest, or the most unusual in shape or color, and not those that are the finest examples of a craftsman's art. Bottles were commercial containers, not works of art. They were originally made to be useful. So many types of bottles have been made that it is hard to know where to start, but a few rules have been set forth in the available writings that will help to make future study easier. Right or wrong, some of the classifications now in use follow.

There are roughly four types of bottles: whiskey bottles or flasks (including glass and ceramic), bitters bottles (the 1840–1900 types), figural bottles (any bottle of an unusual shape—and it may be part of one of the other classifications), and household bottles (shoe polish, ink, canning jars, milk bottles, and other such household items). There are a few rules that can aid in the dating of old glass bottles; all the rules are based on the method of manufacture.

The first American bottles to gain favor with the collectors were the whiskey flasks made in the 1750 to 1860 period. Most of them were pint size and were made by a pattern or blown-mold method and with impressed or raised decorations on the glass. Because consumers feared that the size of blown bottles varied so that they might be cheated, the factories developed a molded bottle that was always the same size. The historic flasks that became popular about 1810 were the result of this search. Books have been written about the "historics," and pages of clear pictures can be seen in relevant books in most libraries.

Here are a few Instant Expert tips for the very inexperienced: THE CHANCES OF FINDING A RARE HISTORIC FLASK ARE ALMOST NON-EXISTENT. REPRODUCTIONS OF DOZENS OF THE PATTERNS HAVE BEEN MADE AND SOLD DURING THE PAST TWENTY-FIVE YEARS. HISTORIC FLASKS ARE LISTED AND GROUPED BY RARITY. IT IS THE RARE, PERFECT BOTTLE THAT IS HIGH-PRICED, NOT THE MORE COMMON TYPES. Since a rarity may differ from a common flask only by the number of stars impressed in the design, it can be a long process to determine whether a flask is good, very good, or WOW!

The flask had a companion on the store shelf by 1830, as the more unusual liquor bottles gained favor. A firm named Bininger made many sizes and shapes of bottles that held liquor. ANY BOTTLE WITH THE NAME BININGER IN THE GLASS IS OF VALUE.

Odd-shaped bottles made like clocks, cabins, or barrels are of interest because they are unusual, fun to own, and are what the decorators call a "conversation piece." Bottle collecting is a supply-and-demand hobby because so little is known about the number of bottles available in any one of the special shapes. If the bottle interests you because of its color, label, or shape, it should interest others.

The Booz bottle is a classic among famous liquor bottles. It says "1840" on the bottle, but there is good reason to believe that it was not made until about 1860. Mr. E. G. Booz ran a tavern in Philadelphia, and the bottle was made for him to sell. Three versions of the bottle were made for the original Mr. Booz, but dozens of recent copies have been made. It often takes an expert to determine the new from the old.

Perhaps some of the unusual Christmas-gift decanters offered by liquor companies have added to the growing interest in collecting liquor bottles, for the new and often limited-edition bottles and decanters have become collectors' items. The liquor bottles of prohibition days are another rich source for collectors. The illegality of the bottle and its contents made the supply scarce, and many bottles of the 1920's are now in great demand.

Most governments require every whiskey bottle to have a permit number molded into it, and each distiller has a number that is recorded with the government and can be traced. Bottle factories also have mold numbers on record that will help to tell the age, but many illegal bottles were made without these numbers. Bottles were made by hand until 1913, when the first semiautomatic equipment was used, and after 1922 almost all bottles were machine made.

Bitters bottles

Most of the bitters bottles should really be classed as liquor bottles, because their contents were usually higher in alcohol than whiskey. Bitters were the "medicine" of the last half of the nineteenth century. Many types of bitters bottles were made from about 1840 to 1900, and a few even later. Bitters were made from mixtures of various herbs, roots, spices, and barks, which were blended with alcohol. Bitters were taken by the spoonful and frequently

Dr. Baker's Pain Panacea was one of many drinks of the bitters type made in the late nineteenth century.

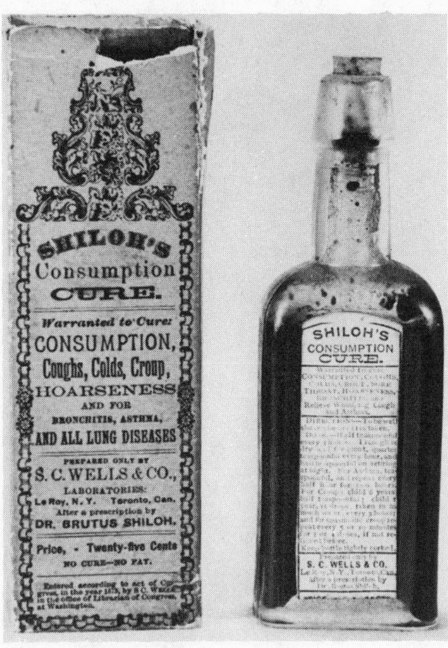

The best bottle for the collector is one that is old and has both label and original box. Shiloh's Consumption cure was packaged in this bottle.

Vermifuge, a medicinal drink, was sold in this bottle with embossed lettering. About 1880.

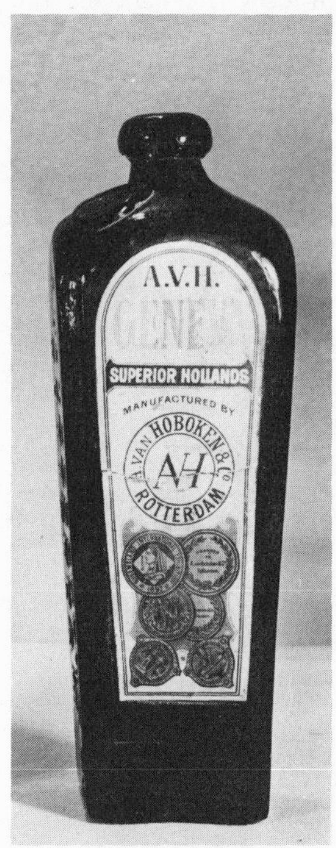

The shape and seal molded into the bottle are typical of special types of liquor bottles.

by the full bottle, and they were the wonder drugs of the times. According to the labels, the contents could cure anything. The label on one bottle claimed the contents would cure "biliousness, liver complaint, fever blisters, constipation, Bright's disease, dyspepsia, malaria, ague, hypochondria, sleeplessness, and others." Bitters were originally invented to avoid the tax on gin in England, because it was a simple process to mix the gin with herbs and call it "medicine." It was easier to tell your wife that the bitters would help your digestion than to admit you were drinking liquor, and therefore the popularity of bitters went on and on—and on.

The collector of bitters bottles prefers A BOTTLE WITH THE NAME BITTERS IN THE GLASS OR ONE WITH A PAPER LABEL. A labeled bottle with the contents, cork, and outside box explaining the curative powers of the bitters is the most desired. Over four-hundred bitters makers have been listed for the United States, and because many of them used several different bottles, the varieties of bitters bottles are numerous. Several books now list the bitters bottles by shape, color, rarity, and even price. (See the bibliography at the end of this chapter.)

Household bottles

Canning jars are becoming popular in the West, but they are not yet in favor with collectors in the East. The famous Mason jar with the words "Mason 1858" is one of the most misunderstood bottles today. The "1858" is the date of the original patent, and not all the Mason jars were made that early. Variations of the Mason jar were made, and the same date could be seen on the jars for over thirty years. Dozens of other canning jars that were made after the original Mason jar was invented are some of the as yet ignored bottles still awaiting the collector.

Milk bottles are the "newest" field for collectors. Paper cartons have replaced the bottle in many stores, and the returnable milk bottle seems destined to disappear. OLD MILK BOTTLES WITH A COMPANY NAME EMBOSSED OR PRINTED ON THE GLASS ARE NOW WANTED BY COLLECTORS. The famous Thatcher milk bottle, picturing Dr. Thatcher milking a cow, was made in 1884, and copies of the bottle have been made for sale in gift stores. The milk bottles collected today were made from about 1900 to 1950.

The famous Mason canning jar has a screw top and raised lettering. The date 1858 appears on many later jars; this is a bottle dating about 1860.

"Ruby Beets" were packaged in this bottle for the grocery store of 1890.

Baby bottles are wanted by a different group of collectors. The first baby feeding bottle, the O'Donnell bottle, was introduced at the Great Exhibition of 1851 in London, England. It had a long tube with a nipple end, and it was the first of dozens of types of glass nursing bottles.

Commercial bottles for foodstuffs were made in the late nineteenth century. THE GOTHIC PANEL BOTTLE favored by pepper-sauce makers is one of the special designs wanted by collectors.

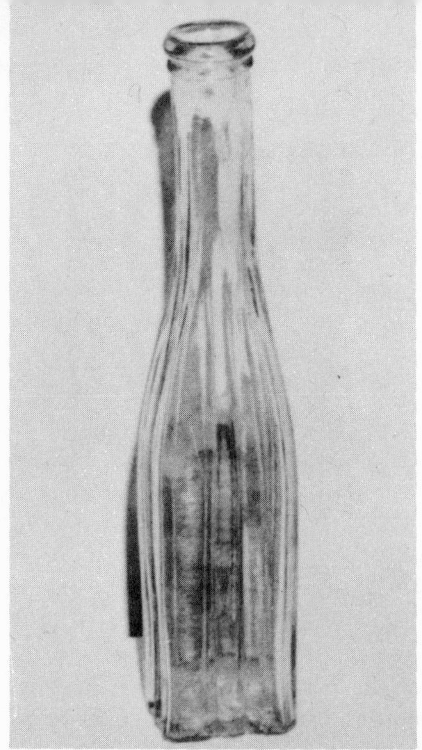

A Gothic panel bottle often used for pepper sauce and other food products.

"Extra Fine Tomato Catsup" was sold in this bottle about 1880.

Pottery bottles from England were often used for ink, beer, or foodstuffs. This bottle held preserves about 1880.

Small ink bottles

Ink bottles with large bases and small necks are another of the nineteenth-century bottle shapes that are no longer made. The bottle with many protruding bumps that indicated it contained poison is another of the unusual household types.

Cosmetic bottles that were often milk-glass jars with metal screw tops are a special class of household bottle. Hair oils, face creams, shaving cream, and other beauty aids came in a variety of bottles.

Shoe polish was held in this small barrel-shaped bottle.

Figural bottles

It is impossible to list the hundreds of types of bottles classed by collectors as "figural" bottles. Any bottle, regardless of whether it is old or new, that is shaped like a recognizable person or object is a figural bottle. Large whiskey flasks, ceramic or glass; decorative bottles that held pancake syrup, mustard, ink, or any of the many products sold in fancy bottles, are included. The small penny candy bottles that were sold in dime stores about 1900 and later form a special group of figural bottles. We know of no complete, or even adequate, listing of figural bottles. It is an interesting collection, and one that is as yet relatively unexplored.

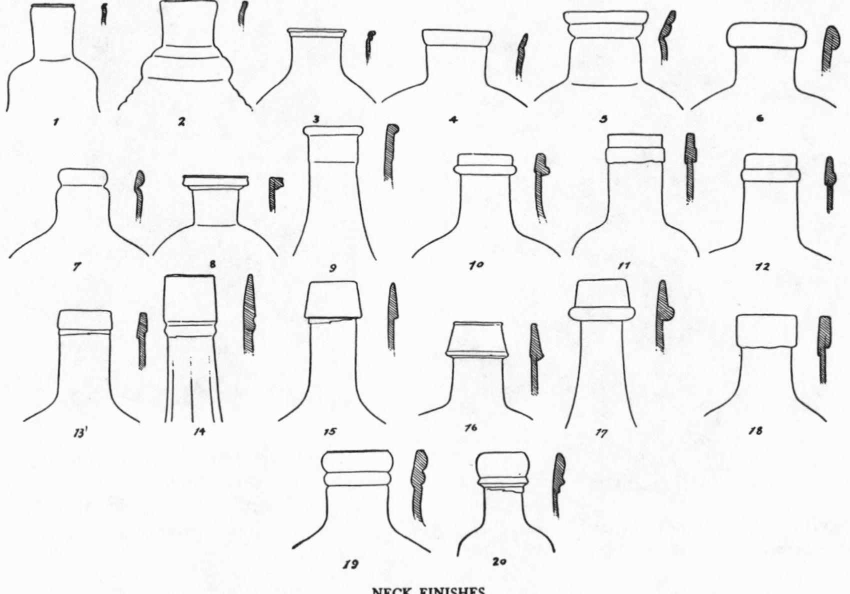

NECK FINISHES

EXPLANATORY NOTES

Neck Finish

The following line drawings, Nos. 1 to 20 inclusive, show the various types of neck finish encountered in historical bottles and flasks. The designation of the flask under each number indicates the particular variety from which the line drawing was made.

1. Plain lip, whetted or cracked off without fire polishing showing rough edges. Half-pint scroll flask, 34, Scroll Group IX.
2. Plain lip, fire polished, "Jared Spencer" flask, 24, Miscellaneous Group X.
3. Folded or welted lip, slightly flanged and infolded, an unusual treatment in flasks. Pint Zanesville Masonic and Eagle flask, 32, Masonic Group IV.
4. Tooled lip, characteristically encountered in heavy Keene Masonics. Masonic "JKB" flask, 4, Group IV.
5. Plain double-tooled lip. Masonic, large star in oval frame beneath eagle, 6, Masonic Group IV.
6. Plain, rounded rolled over collar. Masonic "JKB" flask, 3, Group IV.
7. Tooled and pinched in, a very unusual treatment. Pint Lafayette-Masonic, Vernon Glass Works, 88, Portrait Group I.
8. Flanged lip with flat top and squared tooled edge. Half-pint Washington "Albany Glass Works" flask, 30, Portrait Group I.
9. Slightly flanged, rounded tooled lip with flat tooled three-quarter-inch band below. Quart Calabash Washington and Tree in blue, 35, Portrait Group I.
10. Thickened plain lip with narrow ring below. Pint flask; rider wearing derby hat on galloping horse to right. Reverse: hound walking to right. Van Rensselaer's 34, Group VI. Not listed in our charts.
11. Thickened plain lip with flat ring below. Quart scroll flask, 3, Scroll Group IX.
12. Tooled, plain lip with broad rounded ring below. Quart Pikes Peak with prospector on each side. Not listed by Van Rensselaer and not listed in our charts. Plate 260, Nos. 1 and 2.
13. Thickened plain lip with narrow beveled fillet below. Quart Corn for the World flask, 4, Baltimore Monument Group VI.
14. Tooled, broad sloping collar terminating in beveled ring. Kossuth and Tree, Calabash, 113 Portrait Group I.
15. Tooled, plain broad sloping collar. Quart Washington and Taylor Dyottville flask, 42, Portrait Group I.
16. Tooled, with broad sloping collar having terminal ridges at top and bottom. Quart Sheaf of Rye resting on crossed rake and fork. Reverse: inscription "Traveler's Companion" with eight-pointed circular star. Van Rensselaer's 107, Group VI. Not listed in our charts.
17. Tooled, with broad sloping collar terminating in undercut rounded ring. Calabash Washington and Tree, 35, Portrait Group I.
18. Tooled, with broad verticle sided collar, lower edge not tooled. Quart Washington and Taylor "Dyottville Glass Works" flask, 37, Portrait Group I.
19. Tooled, double rounded collar, upper ring much larger, neck slightly pinched in at base of collar. Quart Lockport Glass Works bust of Washington each side, 61, Portrait Group I.
20. Tooled, with broad rounded collar terminating in beveled ring. Half-pint scroll flask, 33, Scroll Group IX.

EARLY BOTTLE SHAPES

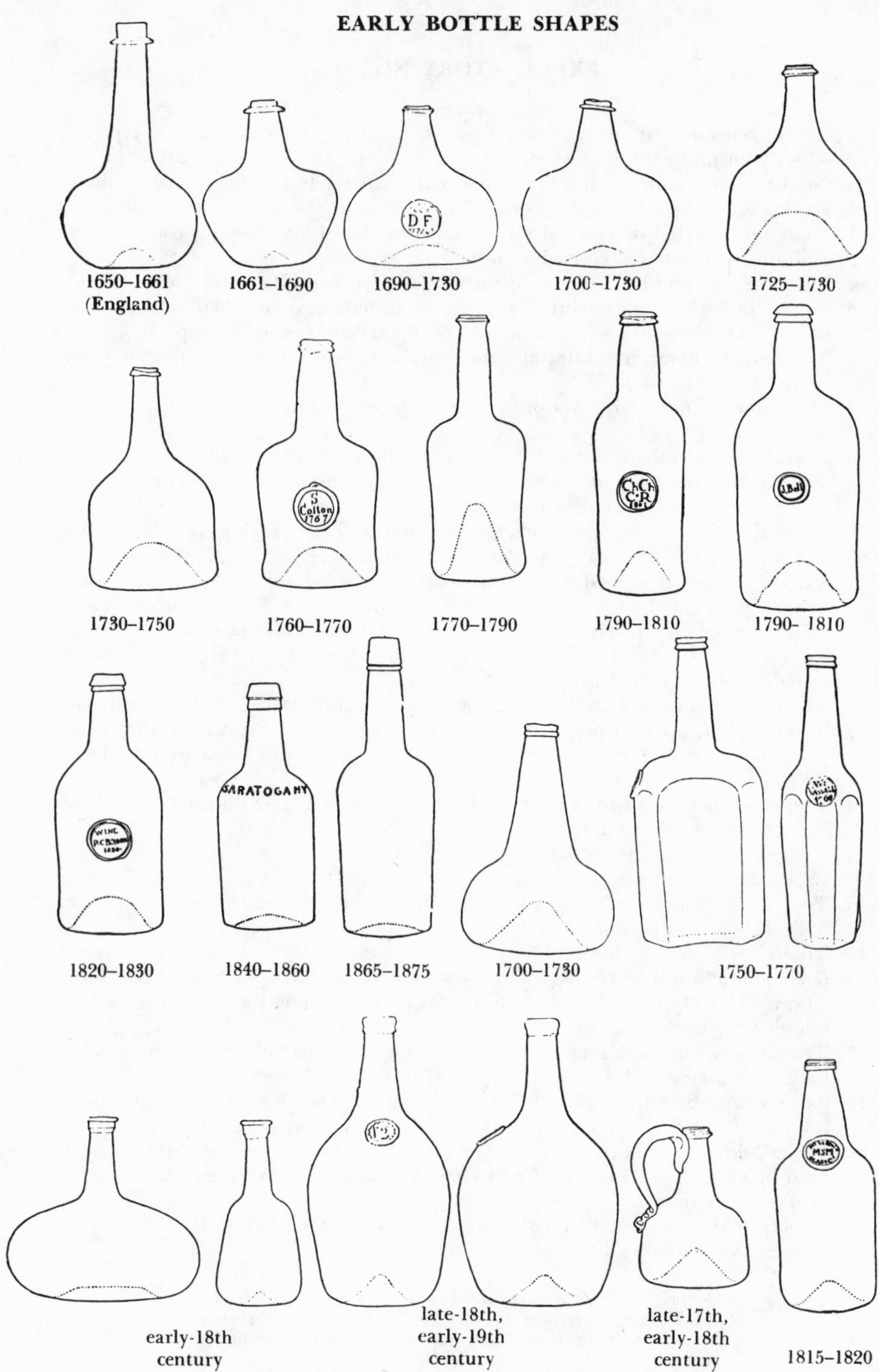

Above drawings reprinted from *American Glass* by George S. and Helen McKearin, copyright 1941, 1948 by Crown Publishers, Inc., New York. Used by permission of Crown Publishers, Inc.

Bottles: Bibliography

General

Covill, William E., Jr. *Ink Bottles and Inkwells.* Taunton. Massachusetts: William S. Sullwold, 1971.
1,780 pictures of ink bottles make this a comprehensive guide for ink bottle collectors.

Eikelberner, George and Serge Agadjanian. *American Glass Candy Containers.* Privately printed, 1967. (Order from Serge Agadjanian, River Road, Belle Mead, New Jersey 08502.)

———. *More American Glass Candy Containers.* Privately printed, 1970. (Order from author.)
These two books are line drawing directories of glass candy containers. Limited information is included.

Freeman, Larry. *Grand Old American Bottles.* Watkins Glen, New York: Century House, 1964.
Informative book about all types of bottles, illustrated with photographs and reprints of old catalogs; bibliography but no index.

McKearin, George S. and Helen. *American Glass.* New York: Crown, 1959.
The authoritative book about glass, including sections on historical flasks and old bitters and medicine bottles.

Munsey, Cecil. *The Illustrated Guide to Collecting Bottles.* New York: Hawthorn, 1970.
An excellent book for beginning bottle collectors. All types of bottles are described and a bibliography is included.

Revi, Albert Christian. *American Pressed Glass and Figure Bottles.* New York: Nelson, 1964.
Well-indexed, well-authenticated information about figural bottles. Many illustrations, patent records, and so on; a scholarly, important book for the collector.

Toulouse, Julian Harrison. *Bottle Makers and Their Marks.* Camden, New Jersey: Nelson, 1971.
This is a very technical alphabetic listing of marks found on bottles. Extensive factory history.

———. *Fruit Jars.* Camden, New Jersey: Nelson, 1969.
This book is a "must" for fruit jar collectors. History, trademarks, and bottles are described in detail.

Umberger, Jewel and Arthur L. *Collectible Character Bottles.* Tyler, Texas: Corker Book Company, 819 West Wilson, 1969.
This is an alphabetic listing of figural bottles with sketches and no photographs. It is of limited value.

Unitt, Doris and Peter. *Bottles in Canada.* Peterborough, Ontario, Canada: Clock House Publications (P.O. Box 103), 1972.
This book describes many of the bottles found in Canada and often in the United States. The Canadian glass factories are listed.

Watson, Richard. *Bitters Bottles.* New York: Nelson, 1965.

———. *Supplement to Bitters Bottles.* New York: Nelson, 1968.
Two extensive lists of bitters bottles, manufacturers, variations, rarity, and measurements. The

books are illustrated with line drawings and include lists of known bitters bottles.

Wearin, Otha. *Statues That Pour.* Denver: Sage Books, 1965.
The story of many types of figural bottles, old and new. Photographs, bibliography, and index.

Ferraro, Pat and Bob. *The Past in Glass.* Sparks, Nevada: Western Printing & Publishing Co., 1964.

Freeman, Larry. *The Medicine Showman.* Watkins Glen, New York: Century House, 1957.

Jones, May. *The Bottle Trail* (Vols. 1, 2, 3, 4, 5, 6). 1963. (Order from author, P.O. Box 23, Nara Visa, New Mexico.)

Kauffman, Don and June. *Dig Those Crazy Bottles.* 1966. (Order from authors, 3520 Laramie Street, Cheyenne, Wyoming.)

Kendrick, Grace. *The Antique Bottle Collector.* Sparks, Nevada: Western Printing & Publishing Co., 1964.

Kincade, Steve. *Early American Bottles and Glass.* Clovis, California: Clovis Printing Company (619 Fifth Street), 1964.

Maust, Don. *Bottle and Glass Handbook.* Uniontown, Pennsylvania: E. G. Warman Publishing Co., 1956.

Putnam, H. E. *Bottle Identification.* 1965. (Order from author, P.O. Box 517, Jamestown, California.)

Reed, Adele. *Old Bottles and Ghost Towns.* 1961. (Order from author, Route 1, Box 96, Bishop, California.)

4

Furniture and Furniture Construction

ONE CHAPTER in a book could hardly explain everything about antique furniture, but we have organized the world of chairs and tables in such a way that you should be able to make a sensible guess about the age of many pieces of furniture. Understanding antique furniture requires organization and good sense, as well as an innate sense of suspicion, because furniture, more than any other antique, is forged, copied, and embellished.

First, there is country furniture, and there is formal furniture. Most of the experts don't really know which is which, but to talk a good game of antiques you must have the general idea. There is furniture from Spain, England, France, Canada, Pennsylvania—in fact from anywhere and everywhere. In this book we are concentrating on the American, Canadian, and English pieces that might cross your path. In antiques, as with the other arts, a picture is worth a thousand words. Follow the pictures, and you should know how to date and determine the *style* of furniture. If you wish to decide if it is really as old as it appears, you must read the section "Furniture Construction" and learn about nails, miter joints, and finishes.

Stuart

The first period of design that could be found hidden in an antique shop or someone's attic is based on the English Stuart period from about 1600–1688, when furniture was heavy and massive. Furniture designing is much like dress designing: if the hem is down, the only thing to do is make it shorter; and when it is short, drop the length of the skirt. If the furniture has been light in weight with straight legs for twenty-five years, then make the legs heavier, curve them, and use dark colors; if massive designs were the style, then develop simple, lightweight chairs. A few outside influences will always vary this pattern, but furniture design has gone from heavy to light to heavy to light, both in color and weight, since 1600. Special exhibits have caused short fads, such as the use of bamboo, and special new materials have enabled designers to construct furniture in different ways, such as the molded plastic chairs of today.

STUART CHESTS can be easily identified. The cabinetmaker used A STYLE CALLED "RECTANGULAR PANEL CONSTRUCTION." That means he took four boards, made a rectangle, then filled the middle with a large flat board. The rectangular panels were the sides of chests, the front doors of cabinets, and so on.

THE GATELEG TABLE WAS FIRST MADE AT THIS TIME. (Instant Expert tip: THE MORE LEGS ON THE GATELEG TABLE, THE BETTER THE TABLE.) Small tea tables, stools, and chairs were also introduced at this time. Most of the furniture from England was made from oak or walnut.

In America most of the designs were passed on by the craftsmen who had recently arrived from England. This period is called the "Pilgrim Century," and until about 1700 the styles were simplified versions of the English Stuart pieces. The rectangular panel construction had traveled by boat to the new colonies, along with many other designs. Trees were so plentiful in America that the furniture was made from solid wood with no veneers. Cabinetmakers used wooden drawer pulls, made from any type of wood that grew in the area and was usable. Most cabinetmakers preferred oak, ash, or maple, but many other woods were also chosen. The most romantic furniture names to appear at this time were the Carver and Brewster chairs. Traditionally, one type of chair was used by the Carver family and another type by the Brewster family, so the chairs made after that were named for each family. One had more spindles than the other, but it really is of little concern to the average collector. Match your chair against the picture and see which family you prefer, but before you do, here is a word of warning: THOUSANDS OF COPIES OF CARVER AND BREWSTER CHAIRS WERE MADE IN VICTORIAN TIMES, AND IT IS VERY, VERY DOUBTFUL THAT YOURS IS ANYTHING BUT A COPY. Let us stop for a moment and be realistic: How many chairs do you think the original Pilgrims would have used?

The gateleg table was an early design in America. This maple table was made about 1700. (Metropolitan Museum of Art; gift of Mrs. Russell Sage)

The trestle table is one other form of furniture that appeared with the Pilgrims. Remember all the drawings that pictured the dozens of Pilgrims eating their Thanksgiving dinner at a long table? That is really not what it was like, because, though tables that long were made, the long thin table had to be small enough to get into a house.

William and Mary

The monarchs William and Mary are the easiest of the English rulers for the antique furniture buff. The Dutch influence came in at this time,

The burled walnut and burled ash William and Mary lowboy has two small balls hanging from the front apron. (Lyman Allyn Museum, New London, Connecticut)

William and Mary furniture can be recognized by the "round ball syndrome." This American highboy with the ball feet was made about 1690-1720. (Baltimore Museum of Art, Baltimore, Maryland)

and furniture developed its "round ball" syndrome. Look at a William and Mary table stretcher, chair stretcher, lowboy, or almost any piece made during the period. Somewhere, somehow the designer almost always included a fat ball. It is just about a sure thing that IF THE FAT BALL APPEARS, THE FURNITURE IS A WILLIAM AND MARY DESIGN. This strange design element disappeared by the time of the next ruler, Queen Anne. The William and Mary style (1688–1715) was in vogue in America from about 1700 to 1720. It took a few years for designs to cross the ocean in the minds of the newly arriving cabinetmakers, by paintings, or by pictures in design books.

American furniture developed the "fat ball" and the Spanish foot that was so popular in England. Inlay, marquetry, and veneer were popular in England, but the Americans settled for burled veneer with teardrop brass handles as part of the design. Designers seemed to like FURNITURE WITH MANY LEGS, such as the gateleg table. A room decorated with pure William and Mary design appears to be a forest of wooden legs. This is the time of the first high chests, or what is later called the highboy. The slant-top desk, the daybed, and the upholstered easy chair were also introduced.

The cabriole leg and pad foot appeared on tables, chests, and chairs of the Queen Anne period. This American highboy is made of curly maple. (Old Sturbridge Village, Sturbridge, Massachusetts)

Queen Anne

Queen Anne's designs ruled furniture in England from about 1715 to 1750. An abrupt change in design had occurred. The heavy furniture seemed a bit less bulky, less blocky, and slight curves appeared. The Queen Anne chair had the CABRIOLE LEG AND THE PADFOOT. This curved leg appeared on tables and chests; and almost every piece from that period had the graceful cabriole leg. Curves appeared at the top of the chair, at the crest of a mirror, and the domelike "bonnet" of a highboy. The furniture had simplicity and grace and WAS USUALLY MADE OF WALNUT. The hardware had been slightly enlarged, and the bail handle appeared with an escutcheon. Designers also had developed some new forms, such as the corner chair, card table, and the tilt-top table. This is also the period when secret drawers were hidden in most large pieces of furniture containing any drawers at all.

The expert examining the Queen Anne chair should look for five things. (1) The top of the back is curved. (2) The splat rests on the rear of the seat and does not end above the seat. (3) The front legs

This Queen Anne chair has all five clues: the curved top of the back, the center splat resting on the seat, the cabriole legs, pad foot, and stretchers between the legs. (Old Sturbridge Village, Sturbridge, Massachusetts)

Chippendale pieces featured big brasses and the ball-and-claw foot. This desk was a large, heavy wooden piece made of mahogany. (Taylor and Dull)

are cabriole. (4) The front feet are Dutch, club, or ball and claw. (5) There may or may not be stretchers between the legs. The later the Queen Anne chair, the less chance of stretchers, as they became a discarded part of the William and Mary design that had been necessary for structural support. Because the curve of the cabriole leg held the width, a stretcher was not needed.

Chippendale

Imagine being a furniture designer with a Queen Anne chair to redesign. The new design must be different enough, but not so strange that it would appear awkward or ugly. It is the same problem that must face designers of new automobiles each year. Much thought, plus a sense of what the public would accept and buy, and the Queen Anne chair with its curved leg, solid-splat high back, became the Chippendale chair—just a few changes, but what a difference!

We will discuss the chair of Chippendale, but let us briefly go back in history. Furniture designs were named for the ruler of the country until 1750. Then, in 1754, furniture designing was revolutionized when Thomas Chippendale of England, the twice-married father of eleven children, and a cabinetmaker of some fame in London, published a book, *The Gentleman and Cabinet-Maker's Director*. There were 160 designs pictured in the book. The designs were based on the early Georgian period (1715–1750), with the slight changes in the Queen Anne style that was to be expected, plus the designs based on the outside influences of French and Chinese pieces (thus the term "Chinese Chippendale"). The cabinetmakers of the day used the book and the several other editions that followed, and a new name was given to the English furniture of the 1750–1785 period—Chippendale. (Experts are still debating whether Chippendale did the designs or if they were done by several of his employees.)

There are Gothic, French, and Chinese styles of Chippendale furniture, but several characteristics are found in all of them. The entire proportion of the chair changed and the back was lowered. MEASURE THE CHAIR FROM THE TOP OF THE BACK TO THE FLOOR. IT SHOULD MEASURE 3 FEET 1 INCH TO 3 FEET 2½ INCHES. Later chairs are lower, earlier ones much higher.

Two types of legs were used, the ball-and-claw foot on a curved leg or a square, rather straight leg. Stretchers were omitted from chairs and other four-legged pieces. In America, especially in the eastern cities where many gifted cabinetmakers worked, some typically American designs finally appeared. It is possible to look at a picture of a Philadelphia Chippendale piece and know it was not made in any other city because of the ornate carving and many of the design characteristics, such as the Philadelphia "peanut." Unless your family still has the ancestral furniture from pre-Revolutionary days, you will probably never find a Philadelphia highboy, but it is still nice to know about them. Copies have been and are being made, but good copies cost thousands of dollars.

Chippendale is the period of THE BIG BRASSES. Look at any piece with drawer pulls; it is obvious that the pulls are not just useful, but are an important part of the decoration. The designers developed the piecrust table, the chest-on-chest, and the large upholstered sofa. Large, heavy carved wooden pieces of polished mahogany were the masterpieces of the American craftsman, and some of America's finest furniture was made at this time.

Hepplewhite

The car designer must find a new style each year to keep the public buying, and the furniture makers have a similar problem after short periods of years. Heavy carved dark wooden pieces with curved legs and backs were in vogue, so of course it was time for a change. From about 1785 to 1810, the Hepplewhite period was "in." Once again, a period was named for a cabinetmaker. *The Cabinet Maker and Upholsterer's Guide* was published in 1799 by A. Hepplewhite and Co. George Hepplewhite had died, but his wife, Alice, continued the business, and it was she who published the book. The volume pictured the designs that were in style, most of them inspired by the work of the Adam brothers. The Adams were architects, and after they had designed large rooms with light-colored walls and restrained classical decorations, they decided to design a style of furniture that would look best in such rooms. These designs became popular with the general public.

The Chinese Parlor is papered with painted Chinese wallpaper and furnished with American-made furniture of the Chinese Chippendale style. (Henry Francis du Pont Winterthur Museum, Winterthur, Delaware)

There are several quick clues in recognizing a Hepplewhite chair. The back of the chair is approximately 3 feet 1 inch from the floor. A shield-back type of chair became popular. The center back of the chair did not touch the seat. To make the design work, the oval, heart, wheel or shield-shaped back was used. The chair had slenderer lines than Chippendale, with delicately carved straight tapered legs and a general feeling of delicacy that differentiated the Hepplewhite period from the heavier Chippendale styles. Once again, special forms were introduced, and the period (1785–1810) saw the introduction of the extension table, the sewing table (the little table with a single drawer and a cloth bag hanging beneath it), the tambour desk and, of course, the

The sewing table is a design that became popular about 1800. This mahogany and satinwood table was made in Salem, Massachusetts. (Index of American Design)

The square leg of Hepplewhite is seen in this American table made of mahogany about 1780. (Minneapolis Institute of Arts, Minneapolis, Minnesota)

sideboard. The light feel and appearance of the design made several forms incongruous, and the high chest of drawers was discontinued.

Hepplewhite furniture was made from mahogany, satinwood, and other fancy woods. Inlay was popular. The brasses had oval-shaped backs with bail-type handles.

Sheraton

Thomas Sheraton of England was making furniture at about the same time as the Hepplewhite company. He had talent, and printed a design book for the use of other furniture makers. There is some question whether Thomas Sheraton personally ever made furniture. He published his first design book in 1791, and by 1805 he had written six publications of this kind. His earliest printed designs were reminiscent of Chippendale work, but his later pieces showed a decided French influence.

At this point it should become increasingly clear that words don't always mean exactly what they say. Sheraton style has one meaning to a museum curator and another to an antique dealer, yet both meanings are correct. The traditional, pedantic view of Sheraton is that the furniture style was graceful, delicate, simple, and with classical lines. Straight lines were favored. The chairs had rectangular backs with a minimum of carved decorations, while the legs were often rounded and reeded. Some of the designs required the return of the stretcher between the legs, which was really an old idea that had been redesigned for the lighter-weight chairs and tables.

Sheraton's later designs featured vase- or lyre-shaped table pedestals, a style that merged almost imperceptibly with the Empire or Federal period.

Many people, while discussing Sheraton styles, often do not picture the lightweight inlaid, early Sheraton, but the heavier, darker, later designs. Some books about antiques use, reuse, and misuse the names until it is almost necessary to take a vote among the printed authorities to learn what is the true meaning, for the true meaning should be the one that is a part of our everyday communication, and not the formal definition of an art professor. A study of various furniture books shows that Sheraton and Hepplewhite styles could be divided and described in several ways, so we have chosen those of the most common usage.

If a chair has a rectangular back it is Sheraton, while a shield-shaped back is Hepplewhite. If the chair leg is square, it is Hepplewhite, while if it is round it is Sheraton. If the sideboard is widest in the center, it

The Federal period in America is illustrated by the Du Pont dining room. The furniture is in Sheraton and Hepplewhite styles, and shows the square back and square leg and straight-lined simplicity popular about 1800. (Henry Francis du Pont Winterthur Museum, Winterthur, Delaware)

Late Sheraton furniture in America featured the round leg, often reeded, and a simple turned wooden knob if the maker was from the country. This cherry nightstand was made about 1800–1820. (Western Reserve Historical Society, Cleveland, Ohio)

is Hepplewhite, and those that are widest at the ends are Sheraton. A chair with square legs and a square back would be transitional Hepplewhite or transitional Sheraton. It isn't really that easy, but the most important problem for the average collector is to determine the age of the chair. Using either the name Sheraton or Hepplewhite can mean furniture that was made about 1800.

Much late Sheraton furniture is obviously Sheraton. It has substantial rounded legs that are reeded, with simple wooden surfaces often made of a wood like curly maple. The oval brasses are a favorite shape in Sheraton designs. The late American Sheraton often appears in "country furniture," and is one of the most popular types purchased by those who want to decorate in "Early American."

Instant Expert note: SHERATON MADE THE FIRST TWIN BEDS.

Duncan Phyfe

There really was a man named Duncan Phyfe and he did make furniture, but he made it for so many years that he has completely confused the American student of design names. If there is a Duncan Phyfe style (we suspect there is not), it has to be the style of furniture made by Mr. Phyfe in his own workshops, in New York, from 1792 to 1847. Duncan Phyfe worked in several styles, including the Sheraton and the Empire. Some authorities believe that his early work was very fine and much of his later work inferior. Styles such as the lyre-shaped pedestal table called "Duncan Phyfe" were really the Empire designs of his day.

Empire

The word "Empire" refers to the furniture made and designed in France from about 1804 to 1830. It began with the designs of two French architects who redecorated Napoleon's palace. The style was stiff and formal, and once again it appeared heavy with Greek, Roman, Egyptian, and Pompeian motifs. The

Duncan Phyfe worked in many styles. This room is furnished with some of the earlier pieces made by Phyfe, about 1807. This too is American Federal style. (Henry Francis du Pont Winterthur Museum, Winterthur, Delaware)

furniture was made for looks, not comfort, and straight backs, hard seats, and other unyielding pieces appeared. Gold was everywhere in the ormolu mountings used on the furniture. Even construction joints were often hidden by a piece of ormolu placed as decoration. The woods were painted or stained black; the fabric colors were dark and muted, and the gold appeared as the only bright spot. There was no doubt that Empire was a heavy, stiff, formal, dark period of furniture.

The Greek Revival style was the later part of the American Federal period. This room is furnished with the dark woods and gold decorations popular in the 1830's. (Henry Francis du Pont Winterthur Museum, Winterthur, Delaware)

The Victorian fashions called for pattern on pattern. The furniture by makers like John Belter added to the pattern of the room. (Thorne Miniature Rooms, Art Institute of Chicago, Chicago, Illinois)

Federal

The term "Federal American" actually means anything made after the Federal government began in 1789. This would include the Hepplewhite, Sheraton, and Empire styles. Most people when referring to "Federal" mean furniture made in the Empire style in America. It is unfortunate that the word has been misused, but the true meaning of Federal covers many types of furniture.

Victorian

The heavy square furniture of the Empire period had to be redesigned as the Victorian era arrived. Heavy, massive, and very ornate furniture appeared during the years from 1837 to 1900 that we now call "Victorian." It is the "newest" period to receive recognition by many of the serious students of antiques, and it is possible to find that some of the books have differentiated between the various types of Victorian furniture, particularly the Eastlake Gothic, Renaissance, and rococo designs for formal furniture and the country-favored spool and painted styles. Unless you plan to specialize in Victorian furniture, it is necessary to know only a few instant clues to decide whether the chair is Victorian or earlier.

The Victorian designer continued with the Empire theory that comfort was of little importance. Try sitting on a carved Victorian chair, and you will notice that the carving will often protrude at some of the same spots as you will—a situation that does not add to the joy of being seated. Scrolls, curls, and intricate designs appeared because of the invention of the jigsaw. It was almost as if the designer and furniture maker became intoxicated with new developments and the advent of the Industrial Revolution. Handmade and handcrafted furniture almost disappeared as mass production became a reality. Marble tops, heavy furniture, and dark woods (especially rosewood and mahogany) filled each room. The Victorian disliked the undecorated surface, and pattern appeared against pattern. Measurements of chairs varied from those larger than Chippendale to those smaller than Hepplewhite, so that size alone will be of no help. It is the general feeling of the period that makes it possible to identify it, the ornate wonder of it all.

Many of the chests had mushroom-turned wooden knobs, but by the later part of the Victorian era the leaf-carved handle or the molded mass-produced leaf handle was used. (See section in this chapter on handles and hardware.)

And then—

The history of antique furniture doesn't end with the Victorian era. Collectors have discovered William Morris and his Mission furniture, which is a plain, rectangular wooden furniture with straight lines and no nonsense. It is reminiscent of the Spanish mission pieces. The "golden oak" of the early 1900's, with its yellow color and massive lines, and the wicker of the 1930's have already been "discovered."

Country furniture

It is hard enough to write a book about a particular subject, but then bravely to write a few paragraphs that discuss the subject of the entire book would be foolhardy. *American Country Furniture 1780–1875* by Ralph and Terry Kovel (Crown, 1965) is filled with information about all sorts of country pieces, but for most collectors there are only a few types that are of immediate importance.

The Windsor chair

Windsor furniture began in England during the sixteenth century, and gradually developed into the type of chair used in America before the Revolution. It has a shaped seat with spindles that made up the back and legs, which were turned and placed at an angle. THE MORE SPINDLES ON THE CHAIR, THE OLDER

The more spindles on the Windsor chair, the older and better the chair. This thirteen-spindle New England armchair was made in Rhode Island in the eighteenth century. (Taylor and Dull)

AND BETTER THE CHAIR. That tip alone can save you from most mistakes concerning a Windsor chair. Of course, there are variations in quality and design, but just try counting the spindles. Never buy a Windsor chair, or any other for that matter, with a large round hole in the center of the seat, because it was made as a "comfort" chair, and the value is well below that of any other chair of its period.

Windsor construction was used in chairs for many years, and the style was gradually simplified to the famous captain's chair. That type of construction was suited to chairs and perhaps benches, but there was only a handful of tables, and no other types of furniture, made in the same manner.

Spool furniture

From about 1815 to the mid-Victorian era a special type of furniture, called "spool furniture," was in style

Any furniture that is partially made with spool turnings comes under the general heading "spool furniture." It was a country furniture style popular from 1815 to 1875. This crib and bedside table (right) are typical examples of the style. (Western Reserve Historical Society, Cleveland, Ohio)

in many country homes. A new lathe was developed that made it possible to create elaborate turnings that were cut apart to make buttons or spools for thread. Some furniture makers believed the turnings would be unusual as part of chairs, beds, and tables, and so began the development of spool furniture. Instant Experts realize that common sense is always important and invaluable in dating spool furniture. It is easier to make long straight pieces of spool turnings than to curve the corners. THE EARLIEST BEDS HAD ANGLED JOINTS, WHILE SOME OF THE LATER ONES CURVED. IT WAS ABOUT 1850 THAT THE FURNITURE MAKERS DISCOVERED A METHOD OF BENDING THE STRIPS OF SPOOL TURNINGS. Spool furniture is still not expensive or popular enough to be copied.

Painted furniture, the Sheraton painted fancy chair, and the Hitchcock-type furniture now collected were popular from 1800 to 1845. The style of the stenciled design, the shape of the arm, the handgrip top, and the shaped slat all hint that this chair was made in Pennsylvania about 1820. (Taylor and Dull)

Painted furniture, or Hitchcock type

Painted furniture was used from about 1800 to 1845 in America. (See Zilla Lea, *The Ornamented Chair,* in bibliography at the end of this chapter, for complete history.)

One important thing to remember is: NEVER BUY A REPAINTED CHAIR IF YOU CAN BUY ONE WITH ORIGINAL PAINT. NEVER STRIP THE PAINT FROM A CHAIR WHERE YOU CAN RESTORE THE ORIGINAL PAINT. Altering painted furniture lowers the value and can destroy much of the beauty, but sometimes that is the only way a chair can be made usable. If a chair must be repainted or the paint removed, it is no longer the antique it was, and the interest and value are sharply reduced.

Other clues about the age of furniture can be found in the discussion of hardware and construction in the following section. Not the general design of the piece but analysis of small details will expose the fraud or the reproduction. Now that you have decided the age of your furniture from the design, search further and see if it is really as old as it appears.

The Carver chair was one of the earliest styles known in America. (Pilgrim Society, Plymouth, Massachusetts)

William and Mary style featured the "round ball"; notice the center of the stretcher, and Spanish feet. (Henry Francis du Pont Winterthur Museum, Winterthur, Delaware)

An American Hepplewhite side chair with the typical shield back made in Philadelphia about 1790. (Henry Ford Museum, Dearborn Michigan)

The Chippendale style often featured the pierced splat and ball-and-claw feet. The elaborate carving of this Philadelphia mahogany chair (c. 1770) is unusual. (Henry Francis du Pont Winterthur Museum, Winterthur, Delaware)

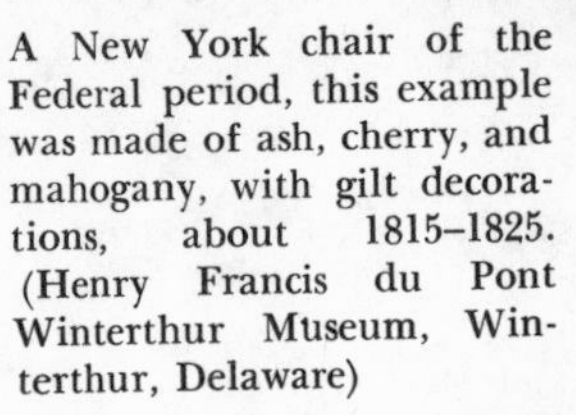

A New York chair of the Federal period, this example was made of ash, cherry, and mahogany, with gilt decorations, about 1815–1825. (Henry Francis du Pont Winterthur Museum, Winterthur, Delaware)

This square-back chair is typical of the Sheraton-Hepplewhite style made in the 1800's in Philadelphia. (Henry Ford Museum, Dearborn, Michigan)

Victorian chairs had many styles and shapes. This example by John Belter of New York, made about 1850, represents the finest in Victorian design. (Henry Ford Museum, Dearborn, Michigan and Cooper Union Museum, New York City)

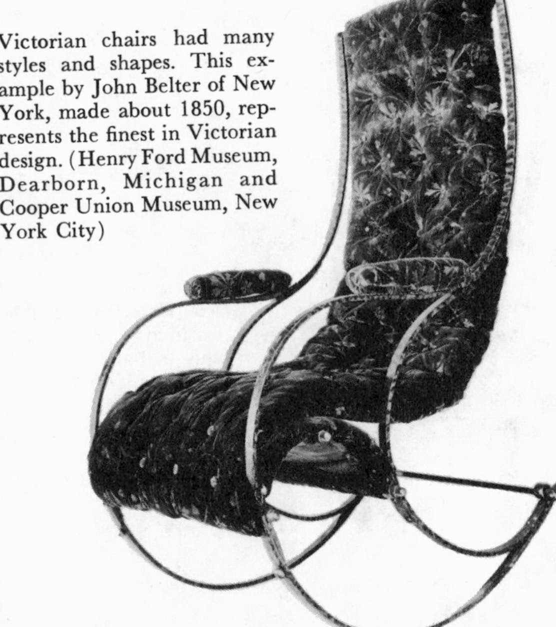

Sometimes a piece of furniture is a special design, unrelate to the mainstream of fashion but indicative of styles to com The Peter Cooper rocking chair was made of painted ste and pressed velvet in New York about 1855. It led the wa into some of the twentieth-century designs. (Cooper Unio Museum, New York)

FURNITURE CONSTRUCTION

This entire section should probably be labeled as one huge Instant Expert Tip, because the only way really to know the age of a piece of furniture is to know how it was constructed. Part of the information is technical, but most of it can be used by any antique buyer out for a day's shopping spree. This is not meant to verify the age of a museum-quality, eighteenth-century Baltimore piece that might really be a very fine and expensive Victorian copy (even the White House staff was fooled for a while with one of them), but it will help when a medium-priced antique appears that may or may not be old. If you plan to buy furniture that costs thousands of dollars, our advice and the best tip we can offer is to find a reliable antique dealer who will stand behind his sales. All legitimate dealers will always take back a piece that turns out not to be as it was represented when sold. Mistakes are often made through ignorance, not through greed, and most dealers are eager to restore your money and your confidence. The long-established dealer is not the difficulty. The problem is the antique that is hurriedly bid on at an auction or quickly purchased at a sale as a bargain. These tips will tell you how to check that bargain.

The antique furniture buyer's Instant Expert "kit" should contain a tape measure, magnifying glass, magnet, and a flashlight. With these simple tools tucked into a pocket or purse, it is possible to learn much about the age of that "may-be" antique in the damp, dark barn of Great-Aunt Susie's neighbor. It wouldn't be polite even to hint that the furniture is anything less than the neighbor claims, but experience will prove that most people know almost nothing about the age of an antique. Blatantly carved and curved Victorian pieces have been represented as "two hundred years old because it belonged to my great-great-grandmother, and she died at 103." This is not a deliberate falsehood, but an honest mistake, which is the hardest type to handle. An antique dealer should let you examine the furniture, remove drawers, or even unscrew the screws, unless he has something to hide. It is the antique that is to be quickly bid at auction or purchased from a friend that calls for the Instant Expert kit.

Measure any part of the table that should be round. This includes the top of a round table, the round legs, round drawer knobs, and round pegs. This is the reason for the tape measure. IF THE ROUND PARTS ARE TRULY ROUND, YOU HAVE FOUND A FAKE. Wood shrinks slightly in only one direction, and a round tabletop should be oval after forty years. Slide your magnet over the brass hardware, and if it clings to the hardware it is iron or steel that has been plated, and not the copper or brass it may seem to be. Remove a drawer and check the dovetailing for age (see below); then examine the back of the hardware to see if the screws are old. (This is where the flashlight will come in handy.) Large pieces, such as cupboards and sideboards, were made using wide boards across the back. See if the boards are wider than usual and of various widths. The cabinetmaker of the early days would cut down a tree, and use the random-width boards. Measure the thickness of the boards. Seven-eighths of an inch is standard today. Knots might appear in the wood where it does not show, but no good cabinetmaker would ever make furniture from what we now call "knotty pine." The old-time cabinetmaker knew that knots would fall out and leave very undesirable holes after the wood shrank.

If a raw sawed surface of the wood can be easily seen with a flashlight, check the saw marks. An old saw left straight marks, while the circular saw, which was used after 1850, left a curved mark. A trained touch or a straightedge rule plus a flashlight will help to check the wood for "hand dressing." Early cabinetmakers planed the wood, leaving small grooves that can be felt over the entire surface. If you don't know how to feel for the grooves, hold a straightedge along the wood and shine a flashlight from behind it, and the light will show each groove.

The rest of the search for the truth rests on intuition and common sense. After examining antique furniture in museums, shops, and collections, you will know how an expert can walk to a table of glassware and from forty feet away spot the one rare example, or how he can enter a room and recognize the only drop-leaf table worth examining. It seems to be a sixth sense that comes with intensive study, together with appreciation and common sense.

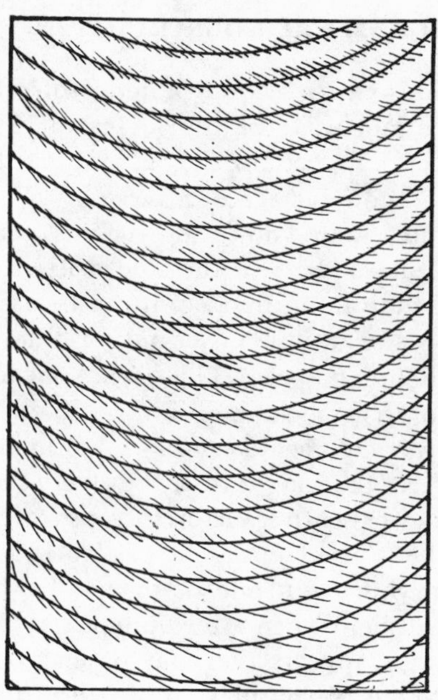

Circular saw marks that appear on furniture made after 1850.

IS THE CHAIR WORN WHERE A CHAIR SHOULD BE WORN? Are the back legs worn at the back from being dragged on the floor? Are the small finials on a ladder-back chair worn where the chair leaned against the wall? Are the rungs worn from the rubbing of many pairs of shoes? Does the low cupboard door show marks where it was kicked shut by a busy housewife? Is the wood near the brass hardware discolored from years of extra rubbing by the polish that dripped? Did the screws in the hinges that had the most use fall out and need replacing? Is the piece all one piece or were they two dissimilar antiques, such as a table and shelf, that were "married" into one strange new one? Does the finish look old or new? Don't expect antiques that have been stored in barns to be in an unblemished condition, but many pieces purchased from elaborate mansions often had perfect care.

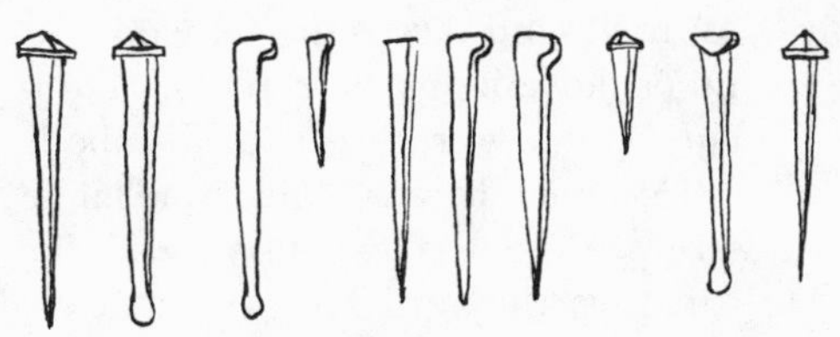

Nails

There is a legend in the world of the antique beginner that a square-headed nail indicates an early piece of furniture. This is only partly true, for square-headed nails are still being made and sold. There are even some shops that straighten old square-headed nails that are salvaged from old houses and sold to customers who are building authentic reproductions or restoring an old home. It is fairly safe to assume that a square-headed nail is an old nail unless there are other problems with the piece of furniture.

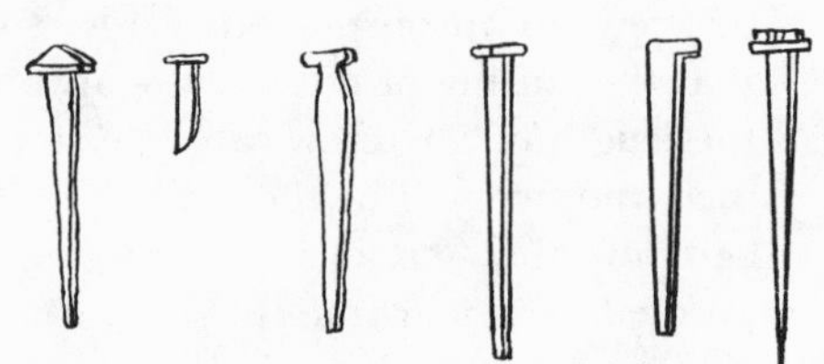

Nails have changed in shape through the years. Top row: hand-wrought nails of the seventeenth, eighteenth, and nineteenth centuries; in the second row are machine-cut nails from the eighteenth century to the present: left to right, two nails made 1790–1820, one nail made from 1815–1830, one nail made from 1820 to the present, one nail after 1810, and one nail c. 1799.

HAND-WROUGHT NAILS WERE MADE FIRST, AND WERE USED UNTIL ABOUT 1820. SQUARE-HEADED, OR CUT, NAILS WERE MADE BY HAND FROM ABOUT 1790 TO 1820. MACHINE-MADE NAILS (SOMETIMES WITH SQUARE HEADS) WERE MADE FROM ABOUT 1815 TO 1850. THE ROUNDHEADED MACHINE-MADE NAIL USED TODAY WAS MADE AFTER 1850. THE WIRE NAIL WAS NOT IN GENERAL USE UNTIL THE 1880'S.

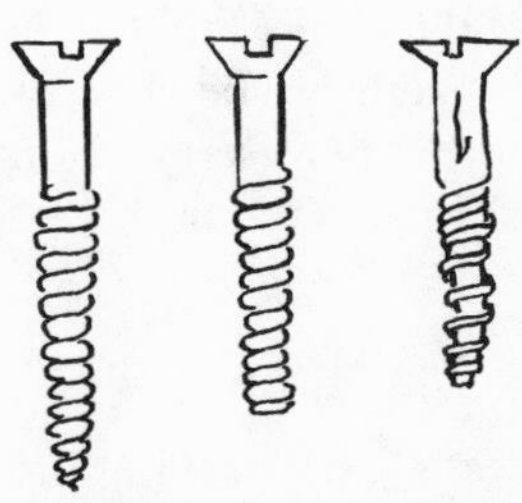

The modern screw is made with an even thread and a centered notch on the head (left); the machine-cut screw of the 1810–1845 period is pictured in the center; the handmade screw (right) of about 1800 was made with uneven threads and a narrow notch in the head.

Screws

The screw is not a recent invention, and the proper type of screw could appear on an antique of any age. The wood screw was made by hand in the United States, and was in use by many furniture makers by the early eighteenth century. Because of the design of the screw, it was able to hold and keep the hinges and other movable parts in place. Hand-cut screws were used until about 1815, but because machine-made screws were less expensive and far superior, they quickly gained favor. It is possible to recognize handmade screws by the off-center slot in the head; but there are better methods if it is possible to remove the screw from the antique. Some dealers will unscrew an inconspicuous screw so that the cutting of the screw shaft or the length of the screw can be examined (no two will be the same). The end of the screw is blunt, not pointed. The machine-cut screw that was made from about 1815 to 1845 has a blunt end, even screw threads, and a round, even head; modern screws have a pointed end. When looking at screws and hardware, remember that usage caused damage, and a screw often fell out and was replaced with a later type. This is not an objectionable repair. It's the finding of an old screw that helps to determine age, never the lack of one. When a screw is removed and replaced, the hole in the wood is changed slightly; be careful, therefore, if the new screw is from an obviously perfect hole.

Hinges

A picture is worth a thousand words, so carefully examine the difference between the butt hinge made about 1815 to 1840 and the type made after 1840. More metal was used in the early type. One problem is that the mid-Victorian Canadian hardware was sometimes made like the early pieces in the United States.

Handles and hardware styles

Find the pictured piece of hardware that most resembles the one on your furniture. The style of hardware changed with the style of furniture, and the hardware should match the rest of the piece. It is not unusual for a piece of furniture to be "updated" by the owner by the addition of newer-style hardware. Unless the same holes are used, the holes from the original hardware will be plugged, and a quick look should tell you so. The inside surface of a drawer front often shows the old holes. A piece of furniture with its original hardware is best, although it is acceptable to replace the hardware with the proper type. Hardware reproductions of all periods can easily be purchased.

Much of the reproduction hardware is almost too well made, and can easily fool the beginner. Check

Hinges. Top–1840; bottom–1815–1840

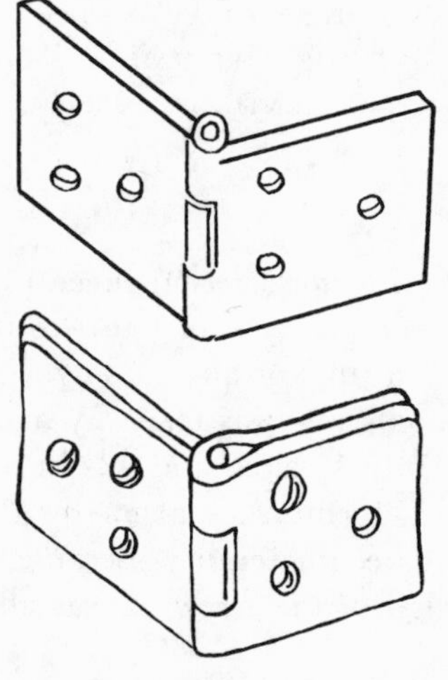

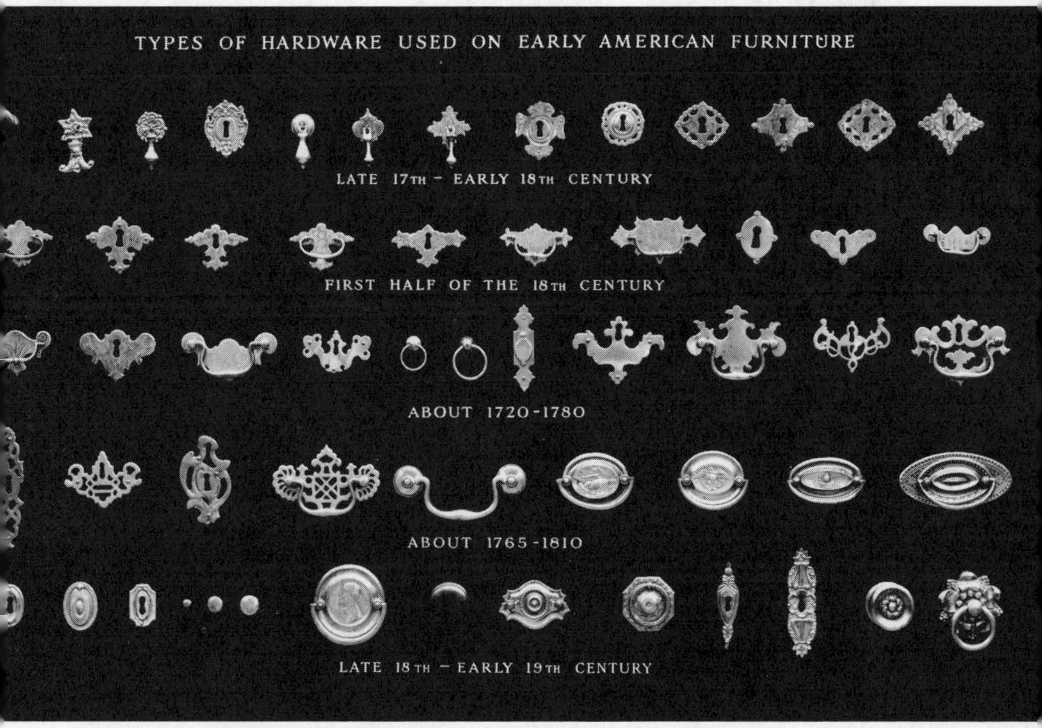

TYPES OF HARDWARE USED ON EARLY AMERICAN FURNITURE

LATE 17TH – EARLY 18TH CENTURY

FIRST HALF OF THE 18TH CENTURY

ABOUT 1720-1780

ABOUT 1765-1810

LATE 18TH – EARLY 19TH CENTURY

Types of hardware used on early American furniture. (Metropolitan Museum of Art, New York City)

the screws that hold the hardware, and be sure they are of the old type. This method is not infallible, because the best reproduction hardware is being made the old way, including an old type of screw.

Dovetailing

THE GENERAL RULE ABOUT DOVETAILING IS: THE FEWER NUMBER OF JOINTS, THE OLDER THE PIECE. AN EARLY EIGHTEENTH-CENTURY DRAWER WAS JOINED WITH ONE HUGE DOVETAIL OR WAS PEGGED TOGETHER. Several small dovetails (ranging from three to five) were used on a drawer. Each one was cut out by hand, and the spacing and size of each was uneven and different. Early Victorian furni-

Left, typical dovetailing of the 1725–1800 period; right, early-nineteenth-century dovetailing, sometimes found as late as 1890.

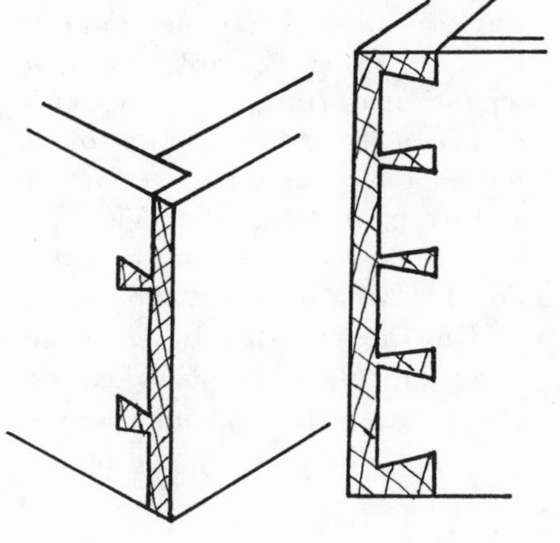

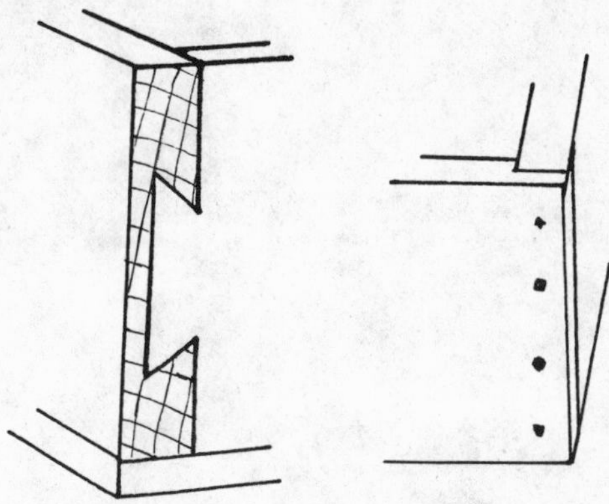

Two kinds of early-eighteenth-century dovetailing.

ture was made with machine-cut dovetailing, often with eight or more small dovetails on a drawer. The dovetails are evenly spaced, symmetrical indications that the drawer is less than a hundred years old. Some Victorian dovetailing was made with scallops and pegs, which are an almost positive indication of its late 1800 origin.

Glorification or its reverse

There was a time when early Chippendale or Queen Anne furniture was carved and redecorated to make it appear to be the work of a more sophisticated craftsman. The knee of a chair leg or the top of a round-topped table was often recarved to add more "interest." The Victorian wanted more pattern, and the additional carving increased the eye appeal to the Victorian buyer. Sometimes an entire Hepplewhite sideboard was given elaborate veneer and inlay work. Today, the process seems to be "glorification in reverse," as much of the Victorian furniture is not primitive enough for the collector of "early American." Carvings have been planed from legs, backboards removed from washstands to produce cupboards, and paint stripped or veneer soaked from early 1900 pine pieces. Spotting one of these "simplified" antiques requires a good basic knowledge of the type of wood, hardware, and furniture style of the desired period. Small details determine the secret. Early chests are being reproduced for bedrooms with the piece being made so that two chests can touch each other. The early chests often had legs or molding that protruded at the sides, making a pair of flush chests impossible.

SOME MORE FURNITURE TIPS

Age by ownership

If you are sure a chair was owned by your Great-Aunt Rose, there is a simple yet fairly accurate way of dating the chair—not Aunt Rose. Take your age and add twenty-five years for each generation, and you will see how simply and accurately you can date your grandparents' or great-aunt's furniture. The rule of thumb is twenty-five years to a generation. This might seem strange at first, but remember that furniture was usually purchased after marriage; also, it was frequently replaced after twenty years. Remember all this, plus the fact that the generations that preceded us had a life expectancy of less than sixty years. Now, if your grandmother bought a chair on her wedding day, and she died at sixty, how old was the chair? Just find out how old she was when she got married, and subtract that number from the date of her death. It should give you the approximate age of the furniture. If you were born when she was twenty-five or so, the chair arrived almost when you did, and her age at death is really of little importance in dating the chair.

The chair that was often thought to be Great-Aunt Susie's isn't at all, and it has picked up history while getting older. The best and surest way to date furniture is by the style and construction.

Veneer

Veneer is a thin piece of wood that has been glued to a thicker piece of wood used as a backing. The top thin layer is for appearance, and the thick back layer for strength. The veneer process has been used since the ancient Egyptians, but in the seventeenth century a new type of saw made a very thin veneer possible. Antique furniture may or may not be veneered, and veneering is of no help in deciding the age.

Bamboo

Chairs made to look like bamboo were first made in Europe by Thomas Chippendale in the eighteenth century. An exhibit of Japanese bamboo furniture started a rage for imitation bamboo furniture at the Centennial Exposition in 1876. A full line of furniture based on the Chippendale bamboo designs was reproduced during the 1960's. Imitation bamboo furniture can date from any time after 1770.

Ladder-back and Windsor-chair age

The ladder-back, or slat-back, chair can be dated by the number of rungs at the back. The more rungs, the earlier the chair. If the posts holding the rungs are decorated with turnings, the chair was probably made during the eighteenth century. The Windsor chair with nine spindles is older than a chair with four spindles. The same rule applies to the Windsor as to the ladder-back because workmen simplified each design to its least difficult stage before turning to a new one. The less skilled workman of the nineteenth century used the simplified version of the eighteenth-century ladder-back or Windsor before he tried the elaborate new Victorian designs.

The chair rung

If there is a rung across the front of a chair joining the legs, it was placed there for added strength, and does not indicate age. Rungs were first used with straight-leg chairs to keep the legs from coming apart when a person's weight was on the chair. When curves changed the design and stress, the rung was removed. Most straight-leg chairs have rungs or stretchers, while most chairs with curved legs do not.

Lacquered furniture

Wrap a coin in a slightly damp handkerchief. Rub the edge of the coin against the lacquer finish of the chair, and if any color rubs onto the handkerchief the lacquer and the chair are new.

Hitchcock chairs

The new Hitchcock chairs marked "L. Hitchcock, Hitchcocksville, Conn. Warranted," are also branded with the letters "H. C. Co."

Breadboard top

Picture a breadboard with a board at each end going the width of the piece and joined to the other boards running the length of the piece. This construction was used for added strength, and kept the wood from warping. The method has been known and used by cabinetmakers in the United States since the seventeenth century.

Breadboard top.

Casters

The ball caster that attaches to the leg of a large piece of furniture was used as early as 1830.

Rope beds

Mattresses and springs were used until about the first quarter of the nineteenth century, when the ropes that held the mattress were replaced by slats. All beds either had knobs or holes for the ropes before 1825, while after 1850 almost all of them had slats and no holes or knobs.

Brass beds

The brass bed was developed at the turn of the twentieth century. It was popular only until about 1915, but it has been made again in the 1960's.

Lazy Susan tables

Most lazy Susan tables were made by country furniture makers in the Pennsylvania area from about 1840 to 1880.

Wicker

Wicker furniture was made in the United States about 1850, and by 1880 the elaborate, fantastic types were made. Some were even painted gold. The twentieth century ignored the ornate pieces, but developed a plainer style of wicker in the 1930's. All types of wicker have come back into style.

Spring-type rockers

The American standard, or platform, rocker was made about 1870. It was a chair on springs, and was attached to a platform. The chair moved but the base remained stationary, and the carpet did not wear out.

Hints on care of furniture

Wooden furniture should be washed with a gentle soap and a minimum amount of water. After the old layers of dirt are removed a good wax polish will give it the best care. To keep the wood from drying out, first feed the furniture about once a month, and when the wood is "no longer hungry," twice a year. Mix equal parts of boiled linseed oil, white vinegar, and turpentine and apply it to the underneath unfinished parts of the wood. This will protect it from cracking and drying. Do not polish furniture more than is absolutely necessary. Wax will build up over the years and hide the original finish.

If there is any possibility of worms or bugs in the wood, use a DDT spray on the furniture before bringing it in the house.

Wicker furniture of about 1925 has begun to interest the collector. Whimsical pieces like the combined planter, goldfish bowl, and lamp table are even now in demand. (Henry Ford Museum, Dearborn, Michigan)

Furniture: Bibliography

See the bibliography of general books about antiques at the end of this volume for other books that contain a few chapters about furniture. This list includes only the most current, authoritative books about American furniture. Many good books about American furniture, and many good publications about English furniture, have not been included in this list.

Bjerkoe, Ethel Hall. *The Cabinet Makers of America.* Garden City, New York: Doubleday, 1957.

An alphabetical listing and short history of the known American furniture makers from the 1600's through the early 1900's.

Comstock, Helen. *American Furniture.* New York: Viking, 1962.

Over 700 pictures show the history of American furniture design from Jacobean to early Victorian.

Downs, Joseph. *American Furniture: Queen Anne and Chippendale Periods.* New York: Macmillan, 1952.

Over 400 photographs of furniture from the Winterthur collection illustrate this, the most important book available that tells about the finest American furniture made in the Queen Anne and Chippendale periods. (It is a companion book to *American Furniture: The Federal Period* by C. F. Montgomery.)

Fales, Dean A., Jr. *American Painted Furniture 1660–1880.* New York: Dutton, 1972.

A beautiful scholarly study of American painted furniture, filled with black and white and color pictures of the best pieces.

Kenney, John Tarrant. *The Hitchcock Chair.* New York: Clarkson N. Potter, 1971.

The history of Mr. Hitchcock and the Hitchcock factory. The author has not only researched the works of Lambert Hitchcock, but he reopened the factory in 1949.

Kovel, Ralph and Terry. *American Country Furniture 1780–1875.* New York: Crown, 1965.

Over 700 pictures help to tell the story of the less formal furniture of America. Included are sections on Canadian, Shaker, Pennsylvania, and Western types of furniture, as well as a chapter about the tools now used in homes: the cobbler's bench, pie safe, and so on.

Lea, Zilla Rider. *The Ornamented Chair.* Rutland, Vermont: Tuttle, 1960.

Painted furniture in America is illustrated by means of photographs, and the characteristics and techniques of each type are explained in detail. Anyone interested in painted Sheraton "fancy" chairs or Hitchcock furniture should use this book.

Lockwood, Luke Vincent. *Colonial Furniture in America.* New York: Scribner's, 1913; revised, Castle Books, 1957.

The classic first book about American furniture, still of importance to the collector. The material is illustrated and interesting, but slightly dated because of the new information made available in the past 50 years.

Montgomery, Charles F. *American Furniture: The Federal Period.* New York: Viking, 1966.
Almost 500 separate pieces of furniture from the Winterthur collection are photographed, 127 in color, in this excellent, authoritative book about the furniture of the 1790–1825 period. The chapter about woods and inlay patterns, including color pictures, is most helpful. (It is a companion book to *American Furniture: Queen Anne and Chippendale Periods* by Joseph Downs.)

Nutting, Wallace. *Furniture of the Pilgrim Century.* New York: Old American, 1924; paperback reprint, Dover, 1965.
Pictures and text about furniture of the 1620–1720 period.

———. *Furniture Treasury.* New York: Macmillan, 1961.
About 5,000 illustrations of furniture in America before the Empire period.

———. *American Windsors.* Boston: Old America, 1917.
This very rare book is a picture listing, with complete description and history, of about 100 Windsor chairs of all types.

Ormsbee, Thomas H. *The Windsor Chair.* New York: Deerfield Books, 1962.
A picture listing of 80 Windsor chairs. A checklist of known makers of Windsor chairs is included.

Sack, Albert. *Fine Points of Furniture: Early American.* New York: Crown, 1950.
The good, better, best arrangement of pictures makes this a valuable teacher for the furniture collector.

Canadian

MacLaren, George. *Antique Furniture by Nova Scotian Craftsmen.* Toronto: Ryerson, 1961.
A good book about the limited subject of furniture made in Nova Scotia before 1900.

Minhinnick, Jeanne. *Early Furniture in Upper Canada Village.* Toronto: Ryerson, 1964.
A pamphlet showing the Canadian furniture collection that is part of the Upper Canada Village.

Palardy, Jean. *The Early Furniture of French Canada.* Toronto: Macmillan, 1963 (published in either French or English).
An authoritative, well-illustrated, excellent book about the furniture made in French Canada from the seventeenth century to the first half of the nineteenth. This is the most important book available concerning Canadian furniture.

Ryder, Huia G. *Antique Furniture by New Brunswick Craftsmen.* Toronto: Ryerson, 1965.
A good book about a limited subject; photographs of furniture and a checklist of makers working in New Brunswick before 1900 are included.

Several reprints of articles from *Woman's Day* magazine are available. These are pictures of furniture that appeared in the magazine. See *Dictionary of American Painted Furniture, Dictionary of American Federal Furniture, Dictionary of Furniture,* and *Victorian Furniture.*

Construction

"Nail Chronology as an Aid to Dating Old Buildings, Technical Leaflet 15," American Association for State and Local History, 151 East Gorham Street, Madison, Wisconsin 53703.

This is one of a group of technical leaflets about antiques.

Yates, Raymond F. *Antique Fakes and Their Detection.* New York: Harper, 1950.

Fakes of all kinds are mentioned in this book; there is a chapter about furniture construction, and one about hardware.

Shaker Furniture

Andrews, Edward Deming and Faith. *Religion in Wood.* Bloomington, Indiana: Indiana University Press, 1966.

———. *Shaker Furniture.* New York: Dover, 1950.

Meader, Robert F. W. *Illustrated Guide to Shaker Furniture.* New York, Dover, 1972.

Shea, John G. *The American Shakers and Their Furniture with Measured Drawings of Museum Classics.* New York: Van Nostrand Reinhold, 1971.

The type of fuel can help to date a lamp. Right to left: the kettle lamp, which used any sort of oil, was popular in Pennsylvania in the first half of the nineteenth century; the Kinnear patent lamp of 1851 was made to burn lard oil; and the Smith and Stonesifer patent lamp (c. 1854) used solid lard as the fuel. (Henry Ford Museum, Dearborn, Michigan)

5

Lighting Devices

THERE ARE thousands of homes filled with the joys of the lamp collector. In this country a perfectly sane woman could have two hundred oil lamps displayed on a shelf in the living room because she knows and appreciates old lighting devices.

Most collectors don't specialize in this way, and a few old lamps are usually enough for one home. It is true that ANY OLD LAMP (AND THIS INCLUDES EARLY LIGHT BULBS) IS OF INTEREST TO EITHER A COLLECTOR OR A DECORATOR. The very old oil-burning Betty and Phoebe lamps appeal to those who want the rustic historic mementos of the past. The elaborate china oil lamps, the candle-burning glass fairy lamp, or the leaded glass shade of the *art noveau* electric lamp can be found in homes that are modern in every other detail.

The clue to old lamps is an easy one. IF IT LOOKS DIFFERENT, IT IS OF WORTH. The problem here is that what seems unusual to the novice may be ordinary to the experienced collector. Some study in the many books about lighting devices will help.

Lighting devices—including candlesticks and chandeliers

The easiest and most obvious way to date a lamp is to find out which type of fuel was used as the source of light. Animal fats, vegetable fats, whale oil, kerosene, electricity, and other types of fuels have been successful lights. See the Instant Expert table below:

FUEL	DATE
pine splint	Colonial America
candlewood	Colonial America
grease	Colonial America
heavy oils	Colonial America
candles	Colonial America
whale oil	1800–1840
Argand	1830
lard oil	used 1820, popular 1833–1863
camphene	1828
turpentine and alcohol	circa 1840
gas (coal gas)	early 1800's, popular 1850–1879
kerosene	1860–
electricity	1879–

(Above) The grease lamp was one of the early forms of lighting devices. This metal lamp was made about 1700. (Above right) The porcelain grease lamp was made c. 1700. (Henry Ford Museum, Dearborn, Michigan)

(Below) Grease lamps have changed very little through the ages. This grayish-green alabaster lamp was used about 2500 B.C. (Henry Ford Museum, Dearborn, Michigan)

(Below right) The Betty lamp was an improved form of grease lamp. This lamp on a stand was used in the nineteenth century. It has a wick pick.

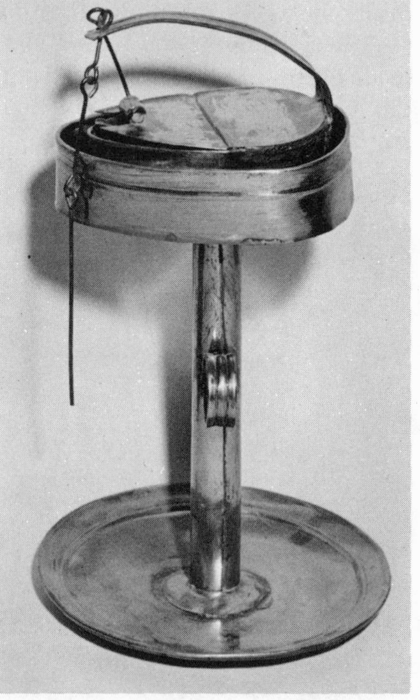

Sometimes it is difficult to determine which type of fuel was used in a lamp. The shape and design of the lighting device should help with that problem. If you were a pioneer in a wild country and needed a light source, you would do just what our ancestors did. The easiest source of light to find is a flame, and wood was the most available fuel.

The first lighting devices in America were long pieces of wood with a light or fire burning at one end. Improvements came rapidly. Candlewood, splints, and resinous wood all had the same purpose as a source of light. SPLINT LIGHTS were slivers of wood. Pine was the most obvious choice of candlewood in the New World, and thin slivers, ranging from eight to ten inches in length, were cut for use as lights. The pitch in the wood burned brightly, but the tarlike residue dropped to the floor in a sticky mess. The colonists were not the first to use this as a light source. The Indians had been using it for many years. No collector will find an old piece of candlewood, but the holders for the wood are very desirable. Early stands made of wood or wrought iron held the splint. This type of stand also held rushlights. It is easy to tell one of these stands from a candlestand, as the holder for the candle had to be either a rounded cuplike holder or a spike to impale the candle. Holders for rush or splint have clips, clamps, or metal pieces that grip the candlewood.

Grease lamps were the next to be used by the light-seeking pioneers. The BETTY LAMP was the first of these lamps. It is said that Captain John Carver, first governor of the Plymouth Colony, bought an iron Betty lamp in Holland to bring to America.

The Betty lamp was a shallow dish that could be oval, round, or triangular. The dish ranged from two to three inches in diameter, and was made from various types of metals, such as pewter, iron, brass, and even silver.

A "nose" protruded for one to two inches on one side of the dish. The bowl was filled with tallow or grease. A wick made by using a twisted rag or rushes was placed in the grease and pulled through the "nose" until a short end was visible. The visible end was lighted.

Betty lamps were often hung on a chair. The name "Betty" came either from the word *betyng,* an oil used in the lamp, or from *besser,* the German word for "better."

The PHOEBE LAMP was next. It is really a Betty lamp with a cup beneath the wick that caught the oil drippings. Most of the early lamps were made with a spike and chain so the lamp could be hung anywhere on a wooden wall. The Betty or Phoebe lamp occasionally was placed on a stand. They were in use in America from the time of the Pilgrims to the days of the Civil War.

Rushlight

The rushlight is another of the early lighting devices based on a flame. Rush is really a plant. The rush was peeled, and the white inside pith

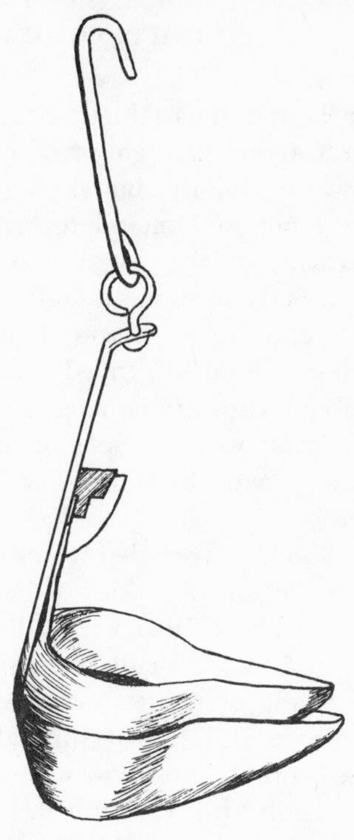

Phoebe lamp.

was dried and later oiled with any available household fat. The fatted rush was held at an angle in the tweezer-like end of the rushlight holder.

Candles

The candle was first used in Roman times, and in Europe about the eleventh century. It was slightly different from those that we use today. Candles were scarce and expensive in the colonies because there were no domestic animals from which to obtain the tallow. Beeswax and bayberry were found in small amounts. Animal fat tallow (usually beef) and whale spermaceti candles were made after 1750. The spermaceti candles were the finest made because they were translucent, attractive, and gave more light than a tallow candle. The term "one candlepower" was measured in terms of a pure spermaceti candle.

Candlesticks and chambersticks

The shape of the candlestick is an indication of its age. In general, the Instant Expert rule is that THE EARLIEST CANDLESTICKS WERE MADE FROM SOLID CAST BRASS OR WROUGHT IRON. THE HOLLOW-STEM CANDLESTICK WITH THE SLIDING KNOB THAT COULD RAISE THE CANDLE WAS USED ABOUT 1710. SHEET-IRON CANDLESTICKS WERE USED IN THE EARLY 1800'S. MOST OF THE SPRING CANDLESTICKS WERE USED DURING THE MIDDLE OF THE 1800'S.

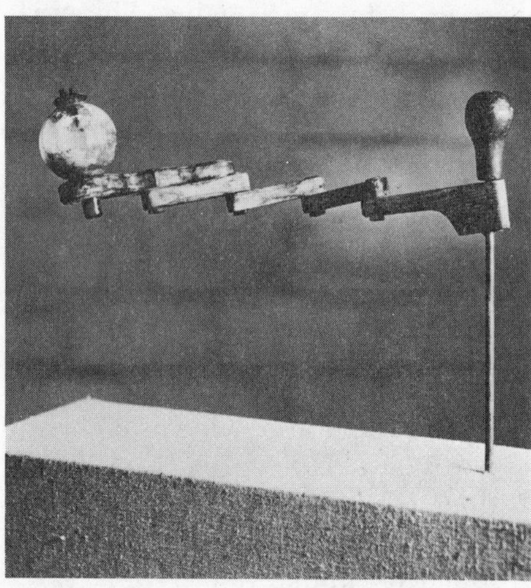

Whale-oil lamps took many forms. The wooden toggle arm supports a glass whale-oil peg lamp made about 1825. (Old Sturbridge Village, Sturbridge, Massachusetts)

(Opposite) Canfield & Brothers of Baltimore, Maryland (1812-1865) made this pair of whale-oil lamps used by John Marshall. (Association for the Preservation of Virginia Antiquities)

The candle was pushed down the tube holder and was held against a spring. The spring forced the candle up as the candle burned.

THE SPIKE, OR PRICKET, HOLDER FOR CANDLES WAS USED FROM THE FIFTH CENTURY. IT IS SELDOM FOUND ON AMERICAN CANDLEHOLDERS, AND WAS OUT OF STYLE BY THE NINETEENTH CENTURY.

Silver and brass candlesticks changed in shape from one decade to the next. (For more details of this shape change, see Chapter 6, "Silver.")

Whale-oil lamps

Whale oil was very important as a fuel for lamps during the nineteenth century. It was used in homes, for street lighting, in lighthouse beacons, and even for locomotive headlights. The great demand for whale oil helped create the giant whaling industry in America. The demand for whale and sperm oils declined about 1840.

The common whale-oil lamp was made after the invention of the flat wick burner in 1783. That patent, plus another for an upright wick tube, made the development of the closed-in reservoir for fuel possible. The lamp had a closed-top reservoir and a vertical wick tube. Whale oil is heavy, and it was necessary for the tube to enter the reservoir to a great depth, with a short tube extending above the lamp. If you find a WHALE-

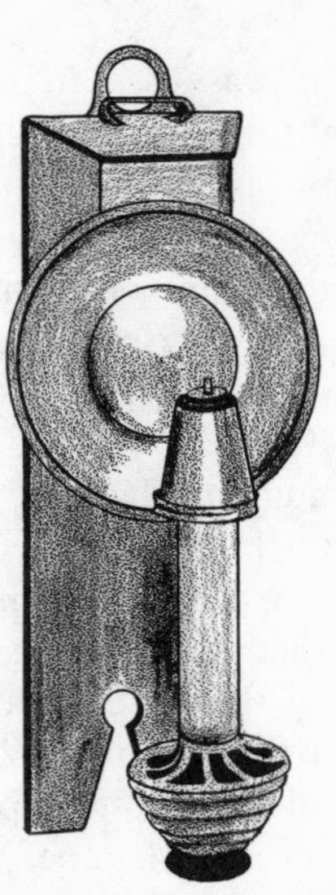

The Argand lamp had a special hollow wick and a base that permitted air to reach the flame. These examples show this burner. The hanging lamp was made about 1843. (Henry Ford Museum, Dearborn, Michigan)

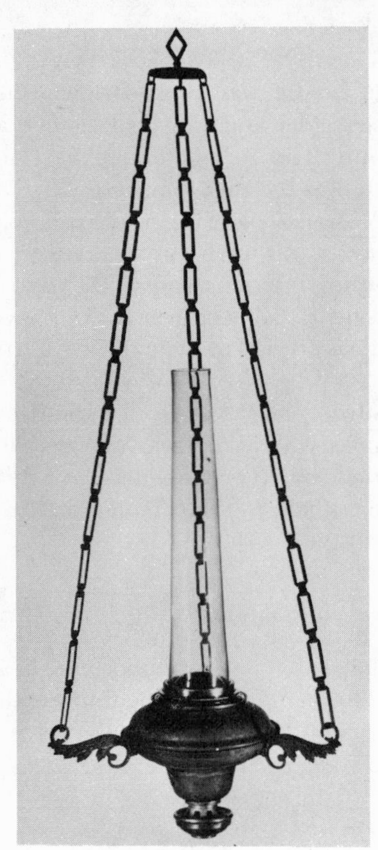

OIL LAMP WITH A ROUND TIN WICK TUBE INSERTED THROUGH A CORK AND CAPPED BY A TIN DISK MARKED "PATENT," THE LAMP DATES ABOUT 1810. If the burner of the whale-oil lamp was screwed into a metal collar on the lamp with a threaded screw, the lamp dates after 1830.

Argand lamps

Many different fuels were burned in lamps were made to overcome the combined turpentine with alcohol, and were highly explosive. Cheap fuel that gave a bright light was desirable, and several new types of lamps after 1830. Some mixtures dangers of explosion.

Aimé Argand, a Swiss, invented his lamp in 1782. It was a specially patented type that burned sperm oil, lard oil, and even camphene. The hollow wick permitted more oxygen to reach the flame, and resulted in a brighter light. After the new wick was developed, a glass chimney to protect the flame from a draft was introduced.

By 1840, a burner was designed with a tall tapered wick tube that was held above the fluid. The tube had a cap so it could be covered when not in use, and in that way the fluid could neither evaporate nor be smelled.

Kerosene lamps

Kerosene and coal oil are the same, and they were the best of the oils used for light. About 1850, Samuel M. Kier of Pittsburgh, Pennsylvania, made lamps that burned kerosene he distilled from surface oil. When Colonel Edwin L. Drake struck oil in Pennsylvania in 1859, the first economical source of kerosene was found. Almost immediately all the earlier oil lamps were obsolete, and the kerosene lamp was "in." At first, whale-oil burners were used with the kerosene, but by 1860 a solid round wick was used. A gadget that turned the wick up, and a glass chimney, were added later.

The "Gone with the Wind" lamp is one of the most familiar types to collectors. It is the attractive shape of the font and the shade that appeals to the buyer of this lamp. Many other types of lighting devices are collected because of their unusual mechanism or age. The "Gone with the Wind" lamp was named after the famous novel about the Civil War. The name is not the one that was originally used by lampmakers. The lamps were originally called "banquet lamps." Millions of them were made in the 1870's and later. The complete lamp has a glass shade with a metal, glass, or porcelain kerosene reservoir and stand. All the lamps had a glass chimney.

ANY SIZE KEROSENE LAMP WITH A HANDLE WAS MADE AFTER 1870. The handle made it safer to carry the lamp.

Kerosene was a popular lamp fuel. The "Gone with the Wind" Lamp was made about 1870. The nutmeg lamp was a miniature lamp that used kerosene as a fuel about 1880.

Lusters

A luster is an elaborate type of candlestick decorated with many hanging glass prisms. The cut-glass prisms and drops were probably first made in England and Ireland. Some of the lusters found in America were made by New England glassmakers, but the majority were made in Europe. All the finest prisms seem to be of European origin. This type of mantel candelabra set was in vogue during the first half of the nineteenth century. A large center-branched candleholder and two single candleholders for the ends of the mantel were usually used together. The base of the stand was made of cast metal, and very often of French gilt. Some of the bases were made of marble. Many different shapes of animals and figures were used as the base of the stand. This type of candle set was popular and not easily damaged, and many are still available.

AND MANY OTHER KINDS

Slut

The slut is an early form of lamp dating from the seventeenth century. It had an open cup that held the fat and a wick.

Chamberstick

A chamberstick is really a candlestick that was used to light the way to the bedchamber. It was usually made with a wide saucer-like base that caught the wax drippings.

Candlestand.

Candlestand

A candlestand is a candleholder that stands on the floor. A candlestick is any device that holds a candle.

Toe candlestick

A toe candlestick is a famous type of candlestick shaped like a foot wearing a sandal. The candle was held in a hole near the big toe. It was made of brass. The first toe candlestick was made by the ancient

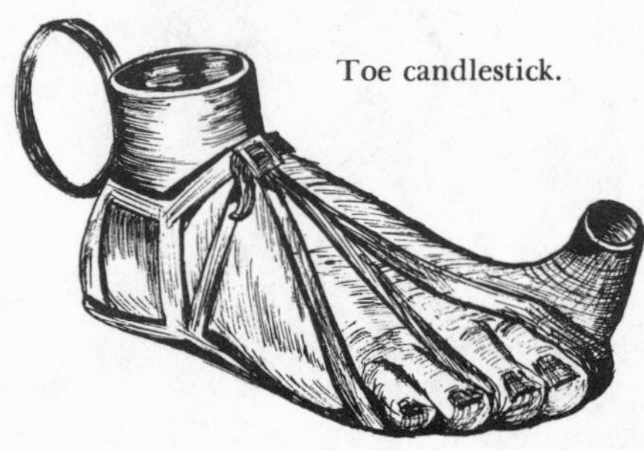

Toe candlestick.

Romans. Benjamin Schlick of the Elkington Company of Birmingham, England, copied the toe candlestick in 1844. He made the mold from an early Roman candlestick.

Fat lamp

A fat lamp is any lamp that used fat as fuel. A Betty lamp could be considered a fat lamp.

Peg lamp.

Peg lamp

Any lamp with a small knob on the bottom that could fit into the top of a candlestick is called a peg lamp. It gave better light because of the added height.

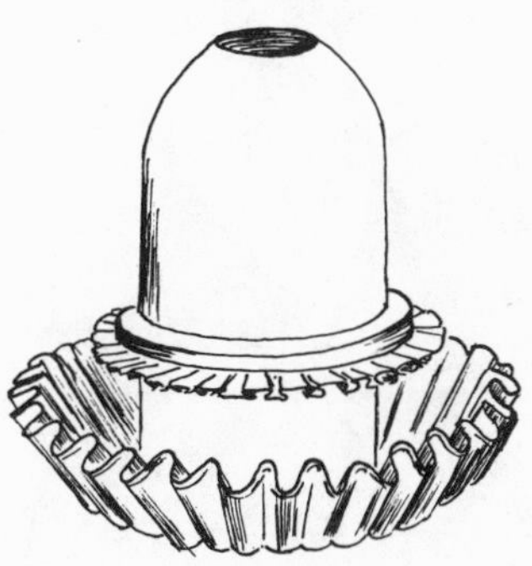

Fairy lamp.

Fairy lamp

A small squatty candle was developed and patented by the Clarke Company of England. This one- or two-wick candle was a great lighting improvement, and was sold all over the world in the 1870's.

Many types of fairy lamps were made to hold the fairy candles. Glass, china, and metal bases were made, with the covering shade made from a similar material.

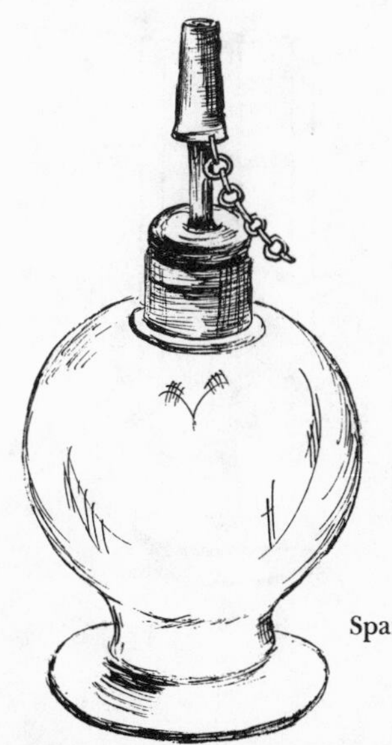

Spark lamp.

Spark lamp

The tiny kerosene lamp often called a "spark lamp" was used about 1870. It was used as a night-light for the nursery or as a small light when a girl entertained her beau.

Burglar's horror

A tall glass holder with a high stem held a small fat candle that would burn for about eight hours. Placed in a room, it would burn all night. The idea was that a light in the house all night would keep a burglar away.

Perfume lamp

The perfume bottle lamp was made in many shapes, and was popular about 1900. One of the most interesting styles was a miniature lamp and perfume bottle in the shape of the famous reporter Nellie Bly. It was about four inches in height to the top of the lamp chimney.

When the bottle lamp was filled with perfume, the original cost was about twenty-five cents. This type of gift was often given by the proprietor of the corner saloon to his New Year's Eve patrons. The label jokingly read "Filled with the best $100-a-quart whiskey."

Bouillotte lamp

Many French gamblers played a card game similar to poker, but called "bouillotte." The lamp was used at the gaming table. It held two or three candles in a brass or bronze doré frame. The bouillotte is an eighteenth-century French design, but there are several "American" versions being made. The lamp had a metal shade that was usually painted dark green, with a metal finial at the top of the lamp. The height of the candleholders and the shade could be changed by using a screw key.

Rabbi's lamp

A rabbi's lamp is a special type of spout lamp made from coin silver or copper. The part of the lamp that held the fuel was a round bulb-like form with a spout that held the wick. The spout and the reservoir were on the top of a stand that resembled the shape of a candlestick.

This type of lamp has been used for hundreds of years, and has also been known as a pastor's lamp, mill lamp, or kyal.

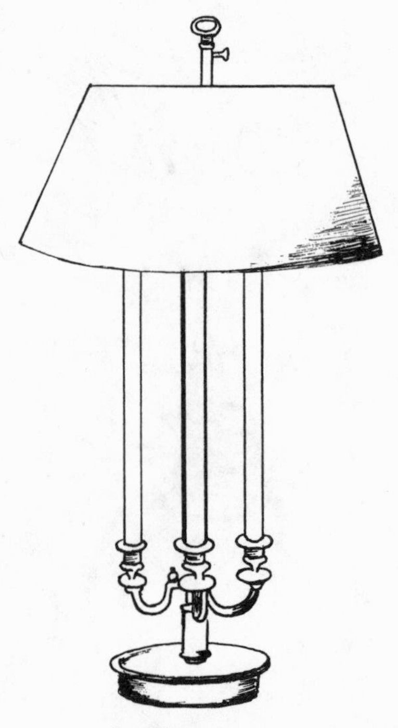

Bouillotte lamp.

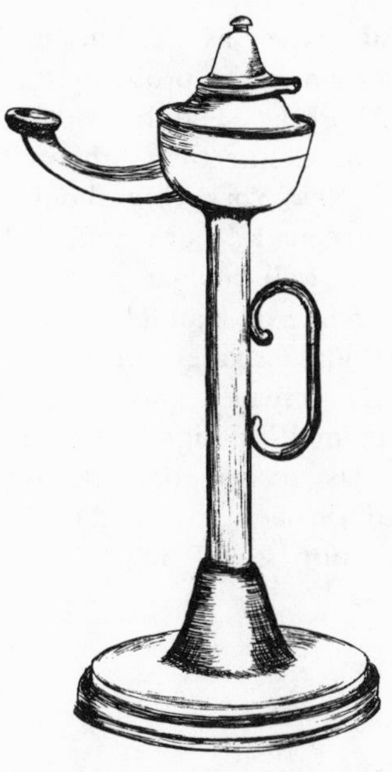

Rabbi's lamp.

the water produced an even glow. These lamps were often made with several bottles of water surrounding one candle. A workman sat near each bottle, and in that way one candle could furnish the light for four men.

Cresoline lamp

Cresoline is a mixture of cresol and resin. The mixture was used as a disinfectant and a deodorant, and was often burned in sickrooms. The Cresoline lamp was used during the late 1800's and the early 1900's.

Dearest lamp

The dearest lamp is one of many Victorian items that used a novel decorative device. Stones were colored to resemble diamonds, emeralds, amethysts, rubies, sapphires, and topazes, and were set into the lamp. In sequence, the first letter of the name of each jewel spelled "dearest." Jewelry was often made in the same manner.

Shoemaker's lamp

The shoemaker's (or lacemaker's) lamp is an ingenious arrangement that uses a candle and a bottle of water. The light from a single candle was not very intense, and the workman who required more light placed a candle behind a bottle of water. The light that came through

Shoemaker's lamp.

Cresoline lamp.

Tiffany lamps and others

L. C. Tiffany was a glassmaker of great reknown who worked in the United States at the turn of the twentieth century. Collectors still treasure his glass and his lamps. (There is a complete discussion of Tiffany glass in Chapter 2.)

The lamps made by Tiffany had iridescent and colored glass shades and green bronze bases. TO BE SURE YOU HAVE A TIFFANY LAMP, YOU MUST FIND THE WORDS "TIFFANY AND CO." PRINTED ON THE METAL BASE. The glass shades were also marked "L. C. Tiffany," or just with the letters "L. C. T." According to the records of The Tiffany Company, all these lamps were marked.

There were several other companies that made lamps of the same general type as Tiffany's. The Handel lamps are probably the best known. Philip Handel worked in Meriden, Connecticut, about 1885, and in New York City about 1900. His firm made many types of art glass, as well as gas and electric lamps. Some of Handel's lamps had leaded glass shades; others had a specially prepared glass shade with hand-painted designs. When the light was turned on, the picture showed through the shade. Handel worked until the 1930's.

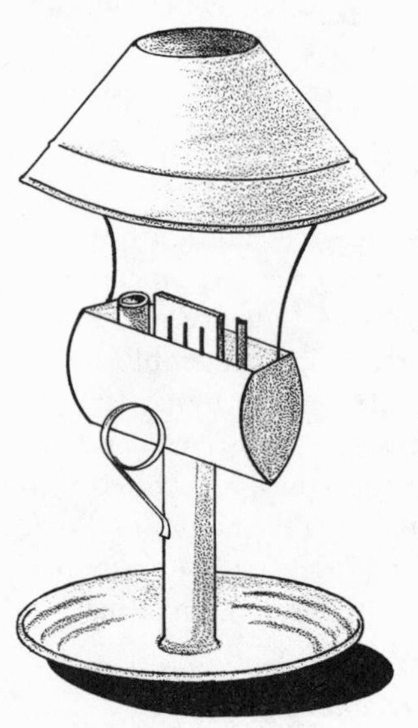

Kinnear patent lamp.

Chandeliers

Early taverns or large living rooms of many early American homes had a center fixture. The smaller rooms, such as the bedroom or kitchen, did not have a center light.

The word "chandelier" originally meant a branched fixture that held candles. The center lights, or chandeliers, were filled with candles that were lighted by a taper on a long pole. It was not a convenient source of light.

The chandelier of early America was sometimes a piece of locally made tinware or wood. Some of the wealthy homes had factory-made chandeliers that were made from brass. It has been said that all the brass chandeliers used in England before the late eighteenth century were made in Holland. This was not so, as many of the eighteenth-century chandeliers were also made in England. It is believed that the earliest English-made chandelier was produced about 1675 for a church. Wealthy Americans had Dutch- or English-made chandeliers.

Wooden chandelier with iron arms and pricket candleholder made about 1800. (Old Sturbridge Village, Sturbridge, Massachusetts)

Chandeliers took many forms. A Dutch example, of brass, made in the middle of the seventeenth century. (Toledo Museum of Art, Toledo, Ohio)

Though the brass chandeliers of Holland and England are similar, they can nevertheless be distinguished by their method of construction and other small details. Doves were often used as finials on London-made lights, while Dutch chandeliers were heavier, and often had eagle-shaped finials.

The pricket candleholder was used on chandeliers, as well as the single candleholder. The candle was held by impaling it on a sharp spike. The pricket-type candleholder was first

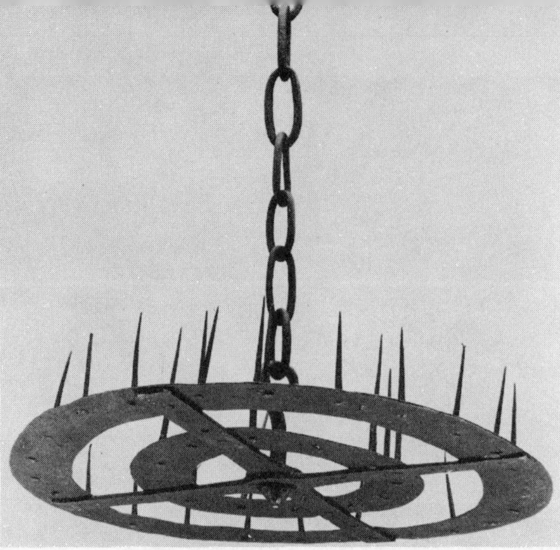

Undated early American candle chandelier. (Old Sturbridge Village, Sturbridge, Massachusetts)

made in Europe during the fifth century. It has been used ever since. The obvious advantage is that any size candle will fit the fixture. The pricket remained popular until the middle of the nineteenth century.

A footnote about crystal chandeliers

There is one Instant Expert tip that can be given about the large center chandelier hung with many crystal prisms. It takes an expert to tell the old from the new, and the very fine from the good—but there is a hint: THE EARLY PRISM-SHAPED DROPS HAD FOUR, SIX, OR EIGHT SIDES. THE LATER ONES HAVE THREE SIDES. The cost of labor made the many-sided prism too expensive.

The age of prisms may also be discovered by the design cut into the glass. THE EARLIEST PRISMS HAD SMALL STAR CUTTINGS. LONG, FINER SHAPED NOTCHES WERE MADE LATER. THE ENDS OF A PRISM OF THE MID-1800'S HAD AN ARROW OR A HEAVY ROUND BALL. That's the clue; but it is a hint, not an authority. Copies of many of the early styles of prisms are being made, so count the sides and watch the design; but, best of all, to be sure it is old, know your source.

Tin chandelier, probably made in New England c. 1800. (Old Sturbridge Village, Sturbridge, Massachusetts)

Wooden chandelier with carved leaves, probably New England about 1800. (Old Sturbridge Village, Sturbridge, Massachusetts)

Lighting: Bibliography

Hayward, Arthur H. *Colonial Lighting.* New York: Dover, 1962.
A paperback reprint of a good general book about early lighting devices. It has an index and many photographs.

Hebard, Helen Brigham. *Early Lighting in New England 1620–1861.* Rutland, Vermont: Tuttle, 1964.
A small, informative book discussing about ten types of lighting devices.

MacSwiggan, Amelia E. *Fairy Lamps, Evening's Glow of Yesteryear.* New York: Fountainhead, 1961.
A well-illustrated book about fairy lamps.

Smith, Frank R. and Ruth E. *Miniature Lamps.* Camden, New Jersey: Nelson, 1968.
A picture listing of miniature oil and kerosene lamps. Very little history is given.

Thwing, Leroy. *Flickering Flames.* Rutland, Vermont: Tuttle, 1958.
A very good general book about lighting, including a dictionary of terms.

———. "A Glossary of Old Lamps and Lighting Devices, Technical Leaflet 30," American Association for State and Local History, 132 Ninth Avenue North, Nashville, Tennessee 37203.
A listing of terms and types of lamps, with line drawings. A bibliography is included.

———. *Old Lamps of Central Europe and Other Lighting Devices.* Rutland, Vermont: Tuttle, 1963.
A reprint of a 1905 German book. This is of limited use to American collectors.

6

Silver

ALMOST EVERYONE realizes that silverware has a value, but oddly enough not everyone can recognize a piece of solid silver. One way to identify a piece of silver or silver plate is by turning the piece over and looking for the mark. Once in a proverbial blue moon a mark is forged, but that would only be a mark that is so rare and valued the forgery is worth the effort. REVERE, the mark of Paul Revere, the horseman, silversmith, and patriot of Revolutionary War fame, is one of the few American marks that ever was forged. The English had such severe penalties for tampering with silver marks that a good forgery is rarely seen. It is only the "glorified" piece of silver, one that was plain originally and has been reworked into a more glamorous item, that has marks that might be misleading.

Pick up a teapot, spoon, or platter and examine the marks. Usually, the mark is conveniently located on the bottom. If there is no mark, look near the edges of the front of the piece. There are several interesting possibilities. Most often seen is a group of small hallmarks, or little pictures, indented into the silver. If four or five separate little pictures appear on the silver, it is probably English. Examine these hallmarks carefully; use a magnifying glass if you aren't nearsighted enough to see them clearly. A lion means "solid silver," or what we Americans call "sterling." A king's head or queen's head means "English made in the reign of the monarch pictured." Both King Georges (III and IV) faced to the left; Queen Victoria faced to the right. Even if you aren't positive who is in the hallmark, you can tell which way the monarch is facing and can get an approximate date on your silver. The other marks are important, but they must be located in one of the many books on silver. The letter gives the exact year; a mark with several letters would probably be the maker's initials. A leopard's head means "made in London," a thistle refers to Edinburgh, a harp, Ireland, etc. So, to be an Instant Expert in silver, LOOK FOR THE KING'S HEAD OR QUEEN'S HEAD AND THE LION.

If the head is missing but there are several small marks (perhaps three), the piece probably is European but not English. Some of the marks are self-explanatory as to the country of origin, that is, Russian letters mean a Russian maker; but additional research in a book is necessary to determine the maker and the date the piece was made.

If the piece of silver has just initials or just a name pressed into the bottom, it is probably American. Both the Canadian and United States makers used their last name and first initial or just their initials as the marks. Only the very earliest American silver (eighteenth century or earlier) had marks that were anything but the maker's initial. Again, there is the exception to the rule. Many silver makers working during the Victorian era used more than initials. The general rule when looking at American silver made prior to 1850 (a hand-hammered silver that is not thick or cast and is usually referred to as coin silver) is: IF INITIALS APPEAR, IT IS PRE-1800; IF THE NAME APPEARS, IT IS PRE-1850.

Some American pieces have "pseudo hallmarks." These were impressed pictures of an eagle's head, a hand, star, or some cartouche that was originally placed on the silver to convince the buyer that the silver was of the same quality as the similarly marked English ware. This should not even cause confusion to our new Instant Experts, because the king's head and the lion were never used on American pieces.

The only American silversmiths ever to try a marking system like the English were those working in Baltimore, Maryland.

An assay office was legally established in Baltimore in 1814, and marks were placed on all the silver

American silversmith's mark 1839–1852.

American silver marked with "pseudo hallmarks." A maker's name might also appear.

English silver marks.

Baltimore silver marks.

sold. Silver marked after 1814 had a head of liberty that told the quality of metal, a date letter, and the arms of Baltimore to indicate the city, and the maker's initials or name.

The Baltimore dating system was discontinued in 1830, and the silversmiths developed their own system of marking. Numbers like 10.15, 11 2, or 11/12 were stamped on the silver and told the percentage of pure silver in the metal.

Perhaps the piece of silver is large and heavy, with ornate designs or engraving. It could be an eighteenth-century or early-nineteenth-century piece, but it most probably is an example of Victorian silver plate. Victorian silver plate was made from either copper or white metal (similar to a pewter or Britannia), and electrically coated with a thin layer of silver.

A special type of hand-rolled silver on copperware was made in the town of Sheffield, England, during the eighteenth century. It is called Sheffield silver. Many other types of silverware, including the chemically plated wares now made, have been made there and referred to as "Sheffield ware." The collector of Sheffield is looking for the old hand-rolled, silver-plated copper, and not the nineteenth-century pieces. Instant Expert tip: to spot the old hand-rolled (and rare) Sheffield, SCRATCH YOUR FINGERNAIL UNDERNEATH THE BORDER OF THE PLATTER, CANDLESTICK, OR WHAT-HAVE-YOU. HAND-ROLLED SILVER WAS PUT ON IN A SHEET, AND THE FINGERNAIL WILL CATCH THE EDGE OF THIS SHEET OF SILVER. Second quick clue: HOLD THE PLATTER NEAR YOU, AND WHERE IT IS ENGRAVED, "HUFF AT IT" UNTIL YOUR BREATH CLOUDS THE SILVER. OLD SHEFFIELD WILL HAVE AN INSET PIECE OF SOLID SILVER FOR THE ENGRAVING (so the copper won't show through), AND THE BLOCK OF SILVER SHOULD BE FAINTLY OUTLINED BY YOUR BREATH.

Chances are, the silver piece being checked is not the old Sheffield, but a newer Victorian plated ware. They were marked in England with strange combinations of shields, designs, and names. THE LETTERS "EPNS" OR "EPWM" INDICATE A VICTORIAN SILVER-PLATED PIECE. The letters stand for Electroplated Nickel Silver or Electroplated White Metal. Other marks also hint at the non-silver metal in the center, because all solid English silver was marked with the quality hallmarks, and the familiar lion would appear.

American plated silver is easy to spot from the marks. Insignias were favored, especially circles with the maker's name inside. The words "triple," "quadruple," "Al," "plate" all indicate that it was plated silver. Most of the marks are listed in available books, and can easily be verified. Actually, a few hours of examining solid silver and Victorian plate is all that is required to make you an expert at telling them apart.

IF THE WORDS "ENGLAND" OR "MADE IN USA" OR SOME OTHER INDICATION OF THE COUNTRY APPEARS, THE PIECE OF SILVER OR SILVER PLATE WAS MADE AFTER 1891. IF THE WORDS "STANDARD," "QUALITY," "COIN," OR "PREMIUM" APPEAR, THE PIECE IS AMERICAN COIN SILVER OF THE MID-NINETEENTH CENTURY. IF THE WORD

"STERLING" APPEARS, IT IS EITHER AN IRISH PIECE MADE AFTER 1720 OR AN AMERICAN PIECE MADE AFTER ABOUT 1860. NUMBERS SUCH AS 800 OR 900 ARE USED TO INDICATE THE QUALITY OF THE SILVER. Pieces marked in this manner are considered solid silver, and are usually German, Italian, or Russian. At least 925 parts out of 1,000 must be silver in the United States or England to be considered solid or sterling silver.

This is just a general quick way to help determine what you may have, but most of the marks on silver can be found listed in books on the subject. Just be careful when searching that you use the proper book. A book published in England called *Hallmarks on Plate* will be about solid silver only. The term "silver plate" in England means what "sterling" means in the United States. The words "silver plated" in the United States mean a thin layer of silver on another metal.

Every silver form and every silver serving piece had to be developed for a special time and place. We have come a long way from the caveman's habit of eating with his fingers to the complex variety of silver serving pieces. The fork, knife, and spoon were the earliest to be invented, but all sorts of equipment for the serving of alcoholic drinks, tea, coffee, heating and cooking units, and other devices have been made. It is possible to determine how old a piece *could not* be with just a little logic. The porcelain-lined large silver-plated pot often referred to as a coffeepot is really a Victorian ice-water pitcher, and can never be older than mid-nineteenth century. The large teapot came after the small two-cup size; the tea-caddy spoon almost disappeared after the eighteenth century. It is of great help to know what the piece was and how it was used. Once again, common sense is your best guide to the age of some antiques. The chafing dish made to hold a can of Sterno can't be older than the introduction of the can, but the chafing dish that was lighted with alcohol may be from the eighteenth century.

Shapes—knives, forks, and spoons

The shape of an American silver spoon will usually tell its age. MOST SPOONS WERE MADE FROM TWO PIECES OF SILVER BEFORE 1800. The bowl of the spoon was hammered to shape, and the handle was soldered to the bowl. The joint where the two pieces were joined is easily seen. MOST SPOONS WERE MADE FROM ONE PIECE OF SILVER AFTER 1800. A piece of silver shaped like a lollipop was cut from a flat sheet; the bowl was shaped and the handle finished. The handle of the finished spoon was flattened slightly, and the long "tongue" on the end went down the back of the rounded bowl. The piece of stem was pointed, and gave the spoon its name "rattail." The "rattail" spoon was made after 1660.

The shape of the bowl of the spoon will also aid in dating silverware. The early-seventeenth-century spoons had fig-shaped and then elliptical bowls. The nineteenth-century spoon was shaped like the

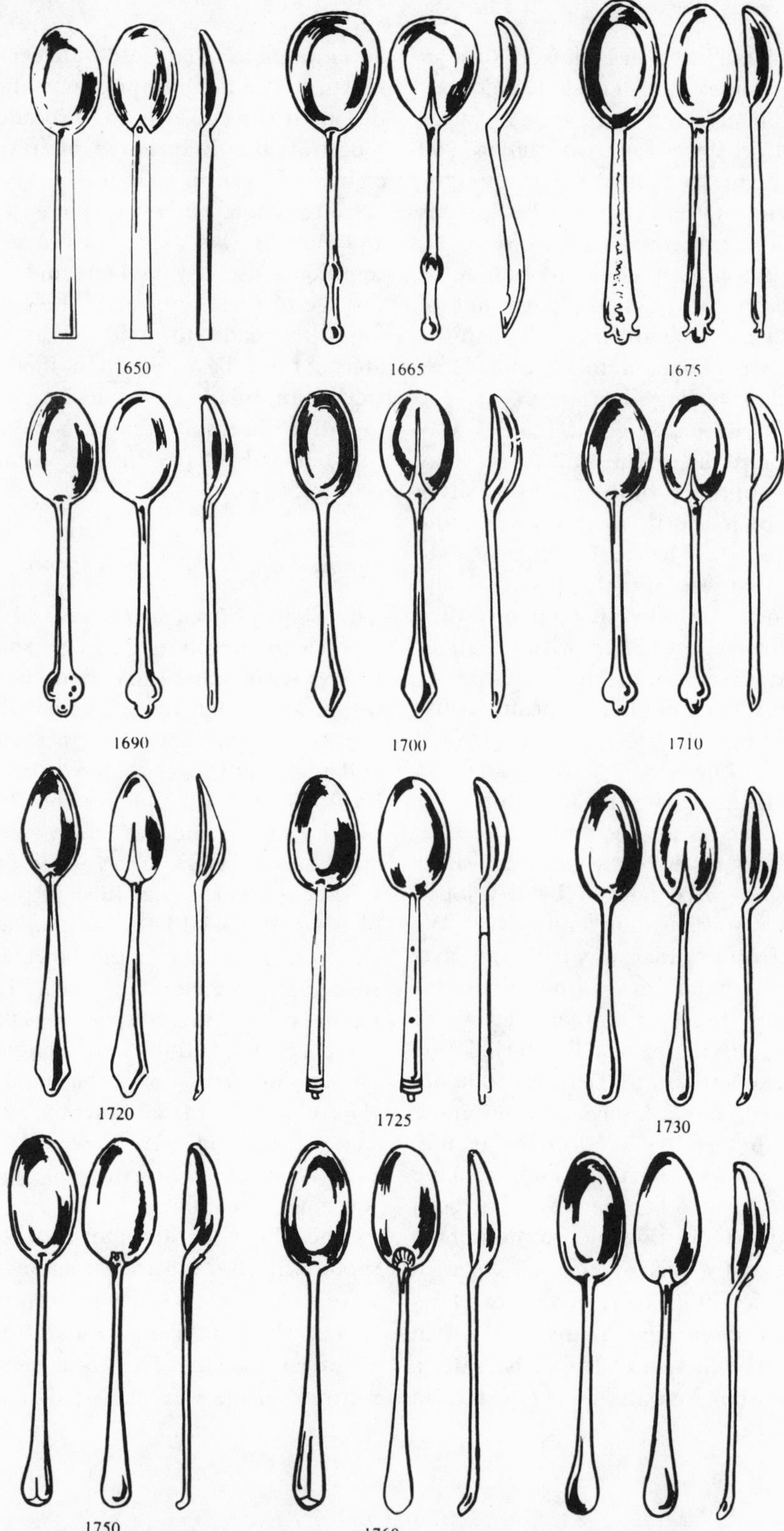
1650
1665
1675
1690
1700
1710
1720
1725
1730
1750
1760
1770

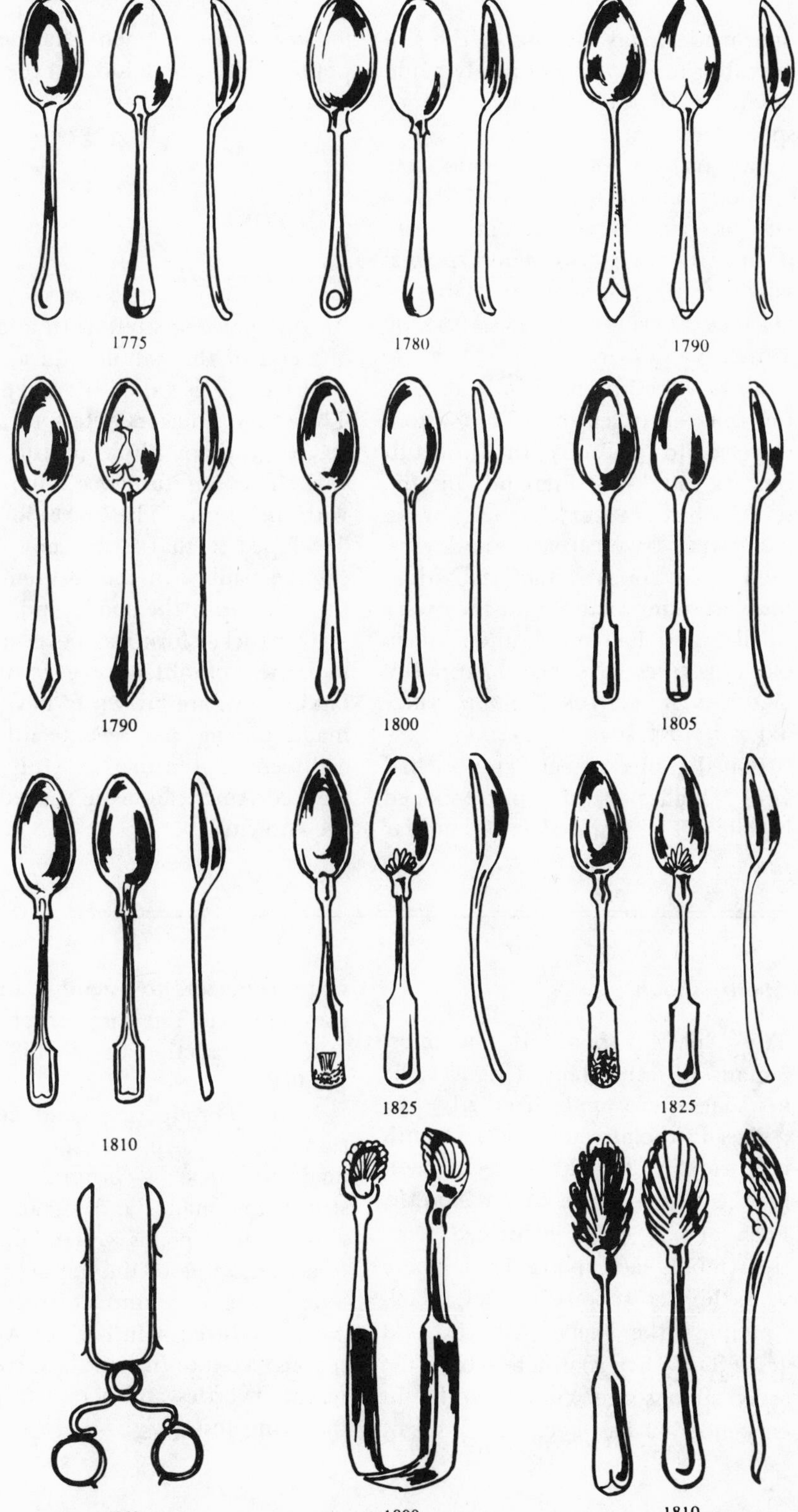
1775
1780
1790
1790
1800
1805
1810
1825
1825
1760
1800
1810

ones made today. Spoons of the size we call a teaspoon were rarely made before 1700. The earlier dinner spoons were much larger.

THE HANDLE OF THE SPOON WAS STRAIGHT AT FIRST, BUT BY 1730 THE TIP OF THE SPOON HANDLE BENT DOWN. THE TIP OF THE SPOON HANDLE TURNED UP ABOUT 1830. ALL THE FIDDLEBACK PATTERNS ARE EXAMPLES OF THE UPTURNED TIP.

Forks were first used in France in the thirteenth century. The custom traveled to Italy by the fifteenth century, and to England in the seventeenth century. FORKS WERE ORIGINALLY TWO-PRONGED, and were used only for serving. Individual forks were used later, and they were smaller and had more tines. THREE OR FOUR TINES WERE POPULAR IN THE EIGHTEENTH CENTURY. FOUR TINES ARE ON MOST FORKS TODAY.

Bone-handled steel knives had steel blades and pistol-shaped handles. The knife that is familiar today is a development that became popular after the middle of the nineteenth century.

ODDITIES IN SPOONS AND FORKS

The sucket fork

An odd piece of silver with a fork at one end of the handle and a spoon at the other is called a sucket fork. The name "sucket" refers to a preserved grape or plum mixture. The sticky fruit mixture was often eaten with the fingers. The sucket fork was developed so that is was possible to eat the fruit with the fork end and the juice with the spoon end.

The sucket fork was never a common piece of tableware, even in England. A few are known to have been made during the seventeenth and eighteenth centuries. Only ten marked American-made sucket forks are known.

Apostle spoon

The Apostle spoon is the most famous of all spoon designs. The first ones were made from silver or pewter in the fifteenth and sixteenth centuries. At the tip of each spoon handle was a figure of an Apostle. Each one is easily identified from the symbols each apostle held. There were thirteen spoons in a set, which contained the twelve Apostles and Jesus. Only five complete sets of the early spoons are known to be in existence. It has been the goal of many collectors to assemble another complete set. The last complete set sold at an auction in the 1930's for $25,000.

Many reproductions and adaptations of the Apostle spoons were made in 1850. Reproductions are still being made, and in all probability, any spoons you might find today are some of the newer spoons. The Gorham Manufacturing Company produced a full set of Apostle spoons, containing the twelve different Apostles and a master spoon picturing Jesus.

Mote spoon

When tea was brewed in the eighteenth century, small bugs, twigs, and other unappetizing items floated to the surface. These undesirable bits were strained from the tea with a mote skimmer. The handle of the spoon was small, straight, and pointed. It was used to poke the tea leaves from the inside of the teapot spout. Small decoratively placed holes in the bowl of the spoon were used for straining the tea. The eighteenth-century mote spoon was the size of a very small teaspoon.

A larger type of perforated spoon was used in the nineteenth century to remove berries from their juices, and even today small condiment spoons are made with holes.

Toy coin silver spoon

Several museums own spoons that were originally children's toys. They are tiny thin coin-silver spoons about two inches in length. Most of the known examples have fiddle-shaped handles. Because they are so rare, each spoon should be treasured. They were made from American coin silver, probably about 1830.

Orange and grapefruit spoons

The oddly shaped spoon bowl that seems pinched near the end so that it is pear shaped was made to remove fruit sections from oranges and grapefruit. It was a popular Victorian type of spoon.

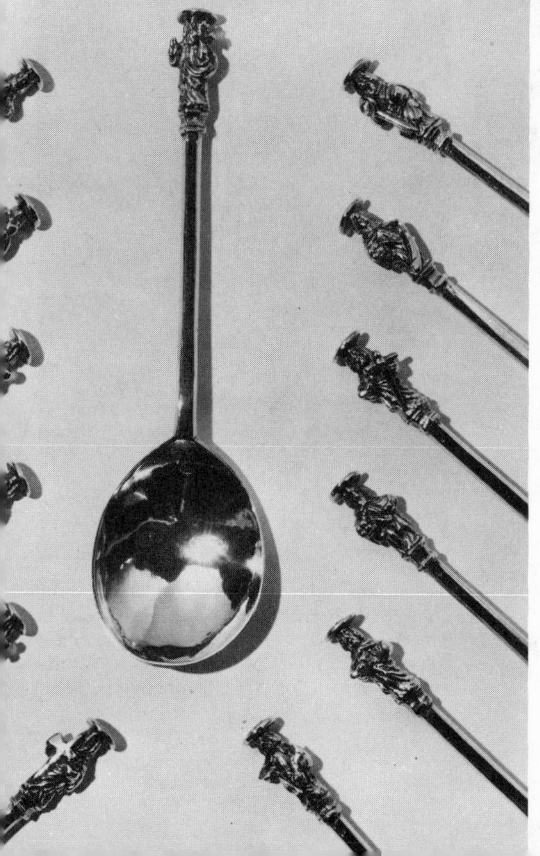

The apostle spoon had a figure of an apostle at the end of the handle. Many versions of this spoon have been made from the fifteenth to the twentieth centuries. This set, marked "I.S.," was made in London in 1617. (Henry Ford Museum, Dearborn, Michigan)

Toy silver spoons for dolls were made in America in the nineteenth century in the same styles as the larger ones. The long twisted handle of the mote spoon was used to push leaves from the teapot spout; the bowl served as a strainer. A fish slice of this style was one of many new designs for silver developed in the mid-1800's.

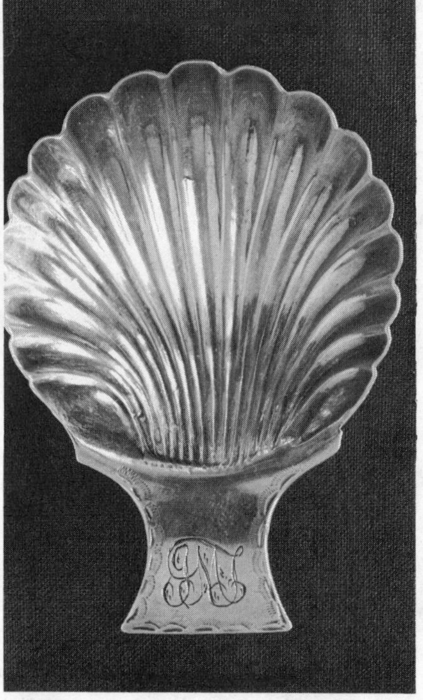

Tea scoops were used in England in the eighteenth century, and the style spread to America. This scoop was made by Paul Revere in Boston, Massachusetts. (Minneapolis Institute of Arts, Minneapolis, Minnesota)

Tea-caddy spoons

The caddy spoon is a short-stemmed silver tea scoop that was first used about 1770. The caddy spoon had a short handle and was kept inside the tea canister. Some caddy spoons were shaped like shells, grapeleaves, shovels, feathers, jockey caps, eagles, flour scoops, and leaves. They were made until the end of the eighteenth century, and went out of style after that time.

OTHER SILVER SERVING PIECES AND ODDMENTS

Fish slice

The earliest fish slices, or silver fish servers, were made in the eighteenth century. The first ones were shaped like the trowel used by a bricklayer. By the nineteenth century the silver server was shaped like a hatchet, fish, or large table knife.

Sugar tongs

During the eighteenth century sugar was usually purchased by the loaf, and a sugar nippers was used to cut the large lump into usable pieces.

The early-eighteenth-century sugar tongs resemble scissors with a spoon-like end. THE BOW-SHAPED TONGS THAT RESEMBLE TWO SPOONS JOINED BY AN ARCH WERE MADE AFTER 1750. Many varieties of the nineteenth-century tongs were made to match the pattern of the silver tableware.

Candlesticks

Candlelight has always added romance and charm to the dining-room table. It is still fashionable today, and the candlesticks of another century add to the setting.

The seventeenth-century candlestick was made with a square base and fluted column. Gambling was widespread by 1695, and a smaller candlestick base became popular be-

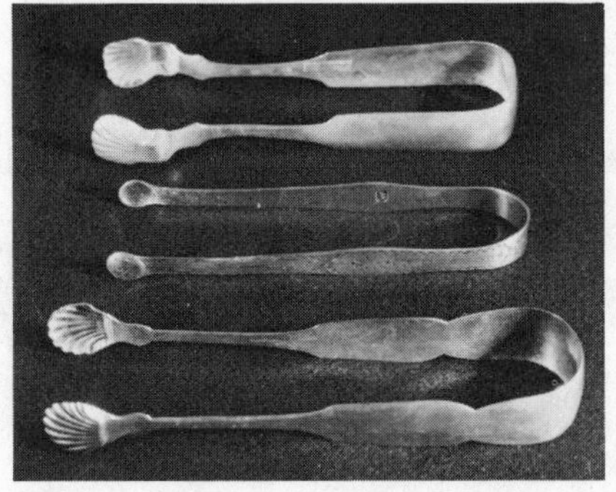

Two American coin silver tongs with shovel tips are seen next to an English eighteenth-century tongs.

The acorn grips on this sugar tongs is one of several types made in the United States in the first half of the nineteenth century. William Moulton (1772–1861) made this piece. Notice the typical name stamp. (Towle Silver Co.)

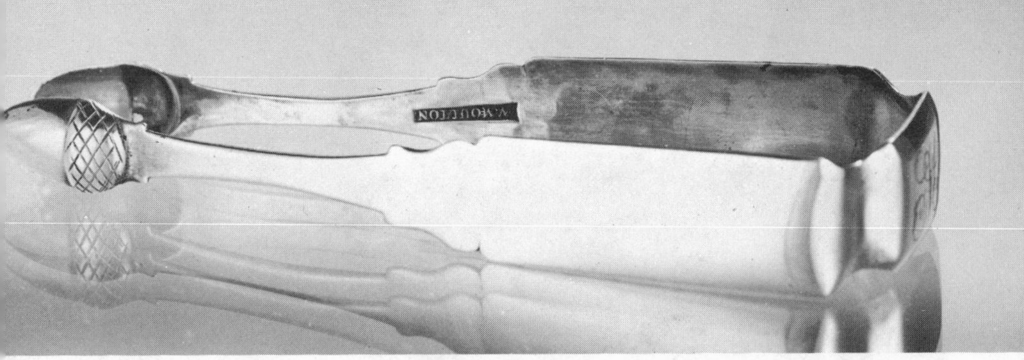

In these American candlesticks the wide base with slight indentation was made to catch the candle drippings. They were made by George Ridout in the eighteenth century. (Minneapolis Institute of Arts, Minneapolis, Minnesota)

The complete silver service of the late eighteenth century could have many pieces. This set by Paul Revere includes a teapot and stand, sugar bowl with tongs, cream pitcher, tea caddy and stand, caddy spoon and caddy strainer. (Minneapolis Institute of Arts, Minneapolis, Minnesota)

cause it required less space on the gaming table. The eighteenth-century candlestick had a variety of hexagonal or ornamented bases.

The nineteenth-century candlestick became larger and more ornate. By the middle of the century it was used more for decoration than for light. Oil lamps and finally electricity replaced the candle as a main source of light.

Let's have tea—and the silver tea service

When tea services were first made, all the pieces did not match. Tea was a scarce and expensive drink when it was first introduced in England during the eighteenth century. Early teapots were designed to hold just one cup of tea. By the mid-1700's the teapot had been enlarged, and it held several cups of tea. The teapot became the large size we know today after 1800.

At first tea was served plain; later, sugar, cream, lemon, and spices were also used. The tea service became part of an elaborate ritual. By 1800 the complete tea service contained a teapot, sugar urn, creamer, and perhaps a tray. It could also have a pair of sugar tongs, tea caddy, tea scoop, tea strainer, and small trivets to hold the teapot and tea caddy. Some sets even included a coffeepot, hot-water pot, or chocolate pot. All the pieces would never appear in one service.

Because the proud buyer of a silver teaset usually ordered one piece at a time, a set was often made by several makers.

The teapot

The tiny eighteenth-century teapot not only grew in size with the passing years; it also changed in shape. THE POT WAS ROUND FROM 1730–1760. THE PEAR-SHAPED POT WAS POPULAR ABOUT 1730. ABOUT 1750 TO 1775 THE INVERTED PEAR SHAPE WAS USED. FROM 1790 TO 1810 THE POT HAD STRAIGHT SIDES. FROM 1810 TO 1835 THE BODY OF THE POT GOT ROUNDER AND FATTER, AND GREW A BASE.

There are other clues that can be used in dating teapots, such as the shape of the spout, the type of handle, the way the lid fits. (See Chapter 1, "Pottery and Porcelain," in the section "The Shape Tells the Tale.")

The tea urn

The tea urn became popular at the end of the eighteenth century, and is still being used. The urn originally held hot water, but it was later used to serve strained tea. The urn replaced the kettle. The tea urn usually had a spigot similar to that used on a beer keg. The teapot has a pouring spout.

The coffeepot

The shape of the coffeepot corresponded to that of the teapot. The early ones that were made about 1715 had straight sides. After that, the pear shape became popular; later, the inverted pear, and the straight-sided pot of 1790, and finally, the fatter, rounded pots of

COFFEEPOTS

Reprinted from *A Directory of American Silver, Pewter and Silver Plate* by Ralph and Terry Kovel. © 1961 by Crown Publishers, Inc. Used by permission of Crown Publishers, Inc.

1730-1760
1730-1760
1750
1760-1775
1760
1780
1790
1790
1800
1810
1820
1835
1825

Tea and coffee urns were made with a spigot at the bottom. This typical silver-plated example was made by the Meriden Britannia Company, of Connecticut, in 1878. (International Silver Co.)

the early 1800's. Victorian teapots tended to become larger and more ornate, with no definite shape.

IF YOUR TEAPOT HAS AN ALL-METAL HANDLE, IT WAS PROBABLY MADE AFTER 1850. Almost all the silver and silver-plated teapots had carved wooden or bone handles because metal handles became too hot to hold. In 1849 Henry Reed made handles by using pieces of oystershell as insulation. Later, ivory or wood insets were used to keep the heat from the handles of a coffee or teapot.

Cream pitchers

"Lemon or milk?" is still the question when the English serve tea. When tea was first introduced to England from China, it was served plain. Evidently, the unfamiliar tea taste was too strong for the English, and milk or cream was added. To serve the cream and sugar, new utensils had to be designed by the silversmith.

The first silver cream pitchers were made in England about 1725. The early pieces were hammered from a flat sheet of silver, and there was no seam on the side of the pot. The rim and the lip were added to the hammered body.

The period of George II brought a deeper rim and often feet for the pot. The feet of the cream pitchers reflected the furniture styles of the period. A chair leg was often the model for the small silver cream-pitcher leg.

Early cream jugs were pear shaped, and by 1770 the pear shape had a stem with molded feet, instead of the three small feet that were used earlier. The classic square styles came into vogue about 1800. Larger, fat, bulging cream pitchers were used in the nineteenth century. The nineteenth-century creamer was larger than the early-eighteenth-century teapot.

The American silversmith copied the English designs, and it is possible to date an early creamer by its shape.

The silver cream pitcher changed in shape to match the coffeepot or teapot used in the same tea service. William Hollingshead made the three-legged small pitcher in the eighteenth century (Minneapolis Institute of Arts, Minneapolis, Minnesota). A straight-lined classical creamer became the style about 1785–1790, when this example was made by Daniel Van Voorhis of New York City (Art Institute of Chicago, Chicago, Illinois). The bulbous teapot was matched by the large-footed creamer of the 1820–1840 period in the United States. (Towle Silver Co. collection)

Sugar bowls

Sugar was not as refined as ours is today. A large bowl was needed because bulky lumps of sugar were used. Sugar was imported from Cuba about 1724, and was sold in large sugar loaves. The loaf was snipped with sugar nippers, and the pieces were placed in a sugar bowl.

The sugar bowl changed shape in the same manner as the other pieces of a teaset. The bowl went from a small rounded bowl to a classic urn shape in the late 1700's, and a fat bulging large bowl in the 1820's.

Sauceboats

The first sauceboats were tiny silver dishes made to resemble the hulls of boats. A lip was at each end, and a handle went across the top. They were first made in the early 1700's. The later sauceboats kept the name "boat," but discarded the shape.

A piece resembling today's small cream pitcher developed with a ring of silver at the base. Three small feet held the pitcher after 1745. Today's sauceboats resemble the eighteenth-century examples.

The sugar bowl, or sugar urn, was made in a style to match the other pieces of the tea service. This urn is in the classical style of the 1785–1790 period, made by Daniel Van Voorhis of New York City. (The Art Institute of Chicago, Chicago, Illinois)

Soup tureens and other large bowls

The original custom of serving from a soup tureen developed during the late seventeenth century in England and France. A large bowl, or tureen, was placed on a side table or in the center of the dining-room table. The idea of an attractive large covered bowl for soup has changed very little during the past two hundred years.

A silver punch bowl was really the development of the seventeenth-century silversmith. Hot punch was first introduced about 1790, and a tray was needed under the bowl to protect the table. The monteith bowl was popular in the seventeenth and eighteenth centuries. It is a large punch bowl with notches around the top rim. Cup handles or glass stems were hung in the notches.

Legend says a Scotsman named Monteith was known for his deliciously brewed punch. He always wore a coat with a scalloped bottom. It was so similar to the rim of the punch bowl that the bowl was called "monteith."

The notched rim could be removed from the bowl, and a plain punch bowl remained.

A few monteith bowls were made in Victorian times, but most of them were made in the eighteenth century.

Braziers and chafing dishes

Keeping food hot in a drafty eighteenth-century home was a talent that required ingenuity and special equipment. The wealthy Englishman or American had his breakfast eggs cooked at the table in a saucepan heated by a special brazier.

Large pieces of meat or roasts would remain warm if served in hot metal dishes, but the gravies and sauces cooled quickly.

Saucepans for gravies were usually made of silver, and were kept on the table over a brazier or small stove heated with a special burning charcoal that did not shoot sparks. Later, small spirit lamps furnished the heat.

Eighteenth-century American examples of the heaters are known but are very rare. The silver brazier had a wooden handle with pierced silver sides, and scrolled feet.

The chafing dish with an alcohol burner as a heater was developed in the United States. It has been said that Paul Revere made a chafing dish from copper in the 1780's.

The English chafing dishes were usually heated with hot water.

A fad for chafing-dish meals swept this country about 1885. This was about the height of the great popularity of Britannia ware, and consequently most of the chafing dishes were made from plated Britannia ware, and only a smaller number were made from solid silver. CHANCES ARE THAT YOUR CHAFING DISH WAS MADE AFTER 1885.

This rare American silver brazier was made by Daniel Henchman in the eighteenth century. (Minneapolis Institute of Arts, Minneapolis, Minnesota)

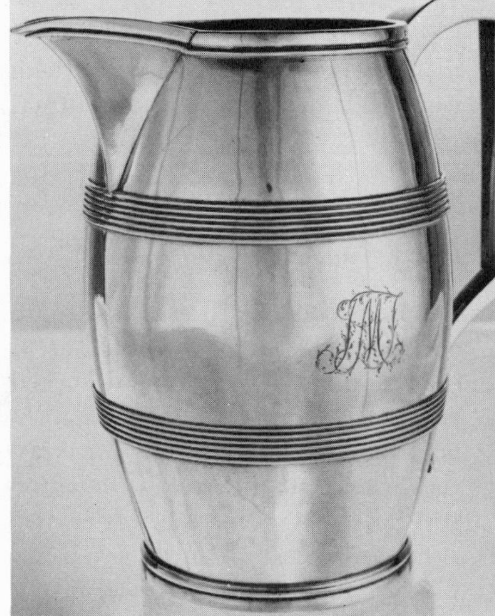

The barrel-shaped water pitcher was made of silver in the late eighteenth century; this example is by Ebenezer Moulton. (Towle Silver Co. collection)

Water pitcher

The silver water pitcher was first made in the late eighteenth century. A favorite nineteenth-century New England pitcher was shaped like a barrel with two bands around it. The pear-shaped pitcher was popular in Pennsylvania, and a similar pear-shaped pitcher having a deeper neck was popular in the South.

Mustard pot

A small silver dish with a lid was used to serve mustard during the eighteenth century. The lid was notched so that a spoon could be kept in the dish. The dish or mustard pot had a glass liner that kept the mustard from staining the silver.

The earliest pot of this sort dated from 1737, but other types of mustard holders were used prior to that time. During the nineteenth century the mustard pot was often included in a castor set that contained cruets and salt and pepper containers.

Porringer or bleeding bowl

The porringer was a bowl with flat earlike handles made from wood, pewter, silver, or other metals. Porridge is a thick soup. You either ate it with a spoon or drank it while holding the large handle. The porringer was used for porridge or other types of liquid food. It is an eighteenth-century form.

Some experts have claimed the porringer was kept in the bedroom for use as a bleeding bowl; but a smaller bowl, similar to the porringer, was used when "bleeding" a patient. The bleeding bowl would hold up to sixteen ounces of blood that the doctor removed from a patient. The number of ounces was usually marked by rings on the side of the bowl.

The porringer was a useful bowl for semiliquid foods like porridge. This American example was made about 1744. (Henry Ford Museum, Dearborn, Michigan)

The eighteenth-century silver tankard is an aristocrat among American antiques because of its beauty and rarity. This (1705–1720) tankard was made by John Coney of Boston. (Art Institute of Chicago, Chicago, Illinois)

Any small child would have enjoyed this whistles-and-bells rattle made of silver about 1725, but only the wealthy could have owned it. (Henry Ford Museum, Dearborn, Michigan)

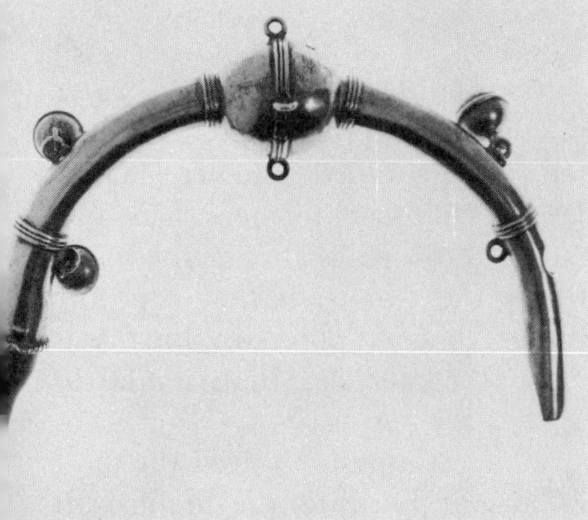

Tankard

The original tankard held water, and was made from hollowed logs bound with iron. The word "tankard" finally came to mean any wooden or metal drinking vessel. The tankard has been used since the sixteenth century, but it reached the height of its popularity during the eighteenth century.

Whistles and bells

The silver baby rattle of the late-eighteenth or early-nineteenth century often had a piece of coral at one end. The coral was used for teething. The other end had noisemaking whistles and bells for the baby's amusement.

Decanter labels

Bottle tickets were renamed "decanter labels" about 1790. They were first made when glass decanters became popular. Before 1790, liquor bottles were made from blue-and-white pottery, with the name of the liquor as a part of the design on the bottle. After the glass decanters came into style, some sort of label was necessary to determine what was in the bottle.

From 1740 to about 1860, metal shields hung with a chain were popular, and are sometimes seen today. The paper label was put into widespread use after 1860.

Decanter labels were made from silver, bone, leather, wood, or any hard durable material.

Epergne

The epergne is a large table centerpiece that was usually made from silver and glass. A large center bowl or basket and several smaller bowls were placed together to hold flowers, fruits, sweetmeats or cookies. It is a seventeenth-century design that was also used during the eighteenth and nineteenth centuries.

A Chinese pagoda inspired the silver epergne made in 1762 by Thomas Powell of London, England. The baskets held flowers, fruits, or bonbons. (Colonial Williamsburg, Williamsburg, Virginia)

Miniatures

Miniature silver was made during the seventeenth, eighteenth, and nineteenth centuries in a style that was in vogue at the time. They may have been toys or gifts or even salesman's samples, as some have suggested. Some English silversmiths made only miniature silver pieces, never full-sized ones.

The tilting water pitcher, or the double-wall pitcher, was a Victorian design popular after 1865. (International Silver)

THE SHAPES OF VICTORIAN SILVER AND SILVER PLATE

Double-wall water pitcher

The large silver-plated pitcher with a porcelain liner is an ice-water pitcher. Several patents were granted for double-walled pitchers about 1850. The first pitchers had two metal walls with an air space between the two walls that kept the liquid cool. A porcelain liner was used at a later date. It is similar to a Thermos jug.

James Stimpson received the most important patent for the double-wall pitcher, and permitted four companies to use it after 1854. Remember NO MATTER HOW OLD YOU THINK IT IS, ANY SILVER PITCHER OR "COFFEEPOT" WITH A PORCELAIN LINING WAS MADE AFTER 1854, PROBABLY AFTER 1865.

Castor sets that held bottles for oil, vinegar, and other condiments were popular after 1850. The cathedral castor opened to show the glass bottles inside (patented 1857); the Ferris-wheel design was a fad after the Civil War (International Silver). Most housewives liked the more common type of revolving castor.

Castor sets

The standing salt and pepper castor sets were used during the seventeenth century. The sugar castor, mustard pot, spice dredger, bottles for vinegar and oil, and other spice holders were introduced within a few years. All the containers were made from silver, gold, pewter, china, or glass.

It became stylish in the early eighteenth century to have a silver stand that held oil and vinegar. A matching set of silver castors for several types of spices and sugar were also used. The two sets were joined together in one large silver frame as early as 1705.

Most of the stands held five bottles or shakers in a frame. The design of the castor set changed about every ten years. The early sets were made from silver or English Sheffield plated ware during the late eighteenth and early nineteenth centuries.

The condiment jars rested on a heavy footed tray. The center of the tray had a handle that supported the rings that held the jars in place. The set often included glass salt dips.

Some of the later sets had pierced bands that surrounded the bottles. They were made to hold six bottles.

The castor sets were often made from Britannia metal (a silver-colored alloy) by the middle of the nineteenth century. They became more ornate each year, and by 1860 castor sets became elaborate cathedral-like creations. Small doors opened and exposed each of the bottles. The designs became heavier and the sets became higher. The lower designs returned to their popularity by 1880. The lazy-Susan type of castor set that was the fad for almost ten years went out of style, and smaller sets, which contained three or four bottles, came into fashion. The racks were just wide frames designed to hold the popular colored glass bottles by 1890.

The "more common type" of castor.

Pickle castor

The pickle castor was a glass jar about six inches in height, and it became popular in 1890. The jar had a top that was usually made from silver or silver plate. The castor was set in a metal frame with a base and tall handles that went up to an arch above the jar. A pair of tongs hung from the frame. The pickle castor was usually made from colored glass and silver-plated Britannia metal. It remained popular for only about ten years. THE PICKLE CASTOR CAN DATE ONLY FROM ABOUT 1890 TO 1900.

Napkin rings

The first napkin-ring patent was issued in 1867. The 1877 silver catalog of the Meriden Britannia Company had six pages devoted to the sale of napkin rings. The fad lasted until about 1886, and by 1900 the napkin ring was almost completely out of vogue. The napkin ring is strictly a late-Victorian piece.

The pickle castor with a glass jar and tongs was a popular form in the 1890's. It was usually made of silver-plated Britannia metal.

Dirty napkins were not tossed in the washer, but held primly in place for the next meal by the Victorian silver napkin ring. Thousands of styles were made in silver or silver plate, and in pottery, glass, or other materials.

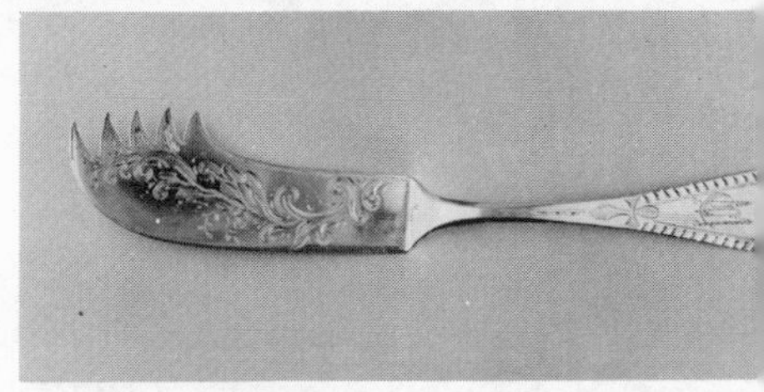

The Victorian silversmith liked to design unusual, amusing pieces of silver and silver plate. The egg frame (at left) held the breakfast egg and spoons (Reed and Barton). At bottom is a silver nutbowl of the 1890's (International Silver). The butter knife (above) cut with the blade, and served with the fork-like ends (Towle Silver). Twisted wire was used to make the handle of this Victorian gravy ladle below. (Towle Silver)

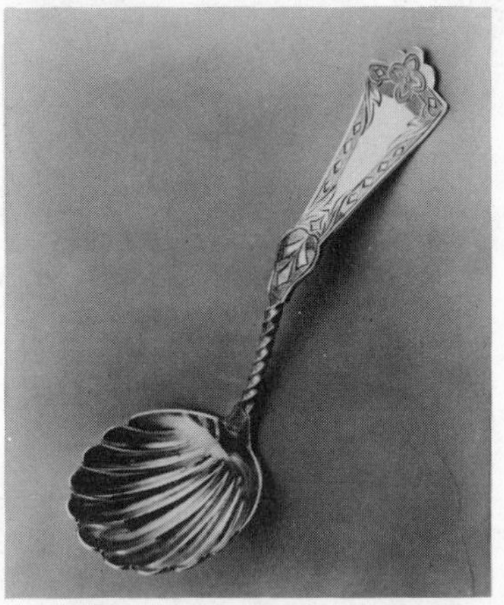

And the thousand of others—

A complete silver service in Victorian times had several types of spoons, with a different one for coffee, demitasse, soup, cream soup, ice cream, and dinner. It also had dozens of different serving pieces, and no one would ever use a cold-meat fork for hot meat. Fish servers, crumbers (to remove crumbs from the table), stuffing spoons, sugar scuttles (popular about 1875 to 1900), cheese scoops, marrow scoops, and others were made. Card holders, sardine boxes, mustard jars, covered butter dishes, spoon holders, syrup pitchers, toothpick holders, and knife rests were also to be found in every well-to-do Victorian home.

Souvenir spoons

The souvenir spoon was a popular fad during the 1880's and 1890's. Teaspoons, orange spoons, sugar spoons, demitasse spoons, and even larger spoons were designed and sold to commemorate important places or events. The handles of the spoons and the inside of the bowls pictured various buildings, exhibitions, or people. Some of the spoons were enameled, while others were just given a gold wash or left as plain silver.

Souvenir spoons are still being made, and the supply of old and new spoons is almost unlimited.

SOME TIPS THAT DON'T SEEM TO BELONG ANYWHERE ELSE

Several names appear on what seems to be silver but really isn't silver. These names confuse everyone. "Brazil silver" is a name used by the Globe Nevada Silver Works of Birmingham, England, on a nickel silverware that was not sterling or silver plate. "Siberian silver" is an English silver on copper made by Hayman and Company of Birmingham, England, in the late 1800's. "African silver" is not African, but is English plate made after 1850 by Hills, Menke and Company of Birmingham. "Oregon silver" is a trade name used on a silver-plated ware made in England about 1880. "German silver" is a clever German substitute for silver. It is a silver-colored metal made from nickel, copper, and zinc. German silver resembles silver, and was frequently used as a base metal for silver-plated pieces. "Waldo" is a gold-colored metal tableware made by the Waldo Foundry in Bridgeport, Connecticut, about 1894. It was made until 1905. (BRITANNIA METAL—for a complete history see Chapter 7, "Pewter.")

Should it be replated?

Should my silver be replated? The classic question about silver tableware has an easy answer. All modern silver plating destroys the charm and color of the old hand-rolled plated ware. Do not replate your old English Sheffield silver, but enjoy the worn patina even when the copper is evident. If you really object to the appearance of the copper, don't buy old silver-plated pieces, but buy later Victorian silver plate that has been electrically covered with silver. Replating the later pieces will not hurt them.

It is possible to remove initials on old solid silver by having a jeweler buff out the initial, but don't do it. The initials on early silver were beautifully engraved, and usually are a part of the overall design. Removing the initials may impair the value of the silver. Why not invent a great-aunt with that initial, and enjoy the family "heirloom"?

Hints on care of silver

Use a good commercial silver polish, and follow the directions. Never use an "instant" dip. The tarnish-preventing polishes are safe for all silver.

Silver: Bibliography

Buhler, Kathryn C. and Graham Wood. *American Silver in the Yale University Art Gallery,* Volumes I & II. New Haven, Connecticut, 1970.
The Yale University collection of American silver is one of the finest in the country. These two books give the collector a picture and history of each piece.

Fales, Martha Gandy. *Early American Silver for the Cautious Collector.* New York: Funk & Wagnalls, 1970.
A guide for the beginning collector of eighteenth-century American silver. Style, history, care, and even fakes are discussed.

Flynt, Henry N. and Martha Gandy Fales. *The Heritage Foundation Collection of Silver, with Biographical Sketches of New England Silversmiths, 1625–1825.* Old Deerfield, Massachusetts: The Heritage Foundation, 1968.
This book is based on the Heritage Foundation collection of silver in Deerfield, Massachusetts. Two-thirds of the book is an alphabetic listing of silversmiths, including personal history and a picture of a mark.

Wood, Graham. *American Silver.* New York: Praeger, 1971.
A history of silver styles in America from 1650 to 1900. This is a well-illustrated and well-documented book.

Knittle, Rhea Mansfield. *Early Ohio Silversmiths and Pewterers 1787–1847.* Ohio Frontier Series. Cleveland, Ohio: Calvert-Hatch, 1943.
A pamphlet listing makers and the cities where they worked.

Kovel, Ralph and Terry. *A Directory of American Silver, Pewter and Silver Plate.* New York: Crown, 1961.
A listing of silversmiths, with locations, dates, names of partners, facsimiles of marks, and a complete bibliography.

McClinton, Katharine Morrison. *Collecting American 19th Century Silver.* New York: Scribner's, 1968.
This book is written for the collector of nineteenth-century American silver. Tea sets, spoons, silver overlay glass, presentation pieces, inkwells, bells, jewelry, spoons, and other small pieces are included.

Wenham, Edward. *Practical Book of American Silver.* New York and Philadelphia: Lippincott, 1949.
Excellent, detailed, illustrated discussion of forms and styles of American silver to 1825.

Silver Plate, American and English

Freeman, Larry, and Jane Beaumont. *Early American Plated Silver.* Watkins Glen, New York: Century House, 1947.
An interesting story of the silver-plating industry in America, illustrated with reproductions of early catalog pages.

Hardt, Anton. *Adventuring Further*

in Souvenir Spoons. New York: Privately printed, 1965.

———. *Souvenir Spoons of the 90's*. New York: Privately printed, 1962 (Order from Anton Hardt, 343 Bleecker St., New York, N.Y.)

Catalog reprints of information about souvenir spoons of the late nineteenth century.

Kovel, Ralph and Terry. *A Directory of American Silver, Pewter and Silver Plate*. New York: Crown, 1961.

A listing of the marks used by silver plate manufacturers in America is included.

Rainwater, Dorothy T. *American Silver Manufacturers*. Hanover, Penn.: Everybody's Press, 1966.

A complete list of Victorian silver and silver plate manufacturers.

Wardle, Patricia. *Victorian Silver and Silver Plate*. New York: Nelson, 1963.

An excellent general history of English Victorian silver and silver plate, with many photographs.

Wyler, Seymour B. *The Book of Sheffield Plate*. New York: Crown, 1949.

An interesting book, with descriptive chapters and a partial list of Victorian English silver-plate makers.

English Silver

Banister, Judith. *English Silver*. New York: Hawthorn, 1966.

———. *Old English Silver*. New York: Putnam's, 1965.

Douglas, Jane. *Collectable Silver*. London: Countrywise Books, 1963.

Henderson, James. *Silver Collecting for Amateurs*. London: Muller, 1965.

Hughes, Bernard. *Small Antique Silverware*. New York: Bramhall House, 1957.

Hughes, Bernard and Therle. *Three Centuries of English Domestic Silver*. New York: Funk, 1952.

Wenham, Edward. *Old Silver*. London: Spring Books, 1965.

All these books are good general reference books about English silver. All are well illustrated, and are interestingly written.

Canadian Silver

Langdon, John E. *Canadian Silversmiths 1700–1900*. Lunenburg, Vermont: The Stinehour Press, 1966.

A history and alphabetic listing of known Canadian silversmiths. Many marks are shown in photographs.

Unitt, Doris and Peter. *Canadian Silver, Silverplate & Related Glass*. Peterborough, Ontario, Canada: Clock House Publications (P.O. Box 103), 1970.

A catalog-like listing of jewelers and silversmiths of nineteenth-century Canada.

7

Pewter

BECAUSE gold and silver have always been expensive, it was necessary for many of our ancestors to buy pewter and other less costly metal dishes and spoons. American pewter was made as early as 1639. The first colonists from England brought their molds with them, and American-made pewter shaped exactly like the English wares was soon for sale in the colonies. There is no sure way to tell an English piece of pewter from an American-made one, and it has become one of those antiques that are sold "upside down." Any eight-inch English plate does not have a dollar value anywhere near that of an American-made plate of the same time, even though they appear identical in all respects, with the exception of the maker's mark. Many dealers will display their marked pewter upside down so that the valuable marks can be seen. ALMOST ALL OLD PEWTER, IF MARKED, IS MARKED ON THE BOTTOM, NOT ON THE FACE OF THE PIECE. Beware of some English-made pewter that just appears old—and has been made with a mark on the front of the plate.

Some pewter is dull, while other pieces are almost silver-like in their appearance. Tin, lead, copper, and other metals were mixed in various amounts to make pewter, and the difference is caused by variance of the chemical composition. A simple trick will help a little with the maze of grades of pewter. RUB A PIECE OF PEWTER ON A SHEET OF WHITE PAPER. THE HEAVIER THE MARK, THE MORE LEAD IN THE PEWTER. THE LIGHTER THE MARK, THE MORE TIN AND THE BETTER THE QUALITY.

No mark on the paper means 90 parts tin to 10 parts lead; faint marks have 75 parts tin to 25 parts lead. "Plate" pewter was made from tin and copper. "Trifle" pewter was used in mugs, and was made from tin and antimony. Lead was not used because the makers feared lead poisoning. "Lay" pewter was the most inexpensive type of pewter, and was made from lead, copper, and tin. Britannia is the trade name given to many types of pewter that were made in the late eighteenth and nineteenth centuries in England; it will be discussed later.

Clean any piece of pewter that looks dull. Use a good commercial metal cleaner. NEVER USE STEEL WOOL, CLEANSING POWDER, OR PROFESSIONAL BUFFING. Pewter was meant to have a soft, satiny finish, and it was never made to look like a polished tin can. Buffing will bring the tin to the surface, and the soft appearance will disappear. Once pewter is cleaned, it will stay clean for a long time; but if it was originally a dull, dark piece of pewter with a high lead content, it can never be polished to a soft, silvery color.

Marks on pewter

Pewter marks can be very confusing, since several makers in the United States marked the pieces "London" to fool their customers who wanted to purchase British-made pewter.

There is a very general rule, but it is only 75 percent correct: THE THISTLE IS THE MARK OF THE SCOTCH PEWTER MAKERS, WHILE THE FRENCH MAKERS FROM PARIS USED AN ANGEL WITH THE WORD "PARIS," A FLEUR-DE-LIS, OR A CROWNED ROSE. ST. MICHAEL AND THE DRAGON IN A CIRCLE, A GOTHIC "B," OR A SIX-PETALED ROSE INDICATE IT WAS MADE IN BRUSSELS. AN ARM WITH A HAND WAS USED IN ANTWERP, BUT THE ENGLISH AND AMERICANS ALMOST ALWAYS USED NAMES AND LETTERS.

The mystery of the pewter mark isn't impossible to solve, because there are several good reference books that picture the marks in detail. The easy way to look up a mark is to try the American makers first, since there are fewer of them. If the mark is not in that list, then try the English. SOME OF THE FINEST EXAMPLES OF ENGLISH AND AMERICAN PEWTER WERE NEVER MARKED.

To sound like a collector you must know these terms

Every type of collection has its own jargon, and the pewter collectors are no exception. The "eight-inch-plate era" was from 1750 to 1825. During those years undecorated plates of simple design and of eight-inch diameter were made. There were about ninety American pewter makers working at that time.

The "coffeepot era" was from 1825 to 1850. During that time pewter was made in shapes that imitated silver.

"Sadware" is a term that refers to heavy pieces of pewter, plates and trenchers, or any pewter article hammered out of a single sheet of metal. "Hollow ware" was cast, and included all the hollow forms.

The "boar's-head platter" is really a large pewter "charger," or dish.

Pewter touchmark. 1758–1788.

The boar's-head platter was really just a large pewter platter. This example was made by William Will of Philadelphia, Pennsylvania, about 1761–1793. (Brooklyn Museum, Brooklyn, New York)

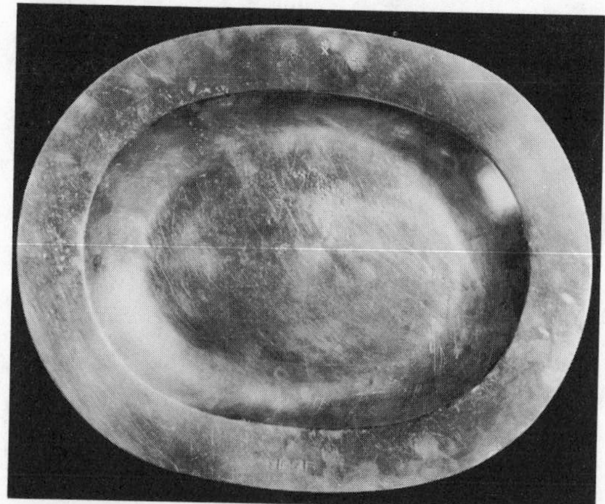

Measures came in many sizes. This old pewter measure held half a gill. (Collection of Eric de Jonge)

The "Rembrandt" tankard was named for its shape. This guild flagon, or tankard, was made in Holland in the eighteenth century. (William Penn Memorial Museum, Harrisburg, Penn.)

Most of them were made at least twenty-six inches in diameter. It is said that these platters were first made in England during the seventeenth century, when they were used to serve a whole roasted boar's head at the dinner table.

The "Rembrandt tankard" is a nickname given to a specially shaped tankard that was similar to the ones Rembrandt liked to paint in his pictures. (The nickname is recent.)

Pewter cups often came marked as a "gill." The bar measures, which came in sets, were usually marked from one fourth of a gill to a pint. A gill is one fourth of one pint.

The shape

Once you have learned the characteristic shapes of silver or porcelain teapots and bowls, you are ready to collect pewter, because the shapes were almost identical. The coffeepot changed shape from small to large, from round to pear shape, then to the inverted pear, and next to the famous pewter shape called the "lighthouse." THE LIGHTHOUSE POT WAS A MID-NINETEENTH CENTURY SHAPE OFTEN COPIED IN TIN AND TOLEWARE.

Porringers are the only other pewter pieces that can't be grouped with the silver shapes. The porringer handles have changed through the years, and a quick study of the typical handles in each region will be sufficient guide for the beginning collector.

After 1850

Many collectors and experts (ourselves included) have made statements in the past that "the pewter makers of America were unimpor-

The coffeepot was made of Britannia metal by the Cincinnati Britannia Company about 1850. The ale pitcher was made about the same time by Homan and Company, Cincinnati, Ohio. (Ohio State Historical Society, Columbus, Ohio)

Porringers have not changed in shape through the years, but the handles did. The handles can reveal the period, region, and sometimes even the maker. The porringers here are from Connecticut, Pennsylvania, New York, and Rhode Island. (Henry Ford Museum, Dearborn, Michigan)

This pewter porringer was made by Gersham Jones in Providence, Rhode Island, in the late 1700's. (William Penn Memorial Museum, Harrisburg, Pennsylvania)

Another style of pewter tankard was this 9-inch example, made about 1800 by the Danforth brothers. (Old Sturbridge Village, Sturbridge, Massachusetts)

tant by 1850." This is not so! To a museum of art, pewter made in America prior to 1850 is really the only pewter to display, but to the collector ANY MARKED AMERICAN PEWTER, EVEN MADE AS LATE AS 1870, IS IMPORTANT. Pewter made at a later date is valuable if it is really pewter, and not the stripped-down silver-plated Britannia that was so popular after 1850.

Many experts will give various explanations of the difference between Britannia and pewter. Actually, there is no difference. Pewter and Britannia were used to make an everyday ware that resembled silver. Pewter was the first name used for the metal.

Most of the early pieces were made by hand. When the sale of pewter began slowing down, some clever English manufacturers called their product "Britannia." The later Britannia pieces were often spun on a lathe. The percentage of tin, copper, antimony, and other metals in pewter and in Britannia varies with each piece and each manufacturer.

James Vickers bought the formula from M. Gowers for the manufacture of Britannia metal in England in 1769. It took eighteen years to perfect the formula and start the actual manufacture of the new ware. James Dixon's sons were exporting it to the United States by 1804.

Britannia ware became very fashionable in the United States in the nineteenth century. The first famous American factory was the Meriden Britannia Company, which started producing in 1808. Seventeen of the independent Britannia factories, including the Meriden Company, joined in 1898 to form the still-operating International Silver Company.

The Babbitt and Crossman Company was founded in 1824, and later became the Reed and Barton Company, a silver concern that is still operating.

John Mead learned the secrets of silver-plating Britannia ware in 1837. He joined William Rogers in 1845. The two men dissolved their partnership, and the 1847 Rogers Brothers Company was founded by

William Rogers. The company made silver-plated flatware that was so good the firm became an immediate success.

About 1850 the Britannia factories decided that silver-plated Britannia metal was most profitable. The Meriden Britannia Company purchased the 1847 Rogers Brothers trademarks. Their name was widely advertised, and became one of the most famous trademarks of its time.

Nickel silver took the place of Britannia ware about 1857. Most of the 128 factories that existed at the time lost money, and by 1879 there were only 55 factories still making Britannia ware. Many of the factories are listed, and their marks can be identified.

Britannia's dark feet

Some of the Britannia ware was made in a dull pewter color. Many later pieces of Britannia were made to be silver-plated. The teapot spout, feet, and handle were made of a harder metal than the body, and were slightly darker in color. The entire pot was then silver-plated, and the dark feet did not show. THERE IS NO CLEANER THAT WILL MAKE THE FEET LIGHTER. IF YOU HAVE A POT LIKE THIS, HAVE IT SILVER-PLATED.

A famous old wives' tale

Somewhere or somehow the idea has come down through the ages that eating from pewter plates would give

Pewter dishes were perfectly safe to use for food. These plates were made by John Brunstrom, Philadelphia, c. 1790 (Love touchmark); Parks Boyd, Philadelphia, c. 1800; and Peter Young, Albany, c. 1785. (Ohio Historical Society, Columbus, Ohio)

you lead poisoning. If that were true, most of our ancestors would have died ahead of their time. It is perfectly safe to serve any type of food from either shiny or dull pewter. Looking at the cheerful side, lead may be poisonous, but the same tin that is in pewter has been used in the cans that store our food.

Marks

Here is an Instant Expert tip for the mark-hunting pewter collector: IF YOU CAN'T FIND THE PEWTER MARK IN A BOOK ABOUT PEWTER, TRY LOOKING AT A LIST OF AMERICAN SILVERSMITHS AND SILVER-PLATE MAKERS. Many of these men worked with all three types of metal.

Hints on care of pewter

Never use steel wool or scouring powder. Clean pewter with a good commercial metal polish. If the metal is badly pitted, it can be soaked in a solution of lye or toilet-bowl cleanser. This can be dangerous, and complete directions from any good book about the care of antiques must be followed.

Pewter: Bibliography

Cotterell, Howard Herschel. *Old Pewter: Its Makers and Marks.* Rutland, Vermont: Tuttle, 1963. This definitive work on English, Scottish, and Irish pewter contains extensive lists of marks, makers, photographs of pewter, descriptions of characteristics.

Jacobs, Carl. *Guide to American Pewter.* New York: McBride, 1957. A picture listing of makers and marks that tells of the rarity of pieces and their approximate value. This book is excellent for the collector who is just starting.

Kauffman, Henry J. *The American Pewterer: His Techniques & His Products.* Camden, New Jersey: Nelson, 1970. This is a study of the techniques, tools, and products of the American pewterer with the emphasis on how he worked; not what he made.

Kerfoot, John Barrett. *American Pewter.* Boston: Houghton Mifflin, 1924. An important book about American pewter, with many photographs, marks, and extensive information about makers.

Laughlin, Ledlie Irwin. *Pewter in America.* Boston: Houghton Mifflin, 1940. This definitive work about American pewter is difficult to obtain but of great value for the collector.

8

Tinware and Toleware

THE names given to painted tin are confusing to many, but the confusion will disappear when you consider that toleware, japanned ware, painted tin, and Pontypool all mean practically the same thing. It certainly is correct to call any painted tin-plated sheet iron by the name "painted tin." The tin-plated iron ware that was painted in the city of Pontypool, England, was given the name "Pontypool ware." The finely decorated ware was first made about 1660. "Japanned ware," or "toleware," almost mean the same, but the toleware was usually more elaborately painted with scenes, fruits, or flowers. When to give the more élite name of toleware is still open to argument.

Japanned ware was first made to imitate the Japanese lacquer wares. Sheets of tin-plated iron were coated with asphaltum, a coal by-product, and baked. When the asphaltum was applied in a thin layer, the finished piece appeared golden brown. The earliest japanned ware was hand painted with designs on the dark brown or black tin. STENCILS WERE USED ABOUT 1820. BLUE, GRAY, OR RED VARNISH WAS OFTEN USED INSTEAD OF ASPHALTUM BY 1840. AFTER 1850, TIN ARTICLES SUCH AS TEA AND COFFEE CANISTERS WERE JAPANNED AND STENCILED WITH THE NAME OF THE PRODUCT. The store-type canisters are the final type of japanned ware, and certainly should not be called "tole."

History of painted tin

Painted tinware was known in most European countries by the seventeenth century. The English Pontypool, the most famous, was made from 1660 to 1822. Eighteenth-century Pontypool and other English painted tinwares can usually be identified from their shapes. METAL OTHER THAN THE TIN-PLATED IRON WAS USED FOR THE FEET, HANDLES, AND FINIALS. Most of the pieces have classic shapes. The background was black, brown, blue, mustard yellow, cream red, or tortoiseshell. The designs were either Chinese- or Japanese-inspired or classical. Tinware was imported into America from England by 1737, and even Paul Revere sold the imported wares. Tinware was made by tinsmiths and young lady amateurs.

Blocked tin was also made in America, and it was a cast metal similar to pewter. This type of tinware was sold across the country by traveling peddlers. The shop of Wil-

Painted tinware like this coffeepot and deed box was popular in New England and Pennsylvania before 1850. The coffeepot is sometimes called either lighthouse or gooseneck style. (Ohio Historical Society, Columbus, Ohio)

liam and Edward Pattison in Berlin, Connecticut, began producing plain tinware about 1740. This was sold plain, or decorated by others and then sold. Connecticut became the center of the American tin industry, and even though business was slow during the Revolution the industry began to boom again by 1800. Some of the other men making the painted tin worked in Maine (Zachariah Stevens, Thomas Briscoe, Oliver Buckley), New York (Aaron Butler), and Pennsylvania (Harvey Filley, Jacob Eichholtz).

Boots and mittens were put on the two tall "arms" of this tin warmer, and hot air blew through the arms to dry the wet clothes. This is an unusual example of nineteenth-century American tinwork. (Shelburne Museum, Inc., Einars J. Mengis)

A rare piece of signed painted tin may be found if you are very, very lucky. Ann Butler or B. Minerva Butler or M. B. were the signatures used by the New Yorker Aaron Butler's daughters. Each of the areas where tinware was painted had special characteristics; much of the Pennsylvania ware was painted red, while the New England pieces were almost always black. The Butler

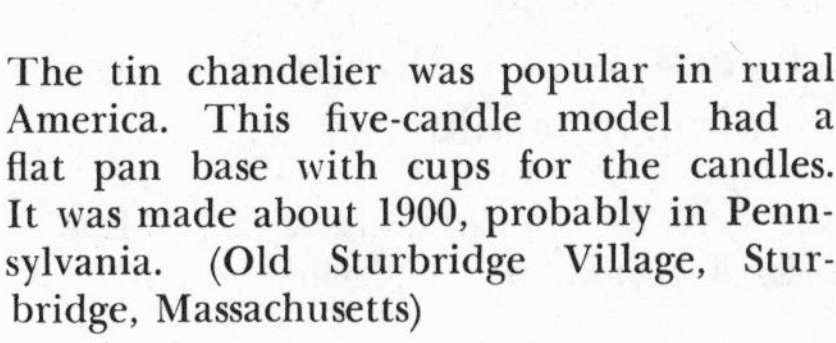

The tin chandelier was popular in rural America. This five-candle model had a flat pan base with cups for the candles. It was made about 1900, probably in Pennsylvania. (Old Sturbridge Village, Sturbridge, Massachusetts)

family used a distinctive elaborate border of flowers and leaves, but the differences are so slight that only study and careful research can verify the source.

Punched tin

Some of the tinware used in America was punched. All sorts of trays, shakers, wall sconces, candlestick molds, cookie cutters, teapots, boxes, and other kitchen utensils were made. Most of the punched tin dates from the 1830 to 1860 period. The dents in the tin, made with a hammer and a nail or a small die, did not break the surface. If the design went through the tin it was called "pierced" tin. Pie safes, colanders, strainers, lanterns, footwarmers, and nutmeg graters were pierced. The tin cans left behind by the soldiers in New Mexico and nearby areas during the 1840's and 1850's were often

The breakfast eggs were cooked at the table in this French painted tin eggwarmer. It is red with gold decorations, and was made about 1800. (Cooper Union Museum, New York)

transformed by the native workmen into wall shrines for saints or as other decorative pierced-tin pieces.

In some cases it is possible to tell an old pierced tray from a new one, but the rules are not infallible. Both were made from heavy tinned sheet iron, with an edge rolled over a wire. The old trays had a flatter edge where rolled, and the edge and holes always faced down, while new trays had holes that turned up.

Hints on care of tin

Old tinware is often rusted, and the paint has flaked. Many of these old pieces have been repainted, so it is best to beware of any piece of tinware with a new finish.

Never scour tinware. Clean it as gently as possible, and dry it completely. Painted tin can be gently cleaned with a diluted solution of liquid household cleaner.

Sheet iron was painted and gilded to make this tray in France about 1830. The picture, by Adrien Victor Anger, shows Napoleon at Frankfort. (Cooper Union Museum, New York)

Sheet metal was shaped to form this metal steer's head that hung in front of a stockman's hotel in Omaha, Nebraska, about 1870. It is a unique example of folk-art work in tin. (Joslyn Art Museum, Omaha, Nebraska)

Pierced tin was used to make this mold or sieve. Notice that the holes are made with the rough edge outside, perhaps so the heart could also be used as a grater.

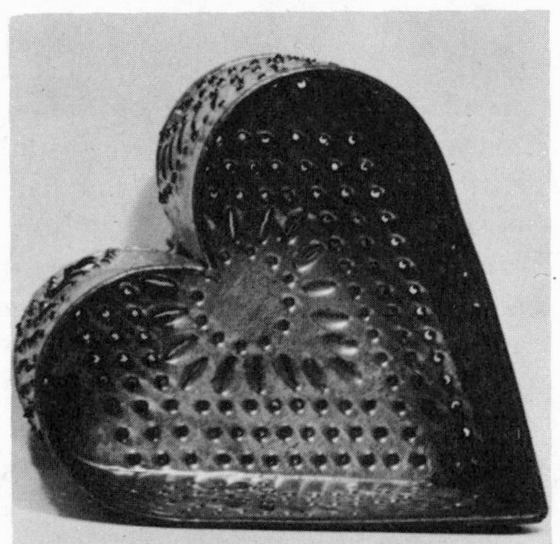

Tinware and Toleware: Bibliography

Coffin, Margaret. *The History & Folklore of American Country Tinware 1700–1900.* Camden, New Jersey: Nelson, 1968.
A book about painted tinware that stresses the history of the makers and types of design. Well illustrated, black and white photographs.

Gould, Mary Earle. *Antique Tin and Tole Ware.* Rutland, Vermont: Tuttle, 1958.
An excellent, important book about early and late tinwares.

Lea, Zilla Rider. *The Ornamented Tray, Two Centuries of Ornamented Trays (1720–1920).* Rutland, Vermont: Tuttle, 1971.
Styles of decoration on antique English and American painted tin trays are illustrated and explained in detail in this book.

Powers, Beatrice Farnsworth, and Olive Floyd. *Early American Decorated Tinware.* New York: Hastings House, 1957.
A good general book about American tinware.

9

Clocks

TIME ALWAYS SEEMS to be of interest to everyone, and clocks, watches, sundials, and other timepieces fascinate a large group of serious collectors. Even the amateur who is interested only in decorating a house needs a clock somewhere, and an antique clock is often the choice. The simple rule for clocks is IF IT IS IN WORKING ORDER, ATTRACTIVE, OR UNUSUAL, IT IS A DESIRABLE CLOCK. A collector's clock should have added features, such as age, excellent condition, unusual features, rarity, and perhaps a label. There are hundreds of different types of American and English clocks that can still be found, and most of them made before World War I could be of some value. To decide if your clock is a collector's gem will require study at the library in any of the many books that list clockmakers and clock types. IF THE MAKER'S NAME APPEARS ON THE AMERICAN CLOCK, IT SHOULD BE LISTED IN *The Book of American Clocks* BY PALMER, and a complete history of the clock factory can be found.

The grandfather clock

From 1680 to about 1840, the grandfather clock was popular in America. It was originally called a tall case clock, and much of the literature written will list it only under that name. The name "grandfather" became popular about 1875 because of the song "My Grandfather's Clock." The name had been used as early as 1835 on a limited basis. There are several clues to help date a grandfather clock. THE EARLIEST GRANDFATHER CLOCKS HAD SQUARE OR ROUND DIALS. THE ARCHED DIAL WAS DESIGNED ABOUT 1715. At first the name of the maker was inscribed on the semicircle or arch, but by 1720 moving figures were added that pictured ships, Father Time, animals, or faces. The first clocks to tell the various phases of the moon were made about 1720. The month, day, and year were shown on some clock faces. THE DIALS OF THE CLOCK WERE MADE OF BRASS WITH SILVER DECORATIONS UNTIL ABOUT 1770. Numbers were engraved on the brass dial from 1770 to 1800, and the name of the maker and some design were often added to the engraving on the face. THE PAINTED DIALS AND THE WHITE ENAMEL DIALS WERE NOT USED UNTIL 1790. A cheap clock face made of printed paper was developed that could be glued to an iron or wooden panel. The paper dial was used only on the cheapest clocks. The cheapest clocks had wooden works, while the better ones were made with metal works.

Next time you are at a party and want to win some money on a gambling game, bet your friends that they can't draw a picture of an old grandfather's clock with the numbers in the correct places. Try it. Almost no one realizes that THE ROMAN NUMERAL VI ON A CLOCK FACE IS PLACED UPSIDE DOWN ON ALL BUT THE MOST RECENT CLOCKS. The bottom of the numeral always faces in toward the center on early clocks or on authentic modern copies. Most early clocks (before 1850) used the Roman numeral IIII instead of IV for 4.

A grandmother's clock is a small grandfather's clock that must be less than six feet six inches in height. They were popular from about 1750 to 1850.

The grandfather clock was originally called a tall case clock. Benjamin Cheney of Hartford, Connecticut, made the clock shown here in front view. It has a wooden movement and a brass face. (Old Sturbridge Village, Sturbridge, Massachusetts)

Lumen Watson of Cincinnati made this clock. He used arabic, not the more common Roman numerals. (Index of American Design)

Wall clocks

The banjo clock is the best known of the hundreds of clock styles that were made to hang on a wall. The name comes from the shape of the clock, which was first made by Simon Willard in 1802. Many other makers followed his idea, and hundreds of banjo clocks were produced by New England makers. BEWARE! THERE HAS BEEN A WHOLESALE FAKING OF WILLARD BANJO CLOCKS. His name has been added to many clocks made by other makers in the nineteenth century. BRASS EAGLES OR DOVES WERE POPULAR ON WALL CLOCKS MADE AFTER 1812, but they too have been copied.

The banjo-clock design became more elaborate, and by the mid-nineteenth century the girandole clock case came into fashion.

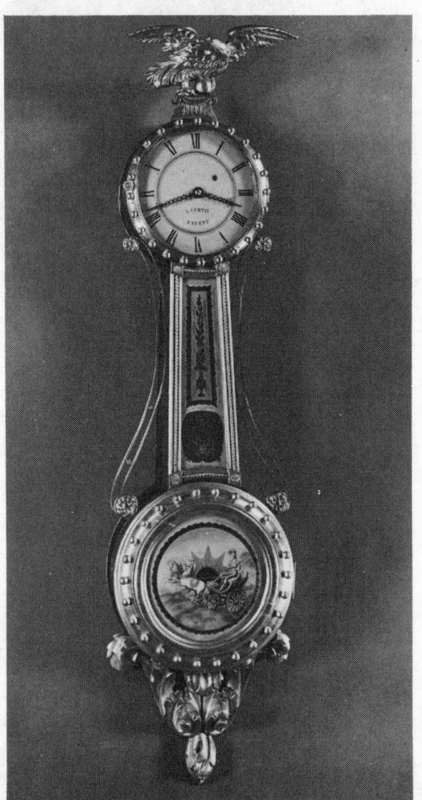

Mantel clocks

An almost infinite number of styles of mantel clocks was manufactured from about 1810 to 1860. The pillar-and-scroll case clock with a wooden movement, the Chauncey Jerome shelf clocks, papier-mâché clock cases (1850), and others in all styles were made.

This shelf clock with a mahogany case was made about 1845 by Birge and Fuller of Bristol, Connecticut. Notice the placing of the Roman numerals on the clock face. (Index of American Design)

The girandole clock was what many collectors call the most beautiful of the American clocks. This 45-inch clock was made by Lemuel Curtis of Concord, Massachusetts, in 1816. (Old Sturbridge Village, Sturbridge, Massachusetts)

Cuckoo clocks and other oddities

The cuckoo clock dates back to about 1730, when the pendulum striking mechanism and the cuckoo idea were developed in Switzerland and Bavaria. It was never a popular design with American manufacturers, but it was purchased by some American families.

A copy of the Christopher Columbus clock was made about 1893, and it pictured his face with the date 1492. The hour hand was the only hand on the clock. The Bostwick and Burgess Manufacturing Company of Norwalk, Ohio, made the clock for sale at the Columbian Exposition.

Clocks have been made to resemble a dancing girl with a clock in her belly. There were clocks that were made to look like sunflowers, animals, or the famous Hickory Dickory Dock clock where a mouse indicates the time. Clocks run by unusual power sources or clocks having unique casings are all eagerly collected. Rarity is important to the clock collector, if not to the housewife who just wants a time piece for the wall.

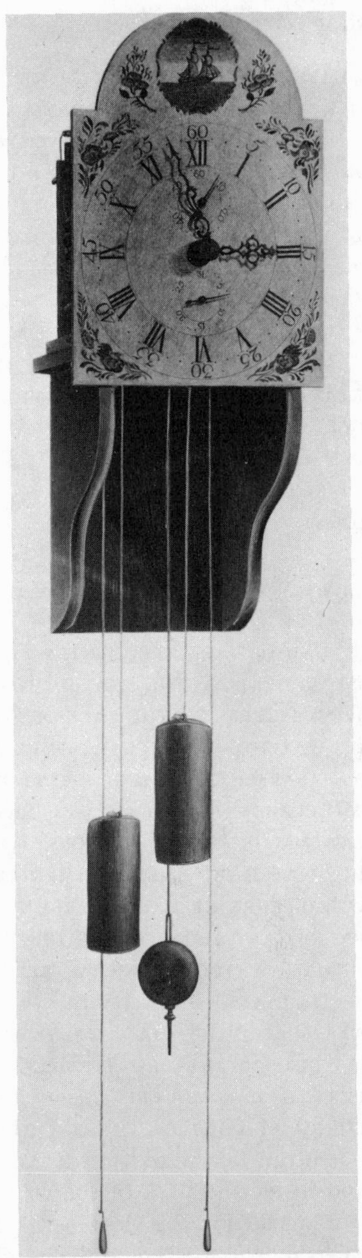

The "wag-on-the-wall" had a pendulum that did wag on the wall. A wooden dial and wooden works complete this clock which was made about 1800.

Wag-on-the-wall

The wag-on-the-wall clock was popular during the mid-1800's. The dial movement, weight, and pendulum were all part of the clock, but there was no case. It just had a hood at the top that protected the works from dirt. The clock was often cased at a later date.

And so remember

TO HAVE VALUE TO A COLLECTOR, A CLOCK SHOULD WORK AND HAVE ALL ITS ORIGINAL PARTS IN GOOD CONDITION, INCLUDING THE GLASS. THE CLOCK SHOULD BE ONE HUNDRED YEARS OLD. IF IT IS A VERY UNUSUAL CLOCK (ONE OF THE NOVELTY TYPES), IT COULD BE FIFTY YEARS OLD OR MORE. ELI TERRY, CHAUNCEY JEROME, SIMON WILLARD, AND SETH THOMAS ARE IMPORTANT NAMES IN THE AMERICAN CLOCK INDUSTRY, BUT EACH MAN MADE THOUSANDS OF CLOCKS. THEY ARE NOT ALL WORTH THE SAME AMOUNT.

Watches

THE UNUSUAL IS FREQUENTLY THE MOST DESIRABLE. THE WATCH WITH MOVING FIGURES ON THE FACE OF THE DIAL, WATCHES THAT PLAY MUSIC OR HAVE ALARMS THAT RING, OR THOSE WITH ELABORATE GOLD CASES HAVE GREAT VALUE TO COLLECTORS. ANY EARLY WATCH SIGNED BY AN AMERICAN MAKER BEFORE HE HAD A LARGE FACTORY, OR ANY HAMILTON, ELGIN, OR WALTHAM WATCH NUMBERED BELOW ONE THOUSAND IS VALUABLE (if it works or can be made to work). DON'T DISCARD THAT LITTLE PIECE OF PAPER THAT MIGHT BE INSIDE THE WATCHCASE! The most valued part of a watch can be the old watch paper found inside the back of the watch. It was an ad for the clockmaker or repairman who worked on the watch. The papers were engraved, printed, lithographed, or hand written. The ads can furnish much of the history of the watch industry in America. Most watch collectors search for old watch papers.

Sundials

The sundial has been known since the beginning of measured time. Pocket sundials have been recorded since the thirteenth century.

The pocket sundial was set with the aid of a compass, and was a great help in enabling the traveler to tell the hour. The permanent sundial is harder to use. The sundial must be set on April 15, June 15, September 1, or December 24, because your watch will then agree with time on the sundial. The sundial will vary as much as sixteen minutes from the actual time on all other days.

Two stray tips that might come in handy

THE SECOND HAND is not a new idea. IT HAS BEEN USED ON WATCHES SINCE 1780, and on clocks before that time. The stopwatch was first used about 1680.

LOOK IN A LISTING OF AMERICAN SILVERSMITHS WHEN CHECKING A CLOCKMAKER. OFTEN THE SILVERSMITHS WERE ALSO JEWELERS OR CLOCK OR WATCH MAKERS, AND SOME CLUES ABOUT DATE AND CITY OF ORIGIN MAY APPEAR.

The pocket sundial could be made of metal or wood. These two examples each measure less than two inches in diameter.

Clocks: Bibliography

Baillie, G. H., C. Clutton, and C. A. Ilbert. *Britten's Old Clocks and Watches and Their Makers.* New York: Bonanza, 1956.

About half of this fine, large book describes clocks, watches, and their construction from 1550 to 1830. The other half is a comprehensive listing of clock and watch makers, and a bibliography.

Clutton, Cecil, and George Daniels. *Watches.* New York: Viking, 1965.

An extensive, well-illustrated discussion of watches from the mid-sixteenth century to the mid-twentieth.

Eckhardt, George H. *Pennsylvania Clocks and Clockmakers.* New York: Bonanza, 1955.

The story of clocks made in Pennsylvania from 1682 to 1850. Illustrated, with a complete listing of clockmakers, and additional information on watch papers, music about clocks, and so on.

Palmer, Brooks. *The Book of American Clocks.* New York: Macmillan, 1950.

An alphabetical listing, the most complete available, of the clock and watch makers in America since 1650.

———. *A Treasury of American Clocks.* New York: Macmillan, 1967.

A picture listing of American clocks dating from eighteenth-century grandfathers to electric clocks of the 1930's. A list of makers is included.

10

Needlework

IF YOU WANT expert advice, the best place to get it is from an expert. Someone among your friends is an expert with a needle who knits sweaters, makes embroidered pillowcases, or does needlepoint chair seats. Anyone who has done difficult sewing can tell if a piece of needlework is good or bad, hard or easy.

There are dozens of types of needlework, and the same rules apply to all of them. Many of the antiques we have discussed are collected because of their historic interest. Needlework, like oil paintings, is collected because of its fine workmanship or for some sentimental reason. Take your treasure of a quilt or rug to an expert who will honestly tell you the truth about its maker's ability as a needleworker. After the shock wears away, keep the quilt or the rug even if it isn't too good. After all, you bought it because of the design or color or perhaps because the amateur needlewoman was really Great-Aunt Helen, and you are her namesake.

Quilts

Patchwork and pieced quilts are different. The patchwork quilt is made of many patterned materials stitched together to make one big piece, which is then quilted. The pieced or appliquéd quilt is made quite differently. A large piece of cloth is appliquéd with small pieces of material. The large background piece and the smaller appliquéd areas are then quilted together.

One of the easiest ways to tell if your quilt is old is to hold it in front of a sunny window or shine a strong light through the fabric. If you can see dark spots in the quilt, they are the cotton seeds that were never "ginned" out. Many claim that the seeds prove the quilt was made prior to 1790, which was the time of the cotton gin. Actually, many quilt makers in rural areas did not use ginned cotton until years later. Nevertheless, DARK SPOTS, OR SEEDS, INDICATE AN EARLY QUILT.

The design of the quilt will also help to tell the age of a nineteenth-century quilt. The all-white quilt was in fashion in the late eighteenth and early nineteenth centuries. The all-white quilt of the early nineteenth century was made with elaborate designs and very fine quilting stitches. The cotton interlining was thin. The quilts often had a large center design with a series of borders. Most of the all-white quilts were made during the first quarter of the nineteenth century. AMERICAN QUILTS

ALMOST ALWAYS WERE MADE WITH A SIMPLE RUNNING STITCH. English and most Continental quilts were made with a backstitch.

The pieced and patched quilts followed the same trend in design. EARLY EIGHTEENTH-CENTURY QUILTS HAD DESIGNS THAT WERE LIKE A TREE, SYMMETRICAL FROM THE BASE UP. THEY HAD NO BORDERS, OR ALMOST NO BORDERS.

BY THE NINETEENTH CENTURY THE PATTERNS WERE MORE FORMAL, AND HAD A CENTER DESIGN WITH SYMMETRICAL BORDERS. THE DESIGN IN THE CENTER OF THE QUILT BEGAN TO CHANGE BY 1825. IT WAS NO LONGER JUST ONE BIG DESIGN LIKE A TREE, BUT SEVERAL REPEATED SQUARES OF DESIGNS.

BY 1860 THE CENTER DESIGNS WERE ALL SMALL SQUARES, WITH THE QUILT BECOMING A SERIES OF LITTLE PATTERNS WITH A BORDER PATTERN. Some of the late Victorian quilts had an overall "crazy" quilt pattern. They were made by using small, irregular pieces of velvet, silk, and satin, sewed together on a backing fabric and embroidered at the seams. Crazy quilts were impractical bedcovers because of the fragile materials, so many were made in smaller sizes for throws on chairs and couches.

There is another clue to the age of a quilt. The first bedcovers in this country were made from imported textiles, usually printed chintz or linen. The first cotton cloth was available from an American factory about 1815, and MOST COVERS MADE AFTER 1815 WERE MADE FROM COTTON. Handwoven cotton fabrics were used by the ambitious housewife before

The Victorian crazy quilt was made of many types of fabric, usually velvet and heavy woolens. The irregular pieces were embroidered, and then joined together to form a colorful quilt. (Western Reserve Historical Society, Cleveland, Ohio)

1815. Printed cotton made in the United States was popular by 1840, but by 1870 the colored quilt had gone out of fashion.

There were many kinds of quilts, and there is a general rule to apply in determining the age of each type. Since the type of quilt changed with the styles, it is possible to guess the age from the style with about 90 percent accuracy. There is always room for error, as some quilts are still being made in a style that has been out of vogue for many years.

THE ALL-WHITE QUILT made from white woven cotton fabric and with cotton wadding used as an interlining DATES FROM THE FIRST QUARTER OF THE NINETEENTH CENTURY. The white quilt had an elaborate design with a central medallion or pattern and a series of surrounding borders.

The quilted woolen bedcover, often called linsey-woolsey, was made from a dark woolen or worsted fabric of blue, green, or brown, a filling of carded wool, and a bottom fabric of yellow or buff woolen. The three layers were quilted together with linen thread. The finished coverlet was used as a blanket is used today. A few of the WOOLEN COVERLETS DATE FROM THE EIGHTEENTH CENTURY, BUT MOST WERE MADE FROM 1800 TO 1850.

The earlier the woolen quilt, the thinner the quilt, the less the amount of stuffing, and the more elaborate the designs. The nineteenth-century quilt was blanket size, but the eighteenth-century quilts were larger because they were used as bedspreads. Sometimes eighteenth-century quilts had the corners cut out for the bedposts.

THE PIECED, OR APPLIQUÉD, QUILT WAS FIRST MADE AT THE END OF THE EIGHTEENTH CENTURY. The nineteenth-century appliquéd quilt was made from a plain or printed fabric with white. GREEN AND RED COTTON APPLIQUÉD QUILTS WERE IN STYLE FROM 1830 TO 1850.

Sometimes many friends would work on one quilt. Each friend would make one block, and sign her name in ink. Later, a party was held and all the blocks were joined into one large quilt. THIS TYPE OF SIGNATURE, OR FRIENDSHIP, QUILT WAS POPULAR FROM 1840 TO 1860.

CRAZY QUILTS MADE FROM SILK, SATIN, AND VELVET WERE POPULAR FROM 1870 TO 1880.

The designs of the appliquéd quilt are numerous. No one is quite sure how it was done, but a new design would often appear in several parts of the country within a few days. Some of the designs were published in ladies' magazines during the Victorian era; but before that, the gossip and word-of-mouth approach made quilt designs available to housewives in all parts of the country.

The size of a quilt has changed slightly during the past centuries. THE EIGHTEENTH-CENTURY QUILT WAS VERY LARGE, AND RANGED FROM NINE TO TWELVE FEET SQUARE. The beds of the period were high, and stacked with pillows. Many of the quilts of the eighteenth century and early nineteenth century resembled a square with two cut-out square corners. The quilt was made for a fourposter bed, with the large part

Coverlet of overshot weave in the "single chariot wheel" pattern.

Double cloth coverlet showing how the colors are reversed on the underside.

Summer and winter weave coverlet. The reverse side is not the same as the front, although the black-and-white picture makes it appear to be. The coverlet is green with red on one side, red with green on the other.

covering the top section of the bed, and the cutout portions leaving room for the high posters at the foot of the bed.

One last Instant Expert tip: MACHINE SEWING STARTED ABOUT 1850. After that date many quilts were still hand sewn, but at least the tip will help if you should find a machine-made quilt with characteristics of the pre-1850 period.

Coverlets

Woven coverlets of blue and white, or brown, red, green, yellow, or other colors, were made during the eighteenth and nineteenth centuries. The colonist furnished his own materials for a coverlet. The wool of black sheep was used for the black wool. The white wool was dyed outside in large kettles. Indigo would dye the wool blue; cochineal (a Mexican insect) made it scarlet; red came from madder root; goldenrod and sumac made yellow; alder bark made tan; hickory or walnut hulls would make it dark brown.

After the wool was dyed and spun on a wheel, the yarn was woven on a loom. The overshot loom was large and was often placed in a special room. The housewife did her own weaving; but by 1800 itinerant weavers worked in New England and the Western Reserve areas, and it was easier and faster to buy the woven product.

There are four kinds of coverlets, and each of them was in style for only a short time. The OVERSHOT was the simplest type of woven coverlet, with a plain weave and the designs in colors. The colored wool skipped over threads in the background and formed geometric designs. The overshot was made on the four-harness home loom. Linen and wool were used during the eighteenth century, and cotton and wool in the nineteenth century. Most overshot coverlets still found were made from 1800 to 1850.

DOUBLE-CLOTH BLOCK OR DOUBLE-WOVEN GEOMETRIC is another type of coverlet, and it is very easy to recognize. Professional weavers did the weaving. The fabric is really two in one, one plain-woven colored woolen, the other plain-woven nat-

A double-woven jacquard coverlet with the "town of Boston" border. (All coverlets from Western Reserve Historical Society, Cleveland, Ohio)

The Jacquard loom was used in America by 1820. It was very complicated, but the weaver was able to produce work with elaborate patterns. Most of the JACQUARD coverlets ignored the geometric designs that were popular with the earlier coverlet makers, and it was possible to have floral and animal designs on the coverlets. Most of the coverlets were made by traveling weavers. Complicated three-color patterns that were impossible to make earlier were woven by this loom.

The earliest dated Jacquard coverlet we know about was made in 1821. The home loom was able to make a strip of woven fabric ranging from only 2½ to 3 yards in length and up to 42 inches wide. Therefore, ALL THE EARLY COVERLETS WERE MADE WITH A CENTER SEAM. The Jacquard loom was much larger, and it was possible to make coverlets from one piece of fabric.

ural-colored cotton. The two fabrics were woven at one time on the loom, and the design was made by interchanging the fabrics. The complete coverlet was reversible. Most popular from 1820 to 1840, THIS TYPE OF COVERLET WAS MADE ON A NARROW LOOM, AND TWO STRIPS WERE NEEDED TO MAKE A COVERLET.

SUMMER-AND-WINTER WEAVE was a closely woven coverlet with a honeycomb appearance. If the design was blue against white on one side of the cloth, it was white against blue on the reverse side. Most summer-and-winter coverlets were made in New York and Pennsylvania from 1800 to 1830.

A single-weave jacquard coverlet of blue and white.

The handwoven coverlets of the nineteenth century came in many sizes. The most common size was made to fit a single adult bed. The smallest coverlet was made for a child's crib, and measured 36 inches by 42 inches. Most coverlets were about 72 inches wide, with lengths that varied from 90 to 108 inches. The widest coverlet was an 84-inch seamless bedcover.

Many of the woven coverlets were signed with the name of the weaver, the county or city, and the date. On some, the name of the owner of the coverlet was woven into one corner. The easiest way to date a coverlet is to LOOK FOR THE NAME. If the date appears, the problem is solved, but if just a name appears there are several books that list the coverlet makers.

A PARTIAL LIST OF MAKERS, WITH A DATE THAT HAS APPEARED ON A COVERLET:

NEW YORK, NEW JERSEY, MARYLAND and NEW ENGLAND COVERLET MAKERS

(Asterisk denotes no date known.)

Alexander, James (Orange County)	1822–1831
Allen, B. Hausman (Groveland, New York)	1839
Ball, H. H. (Orange County, New York)	1830
Bronson, J. and R. (New York)	1817
Brown, John (New York)	1843
Butterfield, J. (New Hartford, Oneida County, New York)	*
Covey, Harriet (New York)	1840
Cunningham, J. (New Hartford, Oneida County, New York)	1843
Davidson, Archibald (Ithaca, New York)	1820, 1832
Deuel, Elizabeth (Saratoga, New York)	c. 1790
Dudley, Samantha Charlotte (Roxbury, Massachusetts)	1830
France, Joseph (Rhode Island)	1814
Garrett, Thomas (Hagerstown, Maryland)	*
Gernand, J. B. (Maryland)	*
Gernand, W. H. (Westminster, Carroll County, Maryland)	1873
Getty, A. (Lockport, New York)	*
Goodwin, Harmon (Maine)	*
Hadsell, Ira (Palmyra, New York)	1849–1867
Hopeman,——— (New York	*
Impson, J. (Cortland County, New York)	1845
Irwin, L. (Pulaski, New York)	1859
Northrup, Elijah (Roanoke, New York)	1826

Petrie,——— (Albany, New York) . . . . *
Phebe, Akin (New York) 1834

Reed, V. R. (Benton, New York) 1883
Rossvilles,——— (New York) 1851

Sherman, John (Mount Morris, Genesee County, New York) 1838

Sternberg, William (New York) 1838

Tyler, Harry (Connecticut) 1834–1858

Van Ness, J. (Palmyra, New York) 1850
Van Nortwic, C. (Asbury, New Jersey) 1840

Witt,——— (New York) 1847

OHIO, PENNSYLVANIA, ILLINOIS and INDIANA COVERLET MAKERS

(Recorded at Ohio State Archaeological and Historical Society Museum are 174 Ohio weavers.)

(Asterisk denotes no date known.)

Adam, ——— (Greencastle, Franklin County, Pennsylvania) 1821

Adolf, Henry (Hamilton County, Indiana) 1851
Allen, A. (Ohio) 1840
Anshutz, P. H. (Carrolton, Ohio) 1820–1840

Ardner, Jacob and Michael (Mount Vernon, Knox County, Ohio) 1858

Baird, James (Switzerland County, Indiana) . . . . *
Balantyne,——— (Indiana) 1845, 1849
Barrett, ——— (Howard, Center County, Pennsylvania) . . . . c. 1850
Bissett, ——— (Franklin, Indiana) . . . . *

Bordner, Daniel (Millersburg, Berks County, Pennsylvania) . . . . *
Brehm, Henry (Womelsdorf, Berks County, Pennsylvania) 1836
Breneman, Martin B. (York County, Pennsylvania) 1861
Buechel, W. (Logan County, Ohio) 1847
Burkerd, E. (La Porte, Indiana) 1845
Cassel, Joseph H. (Skippack Township, Montgomery County, Pennsylvania) . . . . *
Christman, G. (Hereford Township, Berks County, Pennsylvania) . . . . *
Cleever, J. (Easton, Pennsylvania) . . . . *
Cole, J. C. (Vernon Township, Crawford County, Ohio) 1861
Colman, Peter (Ohio) . . 1853
Cosley, G. (Xenia, Ohio) 1851
Craig, J. (Floyd County, Indiana) . . . . *
Craig, William, Sr. (Greensburg, Decatur County, Indiana) 1838

Craig, William, Jr. (Greensburg, Decatur County, Indiana) 1850–1860

Cranston, Thomas (Switzerland County, Indiana) 1855

Crozier, John (Cadiz, Ohio) 1830

Cumbie, Alamo (Indiana) .... before 1850

Dannert, Henry (Allentown, Pennsylvania) .... *

Ettinger, Emanuel (Aaronsburg, Center County, Pennsylvania) 1820–1860

Fairbrothers, William (Henry County, Indiana) .... *

Fatsinger, Adam (either Allentown or Lehigh County, Pennsylvania) 1843

Fehr, C. (Emmaus, Pennsylvania) 1839

Fehr and Keck (Emmaus, Pennsylvania) .... *

Fehr, T. (Lower Saucon Township, Northampton County, Pennsylvania) 1843

Fisher, Daniel (South Bend, Indiana) 1853

Flanagan, George (Mill Hall, Clinton County, Pennsylvania) .... c. 1850

Frances, ——— (Indiana) .... *

Franz, Michael (Miami County, Ohio) 1839

Frazie, J. (Casey, Illinois) 1860

French, B. (Clinton, Ohio) 1840

Gabriel, Henry (Allentown, Pennsylvania) .. *

Gebhart, J. (Pennsylvania) .... *

Gilbert, Samuel (Trappe, Montgomery County, Pennsylvania) .... *

Gilchrist, Hugh (Franklin County, Indiana; later, Iowa) 1869

Gilmore, Gabriel (Union County, Indiana) 1826

Gilmore, Joseph, Thomas, and William (Union County, Indiana) 1826

Goebell, Henry (possibly Bucks County, Pennsylvania) .... *

Goodman, John S. (Black Creek, Luzerne County, Pennsylvania) 1830

Graham, Samuel (Newcastle, Indiana) 1848

Graves, David Isaac (Ohio) 1836

Greenewald, J. W. (Lobachsville, Berks County, Pennsylvania) .... *

Grimm, Peter (Loudonville, Ohio) 1857

Haag, J. (Emmaus, Pennsylvania) .... *

Harting, Peter (Vera Cruz, Lancaster County, Pennsylvania) .... *

Hartman, John (Ohio) .. 1851

Hartman, Peter (Lafayette, Ohio) 1843

Hausman, Benjamin (Allentown, Pennsylvania) 1836

Hausman, Ephraim (Trexlertown, Lehigh County, Pennsylvania) 1850
Hausman, Jacob, Jr. (Lobachsville, Friedensburg, Rockland, Berks County, Pennsylvania) 1842
Hausman, Solomon (Trexlertown, Lehigh County, Pennsylvania) 1848
Hausman, Tilghman R. (Lobachsville, Berks County, Pennsylvania) . . . . *
Heilbronn, G. (Lancaster, Ohio) 1850
Hesse, L. (Ohio) 1847
Hicks, William (Madison County, Indiana) 1850
Hipp, S. (Mount Joy, Lancaster County, Pennsylvania) . . . . *
Hogeland, J. S. and Son (Lafayette, Indiana) . . 1856
Huber, John and Damus (Dearborn County, Indiana) 1840–1850
Hull, Lewis (New Holland, Lancaster County, Pennsylvania) 1831

Inger, J. Fritz (Allentown, Pennsylvania) 1845

Jackson, John Hamilton (Pennsylvania) 1840

Kachel, John (Robeson Township, Berks County, Pennsylvania) . . . . *
Kappel, Gottfried (Ohio) 1871
Kauffman (probably Bucks or Montgomery County, Pennsylvania) . . . . *
Kean, F. A. (Vigo County, Indiana) 1850
Keener, Henry (Womelsdorf, Berks County, Pennsylvania) . . . . *
Kepner, Isaac (Pottstown, Pennsylvania) 1843
Klar, Francis Joseph (Reading, Pennsylvania) 1843
Klein, John (Noblesville, Hamilton County, Indiana) 1861
Klinger, Absalom (Bethel, Berks County, Pennsylvania) . . . . *
Kuder, Solomon (Trexlertown, Lehigh County, Pennsylvania) . . . . *
Kuder, William (Solomon's son) (Norristown, Pennsylvania) . . . . *

La Tourette, John (Fountain County, Indiana) 1826
La Tourette, Sarah and Henry (Fountain County, Indiana) . . . . *
Lashel,——— (Ohio) . . . 1850
Le Bar, Pamela (North Hampton County, Pennsylvania) 1843
Leidig, P. (probably Lebanon County, Pennsylvania) . . . . *
Leisy, Peter (Cocalico Township, Lancaster County, Pennsylvania) . . . . *
Lichty, B. (Bristol, Ohio) 1854
Linderman,——— (Union Township, Berks County, Pennsylvania) *
Lomiller, William (Muncy, Pennsylvania) . . . . c. 1840
Lorenz, Peter (Germantown, Pennsylvania) . . 1846

Loren (t) z, Peter (Wayne County, Indiana) 1838

McKinney, James (Brookville, Indiana) 1813

March, J. H. (Salona, Clinton County, Pennsylvania) 1837–1850

Marsteller, Thomas (Lower Saucon Township, Northampton County, Pennsylvania) .... *

Meily, Charles S. (Mansfield, Wayne County, Ohio) 1837

Mellinger and Sons, John (Seneca County, Pennsylvania) .... *

Metz, L. (Montgomery County, Pennsylvania) .... *

Metzger, F. (Pennsylvania) .... *

Miller, Gabriel (Pennsylvania) 1820

Miller, Robert (Salem, Indiana) 1857–1858

Miller, Tobias (Lagrange County, Indiana) 1867

Milroy (Mifflin County, Pennsylvania) 1851

Morrey,——— (Ohio) .. *

Muir, John (Greencastle, Indiana) 1843

Muir, Robert, Thomas, and William (Indiana) .... *

Mundwiler, Samuel (Hopewell Township, Ohio) 1848

Musselman, S. B. (Hilltown and Milford, Bucks County, Pennsylvania) 1841

Myers, D. L. (Bethel Township, Pennsylvania) 1849

Ney, William (Myerstown, Lebanon County, Pennsylvania) .... *

Nichlas, G. (Chambersburg, Pennsylvania) .. 1840, 1843

Oberly, Henry (Womelsdorf, Berks County, Pennsylvania) .... *

Orms,——— (Malago, Ohio) .... *

Packer, J. (Pennsylvania) 1839

Peters, R. (Heidelberg Township, Lehigh County, Pennsylvania) .... *

Petry, H. (Canton, (Ohio) 1842

Randel, Martha (Chardon, Ohio) 1848

Rassweiler, Ph. (Orwigsburg, Schuylkill County, Pennsylvania) 1844

Rausher, Gabriel (Ohio) 1840, 1853

Renner, P. (probably Lebanon County, Pennsylvania) .... *

Rich, John (Clinton County, Pennsylvania) 1854

Risser, L. D. (Pennsylvania) .... *

Royer, John (New Holland, Lancaster County, Pennsylvania) .... *

Schlabach, Lydia (Lancaster County, Pennsylvania) .... *

Schnee, Joseph (Freeburg, Pennsylvania) 1836

Schnee, William (Freeburg, Pennsylvania) 1838

Schroutz (Dearborn County, Indiana) ..... *
Schultz, J. N. (Mercersburg, Pennsylvania) .. 1850
Schum, Philip, Son and Company (Lancaster, Pennsylvania) .. 1856–1880
Schwartz, M. (Manheim, Lancaster County, Pennsylvania) .... *
Sehr, T. (Lower Saucon Township, Northampton County, Pennsylvania) 1840
Seibert, John (Lowhill Township, Lehigh County, Pennsylvania) 1846
Seibert, Peter (Easton, Pennsylvania) .... c. 1840
Shalk, Jacob (probably Bucks County, Pennsylvania) .... *
Sherman, Jacob (Attica County, Ohio) 1839
Shive, M. (New Britain Township, Bucks County, Pennsylvania) .... *
Shreffler, Henry (Salona, Clinton County, Pennsylvania) 1851
Shreffler, Samuel (Salona, Clinton County, Pennsylvania) .... *
Simpson, George (Switzerland County, Indiana) 1840
Smith, John (Millerstown, now Annville, Lebanon County, Pennsylvania) .... *
Snyder, Daniel (Hanover Township, Montgomery County, Pennsylvania) 1838
Speck, Johan (Pennsylvania) 1725
Stager, H. F. (Mount Joy, Lancaster County, Pennsylvania) .... *
Staudt, Simon (Miami County, Ohio) 1845
Steier, W. (Hanover Township, Montgomery County, Pennsylvania) 1848
Stich, G. (Newark, Ohio) 1839
Stiff, Jay (Pennsylvania) 1843
Stracke, Barnhardt (Hocking County, Ohio) 1856
Striebig, John (Wayne County, Indiana) 1834–1840
Stringer, Samuel (Carthage, Rush County, Indiana) .... *
Strobel, Lorenz (Ohio) .. 1846
Stroud, William (Cadiz, Ohio) .... c. 1830

Thompson, Ritchie (Brownsville, Indiana) 1834

Umbarger, Michael (Dauphin County, Pennsylvania) 1851

Vanvleck, Jay A. (Ohio) .... *
Vogel,——— (Crawfordsville, Indiana) 1846

Weand, Charles (Trexlertown, Lehigh County, Pennsylvania) .... *
Weber, R. (Emmaus, Pennsylvania) .... *

Wiand, C. (Allentown, Pennsylvania) 1854
Wiand, C. (Lehigh County, Pennsylvania) 1843
Wieand, J. D. (Allentown, Pennsylvania) .... *
Williams, H. R. (Mill Hall, Clinton County, Pennsylvania) 1850
Wilson, Henry (Hendricks County, Indiana) 1850
Wingert, H. (Landisburg, Perry County, Pennsylvania) 1838
Wissler, John (later, Whisler) (Milton, Indiana) 1826
Witmer, J. (Lancaster County, Pennsylvania) 1838
Wolf, Adam (Ohio) 1849

Yearous, F. (Ashland County, Ohio) 1853
Young, Matthew (Canton, Indiana) .... *

Zelner, A. (Plumstead Township, Bucks County, Pennsylvania) 1840

M. K. (Springfield Township, Bucks County, Pennsylvania) .... *
P. H. L. M. T. (Bethel, Pennsylvania) 1839
S. S. J. and T. (probably Montgomery County, Pennsylvania) 1837

COVERLET MAKERS NOT KNOWN TO BE FROM NEW ENGLAND, OHIO, PENNSYLVANIA or INDIANA

(Asterisk denotes no date known.)

Adolf, George 1857
Alexander, F. M. 1848
Allabach, Philip (Michigan) .... *

Beil, B. 1846
Biesecker, J., Jr. 1852
Bivenouer, M. 1842
Brick, Zena 1833
Brosey, J., and Brand, D. 1838
Brosey, W., and Brubker, A. 1847
Burns, Martin (West Virginia) 1851

Campbell, Daniel (Bridgeport, West Virginia) ... 1839
Conger, J. .... *
Cook, Harvey (West Virginia) 1851
Coulter, George (West Virginia) 1851

Devarmon, Abraham (Lexington, Kentucky) 1825

Hall, ______ 1869
Hamilton, John (Lanark, Illinois) 1850
Harch, J., and Kump, André .... *
Harper, William (Bridgeport, West Virginia) ... 1839
Hart, J. 1851
Hecht, Abslam (Maryland) 1849
Hohulin, Gottlich 1861
Hoke, M. 1842
Housman, ______ 1839–1845
Hull, Mathias .... *

Ingham, J. and D. 1847

Landes, John	1756
Lutz, J. (Hempfield Township, ———)	1850–1856
MacKeon, Abraham B.	1841
Marr, John	*
Marsh, J.	1840
Mench, E.	1840
Myer, P.	1841
Noll, William and John	1872
Nurre, Joseph	1839
Overholt, Henry O.	1842
Pearsen, J. (Chippeway, ———)	*
Pierce, Merrily	1834
Pompey, L. W.	1831
Richardson, ———	1835
Sayles, J. M. (Knox County, Illinois)	1851
Sheafer, Franklin D.	1849
Sheaffer, Isaac (New Berlin)	1845
Snider, Samuel	1843
Snyder, Jacob	*
Snyder, John	*
Stephenson, D. (Fairfield, Iowa)	1849
Trappe, Samuel J.	1856
Van Doren, ——— (Oakland County, Michigan)	1846
Varick, ———	1835
Warick, J.	1849
Weaver, J. G.	1837
Weddel, Liza Jane (Floyd, Virginia)	1819
Wiand, David	1837
Williams, May (Falmouth, Kentucky)	1817
Yardy, C. (Lampeter Square, ———)	1833
J. K. M. (no further information)	*
Jo K M PAW	1837

If you own a coverlet that has a maker's name and it is not listed here, you may still discover the age and history of the coverlet. Copy the name and photograph your coverlet (a Polaroid will do). Send this information to the Colonial Coverlet Guild (see list of collectors' groups).

Samplers

A sampler is exactly what the name suggests, a sample of the skills of the maker. Samplers have been made for hundreds of years. They reached the height of their popularity during the seventeenth and eighteenth centuries in Europe, but the best American samplers date from 1790 to 1840.

One of the earliest dated samplers known that has the date as part of the design was made in 1630 in England. It was made on linen with silk thread stitches. The earliest-known American sampler was made by Lora Standish, the daughter of Miles Standish. American samplers of the seventeenth century are very scarce, and only five samplers dating before 1700 are known to be in collections today.

THE FINEST AMERICAN SAMPLERS WERE MADE FROM 1790 TO 1840. Once again, the best way to date your antique is to LOOK FOR THE NAME AND DATE. They were often worked into the design. There seems to be no reason to doubt that the samplers were usually the work of young girls.

EARLY SAMPLERS WERE NARROW (ranging from eight to nine inches in width) because the looms that made homespun were not very wide. LATER SAMPLERS WERE WIDER because the looms were larger. BY THE LATE EIGHTEENTH AND EARLY NINETEENTH CENTURY THE SAMPLER WAS WIDER THAN IT WAS HIGH, and that is the shape that is familiar to most of us.

Most of the early samplers were made from materials found at home. Linen, coarse linen, muslin, or canvas was often used. The loosely woven material was easier to embroider. EIGHTEENTH-CENTURY SAMPLERS WERE USUALLY MADE WITH WOOL THREAD. SILK THREAD WAS USED AFTER THE REVOLUTION.

Canvas worked in needlepoint was a favorite type of handcraft for the Victorian housewife. The "do-it-yourself" sampler came with the center design already worked. The Victorian housewife completed the background and added the date. The sampler no longer was the work of a young girl who wanted to display her talents.

The fabric, thread, and of course the design will all help to determine the age of a sampler. Early samplers consisted of the alphabet, examples of types of stitching, perhaps a worthy motto, and the maker's name and date. ALPHABET DESIGNS WERE USED AFTER 1720. MOURNING PICTURES, MEMORIAL PATTERNS, AND MAPS EMBROIDERED ON LINEN WERE POPULAR IN THE EARLY 1800'S. NINETEENTH-CENTURY SAMPLERS PICTURED MILITARY CAMPAIGNS, HISTORICAL EVENTS, HOBBIES, FAMILY PORTRAITS, AND SIMPLE DESIGNS. THE CROSS-STITCH SAMPLERS WERE MADE FROM THE EARLY 1800'S.

SOME CLUE TO THE AREA WHERE THE SAMPLER WAS MADE IS GIVEN BY THE DESIGN. After 1825 the pictured architecture of the area sometimes shows actual buildings with the crow-step gables of the Dutch houses that were known only in early New York. Ships usually appeared on New England works, while sugarcane appeared on southern samplers. Eighteenth-century samplers often had the name of the school where the girl worked, and this helps in tracing the origin of the work.

Our Instant Expert tips regarding samplers are: LONG, NARROW SAMPLERS ARE EARLIER THAN SQUARE OR WIDE ONES. EARLY SAMPLERS FIRST SHOWED STITCHING, THEN THE ALPHABET, THEN NUMERALS, THEN DECORATIVE BORDERS, AND FINALLY PICTORIAL DECORATION AND MOTTOES. Therefore, a sampler with all letters is probably earlier than one that includes flowers in the design.

Paisley shawls

Each year thousands of housewives clean their attics and basements and "rediscover" the paisley shawl that grandmother packed away many years ago. Each year hundreds of these housewives pack the same paisley shawl back into the same box, wondering what can be done

Little girls learned how to sew at an early age in 1828. This cross-stitch sampler was made by Elizabeth Jane Humer. She pictured the New York City Hall. (New-York Historical Society, New York City)

The early paisley shawl was hand embroidered, as can be seen in this enlarged section of the design. The reverse of this shawl is a mass of jumbled threads, with no design. (Western Reserve Historical Society, Cleveland, Ohio)

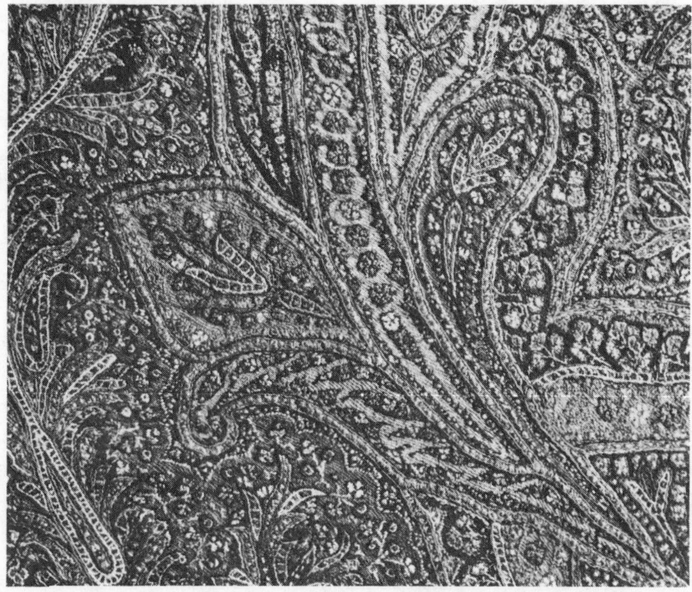

The paisley type shawl was popular for many years. This example was made after 1850. It was a deep border and a black center. (Smithsonian Institution, Washington, D.C.)

with it. What is it worth? Little thought, if any, is ever given to the shawl itself, to its muted colors or popular pattern. Dresses of high fashion today are of fabrics printed to resemble the paisley shawl, yet the shawl itself is ignored and forgotten. If you own one of the early Indian shawls, you have a valuable antique, but if you have one of Victorian vintage you are just saving a dinner for the moths who thrive on the wool of these fabrics.

Grandmother may have owned several types of shawls. If she was extremely wealthy, she may have owned an early Indian patchwork shawl. These shawls will not fold flat, and are rough on the reverse side.

We must go back to India and Kashmir and the year 1420 to understand the origin of the paisley shawl. Shawl, or "shal," was the Persian word for a special woven fabric. Early Indian or Kashmiri shawls were not woven; instead, many small embroidered pieces were sewn together like a crazy quilt.

These shawls can easily be identified because the stitches show clearly on the reverse side. An embroidered shawl took many years to make. A century later the Indians developed a method of sewing thread across the threads of a loom. These shawls were made by two weavers over a period of several years, and cost hundreds of dollars.

Chances are that you are not lucky enough to own one of these early Indian shawls. Your shawl is the result of a war and a desire to make money.

The early shawls were merely the inspiration for the work done at Paisley, Scotland. The Indian shawl traveled from the Orient to Egypt, where it was seen by French soldiers, and purchased as a gift. Its popularity soon spread to England and the United States. The astute businessmen of Paisley realized that they could sell a similar shawl, and went to work copying the Oriental patterns.

Paisley was a town that had long been interested in weaving. The weavers there had been making cotton and silk, homespun, and woolens in striped or checked designs. There were sixty-six weavers working in Paisley as early as 1695, and in 1820 there were seven thousand. They had the looms, the workers, and the demand for Oriental shawls. All that was needed was a way to produce a woven shawl that looked like the hand-sewn shawl of Kashmir.

The way was found in 1808. Silk and wool thread was made in France and sent to Scotland. The dyeing took a very skilled man, because the center of each strand was dyed a color different from that of the ends. A design was sketched, put on paper, and transferred to the looms with exacting accuracy. It took from two to three weeks to set up a loom, and a single error could ruin months of work. There were as many as eight colors used. Because the weaving was done with the material face down, the weaver could not tell how the design looked while it was on the loom.

The town of Paisley continued to prosper, and the weavers copied the Oriental designs, not knowing or caring that the Orientals were copying the European designs. In Kashmir, by 1850, French agents were "improving" their patterns. Instead of the simple primary colors used by the Indians, they introduced magenta and other French colors, rococco designs and altered forms. By 1860 they even convinced the Indians to trim the back of the shawl to make it seem reversible.

A clever Armenian named Khwaja Yusuf decided in 1803 that he could profit from a new type of shawl. He had a seamstress make a needlework shawl that cost about one-third of the loomed Kashmir shawl, a product that could enter England without the 26 percent duty. These shawls were made until 1850, but the quality deteriorated, and the latter pieces were extremely poor.

Most of the odd characters that are a part of the design on the shawl had a meaning. The pine cone represented fertility and abundance. (The pine was originally a palm tree, but the English did not recognize the palm, and used their more familiar pine.) Other motiffs were fantastic plants and birds. Some of the more aggressive salesmen of nineteenth-century England, recognizing the possibilities, promoted the mysterious, and many new and hidden meanings were claimed for the Oriental symbolism of the shawl.

The embroidered shawl came from India, and the loomed and embroidered shawl from Persia, but from Scotland came the mixture of Oriental designs plus European salesmanship that produced the design we now know as paisley. Every well-dressed woman used a shawl in cool weather. Brides were married wearing a shawl. Every girl knew the graceful look of a softly folded shawl over the full-skirted dress. The city of Paisley prospered, and its product was shipped throughout the world.

Queen Victoria was "kirked" in a shawl after her wedding to Albert. The well-dressed woman had a white or scarlet-centered shawl for summer wear and a filled-over shawl for cold weather. In 1842 the queen bought seventeen shawls, one for the christening of the Prince of Wales.

When dress styles changed in 1870, the shawl was unattractive over the new dresses, and the paisley became another victim of the Franco-Prussian War. Added victims were the weavers of Paisley, who starved to death in the famine of 1877 to 1879. Their sensitive hands, attuned to the loom, were too fine for any other form of work. The town went bankrupt.

THE EMBROIDERED PIECED INDIAN TYPE OF SHAWL IS THE OLDEST, AND WAS MADE BEFORE THE NINETEENTH CENTURY. THE WOVEN AND EMBROIDERED INDIAN OR PERSIAN SHAWLS WERE MADE ABOUT 1808. THE FIRST WOVEN PAISLEY SHAWL WAS MADE ABOUT 1820. IT WAS NOT REVERSIBLE. The thread was dyed before it was woven on the early shawls.

ABOUT 1825 THE SHAWL HAD A BORDER WITH A PLAIN CENTER, USUALLY WHITE, RED, OR BLACK. FRENCH DESIGNS AND COLORS WERE USED BY 1840, AND THE EMPTY MIDDLE WAS FILLED WITH AN OVERALL PATTERN. The back-to-back shawl was also made at this time. There were three sizes of shawls in the eighteenth century: 12′ × 5′, 8′ × 5′, or 6′ × 2′. If your shawl seems to have the borders reversed, you need not be concerned. This was really two shawls woven together back to back. Unfortunately, it was twice as heavy as the early shawls. THE REVERSIBLE SHAWL WAS MADE IN 1865, and sold for about 27 shillings ($9.72). The same type of shawl cost about one pound ($4.80) by 1870, and a cotton copy cost a few shillings ($1.08). The paisley shawl that was the mysterious and expensive shawl of the wealthy had become the cheap and gaudy apparel of the poorer classes. IT IS ONLY SINCE 1870 THAT THE DESIGN WAS PRINTED AFTER THE FABRIC WAS MADE.

Broché

Broché, or brochet, is a type of paisley shawl. It has an oval of a contrasting color woven as the center design. The name is said to come from an Indian word meaning "gift of flowers." The entire shawl, except for the solid-colored center, is covered with stylized flowers. These shawls were popular about 1850.

There is another meaning for the word "broché." It refers to any piece of fabric woven with a raised figure. The fabric is usually silk. This type of weaving has been known for hundreds of years, but the broché shawl was not popular until the mid-nineteenth century.

Deerfield blue embroidery

Deerfield, Massachusetts, was settled in 1670. The early settlers did many types of needlework, but blue-and-white crewel embroidery was the most popular during the eighteenth century. A group of interested women rediscovered the blue-and-

Early crewel embroidery at Deerfield, Massachusetts, inspired the Victorian revival of "Deerfield blue embroidery." This spread was made in eighteenth-century Connecticut. The design is worked in wool in three shades of indigo. (Heritage Foundation, Deerfield, Massachusetts)

white crewel embroidery about 1896. The Blue and White Society of Deerfield was organized, and its members made copies of the early American embroidery.

Crewel

Crewel, or crewelwork, is an embroidered fabric. Colored yarn was sewn in designs on a piece of natural-colored linen. The designs were usually of an Oriental type, and pictured imaginary flowers and birds.

Crewel was made in India and sent to all parts of the world. Crewel was used for draperies, to cover chairs, or as bed hangings.

Most fabrics were expensive and scarce in the American colonies, and many women made their own crewel embroidery. To conserve time and the scarce colored yarn, MOST AMERICAN HOUSEWIVES MADE WIDELY SPACED DESIGNS THAT USED LESS THREAD. Many New England pieces were embroidered in the "economy" stitch, which exposed the maximum amount of thread on the top surface, and consequently conserved the thread.

Turkey work

Turkey work was needlework on canvas made to resemble popular and expensive Oriental rugs. The turkey work was frequently used to cover chairs or as table covers. It reached the height of its popularity in the seventeenth century.

Stump work

Stump work is a form of embroidery. It was popular in England and the colonies from the seventeenth century. The embroidery was padded, and the stitches appeared to be raised. Most of today's creative sewers do not do stump-work embroidery.

Needle painting

Needle painting is a special type of art. A picture was made with a sewn stitch of colored silk thread. The stitches were placed in all directions, but the stitch texture and color variations made the picture. NEEDLE PAINTINGS WERE MADE AS EARLY AS THE FIFTEENTH CENTURY.

Stump work was a popular seventeenth-century needlework style. (Below) This elaborate sewing casket is covered with fine English needlework on a white satin background. (Art Institute of Chicago, Chicago, Illinois)

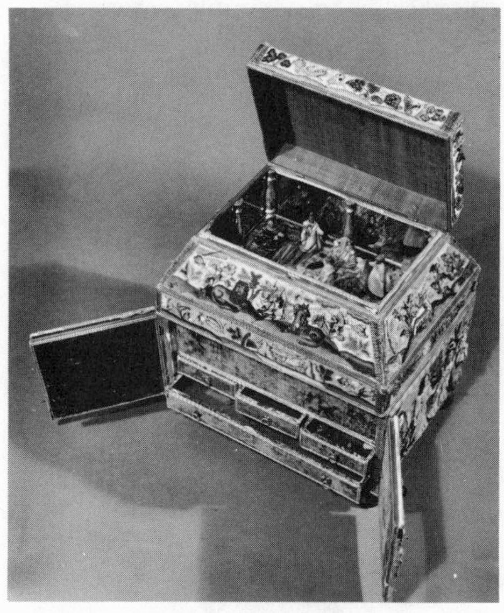

Crosley mosaic

The Crosley mosaic resembles a needlepoint picture. STARTING IN THE 1840's THE CROSLEY MOSAIC WAS MADE IN ENGLAND FOR ABOUT TEN YEARS. The Crosley method was to make pictures from yarn. The yarn was glued to a piece of canvas in such a manner that it resembled needlepoint work. The yarn was bunched together and sliced in the same manner as a jelly roll. The slices were placed flat to make the picture. It took many slices to make each picture.

Battenburg

Battenburg work is also called Belgian lace, Bohemian lace, and Astrid lace. IT WAS USED FOR TRIM ON DRESSES, CURTAINS, AND LINENS IN THE LATE 1890's.

Battenburg work can be easily identified. A tapelike braid outlined the design. Fancy openwork filled the spaces inside the design. It was made by hand and by machine.

Stevengraphs

THE STEVENGRAPH IS A WOVEN PICTURE MADE LIKE A FANCY RIBBON. IT WAS

MARKED "WOVEN IN SILK BY THOMAS STEVENS." The silk pictures showing the Crystal Palace were sold in quantity in 1862 and at the Philadelphia Centennial in 1876. They were made in Coventry, England.

Stevengraphs are eagerly collected today.

Rugs

Straw was one of the earliest forms of floor covering. The first true carpet was seen in Babylonian art about 700 B.C. It is believed that carpets might have been made at an earlier date. The Oriental rug was used in ancient Greece and Rome, but wear

The Stevengraph is a small ribbon of woven silk that had a picture in the weave. "The Lady Godiva Procession" and "The First Over" are examples of this Victorian ribbon. (Stevengraph Collectors Society, New York)

plus time has destroyed them. Some examples of rugs from the 1400's still exist.

Deerskin rugs and rush mats were the earliest types of floor coverings used in the American colonies.

THE EARLIEST RUGS IN AMERICA WERE TONGUE RUGS. They were made with small tongue-shaped pieces of cloth overlapped and sewn to a backing.

BUTTON RUGS WERE MADE A FEW YEARS LATER. They were canvas-backed homemade rugs that resembled tongue rugs but had round pieces of cloth. The background material of the tongue rug is completely covered by the overlapping tongues. The background of the button rug shows between the circles of material that were stitched to the backing. Sometimes the circles were made from braided material, and the canvas area between the circles was covered by sewn wool. The button rug was at the height of fashion during the 1820's. A FEW LATE EXAMPLES WERE MADE FROM BLUE AND GRAY PIECES CUT FROM OLD UNIFORMS IN THE 1870's.

THE BRAIDED RUG WAS POPULAR BETWEEN THE BUTTON RUG OF THE 1820's AND THE HOOKED RUG OF THE 1850's. The braided rug was made from braided strips of worn fabric. The braids were sewn together, round and round, until a large circular rug was made. Of course, it is still made today.

Hooked rugs were made in America by 1700, but reached the height of their popularity from 1850 to 1870, when the cheap factory-made rugs appeared. The artistic housewife was able to draw her own patterns, but those less endowed with talent could buy a pattern from Edward Frost. He sold thousands of patterns, and his factory was still working in the early 1900's.

EMBROIDERED RUGS WERE MADE BY MANY OF THE "WELL-TO-DO" AMERICAN WOMEN OF THE EARLY NINETEENTH CENTURY. Woolen yarn was

The embroidered wool-on-wool rug was rare even when in style in the nineteenth century. This American example was made early in that century. (Art Institute of Chicago, Chicago, Illinois)

Hooked rugs were popular in America about 1850. The patterns were many, and featured flowers, animals, or geometric designs. (Henry Ford Museum, Dearborn, Michigan)

The overlapping petal design was a popular type of early American rug. This carpet of wool was made by Elizabeth Stowell about 1790 (Metropolitan Museum of Art; gift of Mrs. Alexander Cummins, 1940). The embroidered carpet pictured flowers, animals, or familiar scenes.

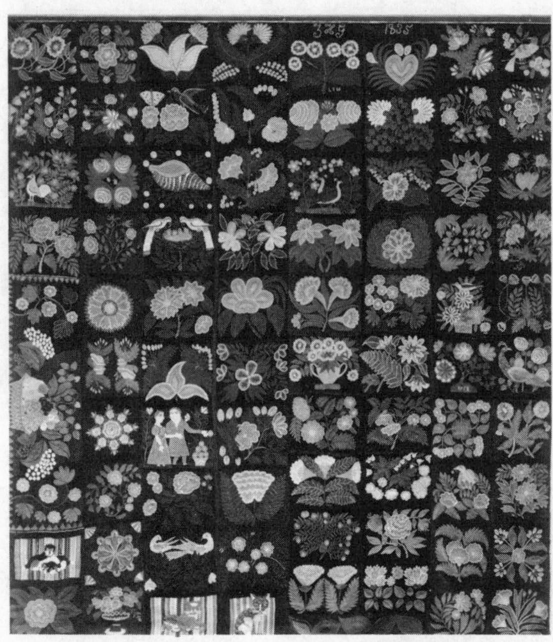

This Vermont-made carpet was embroidered in colored yarn on a woolen fabric about 1832–1835. (Metropolitan Museum of Art; gift of Katharine Keyes, 1938, in memory of her father, Homer Eaton Keyes)

stitched on a heavy material, with the stitching covering the entire surface of the rug. Early embroidered rugs are very rare. A few modern embroidered rugs are being made.

CROCHETED RUGS WERE MADE ABOUT THE MIDDLE OF THE NINETEENTH CENTURY. They were made by crocheting a single stitch of rags with a giant wooden crochet hook. The rug was round, and if it did not lie flat after it was washed, it was starched and flattened to the floor.

Carpets and other floor coverings

Carpets were first made in the United States in 1791. The first carpet factory made finger-tufted rugs by W. P. Sprague in Philadelphia. Oriental rugs were also used in the eighteenth-century home and, of course, afterward. An Oriental rug usually means any of the hand-knotted rugs made in southeastern Europe, Turkey, North Africa, Iran, Pakistan, India, and China. The elaborate designs had symbolic meanings, but most of them were just geometric in design.

The floor did not have to be covered with a rug or carpet, and was often painted in the informal homes of the early 1800's. There were spattered floors as well as floors that were painted with stencil de-

A stenciled sailcloth floor covering of the type used in nineteenth-century America was copied for this room in the General Salem Towne House. Very few of the old painted floor cloths are still to be seen. (Old Sturbridge Village, Sturbridge, Mass.)

signs. A wide border design was painted near the edges, and a smaller, overall pattern was made in the center.

Painted floor cloths were used in England by 1680, and they are shown in several paintings of the period. About ten coats of paint were brushed onto sailcloth and decorated with designs made to imitate marble flooring or just attractive geometric patterns. These floor cloths were used in middle-class homes by 1720. Carpets were used about 1750.

The word "linoleum" refers to various types of coverings. The early floor cloths were covered with canvas and painted with many layers of paint. The covers were then printed with a pattern, and varnished. These were the earliest floor covers of the colonies, and were imported from England.

True linoleum was made by rolling cork dust, wood dust, and coloring on a canvas. The first floor-cloth patents were issued in England in 1636.

Nathan Smith started a factory in Knightsbridge, England, in 1754. He made a floor cloth from resin, pitch, beeswax, linseed oil, and Spanish brown. This was pressed into a canvas.

Early floor cloths were expensive, but in 1844 a new product was developed by Elijah Gallowy, who used rubber and cork dust. The rubber was costly, but in 1860 Frederick Walton invented a way to use oil in place of rubber. He was the first one to make an inexpensive linoleum.

Needlework: Bibliography

Colonial Coverlet Guild. *Heirlooms from Old Looms.* Chicago: Donnelley, 1955.

A privately printed book, filled with photographs of quilts and a list of quilt makers.

Hall, Carrie A., and Rose G. Kretsinger. *The Romance of the Patchwork Quilt in America.* New York: Bonanza Books, 1935.

The history of quilts, pictures of quilts and quilting designs are all included in this book.

Hall, Eliza Calvert. *A Book of Hand Woven Coverlets.* Rutland, Vermont: Tuttle, 1966.

This reprint of a 1912 book is well illustrated with coverlet pictures. General bibliography.

Harbeson, Georgiana Brown. *American Needlework.* New York: Bonanza Books, 1938.

A fact-filled, well-illustrated history of needlework in America before 1900.

Keyser, Mrs. C. Naaman. *Pennsylvania German Coverlets.* Privately printed Home Craft Course, Plymouth Meeting, Pennsylvania, 1947.

Pamphlet with photographs of coverlet weaves and list of makers.

Lane, Rose Wilder. *Woman's Day Book of American Needlework.* New York: Simon and Schuster, 1963.

Beautiful, large color-illustrated book containing the history of needlework from colonial times to the present, with instructions for all types of needlework.

Little, Nina Fletcher. *Floor Coverings in New England Before 1850.* Sturbridge, Massachusetts: Old Sturbridge Village, 1967.

This paperback pamphlet gives hard to find history of the types of rugs and other floor coverings used in American homes before 1850. It is of particular value for the collector who is restoring a home.

Ries, Estelle H. *American Rugs.* Cleveland: World, 1950.

A small book with much information and many color pictures of rugs.

Robertson, Elizabeth Wells. *American Quilts.* New York: Studio Publications, 1948.

A general history of quilts, illustrated, with a list of quilt patterns and bibliography included.

Shelburne Museum. *Pieced Work and Appliqué Quilts.* Shelburne, Vermont: Shelburne Museum, 1957.

A pamphlet listing, describing, and illustrating over 100 quilts from the museum collection.

Sprake, Austin and Michael Darby. *Stevengraphs.* London, England, 1968.

This is an illustrated list of known Stevengraphs including coded information on size, colors and rarity.

11

Jewelry

Collectors of antique jewelry prior to the Second World War had a heyday, as most of the stores that sold new jewelry and every pawnbroker had a box of old "scrap" jewelry waiting to be melted down for the gold content. Some of the ridiculous collectors that wanted to purchase one of the old scrap pieces of jewelry merely paid the value of the scrap metal, and the stones were a bonus. Old jewelry often was traded in as a partial payment for new, modern pieces or for much-needed cash. Times have changed, and if the affluent American does have to pawn Grandma's ring, he redeems it before long. Antique-styled rings and pins are so fashionable that many costume jewelry makers are copying them in inexpensive versions, and the fancier jewelry stores are selling solid-gold replicas of the nineteenth-century-designed jewelry. It is difficult for a beginner to tell an authentic old piece from a good copy, but there are still hints that might help the collector.

Try to select a trustworthy source when buying old jewelry. ANY JEWELRY DEALER IS ABLE TO MAKE A FEW SIMPLE TESTS AND DETERMINE THE GOLD CONTENT AND WORTH OF A GOLD PIN, BASED ON ITS ACTUAL MELT-DOWN VALUE AS WELL AS ITS ARTISTIC WORTH. Gemstones can be identified and appraised by any good jewelry store. IF YOU HAVE AN OLD PIECE OF JEWELRY THAT LOOKS VALUABLE TAKE IT TO AN EXPERT FOR AN APPRAISAL.

There are a few things that should be done before you go to an expert. Examine the piece of gold or silver jewelry for a mark such as "sterling," "18K," or "14K." Pieces marked "gold filled" are late and are not made of solid gold. Those that are unmarked must be tested by an expert with acid.

ODD FACTS ABOUT JEWELRY

Filigree

Silver filigree work has been known since ancient Egypt. The silver filigree wire was made by drawing a wire through successively smaller holes until a very thin wire was formed. The wire was coiled, bent, and soldered into designs with small silver balls. The filigree found today may be old or new, but the technique has remained the same.

Pinchbeck

In 1732, Christopher Pinchbeck, an English watchmaker, developed an alloy of copper and zinc that looked like gold. His new metal was used to make imitation gold jewelry and watchcases in England. The secret of "pinchbeck" died with him, but his name continued to be part of the English language. Many types of imitation gold metals are referred to as "pinchbeck."

Platinum

PLATINUM WAS NOT USED FOR JEWELRY UNTIL AFTER 1890. It did not become popular until the early twentieth century. Most platinum jewelry is marked.

STONES YOU CAN IDENTIFY

Amber

Amber comes in many colors, ranging from a cloudy light yellow that was popular for beads to a clear brownish-red that has been the most desirable. MIX FOUR TEASPOONS OF SALT IN AN EIGHT-OUNCE GLASS OF WATER. AMBER WILL FLOAT IN THIS MIXTURE, and the imitation amber-colored stones will sink. Amber beads were popular in the 1880's, and are still in fashion.

Agate

Moss agate is a stone that looks as if it has fossilized moss inside. It was often found in Victorian jewelry, and it was believed that the moss agate protected the wearer from spider bites and thunderstorms. Plain black-and-white agate has often been used in making cameos.

Cameo

A cameo is made from one piece of shell or stone. The artist carves away part of the stone so that the different-colored layers appear. A cameo will usually have an all-white figure against a black background. LOOK CAREFULLY FOR ANY SIGN THAT MIGHT PROVE YOUR CAMEO IS REALLY TWO PIECES OF STONE THAT HAVE BEEN CEMENTED TOGETHER. This is an inferior cameo, and can be detected. Many cameos were made from two- or three-colored layers of stone, and it really is the skill of the artist that determines the value.

Carnelian

The brownish-red stone chalcedony is called "carnelian," and it has often been used for beads. Napoleon always carried a carnelian to protect him in battle. Superstition claimed that if the carnelian failed to protect, it would at least stop the bleeding if it was placed next to an open wound.

Coral

Coral was particularly popular in Victorian times for beads. The color ranges from white to orange-red to deep coral red. THE DARKER THE CORAL, THE BETTER THE QUALITY. Coral is thought to protect babies from danger, and many small necklaces of coral beads were made for children.

Diamonds

Diamonds have not changed through the years, but the methods of cutting have improved, and modern diamonds have more brilliance than the early ones. Early diamonds (after about 1520) were cut in a shape called "rose cut." The European-cut stone was faceted to reflect the light, while the Oriental-cut stone was cut so the greatest size remained. It was not until the eighteenth century that the brilliant cut was developed in France. It doubled the number of facets on the upper part of the stone, and increased the reflection of light and the brilliance.

The "rose cut," or "old mine," diamonds were often used in Victorian jewelry, and it is only in the past century that the "brilliant cut" has been in fashion. "Old mine" diamonds are worth only a fraction of a full-cut stone, and are now mainly used as replacements for lost diamonds in antique jewelry. Jewelers who specialize in antique jewelry and jewelry repair will buy "rose cut" stones, and most jewelers will buy a piece of Victorian jewelry set with old stones.

It has always been said that a diamond can scratch glass, and this has been a good test for the authenticity of the stone. It is true that the diamond will scratch glass, but so will many other clear white stones, such as zircon, quartz, white sapphire, beryl, topaz, and tourmaline. It is often difficult to determine whether the mark made on the glass is a scratch or a powder line left by the scratcher.

Garnets

Garnet jewelry was fashionable before 1850, but it flourished in Victorian times. It went out of style about 1910 and was revived about 1950. Many copies of the old-fashioned garnet jewelry are being made in Europe, but the new pieces are usually not so well made as most of the old. The new stones are lighter in color, and not the deep red that is most desirable. Some of the faceting is poorly done, and a good garnet must have many facets. Most of the garnet jewelry, whether old or new, is made with clusters of small stones set in prong settings. Because most garnet jewelry is set in silver or gold plate, any solid-gold garnet jewelry would be of greater value. Garnets come in many colors, such as yellow, orange, brown, violet, green, pink or red, but the red garnet has been in the greatest demand.

Garnets are said to be lucky for those born in January. It is claimed that they can cure hemorrhages, calm the wearer, or be deadly if shot from a gun like a bullet.

Goldstone

The reddish-brown stone that looks as if it is filled with gold grains is called goldstone. It is an imitation stone first made about 1840 by spilling copper fillings into glass. Many pieces of jewelry were made with this stone. There is also a natural stone, aventurine, called "goldstone," but it is a dull dark green with metallic spots, and is not used for jewelry.

Jet

Jet is a form of coal, and the best has been found in England. The first jet necklaces were made about 1800, using the dark-black coal and hand carving or turning it on a lathe. Jet jewelry was associated with mourning, and became very fashionable after the death of Prince Albert. Jet is a soft stone, much softer than glass; glass beads are much harder to scratch. The best way to clean jet jewelry is to wash it, dry it, then rub it with fresh white bread.

Moonstones

The moonstone was very popular from about 1885 to 1900. It is a colorless, cloudy stone that seems to gleam from within. Carved moonstones were popular during the late Victorian era. It is considered a "lucky" stone.

Rock crystal

There are several meanings for this term, but for jewelry "rock crystal" is literally the crystal rock that has been dug from the earth. It is as clear as glass if it is of good quality. TRUE ROCK CRYSTAL FEELS COLD TO YOUR HANDS EVEN ON A WARM DAY, BUT GLASS WILL FEEL ALMOST ROOM TEMPERATURE.

STYLES AND ODDITIES

Buckles

Shoe buckles set with precious stones were worn by King Charles II of England in 1665, but it was not until the eighteenth century that the style was generally accepted. The shoestring and shoelace came into fashion in 1790, and men never went back to the buckle style, although women have used them at various intervals.

Choker necklace

The "dog collar," or "choker," necklace was first popular from 1885 to 1900. Ribbon or bead necklaces were worn by the average women high on the neck like a dog's collar, with pearl, diamond, and jeweled chokers being favored by the wealthy.

Earrings

EARRINGS FOR PIERCED EARS WERE THE ONLY KIND WORN UNTIL THE 1900'S. CLIPS WERE FIRST PATENTED IN 1934; SCREW BACKS WERE USED ABOUT 1900.

Mourning jewelry

Mourning rings were popular during the late eighteenth and early nineteenth centuries, and these odd rings seem to have been saved by many families. At a funeral a mourner was given a ring with the name, age, and the date the deceased died. The mourning rings were worn for years in memory of the departed. Hair jewelry (rings, brooches, lockets, bracelets, watch chains, earrings, and other jewelry) was made from the hair of the deceased.

Silver Lockets

Heavy oval silver lockets became the rage about 1880, and were preferred to the gold and jeweled types that previously had been in favor. The old lockets had intricate chased or carved designs, and were hung from heavy elaborate silver chains of medium length. THE EASIEST ONES TO IDENTIFY HAVE THE ENGLISH HALL-MARKS. (See Chapter 6, "Silver.")

Silver Scotch stone jewelry

For many years the heavy jewelry that was made in Scotland for use with plaid clothing was ignored in America. Several manufacturers began to make fine copies of this early jewelry about 1960, and today it is much in demand. The large circle pin with a "niello" (black) inset was not only used to fasten a tartan but was also considered a good-luck charm that kept disease and ill fortune away. Most of the Scotch stone jewelry was set with quartz, agate, chalcedony, and Scotch pebbles. Gemstones were never used. The silver was engraved or chased with designs. When a Highlander went into battle, it was traditional for him to wear a fine piece of silver jewelry. If he were killed in battle, the person who found the body and gave it a decent burial was expected to keep the jewelry as payment.

Thimbles

The first thimbles were known in Roman days. It was a nineteenth-century European custom to give the bride a thimble before an engagement ring. Silver, gold, glass, tortoiseshell, jade, enamel, china, or wood examples of eighteenth- and nineteenth-century thimbles can be found today.

Umbrellas

The first American umbrellas were made in pre-Revolutionary days, with wooden frames and acorn-carved handles. The acorn protected the owner from lightning. STEEL FRAMES FOR UMBRELLAS WERE FIRST USED ABOUT 1850.

Jewelry: Bibliography

Bainbridge, Henry Charles. *Peter Carl Fabergé.* London: Batsford, 1949.
This beautiful book tells the history of the life of Fabergé, the famous Russian jeweler, and pictures many of the famous gold and silver pieces made by his factory.

Burgess, Fred. *Antique Jewelry and Trinkets.* New York: Tudor, n.d.
Jewelry from ancient to recent times is discussed; there are a few illustrations.

Flower, Margaret. *Victorian Jewellery.* New Yorker: Duell, Sloan and Pearce, 1951.
This well-illustrated book pictures hundreds of different styles of Victorian jewelry, and explains the styles popular during the era.

Gregorietti, Guido. *Jewelry Through the Ages.* New York: American Heritage Press, 1969.
A beautifully illustrated book with many color pictures of jewelry dating from Egyptian to Art Deco.

Ross, Marvin. *The Art of Karl Fabergé and His Contemporaries.* Norman, Oklahoma: University of Oklahoma Press, 1965.
This is the catalog of the Marjorie Merriweather Post collection of Russian art, and includes many objects by Fabergé and his contemporaries.

12

Prints, Paintings, Pictures to Hang

THERE ARE many reasons to own a picture or a print. Perhaps it is a picture of a clipper ship, a balloon ascension, or an early baseball game. Any picture of an unusual or historic event is the dream of some collector, so if you aren't eager to own it, someone else will be.

Early prints can easily be identified if the maker's name appears, but if no name appears you can judge the picture by its subject matter or beauty. Pictures of flowers (unless they are from the earliest flower catalogs), people doing nothing but looking like people having their picture painted (unless it is a primitive oil painting), and pictures of religious subjects have a disappointingly low value. Pictures of rare breeds of cows, chickens, horses, sporting events, ships, Civil War battle scenes, and other historic pictures are of value even if the maker is mediocre or virtually unknown. Strange types of pictures, early ads for automobiles, lawn mowers, homemade pastel or crayon pictures, and primitive watercolors are of value.

Perhaps the Instant Expert rule should be: IF THE PICTURE OR PRINT HAS A SUBJECT THAT INTERESTS YOU, IT WILL ALSO INTEREST OTHERS. If it is of a subject that you never even thought about, it is probably of even greater interest.

When you see a picture, the natural reaction is to look for the signature even though you cannot tell whether it is a print, photograph, or painting. We have not included oil paintings, but if you find a signed oil it is a relatively simple task to determine the fame of the artist. Most libraries have books listing artists and their works. *Who's Who in American Art* and *Mallett's Index of Artists* will be helpful. Libraries and museums are usually able to aid in the search for the fame of an artist. The book *Art Prices Current* may help you to check the current sale price of other paintings by the same artist.

The numerous forms of pictures printed on paper have names that will help to differentiate the method of printing and drawing. Etchings, engravings, woodcuts, and lithographs are all printed pictures. Many of them originally were printed to depict the happenings of the day. The photograph has replaced the lithograph as a news medium, but the lithograph still remains as an art form and as a collector's delight.

Look at your print to see if a name appears. It is usually at the bottom of the picture in either the right- or left-hand corner. Some are signed on the picture, while others are signed in the white margin below the picture. IF IT SAYS "PUBLISHED ACCORDING TO ACT OF PARLIAMENT," IT IS AN ENGLISH PRINT MADE AFTER 1735. TO MAKE IT EVEN EASIER, SOME ARE MARKED "PUBLISHED BY ACT OF PARLIAMENT 18—" OR "PUBLISHED LONDON BY MR. JOHN DOE 1845." YOU CAN BELIEVE WHAT YOU READ IN MOST CASES. Unless it is a very modern photographic copy or a late reprint of the original, the words mean what they say. It is the result of the first copyright laws published in England. "ENTERED ACCORDING TO ACT OF CONGRESS IN THE YEAR ——" APPEARED ON PRINTS MADE IN THE UNITED STATES AFTER 1802.

Early engravings and lithographs that were copyrighted tell their own story. The first copyright laws were passed by the United States Federal Government in May of 1790. In April of 1802, engravings were listed among the new items eligible for a copyright under the new law.

The district courts were given jurisdiction over all the copyright applications in February of 1819. The laws protecting artists and writers with copyrights were revised in 1831 and 1909. MOST AMERICAN LITHOGRAPHS WERE NOT MARKED WITH THE YEAR AND COPYRIGHT WORDS UNTIL AFTER 1848.

If your print has the notation "Entered according to the act of Congress," you can get some information about it by writing the Register of Copyrights, Library of Congress, Washington, D.C.

The clipper ship "Flying Cloud" is a Currier print that has been reproduced. This is an original.

If it is an American print, the odds are that it is a CURRIER AND IVES lithograph. Mr. Currier and Mr. Ives made more prints than anyone else in America during the nineteenth century, and consequently more of their prints have survived. THEIR PRINTS WERE ALWAYS MARKED WITH THE NAME OF THE FIRM, AND THEY FREQUENTLY INCLUDED THE COMPANY'S ADDRESS. If there is no name on the print, it is either a copy or the print has been trimmed. It is important for a collector to have the original margins on the picture. A trimmed print is of less value, so

"God Bless Our School," a print by Currier and Ives, 1874.

when you are tempted to trim a picture to fit an old frame, just remember that you might be cutting off dollar bills in the future.

The marked Currier and Ives print is the Instant Expert's delight. The restless firm moved from building to building in New York City, and it is possible to get an almost exact date by CHECKING THE ADDRESS:

CURRIER AND IVES PRINTS

NAME	ADDRESS	DATE PICTURE WAS PRINTED
N. Currier's Lith.	1 Wall Street	1835–1836
Currier's Lith.	1 Wall Street	1835–1836
Charles Currier	33 Spruce Street	1845–1846
N. Currier	148 Nassau Street	1836–1838 (questionable)
N. Currier	152 Nassau Street	1848–1871
N. Currier and C. Currier	33 Spruce Street	1847–
N. Currier	169 Broadway	1842–?
N. Currier	2 Spruce Street	1838–1847
Currier and Ives	152 Nassau Street	1857–1872
Currier and Ives	125 Nassau Street	1872–1874
Currier and Ives	123–125 Nassau Street	1875–1894
Currier and Ives	115 Nassau Street	1876–1886
Currier and Ives	108 Fulton Street	1886–1907
Currier and Ives	33 Spruce Street	1866–1907

"View of New York from Brooklyn Heights," a Currier print.

Some pictures of a controversial nature are labeled with an address but no name.

While both Mr. Currier and Mr. Ives worked separately, THE FIRST CURRIER AND IVES PRINT WAS MADE IN 1857.

It is possible to determine whether a Currier and Ives is an original print produced by the company or whether it is a copy. An insurance firm has printed Currier and Ives calendars for many years by using fine reproductions of the print made by a photographic method.

A new copy of the print, when examined under a magnifying glass, will show a series of small dots. THE ORIGINAL PRINT WAS MADE UP OF A SERIES OF SHORT LINES. The copies made by today's fast methods print the black, white, and color at one time. The original print was printed black on white and was hand-colored or partially printed in color and finished by hand. The inaccuracies of hand coloring show on the old prints. (The first chromo lithographs were made in 1858. These "chromos" had a sharper color. Currier and Ives always hand-colored the lithographs, and never used chromos.)

There are several Instant Expert tips that will help to tell the new from the old in Currier and Ives.

MEASURE THE PRINT. Most of the original Currier and Ives prints were made in three sizes: small folio —7.8 inches by 12.8 inches; medium folio—13 inches by 20 inches; large folio—18 inches by 27 inches. Many of the reproductions were made in different sizes. Some prints were made only in the large folio size, but they have been copied in smaller sizes.

EXAMINE THE COLORING. The old hand-applied colors are not hard to tell from the new machine-run colors.

EXAMINE THE PAPER. Compare it with a print that you are sure is old. Many of the reprints are made on modern, thinner paper.

WATCH FOR RESTRIKES. A "restrike" is a new print made from an old engraving or lithograph. Some of the old prints have been made from the old stones. (Lithographs were drawn on a porous stone, then printed.) "Flying Cloud" and "Grand Republic" are two of these restrikes. Two other very fine forgeries should be mentioned. "View of New York from Brooklyn Heights" is a foreign copy. It has a steamboat in the corner with the word "Vanderbilt" misspelled as "Vanderblue." Another copy of "The Celebrated Ship Grapeshot" is good enough to fool all but the true expert who recognizes the difference in the paper.

Black-and-white prints, as well as color Currier and Ives prints, have a value. As a general rule the countryside scenes or the political cartoons are of most interest. The still-lifes, vases of flowers, heads of children, and religious pictures are of less value. The known works of Currier and Ives have been catalogued in many books. (See the bibliography at the end of this chapter.)

Other United States prints

If the name on your colored print isn't Currier and Ives, it could still be a valuable "antique." Many of the lesser-known American printmakers and artists who signed or published pictures that are now collectors' items are listed here:

Ackerman, Emil	Boston, Massachusetts	1863
Ackerman, George W.	New York City	1829–1864*
Ackerman, James	New York City	1845–1859*
Ackerman, Lewis	New York City	1846
Ackerman, Samuel, & Co.	New York City	1829–1848*
Akin, James	Philadelphia, Pennsylvania	1830–1847*
Alkin, M.	Philadelphia, Pennsylvania	1840
Andrews, J.	Boston, Massachusetts	1827
Annin & Smith Engraving Co.	New York City	before 1831
Annin & Smith-Senefelder Lithographic Co.	Boston, Massachusetts	1828–1834
Appleton, George S.	New York City	1853
Armstrong, Charles & Co.	Boston, Massachusetts, and New York City	1872–1876
Armstrong, Thomas	San Francisco, California	1849–1867 (?)
Arnot, D. H.	New York City	1845
Atwill, Joseph F.	New York City	1843–1849*
Atwill & Co.	San Francisco, California	1850
Atwood, J.	Philadelphia, Pennsylvania	c. 1840
Audibert, Louis	New Orleans, Louisiana	no date
Audubon, J. W.	New York City	1840–1860
Autenrieith, C.	New York City	1850
Ayres, Thomas A.	San Francisco, California	1852–1859
Bachelder, John B.	Boston, Massachusetts	1863
Bachman (n), John	New York City, and Jersey City, New Jersey	1849–1863*
Bailey & Noyes	Portland, Maine	1865
Baillie, James S.	New York City	1838–1855*
Baker, Alfred E.	New York City	1833–1843*
Baker, George H.	San Francisco, California	1849
Baker and Godwin	New York City	1864–1872
Balch, Vistus	Utica, Albany, and New York, New York	1830–1844
Ball, W.	New York City	no date
Balmer & Weber	St. Louis, Missouri	c. 1870
Bancroft, A. L. & Company	San Francisco, California	1877
Bancroft, Monson	New York City	1828–1844
Banly, William	New York City	1861
Barker, J. J.	Philadelphia, Pennsylvania	1832
Barnard & Freeman	Nashville, Tennessee	no date
Barnet & Doolittle	New York City	1821–1822
Barrett, R. C.	Boston, Massachusetts	1856

Barry, Charles A.	Boston, Massachusetts	1851–1859
Bartholomew, V.	Boston, Massachusetts	1853
Bartholomew, W. N.	Boston, Massachusetts	no date
Bartlett, C.	New York City	1841
Bassau	New York City	1842
Bateman, Horatio	unknown	1867
Bauer	Louisville, Kentucky	1843–1849
Baum, C.	Philadelphia, Pennsylvania	no date
Bauncou, J.	New York City, and Philadelphia, Pennsylvania	1832
Bayot	unknown	no date
Beard, James Henry	New York City	no date
Beaugureau	Philadelphia, Pennsylvania	1845
Beaulieu, E.	unknown	1856
Becker, O.	St. Louis, Missouri (?)	c. 1875
Belden, J., Jr.	Hartford, Connecticut	no date
Bellows, A. E.	unknown	after 1860
Belony, J.	New York City	no date
Benade, James	Philadelphia, Pennsylvania	1850
Bencke & Scott	New York City	1867–1880
Bender, C. W., & Co.	Philadelphia, Pennsylvania	1844
Benecke, D.	New York City	1853–1855
Beyer, Ed	Richmond, Virginia (lithographed abroad but American scenes)	1857–1858
Biddle, E. C.	Philadelphia, Pennsylvania	1837
Bien, Julius	New York City	1850–1868*
Bigemann, A.	Philadelphia, Pennsylvania	1856
Bigot, Alphonse	Philadelphia, Pennsylvania	1875
Bingham & Dodd	Hartford, Connecticut	1859
Birch, Thomas	New York City	1821–1890
Birch, Thomas	Philadelphia, Pennsylvania	1807–1851
Birch, William	Philadelphia, Pennsylvania	1794–1834
Birch, William E., & Co.	New York City	1890–1894
Bisbee, E.	New York City	1833–1834
Bisbee, John	New York City	1832–1837
Bischebou	Boston, Massachusetts	1826
Bising & Co.	Cincinnati, Ohio	1868
Bland, E.	New York City	1860
Blane, O. & A.	Utica, New York	no date
Blelock & Co.	New Orleans, Louisiana	no date
Blood & Evans	Boston, Massachusetts	1857
Blumner, F.	New York City	1859
Boell, William	New York City and Philadelphia, Pennsylvania	1854–1868
Boell & Lewis	New York City	1855
Boell & Michelin	New York City	1856–1858
Bohn, C.	Washington, D.C.	no date
Bonar, Thomas	New York City	1848–1867

Bonar & Cumming	New York City	1847–1848
Bonwill, C. E. H.	New York City	1872
Borum	unknown	no date
Bosqui, T.	San Francisco	1846
Botti (s) cher, Lieut. Col. Otto	New York City	1852–1858
Bouker	New York City	1864
Bourne, A.	Montreal and Quebec, Canada	1830–1834
Bourne, George Melksham	New York City, and Quebec, Canada	1827–1832
Bourquin, Frederick	Philadelphia, Pennsylvania, and New York City	1872
Bouve, Ephraim	Boston, Massachusetts	1839–1840 1844–1851
Bouve & Sharp	Boston, Massachusetts	1843–1844
Bouvier, Charles	New York City	1854
Bowen, John T.	New York City, and Philadelphia, Pennsylvania	1834–1844*
Bowker, J.	New York City	no date
Bradford, L. H., & Co.	Boston, Massachusetts	1848–1859
Bradlee, C.	Boston, Massachusetts	no date
Bradley, Lewis	Boston, Massachusetts	1855
Bradley, Milton	Springfield, Massachusetts	1862
Brainard, C. H.	New York City	1859
Brandon & Co.	Washington, D.C.	1833
Brechemin & Camp	Philadelphia, Pennsylvania	1848
Brennan, J.	New York City	1866
Breton, W. L.	Philadelphia, Pennsylvania	1830
Brett, Alphonse	Philadelphia, Pennsylvania, and New York City	1852–1864
Breuker & Kessler	Philadelphia, Pennsylvania	1867–1876
Brewster, Edmund (painter)	Philadelphia, Pennsylvania	1828–1845
Bridport, Hugh	Philadelphia, Pennsylvania	1816–1837
Briem, John	New York City	1875–1880
Briggs, John	New York City	1834–1837
Britton, James	New York City, and San Francisco, California	1847–1870's
Britton & Co.	San Francisco, California	1853
Britton & Rey	San Francisco, California	1849–1870's
Bromley & Co.	New York City	1864
Broughton	Glover, Massachusetts	1854
Brown, A., and Co.	New York City	1863–1866
Brown, B. S.	Philadelphia, Pennsylvania	1861
Brown, E. & J.	New York City	1848
Brown, Eliphalet, Jr.	New York City	1843–1858
Brown, George Loring	Boston, Massachusetts	1835
Brown, M. E. D.	Philadelphia, Pennsylvania	1832–1834
Brown, William H.	Charleston, West Virginia	1846†
Brown & Redmond	New York City	1836

Brown & Severin	New York City	1851
Browne, William R.	New York City	1836–1838
Brownson, William M., & Co.	New York City	1840–1851
Bruckner, Henry	New York City	1859
Buell	Philadelphia, Pennsylvania	no date‡
Bufford, John H.	Boston, Massachusetts and New York City	1835–1871*
Bufford (The) Sons Lithograph Company		c. 1886
Burgess, G. W., Company	Philadelphia, Pennsylvania	1841
Burleigh, L. R.	Troy, New York	no date
Burrill, Edward	Boston, Massachusetts	1860
Burton, C. W.	New York City	c. 1849
Burton, James R.	New York City	1829
Burton & Gurley	New York City	1831–1851
Butler, Benjamin F.	New York City and San Francisco, California	1838–1851
Butler, J. B.	Philadelphia, Pennsylvania	no date
Butt, R.	New York City	1843
Buttre, John Chester	New York City	1865
Cameron, John	New York City	1852–1862*
Camp, J. Henry	Philadelphia, Pennsylvania	1849–1859
Camp & Koeler	Philadelphia, Pennsylvania	1848
Campbell, Thomas	Baltimore, Maryland and Louisville, Kentucky	1834–1845
Canova, Dominick	New York City	1832
Canova & Farby	New York City	1831
Carstensen & Gildemeister	New York City	1852
Carter, Franklin N.	Boston, Massachusetts	1858–1867
Catlin, George	United States and England	1825–1838
Champney, Benjamin	Boston, Massachusetts	c. 1840
Charles Brothers	New York City	c. 1865
Chenard, Anthony F.	New York City	1826–1839
Chicago Lithographing Co.	Chicago, Illinois	1868
Childs, Cephas G.	Philadelphia, Pennsylvania	1823–1858
Childs, John	New York City and Philadelphia, Pennsylvania	1830–1862*
Childs & Inman	Philadelphia, Pennsylvania	1831–1833
Childs & Lehman	Philadelphia, Pennsylvania	1835–1836
Chillas, David	Philadelphia, Pennsylvania	1853
Christman, Charles	New York City	1823–1857 (M)
Clay, Edward	Philadelphia, Pennsylvania	1825–1838
Clay, H. M.	Buffalo, New York	1861
Clay & Co.	Buffalo, New York, and Chicago, Illinois	c. 1865
Clay & Rischmond	Buffalo, New York	c. 1865
Clay, Cosack & Co.	Buffalo, New York	c. 1865

Clayton, Charles	New York City	1867–1868
Coffin, E. H.	New York City	no date
Coggins, E. H.	Philadelphia, Pennsylvania	1854
Colen, J. H.	New York City	1839
Collins, John	Philadelphia, Pennsylvania	1833–1869
Colton, Frederick P.	Hartford, Connecticut	1844–1852
Combe, Voltaire	New York City	**
Compton, Richard J.	Buffalo, New York	1849–1856
Compton & Co.	Buffalo, New York	1853
Compton & Gibson	Buffalo, New York	1854
Conant, Alban Jasper	Boston, Massachusetts	1845
Connolly, A. P.	Chicago, Illinois	no date§
Cook, Charles	Boston, Massachusetts	1840–1853
Cooke, Robert	Boston, Massachusetts	1835
Cooke, W. B., & Co.	San Francisco, California	1850
Cooke & Le Count	San Francisco, California	1852
Cottrell, G. W., & Co.	Boston, Massachusetts	no date
Courier Lithographing Company	Buffalo, New York	no date
Cram	Chicago, Illinois	1871
Crawley, John, Jr.	New York City	1832
Crehen, E. R.	Richmond, Virginia	no date
Crehen, S. G.	all over United States	1850
Crosby, Charles H.	Boston, Massachusetts	1852–1872
Crow, Thomas, & Co.	New York City	1861
Culver, Page & Hoyne	Chicago, Illinois	1862
Darley, Felix Octavius Carr	Philadelphia, Pennsylvania	c. 1848–1860
D'Avignon, Francis	New York City and Boston, Massachusetts	1844–1859
D'Avignon & Brainerd	Boston, Massachusetts	1859–1860
Davis, Alexander Jackson	New York City	1825–1839
Day, Benjamin H.	New York City	1835
De Hollosy	New York City	1835
Degen, George	New York City	1869–1874
Delevan & Company	New York City	1868
Derby, B.	New York City	1862
Desobry, Prosper	New York City	1829–1844
Deutz Brothers	New York City	1869
Dewey, D. M.		no date (F)
Disturnell, J.	New York City	1835
Dodworth, Allen	New York City	1844–1855 (M)
Dodworth, Harvey B.	New York City	1845–1872 (M)
Dodworth, Olean H.	New York City	1866–1871 (M)
Donaldson, William M.	Cincinnati, Ohio	after 1860
Donaldson Brothers	New York City	1878–1879
Donaldson & Elmes	Cincinnati, Ohio	1863
Donnelly, A.	New York City	1844
Dorival, John	New York City	1826–1838

Doughty, H. & T.	Philadelphia, Pennsylvania	1830s
Dovilliers, E.	Columbia, South Carolina	no date
Dow & Duval	Philadelphia, Pennsylvania	1838–1839
Drew, C.	Boston, Massachusetts	no date
Drouaillet	San Francisco, California	1860
Dubois, H. W.	Fall River, Massachusetts	1850
Dubois, William	New York City	1813–1854 (M)
Dubois & Bacon	New York City	1835–1838 (M)
Dubois & Stodart	New York City	1822–1834 (M)
Dubois & Warrinter	New York City	1850–1852
Dugan, A. A.	Philadelphia, Pennsylvania	1852
Dugan, George	New York City	no date
Dumke & Keil	New York City	1855
Dunbar, S. O.	New Bedford, Massachusetts	1836
Dupré, E.	St. Louis, Missouri	1839
Duval, P. S., & John T. Bowen	Philadelphia, Pennsylvania	c. 1863
Duval, Peter S.	Philadelphia, Pennsylvania	1831–1893
Duval & Huddy	Philadelphia, Pennsylvania	1839
Duval & Hunter	Philadelphia, Pennsylvania	1879–1893
Duval & Ludlow	Philadelphia, Pennsylvania	1863
Duval & Son	Philadelphia, Pennsylvania	1857
Eddy, James	Boston, Massachusetts	1838
Edwards, Thomas	Boston, Massachusetts	1829
Ehrgott, Forbriger & Company	Cincinnati, Ohio	1861–1869
Ehrgott & Forbriger	Cincinnati, Ohio	1858–1859
Ehrgott & Krebs	Cincinnati, Ohio	1870
Elliott, John	New York City	1837
Ells, William	New York City	1847
Elton, Robert H.	New York City	1834–1853
Emerson, Samuel	Brighton, Massachusetts	1865
Emmons, William	unknown	1833
Emporium of Arts	New York City	1815
Endicott, G. & W.	New York City	1845–1849
Endicott, George	New York City	1834–1844
Endicott, George (II)	New York City	1887–1896
Endicott, William, & Co.	New York City	1849–1852
Endicott and Company	New York City	1852–1886
Endicott & Swett	New York City	1830–1834
Eno, Henry	New York City	1863–1869
Ensign, Timothy and Edward	New York City	1841–1861
Ernst, Philip	New York City	1840–1868 (M)
Evans, C. H.	New York City	1833
Evans, Charles	Boston, Massachusetts	1858–1860
Eytinge, Clarence	New York City	1853–1854
Eytinge, Robert	New York City	1853–1854

Fabronius, Dominique C.	Philadelphia, Pennsylvania; Cincinnati, Ohio; Boston, Massachusetts; New York City	1861–1888
Farrell, E. D.	New York City	no date
Farrell, P. D.	New York City	1867
Fasel & Valois	New York City	1862
Fatzer	New York City	1859
Fay, A.	Hoboken, New Jersey	1854
Felton, C. B.	New York City	1845 (M)
Fenderich & Wild	Philadelphia, Pennsylvania, and Washington, D.C.	1833–1837
Fern, Henry	New York City	1853–1854
Fern & Eytinge	New York City	1853–1854
Fersenheim & Witschief	New York City	1867
Feusier, A.	Philadelphia, Pennsylvania	no date
Firks, Henry	San Francisco, California	1849
Firth, John	New York City	1815–1820 (M)
Firth, Hall & Pond	New York City	1843 (M)
Firth, Pond & Co.	New York City	1848–1865 (M)
Firth & Hall	New York City	1821–1847 (M) *
Fisher, J.	Boston, Massachusetts	1841
Fisher & Carpenter	New York City	no date
Fitzsimmons, James N.	New York City	1838
Fleetwood, Anthony	New York City	1828–1848*
Forbes, William H., & Co.	Boston, Massachusetts	1867
Forbriger, A.	Cincinnati, Ohio	1858–1869
Foreman, E. W.	New York City	1848
Forsyth, John	New York City	1847
Francis, John F.	Philadelphia, Pennsylvania	1838
Frankenstein, G. N.	Cincinnati, Ohio	1848
Franklin Institute	Philadelphia, Pennsylvania	1824–1874 (M)
Fritsch, F. J.	New York City	1843
Frizzell, S. S.	unknown	1866
Fuchs, F.	Philadelphia, Pennsylvania	1856
Fuchs, Theodore	Philadelphia, Pennsylvania	1859
Fuller, George	unknown	1859
Galt & Hoy	New York City	1879
Galusha, Elijah	New York City	1846
Gast	St. Louis, Missouri	no date
Gay, James D.	New York City	1864
Gebbie, George	Philadelphia, Pennsylvania	1871
Gedney, J. F.	unknown	1867
Geib, Adam	New York City	1844–1847
Geib, John, & Co. Geib, John & Adam, & Co. Geib, John & Son	New York City	1802–1807
Geib, William H.	New York City	1859–1872

Geib & Jackson	New York City	1849–1858
Geissler, L. N.	New York City	1869
Gemmell, S.	Chicago, Illinois	c. 1857
Gerlach, Herman	Buffalo, New York, and Cincinnati, Ohio	1860–1866
German & Brother	Louisville, Kentucky	no date (M)
Geslain, Alexander C., Jr.	New York City	1844 (M)
Geslain, Charles	New York City	1840–1842 (M)
Gibson & Company	Cincinnati, Ohio	1865
Gifford, C. B.	San Francisco, California	1856–1877
Gildemeister, Charles	New York City	1850–1858
Giles, J. L.	New York City	1868
Gimber, Stephen	Philadelphia, Pennsylvania	c. 1830
Glasgow, D.	New York City	1858
Glasgow, J. T.	New York City	1850
Gleason	Boston, Massachusetts	no date
Goddard, G. H.	San Francisco, California	1849
Goff, Joseph	Philadelphia, Pennsylvania	1867
Goldsmith, Morris	New York City	1876
Goupil & Co.	New York City	1852–1857
Gower, J. S.	San Francisco, California	no date
Graham, Curtis B.	New York City and Washington, D.C.	1836–1841
Graham, Curtis B. and John B.	New York City and Washington, D.C.	1835–1836
Graham & Price	New York City	1836
Graphic Company	New York City	no date
Gratacap, George G.	New York City	1845
Green, C. C.	unknown	no date
Green, William	Albany, New York	1843–1845
Greene, William	New Orleans, Louisiana	1838
Greene & McGowran	New York City	1837
Greene & Pishbourne	New York City	1836–1837
Gregson, Donaldson and Elmes	Cincinnati, Ohio	1862
Grow, Thomas, & Co.	New York City	1861 (M)
Grozelier, Leopold	Boston, Massachusetts	1854–1860
Gus, Seymour J.	New York City	1854
Haas, P.	Washington, D.C.	1837–1845
Haasis, J.	New York City	1851
Haasis & Lubrecht	New York City	1871
Haehlen, Jacob	Philadelphia, Pennsylvania	1841–1871
Hailer, John	Northampton County, Pennsylvania	1862
Hall, John H.	Albany, New York	1831–1849
Hall, William	New York City	1841
Hall & Mooney	Buffalo, New York	1839–1850
Hankerson, John	Portland, Oregon	no date

Harris, George	Philadelphia, Pennsylvania	1860's
Harrison & Weightman	Philadelphia, Pennsylvania	no date
Hart, Charles	New York City	1862–1868
Hart, John	Philadelphia, Pennsylvania	1868
Hart, S., & Son	Philadelphia, Pennsylvania	no date
Hart & Mapother	Louisville, Kentucky	1861
Harvey, H. A.	unknown	1848
Haskell & Allen	Boston, Massachusetts	1867–1875
Hastings & Parker	Boston, Massachusetts	1820
Hatch Lithographing	New York City and Boston, Massachusetts	1875
Hatch & Severin	New York City	1853–1873
Haugg, L.	Philadelphia, Pennsylvania	c. 1860
Haven, J.	Boston, Massachusetts	1850
Hawley, Hughson	New York City	1882
Hayward, George	New York City	1834–1861
Hayward, States & Koch	New York City	1868–1872
Heerbrandt & Co.	New York City	no date
Heine, W.	unknown	1856
Heiss, George H.	Philadelphia, Pennsylvania	no date
Hennenberger, J.	New York City	1866
Hensel & Urwiter	Philadelphia, Pennsylvania	no date
Heppenheimer, F.	New York City	1854–1863
Heppenheimer & Maurer	New York City	1872–1884
Herline & Co.	Philadelphia, Pennsylvania	1840–1856, 1870
Herline & Henzel	Philadelphia, Pennsylvania	1857–1860
Hess, B.	Newburgh, New York	no date
Hewitt, James	New York City	1844–1847
Hewitt, James L., & Co.	New York City	1830–1833, 1842–1843
Hewitt & Jacques	New York City	1839–1841
Hickok & Cantine	Philadelphia, Pennsylvania	1845
Hill, Henry	unknown	1850's
Hill, J. H.	Hoboken, New Jersey	1854
Hill, Warren	New York City	1835–1858 (M)
Hill, William, & Son	New York City	1848–1874 (M)
Hillyer, H.	Jersey City, New Jersey	no date
Hobson, R. H.	Philadelphia, Pennsylvania	1832
Hochstein	New York City	1864
Hoen, A., & Co.	Baltimore, Maryland, and Richmond, Virginia	1848
Hoff, Henry	New York City	1850
Hoff & Bloede	New York City	1850
Hoffman, Knickerbocker Co.	Albany, New York	1859
Hoffy, Alfred	Philadelphia, Pennsylvania	1840–1864
Hohenstein, Anton	unknown	1867
Holland, Thomas R.	Boston, Massachusetts	1858–1867
Holland, Thomas R., & Co.	Boston, Massachusetts	1855
Holland & Stimson	Boston, Massachusetts	1856–1857

Holmes, Stimson & Co.	Boston, Massachusetts	1855
Holt, Charles, Jr.	New York City	1847–1849 (M)
Hoover, Joseph	Philadelphia, Pennsylvania	1869
Horn, Charles	New York City	1840–1843 (M)
Howel, J. P.	New York City	1868
Howell, R. H.	Savannah, Georgia	c. 1851
Hubbard, J. R.	Boston, Massachusetts	1822 (H)
Huddy, W. M.	Philadelphia, Pennsylvania	1839–1846
Huddy & Duval	Philadelphia, Pennsylvania	1839–1841
Hudson, William, Jr.	Boston, Massachusetts	no date
Hull, Joseph	Chicago, Illinois	1870
Hunkel & Son	Baltimore, Maryland	no date
Hunt, William	Boston, Massachusetts	1863
Hunt, William Morris	Boston, Massachusetts	1863
Hunter, Thomas	Philadelphia, Pennsylvania	1875
Husted, Thomas, & Co.	New York City	no date
Hutawa, Julius	St. Louis, Missouri	1846
Hutchings & Rosenfield	San Francisco, California	1855
Ibbotson, A.	Philadelphia, Pennsylvania	no date
Ihue, F.	New York City	c. 1880
Imbert, Anthony	New York City	1825–1839
Inger, C.	Philadelphia, Pennsylvania	1886
Inman, Henry	Philadelphia, Pennsylvania	c. 1830
Jackson, J. E.	New York City	1878
Jacques, John D.	New York City	1853–1857 (M)
Jaques, Edward	New York City	1842 (M)
Jaques, James	New York City	1846–1853 (M)
Jenkins & Colburn	Boston, Massachusetts and New York City	1836–1840
Jevne & Almini	Chicago, Illinois	1866
Jewett, W. S.	New York City	1847
Johns, E., & Co.	New Orleans, Louisiana	1837
Johnson, Eastman	New York City	c. 1845
Johnston, David Claypool	Philadelphia, Pennsylvania and Boston, Massachusetts	1865
Jollie, Allen R.	New York City	1829–1866 (M)
Jollie, Samuel C.	New York City	1838–1855 (M)
Jollie & Millet	New York City	1835 (M)
Jollie & Secor	New York City	1829 (M)
Jones, Edward	New York City	1844, 1849–1850
Jones, W. H.	San Francisco, California	1849
Jones & Newman	New York City	1846–1849
Justh & Co.	San Francisco, California	1852
Justh, Quirot, & Co.	San Francisco, California	1851
Kearny, Francis	Philadelphia, Pennsylvania	no date

Keenan, William	Philadelphia, Pennsylvania, and Charleston, West Virginia	1830–1839
Keffer, J. L.	Philadelphia, Pennsylvania	1839
Keith, Charles	Boston, Massachusetts	1843 (M)
Kellogg, E. C.	Hartford, Connecticut	1836–1843
Kellogg, D. W.	Hartford, Connecticut	1833–1842
Kellogg, E. B. & E. C.	Hartford, Connecticut	1843–1865
Kellogg & Bulkley	Hartford, Connecticut	1869–1875
Kellogg & Hammer	Hartford, Connecticut	1844–1845
Kellogg & Thayer	Hartford, Connecticut	1844–1848
Kelly	New York City	1866
Kelly, Thomas	New York City	1870
Kelly, William	New York City	no date
Kelly & Whitehill	New York, and Brooklyn, New York	1868
Kennedy & Lucus	Philadelphia, Pennsylvania	1829–1835
Kerr, Robert	New York City	1844
Ketterlinus,	Philadelphia, Pennsylvania	1842–1876
Kidd, J. B.	New York City	1838
Kidder, James	Boston, Massachusetts	1821
Kimmel & Forster	New York City	1865–1866
King, Louis	Chicago, Illinois	1865
Kipps, A. R.	Boston, Massachusetts	no date
Kiraly, Anderson, & Co.	New York City	1851
Klauprech & Menzel	Cincinnati, Ohio	1840–1859
Knauber, J., & Co.	unknown	1876
Knickerbocker & Company	Albany, New York	no date
Knirsch, Otto	New York City	1852
Kollner, Camp, & Co.	Philadelphia, Pennsylvania	1851–1856
Koppel	unknown	1865
Korff Brothers	New York City	no date
Kraezer, G.	New York City	1851–1859
Kramer, Peter	Philadelphia, Pennsylvania and New York City	1857–1898
Kramer, Sevastian, & Co.	Boston, Massachusetts	1856
Kramp, William	New York City	1836–1842
Krebs, Adolph K., & Co.	Pittsburgh, Pennsylvania	1864
Krimmel, John Lewis	Philadelphia, Pennsylvania	1815
Kuchel, C.	Philadelphia, Pennsylvania	1820
Kuchel & Dresel	San Francisco, California	1856
Kuhl, J.	Philadelphia, Pennsylvania	no date
Kummer, J.	Boston, Massachusetts	no date
Kurz & Allison	Chicago, Illinois	1860–1890's
Lacombe, Theodore	New York City	1853
Laidlaw, J. S.	New York City	no date
Laing, Joseph	New York City	1888
Lambdin, James	Philadelphia, Pennsylvania	(died) 1889

Landis	unknown	1840
Landon, R. R.	Chicago, Illinois	(L)
Landreth, D. & C.	Philadelphia, Pennsylvania	1832 (F)
Lane & Scott	Boston, Massachusetts	1840–1847
Lang & Cooper	New York City	no date
Lang & Lang	New York City	no date
Langton, Samuel W.	Downieville, California	c. 1850
Lapham, J. M.	San Francisco, California	1853
Laurence, John	New York City	1837
Lawrence, Henry	New York City	1852–1862
Lee, Homer, & Co.	New York City	no date
Leefe, George	New York City	1850–1855
Leffingwell, Caroline	unknown	no date
Leggot & Co.	Montreal, Canada	1865
Lehman, George	Philadelphia, Pennsylvania	1830–1870
Lehman & Duval	Philadelphia, Pennsylvania	1836–1838
Lentz, Charles H.	New York City	1865
Leonhardt, Theodore	Philadelphia, Pennsylvania	1849–1876
Lewis, George	New York City	1841–1861
Lewis, J. O.	Philadelphia, Pennsylvania	1835
Lewis & Brown	New York City	1844–1849
Lewis & Goodwin	New York City	1861–1867
Lewis & Grebner	Buffalo, New York	no date
Lion, Jules	New Orleans, Louisiana	1839–1865
Litchfield	unknown	1851
Lopez	Boston, Massachusetts	1831 (M)
Loudenslager, J. L.	Philadelphia, Pennsylvania	1854
Lowenstrom, C.	New York City	1850
Ludwig, Charles	Richmond, Virginia	no date
Lutz, J.	New York City	1851
Lyon & Co.	New York City	1861
Mac, Jacoby & Zellner	New York City	no date
Macbriar & Co.	Cincinnati, Ohio	late 1800's (M)
Mack, Dixon, & Co.	New Bedford, Massachusetts	1834
Magee, John L.	New York City and Philadelphia, Pennsylvania	1844–1860
Magee, R.	Philadelphia, Pennsylvania	1856
Magnus, Charles, & Co.	New York City and Washington, D.C.	1858–1877
Magny, X.	New Orleans, Louisiana	1849–1856
Major, James P.	New York City	1843–1844
Major, Henry B.	New York City	1845–1846
Major, John & Daniel	New York City	1839–1851
Major & Knapp	New York City	1864–1870's
Major & Knapp Engraving, Manufacturing & Lithographic Co.	New York City	1867–1868
Mallory, D.	New York City	c. 1830

Manouvrier, Jules	New Orleans, Louisiana	1849–1867
Manouvrier & Chavin	New Orleans, Louisiana	1843
Manouvrier & Simon	New Orleans, Louisiana	1867–1870
Mansfield, H.	New Haven, Connecticut	no date
Marsden, J.	unknown	1868
Marsden, Theodore	New York City	c. 1868
Marsiglia, Gerlando	New York City	1826–d. 1850
Martin, Charles	New York City	1851
Martin, J. B.	Richmond, Virginia	1817–d. 1857
Mathews, A. E.	Cincinnati, Ohio, and New York City	1870
Maverick, Peter	New York City	1820–1831
Maverick, Peter, Jr.	New York City	1832–1846
Mayer, J., & Co.	Boston, Massachusetts	1863–1872
Mayer, Ferdinand	New York City	1846–1877*
Mayer, Merkel & Ottman	New York City	c. 1884
Mayer & Merkel	New York City	1869
Mayer & Stetfield	Boston, Massachusetts	1861–1862
McDermott, John	New York City	1868
McLaughlin	Philadelphia, Pennsylvania	no date
McLean, A.	St. Louis, Missouri and Washington, D.C.	1858
McLellan, David	New York City	1851–1858
McLellan, David, & Bros.	New York City	1865–1867
McLellan, David & James	New York City	1859–1864
McNevin, M.	unknown	1863
McSpedon & Baker	New York City	1853
Meer, John	Philadelphia, Pennsylvania	1825
Meetz (Meets), Raymond	New York City	1810–1835 (M)
Meisel, Augustus	Boston, Massachusetts	1856–1871
Meisel Brothers	Boston, Massachusetts	1857–1861
Mendel, Edward	Chicago, Illinois	1858
Merrick, W. W.	unknown	no date
Mesier, Edward S.	New York City	1833–1851
Mesier, Peter A.	New York City	1794–1848
Metcalf & Clark	Baltimore, Maryland	1870
Michelin, Francis	unknown	1846–1859
Michelin & Cuipers	New York City	1844–1845
Michelin & Leefe	New York City	1852–1853
Michelin & Shattuck	New York City	1853–1854
Middleton, Strobridge & Co.	Cincinnati, Ohio	1859–1864
Middleton, Wallace & Co.	Cincinnati, Ohio	1855–1858
Miedzielsky, Paulin	New York City	1833
Miller, Alfred J.	Philadelphia, Pennsylvania	1837
Miller, Peter, & Co.	New York City	1834–1869*
Miller, William	New York City	1850
Millet, Frank	New York City	1879
Millet, William E.	New York City	1836–1865 (M)
Millet & Son	New York City	1869–1873

Millet Sons	New York City	1868
Milwaukee Lithographic & Engraving Co.	Chicago, Illinois	no date
Milwaukee Lithographing Co.	Milwaukee, Wisconsin	c. 1896
Mitton, N.	Philadelphia, Pennsylvania	1869
Moeller & Co.	St. Louis, Missouri	no date
Moody, David William	New York City	1846–1847
Mooney, Lawrence	Buffalo, New York	1850–1863
Mooney & Buell	Buffalo, New York	1851–1852
Moore, E. N., Co.	Boston, Massachusetts	1857–1860
Moran, Edward	Philadelphia, Pennsylvania	1855
Moran, Thomas	Philadelphia, Pennsylvania	1860's
Moras, Ferdinand	Philadelphia, Pennsylvania	1853–1899
Morawski & Kruger	New York City	1845
Morgan, W. P.	New York City	1825
Mount, William Sidney	New York City	c. 1850
Mudge, Joseph	New York City	1843
Mueller, A., & Co.		1879
Mueller, J.	Cleveland, Ohio, and Pittsburgh, Pennsylvania	1854
Muntz, C. F., & Co.	Rochester, New York	no date
Murdoch, John	San Francisco, California	no date
Myer, Fritz	New York City	no date
Nagel, Fishbourne & Kuchel	San Francisco, California	1862–1863
Nagel, Louis	New York City	1844–1848
Nagel & Mayer	New York City	1846
Nagel & Weingartner	New York City	1849–1857
Nahl Brothers	San Francisco, California	1863–c. 1880
Narine, James, & Co.	New York City	1839–1843
Natt	unknown	1832
Neal, David	San Francisco, California	1838–d. 1915
Nebel, Carl	New York City	(Mexican War)
Nelke, Louis	Chicago, Illinois	1865
Nesbit (t), George F., & Co.	New York City	no date
Netherelist	New Orleans, Louisiana	c. 1822 (?)
New England Lithographic Steam Printing Co.	Boston, Massachusetts	1867–1872
New Orleans Lithographic Office	New Orleans, Louisiana	1838
Newell, J. P.	unknown	c. 1870
Newsam, Albert	Philadelphia, Pennsylvania	1831–1857
Newton	Pittsburgh, Pennsylvania	no date
Nichols, George Ward	New York City	1870
Niles	unknown	1864
Norris & Baker	New York City	1835
Norton, W. O. V.	Boston, Massachusetts	no date
Nunnus, John	Philadelphia, Pennsylvania	1830
Nutting, B. F.	Boston, Massachusetts	c. 1860

Nutting, Emily	Boston, Massachusetts	no date
Oakley, Francis F.	Boston, Massachusetts	1856–1863
O'Connor	Philadelphia, Pennsylvania	1839
Oertel, Johannes Adam	New York City	1853
O'Grady, W. H.	San Francisco, California	no date
Onken, Otto	Cincinnati, Ohio	1849–1853
O'Sullivan, T.	Philadelphia, Pennsylvania	1840
Otis, Bass	Philadelphia, Pennsylvania	1818–1826 (A)
Otis, F. N.	unknown	no date
Ottman, J.	New York City	no date
O. A. P.	Dubuque, Iowa	no date
Palmer, Cecil	New York City	1884
Palmer, E.	New York City	1844
Palmer, F., & Co.	New York City	1847–1851
Palmer, Francis & Seymour	New York City	1846–1849
Palmer, Seymour	New York City	1844–1845
Parker & Ditson	Boston, Massachusetts	c. 1840
Parkinson, M. B.	unknown	1897
Parsons, Charles	New York City	1863
Parsons & Atwater	New York City	1863
Payot, Upham & Co.	San Francisco, California	no date
Peabody, Charles	New York City	1834
Peabody & Co.	New York City	1831–1843
Peale, Rembrandt	New York City, and Boston, Massachusetts	1827
Pearson, Sidney	New York City	1842–1864 (M)
Pease, E. H.	Albany, New York	1845
Pease, Richard H.	Albany, New York	1834–1855*
Pendleton, J. B.	New York City	1827–1835
Pendleton, W. S.	Boston, Massachusetts	1827–1836
Pendleton, W. S. & J. B.	Boston, Massachusetts	1826–1831
Penniman, John Ritto	Boston, Massachusetts; Baltimore, Maryland; and New York City	1835–1844
Penwork	New York City	1845
Peregoy, Charles E.	San Francisco, California	1851
Pesson & Simon	New Orleans, Louisiana	1857
Pharazyn, H.	Philadelphia, Pennsylvania	1856–1870
Phelps, Humphrey	New York City	1841–1853
Picken, A.	New York City	1835
Pierce, J. H.	Boston, Massachusetts	1846
Pierce, J. H.	New York City, and San Francisco, California	1841
Pilliner, Frederick J.	Philadelphia, Pennsylvania	1859–1861
Pillner, George	Philadelphia, Pennsylvania	1860
Pinkerton, Wagner & McGuigan	Philadelphia, Pennsylvania	1845–1846

Pollard, C. J.	San Francisco, California	c. 1855
Pollard & Britton	San Francisco, California	1852
Ponarede, L. D.	St. Louis, Missouri	c. 1875
Powers, James T., & Co.	Boston, Massachusetts	1852–1860
Powers & Weller	Boston, Massachusetts	c. 1852
Prang, Louis	England	after 1865
Prang, Louis & Co.	Boston, Massachusetts	1861–1864
Prang & Mayer	Boston, Massachusetts	1857–1864
Prestele	Boston, Massachusetts	1847
Punderson & Crisand	New Haven, Connecticut	1862
Purdy, A. H.	New York City	c. 1831
Queen, James	Philadelphia, Pennsylvania	d. 1877
Querner, G.	Washington, D.C.	1865
Quidor, George W.	New York City	1849–1854 (M)
Quintin, D. S.	Philadelphia, Pennsylvania	1841
Quirot & Company	San Francisco, California	c. 1852
Rabuske, Theodore	New York City	1856
Radcliff, C. H.	Madison, Wisconsin	no date
Ratellier, F.	New York City	no date
Rau, T. & Jacob	New York City	1859–1867
Rease, William H.	Philadelphia, Pennsylvania	1844–1860
Reigart & Dellinger	New York City	no date
Reinagle, Huch	New York City, and New Orleans, Louisiana	d. 1834
Restein, Edmund P. & L.	Philadelphia, Pennsylvania	1852–1875
Reynolds, R. F.	Philadelphia, Pennsylvania	1850
Rice & Clark	Philadelphia, Pennsylvania	1843
Richards, T. Addison	New York City	1831
Rider, A.	Philadelphia, Pennsylvania	1835
Righter, Charles	Charleston, South Carolina	no date
Riley, E. (may be two different men)	New York City	1810–1842 (M)
Riley, Frederick	unknown	1842–1851
Risso & Browne	New York City	1832–1838
Risso & Leefe	New York City	1845–1846
Ritchie & Dunnavant	Richmond, Virginia	1852–1856
Ritz, Philip	Walla Walla, Washington	1867
Robertson, Archibald	New York City	d. 1835
Robertson, Seibert & Shearman	New York City	1859–1861
Robertson, William	New York City	1865–1868
Robertson & Seibert	New York City	1854–1858
Robinson, Henry	New York City	1833–1851
Robyn & Co.	Louisville, Kentucky	no date (M)
Rogers, W. C., & Co.	New York City	1868
Rondel (l), F.	Boston, Massachusetts	1870
Root & Tinker	New York City	1885

Rosenfield, A.	San Francisco, California	1862
Rosenthal, (Max, Louis, Simon, and Albert—four brothers)	Philadelphia, Pennsylvania	1852–1870
Ross, T. J.	New York City	1869
Rowse, Samuel	Cincinnati, Ohio	1845, 1848
Rowse, Samuel	Worcester, Massachusetts, and Boston, Massachusetts	b. 1822, d. 1901
Ruckle, Thomas	Baltimore, Maryland	1830
Rudiger & Hill	New York City	1867 (M)
Ruger & Stone—Merchants' Lithographing Co.	Madison, Wisconsin	1870
Russell, B. B., & Co.	Boston, Massachusetts	1863–1872
Russell, Benjamin	New Bedford, Massachusetts	1871
Ryder, J. F.	Cleveland, Ohio	no date
Sachse, Edward, & Co.	Baltimore, Maryland	1851–1866
Sage, J., & Sons	Buffalo, New York	1856–1857
Samyn, Lewis	Cincinnati, Ohio	1838–1843
Sanford, G. T.	New York City	no date
Sarony, Major & Knapp	New York City	1857–1867
Sarony, Napoleon	New York City	c. 1840–1845
Sarony & Co.	New York City	1840–1857
Sarony & Major	New York City	1846–1857
Schaerff	St. Louis, Missouri	1854–1864
Scharfenberg & Luis	New York City	1845–1866 (M)
Schaus, W.	New York City	1850–1861
Schell	Philadelphia, Pennsylvania	1855
Schile, H.	New York City	1870's
Schlegel, George	New York City	1868–1874
Schmidt, L. W.	New York City	1855
Schmitz, M.	Philadelphia, Pennsylvania	1849
Schnabel, E.	Philadelphia, Pennsylvania	1858
Schone, Robert	New York City	1862
Schrader, Theodore	St. Louis, Missouri	c. 1864
Schreiner, Mrs. T.	Philadelphia, Pennsylvania	1845
Schumacher & Ettlinger	New York City	no date
Schusele, Christian	Philadelphia, Pennsylvania	1848
Scott, John A.	Boston, Massachusetts	1849
Scott, Thomas S.	Philadelphia, Pennsylvania	c. 1852
Seaman, James V.	New York City	1822
Seitz, Emil	New York City	1851–1853
Semmell, J.	Chicago, Illinois	no date
Senefelder Lithographic Co.	Boston, Massachusetts	1828–1834
Serrell, Henry R.	New York City	1853–1854
Serrell & Perkins	New York City	1849–1852
Severin	New York City	no date
Sewell, H.	New York City	1835
Sharp, James	Boston, Massachusetts	1842–1843
Sharp, Michelin, & Co.	Boston, Massachusetts	1840–1841
Sharp, Philip	Boston, Massachusetts	1858–1880

Sharp, William	Boston, Massachusetts	1841–1885
Sharp, William, & Son	Boston, Massachusetts	1852
Shaw, J. P.	New York City	1860
Shearman & Hart	New York City	c. 1860
Shecker, Herman	Reading, Pennsylvania	1860
Shepard, C.	New York City	1837
Sherer & Rowse	Cincinnati, Ohio	1847–1850
Sherwin, John H.	Philadelphia, Pennsylvania	1861
Shober, Charles	Chicago, Illinois	c. 1861
Shober & Carqueville	Chicago, Illinois	after 1860
Shobert, Alonzo	Philadelphia, Pennsylvania	1855
Sibell	New York City	1864
Sinclair, Thomas S.	Philadelphia, Pennsylvania	1839–1889
Sintzernich, E.	Albany, New York	no date
Skelly, J. P.	unknown	1865
Slater, J.	New York City	1879
Smart, J. E., & Kahlmann	New York City	1870
Smillie, James David	New York City	1849
Smith, A. B.	unknown	1846
Smith, A. C.	Philadelphia, Pennsylvania	c. 1840
Smith, B. F., Jr.	Philadelphia, Pennsylvania	c. 1850
Smith, Cremens & Co.	Philadelphia, Pennsylvania	1875
Smith, J. B.	New York City	c. 1850
Smith, John	Philadelphia, Pennsylvania	1863, 1869
Smith, John Rubens	Boston, Massachusetts; New York City, and Philadelphia, Pennsylvania	1827
Smith, Peter (thought to be a pen name for Nathaniel Currier of Currier & Ives)		
Smith Brothers & Co.	New York City	1853
Smith & Jenkins	New York City	1853
Smith & Sleap	New York City	no date
Snyder, Black & Sturn	New York City	1855–1870
Snyder, George	New York City	1843–1849
Snyder & Black	New York City	1850–1854
Sonrel, A.	Cambridge and Boston, Massachusetts	1849
Sowle & Shaw	New Bedford and Boston, Massachusetts, and New York City	c. 1840
Spohni, G.	Philadelphia, Pennsylvania	1863
Sprague, Isaac	Cambridge, Massachusetts	1848
Spratt, G.	Baltimore, Maryland	1831
Staines, William T.	Springfield, Illinois	c. 1865
Stansbury, Arthur J.	Washington, D.C.	1823
Stauffer, Jacob	Lancaster, Pennsylvania	b. 1808–d. 1880
Stayman & Brother	Philadelphia, Pennsylvania	1858
Stebbins & Wilson	New York City	no date

Steele, Oliver G.	Buffalo, New York	1839
Steiger, E.	New York City	no date
Stephens, H. L.	New York City	1864–1865
Stephenson & Co.	New York City	1854–1856
Stimson, William	Boston, Massachusetts	1853–1859
Stinson, George, & Co.	Portland, Maine	1871
Stodart†	New York City	pre-1870
Stone, Henry & William	Washington, D.C.	c. 1823
Storey, Alfred & Co.	unknown	1865
Strobel	Philadelphia, Pennsylvania	1853
Strobridge, Gerlach & Wagner	Cincinnati, Ohio	1862–1866
Strobridge, Hines	Cincinnati, Ohio	1859–1864
Strobridge & Co.	Cincinnati, Ohio	1867
Strong, Thomas W.	New York City	1842
Swasey, Captain W.	San Francisco, California	after 1846
Swett, Moses	Boston, Massachusetts; New York City, and Washington, D.C.	1830–1837
Taber, Charles & Co.	Massachusetts	1859–1862
Tabert, Charles & Co.	New Bedford, Massachusetts	1858
Tanner, Benjamin	Philadelphia, Pennsylvania	d. 1848
Tappan & Bradford	Boston, Massachusetts	1848–1853
Taylor & Shuck	unknown	c. 1837
Tazewell	Canada	1833
Teller, A.	New York City	no date
Teller, R.	New York City	1870's–1880's (M)
Teller & Wright	New York City	1870's–1880's (M)
Teubner, George W.	New York City	1832–1845
Thalmessinger, M.	New York City	c. 1882
Thayer, Benjamin W.	Boston, Massachusetts	1840–1851
Thayer & Eldridge	Boston, Massachusetts	1860
Thiebaut	unknown	1863
Tholey	Philadelphia, Pennsylvania	1860's
Thomas, Henry	New York City	c. 1878
Thomas & Enos	New York City	1862–1864
Thomas & Wylie	New York City	c. 1880
Thompson	Unknown	1860
Thompson, Thomas	New York City	1829
Throop, J. V. N.	New York City	b. 1794 (c. 1830)
Thurston, Nathaniel	New York City	1823–1830 (M)
Thurwanger, Martin	Philadelphia, Pennsylvania	1850
Tidd, Marshall M.	Boston, Massachusetts	1854–1870
Tilton, J. E., & Co.	Boston, Massachusetts	1860
Tobin, M. F.	New York City	1892
Tolman, Henry	Boston, Massachusetts	1855 (M)
Tomford, J.	New York City	unknown
Tompson & Ramsay	Boston, Massachusetts	1873
Tone, Robert W.	New York City	1838–1849 (M)

Torp, Otto	New York City	1832–1841
Torp & Love	New York City	1836–1837
Torp & Unger	New York City	1838–1839
Torp & Viereck	New York City	1834
Toudy, H. J., & Co.	Philadelphia, Pennsylvania	1867
Toy & Lucas	Baltimore, Maryland	1830–1834
Traubel, Morris H., & Co.	Philadelphia, Pennsylvania	1853–1869
Traubel, Schnabel & Finkeldy	Philadelphia, Pennsylvania	1850
Trochsler, Albert, & Co.	Boston, Massachusetts	1859–1863
Turgis, John & Jeune L.	New York City	1856–1862
Turgis, W. & John	New York City	1852–1856
Tuthill, W. H.	New York City	1826
Upham & Colburn	Boston, Massachusetts	c. 1852
Usher, James M.	Boston, Massachusetts	1856
Valentine, David Thomas	New York City	1841–1868
Valois	New York City	1840's
Van Best, A.	unknown	1859–1862
Van Valkenburgh, James	New York City	1834
Vance, Parsloe, & Co.	New York City	1875
Vanderbeek, Alfred	New York City	1853 (M)
Vanderbeek, William	New York City	1845–1857 (M)
Vangelder, Abraham	New York City	1845–1853
Vaudricourt, A. De	New York City	1845
Vidal, E. & Sinclair	New York City	no date
Vogel, Emil	Baltimore, Maryland	no date
Vogt, G. H.	Milwaukee, Wisconsin	1876
Wade, F. J.	Philadelphia, Pennsylvania	1875
Waeschle, J.	Philadelphia, Pennsylvania	no date
Wagenbauer, Max Joseph	unknown	no date
Wagner, J. F.	Nashville, Tennessee	no date
Wagner, Thomas	Philadelphia, Pennsylvania	1840–1865
Wagner & McGuigan	Philadelphia, Pennsylvania	1846–1858
Walker, George H., & Co.	Boston, Massachusetts	no date
Walker, O.	Boston, Massachusetts	1852
Waller, Edward L.	Philadelphia, Pennsylvania	1855–1858
Walsh, John, & Co.	New York City	1870
Walton, H.	New York City and California	c. 1836
Ward, Joseph	Boston, Massachusetts	no date
Warner, C. L.	New York City	1837
Waters, Horace	New York City	1853 (M)
Watson, J. Frampton	Philadelphia, Pennsylvania	1835–1861
Watson, J. S.	Philadelphia, Pennsylvania	1850–1860
Webber, Mrs.	Boston, Massachusetts	no date
Weber, Edward, & Co.	Baltimore, Maryland	1835–1854
Webster, Ira	Hartford, Connecticut	1844

Weed, Parsons & Co.	Albany, New York	1865
Wegner, Brueckner & Mueller	Pittsburgh, Pennsylvania	1860
Wehrmann, H.	New Orleans, Louisiana	no date (M)
Weik, John	Philadelphia, Pennsylvania	1857–1870
Weingartner, Adam	New York City	1858–1863
Weiss, F. T.	New York City	1867
Wessbecher, Herman	New York City	no date
West, F.	Salem, Massachusetts	1828–1834
Wetzler, E.	unknown	no date
Wever, Adolphus	Cincinnati, Ohio	1840–1859
Wharton, T. K.	Boston, Massachusetts	c. 1840
Whipple & Damrell	Boston, Massachusetts	1840
White, Edwin	Philadelphia, Pennsylvania; Chicago, Illinois; and Minnesota	1870
Whitefield, E.	New York City	c. 1850
Whitney & Prentice	Boston, Massachusetts	late 1800's
Wiess, Spiegel & Co.	New York City	1869
Wild & Chevalier	Philadelphia, Pennsylvania	1838–1841
Willard, A. M.	Cleveland, Ohio	no date
Williams, C. S.	Philadelphia, Pennsylvania	1846
Williams, Michael	New York City	1826–1834
Williams & Stevens	New York City	1848
Willig, George	Philadelphia, Pennsylvania	1818–1850 (M)
Willis, William R.	New York City	1838–1850
Willis & Probst	New York City	1844
Wiltsie & Hess	Newburgh, New York	no date
Winch, A.	Philadelphia, Pennsylvania	no date
Wirt, Mrs. E. M.	unknown	1837 (F)
Wogram, E. & F.	New York City	1859
Wood, Thomas	New York City	1843–1860
Woodward, Tiernan & Hale	St. Louis, Missouri	no date
Wooll, George	St. Louis, Missouri	no date
Worret, Charles	unknown	c. 1860
Wyeth, Francis	Boston, Massachusetts	1832
Zareski, Alexander & Co.	San Francisco, California	1851
Zeke	unknown	1864

(One asterisk* means "can date from address.")

* Can date from street address after you do further research. (See Bibliography)
† Made silhouettes that were lithographed.
‡ Pictured Grant.
(M) Music publisher.
** Worked for Currier & Ives, Major & Knapp, and others.
§ Civil War pictures.
(F) Flower prints.
(H) Horse prints.
(L) Lincoln picture.
(A) First American lithographer.

Other Prints Often Found in the United States

Alken, H.	Sporting prints	Did paintings, watercolors, etchings, prints. England 1785–1851.
Audubon, John James	"Audubon Prints"	Prints from books published by Robert Havell of London, England, 1827–1838.
Baxter, George	"Baxter Prints"	Aquatint or mezzotint of flowers, landscapes, groups of people. Made in mid-Victorian England.
Godey	"Godey Prints"	Pictures printed in *Lady's Book* or *Godey's Lady's Book* from 1830 to 1898.
Nash, J.	Colored lithographs of Elizabethan interiors	England, 1808–1878.
Nutting, Wallace	"Nutting Prints"	Photographs of birch trees, apple blossoms, landscapes, colonial interiors. Platinum prints, hand colored. Made 1898–1941. (Instant Expert tip: *Platinum finish not used after World War I.*)
Peterson, Charles	"Peterson Print"	Picture printed in *Peterson's Magazine,* women's fashion magazine, from 1842–1898.
Revere, Paul	"Boston Massacre"	An engraving copied from print of Henry Pelham. Original engraving March, 1770, reprint copy, 1832, and others. (Dog sometimes omitted in reprint.)
Wheatley, Francis	"Cries of London"	Thirteen stipple-engraved prints made 1793–1797 and copied later. Color prints of the tradespeople of London.
———	"Balloon Ascension Prints"	1783–1850, any pictures of the history of the balloon.
———	"Marine Prints"	1799–, any pictures of ships, marine battles. *Best if United States flag is seen.*

OTHER TYPES OF PICTURES

Silhouettes

The silhouette is a "cutout" paper picture that still enjoys popularity. It was named for an unpopular Frenchman of the eighteenth century. Étienne de Silhouette was the Controller General of Finances of France in 1759. He was a friend of the Marquise de Pompadour. This friendship, not his ability, got him his job.

The papers of his day were filled with cartoons and jokes about Mon-

John J. Audubon drew many famous pictures for use in his books. This "Golden Eagle" is from *The Birds of America,* engraved by Robert Havell. (New-York Historical Society, New York City)

The silhouette is still made. This 19th-century full figure silhouette shows Dr. John Treadwell of Salem, Massachusetts. (Essex Institute, Salem, Massachusetts)

sieur Silhouette. He required great sacrifices of the nobles because of a high tax rate.

The term "silhouette" came to mean a man reduced to his simplest form. The man taxed by Silhouette was indeed reduced to his simplest state. There was nothing left for him. The word "silhouette," meaning a simple outline picture, was added to the French dictionary in 1835. In eighteenth-century America the word "shade" was used until the French word came into use. The type of picture predates the name.

Any early silhouette is a collector's prize, but the most easily identified American silhouette was marked "Peale Museum" or "Peale's Museum." The silhouettes cut by Charles Willson Peale were all similar in technique. Peale cut the head into a piece of white paper. It was then backed with a dark silk or paper. The finished silhouette was not the usual black pasted on white. It was black showing through a hole in the white.

Most of the Peale silhouettes were made from 1800 to 1810.

One very famous maker, Auguste Édouart, worked in the United States and abroad. He was born in Dunkerque, France, in 1789, and went to England in 1813, where he spent several years making hair pictures and portraits. His first silhouettes were cut in 1825. He traveled from Scotland to Ireland to the United States, where he worked in Boston, Massachusetts, New Orleans, Louisiana, Charleston, West Virginia, Washington, D.C., and New York City. He signed his silhouettes "Aug Edouart."

There is a sad ending to the story of Mr. Édouart. On returning to France with duplicates of his silhouettes (about 50,000 pictures), his ship was wrecked, and all of Mr. Édouart's work was lost at sea. Auguste Édouart was so upset that he never worked again.

Other signed American silhouettes were made by Bache, Brown, Day, and others.

Paper cutouts were a popular pastime in Victorian days. This white paper design was cut and mounted on brown paper by Margaret Isabella Mallett in the United States about 1860 (Cooper Union, New York City) "The Lord's Prayer" is an English paper cutout. (Victoria and Albert Museum, London, England)

Paper pictures

There were many types of paper pictures that gained in popularity during the Victorian era. Elaborate and intricate cutout paper designs were made from about 1840 to the beginning of the 1900's. Most of them were made as personal treasures by ambitious and artistic women. A few exceptionally gifted artists made and sold the cutouts. The white paper was usually mounted on a dark paper, and framed to be hung as a picture.

The general rule is: THE MORE ELABORATE THE CUTOUT, THE BETTER THE PICTURE.

Quillwork

Paper filigree work, or quillwork, was first made in the seventeenth century. Samuel Pepys's diary mentioned it.

Small strips of paper were cut about one eighth of an inch wide, and were rolled into tight spirals of different sizes. The rolled spirals were made about the size of a watch spring, or even smaller, and glued on a background.

The designs were formed by the edges of the spiral rolls, which were painted to add to the design. Some artists even added shells, dried grass, or small pictures to the filigree pattern.

French and English quillwork is still considered the finest, but it must be noted that quillwork was also made in many other countries, including the United States and Canada.

Quillwork was popular during the eighteenth century, and was made as late as 1870.

Rolled-up pieces of paper glued to a wooden background make this box of quillwork. The ends of the paper have been painted orange, green, or gold. Glass covers the finished work. The tea box has the date 1800 worked into the design.

Tinsel pictures

The tinsel picture, or "gravure découpée," was an art form popular in the late eighteenth and early nineteenth centuries. Colored paper was cut to form pictures of fruit or landscapes. It was an art form popular with young ladies of little talent.

Pinprick pictures

A picture made with various sized holes is called a "pinprick" picture, and was very popular in England from 1820 to 1840. Complete instructions and designs for making these pictures were available in books and magazines.

The picture was made by pricking the paper with one of several sizes of pins. The holes could be made from either side of the paper. Some of the more talented of the amateur artists who tried this technique also used watercolors, thereby developing many interesting textures on the picture.

ANY OLD ODD PICTURE MADE FROM PAPER IN AN UNFAMILIAR STYLE IS PROBABLY A WORTHWHILE ANTIQUE.

Hair pictures

Hairwork of all kinds was a popular form of the arts during the early eighteenth century, and remained in style until about 1890. Flowers, fruit, portraits, and jewelry were woven from human hair.

The mourning picture made from human hair was a rather grisly fad.

A neglected "art" form is the pinprick picture. It was popular in England before 1840, but has been of little interest in recent years. This picture of a woman and two children was made in England. (Victoria and Albert Museum, London, England)

Any odd picture made from paper in an unfamiliar style is probably of interest to the collector. This penmanship horse was made in Pennsylvania in the mid-nineteenth century. It is one of many examples of calligraphy, a popular nineteenth-century pastime. (New-York Historical Society, New York City)

It was made in memory of a dear departed, but the hair of the deceased was not always used, as the supply was too limited to risk removal in some cases.

Love tokens and baby hair in lockets were also popular. IF IT'S MADE FROM HAIR IT IS RARE, BUT NOT ALWAYS WANTED BY COLLECTORS. (There is a limited market for items made of some unknown great-grandmother's hair.)

The grisly custom of making pictures from the hair of the deceased was in style until the 1890's. This hair picture of Rubens was not a memento of the dead, but the work of an interested English artist. (Victoria and Albert Museum, London, England)

Burned wood pictures

Hot poker pictures were popular from about 1850 to 1870. Landscapes and portraits were made by talented workmen who burned the pictures into basswood by using a red-hot poker as the only tool. The earliest ones we know of were made about 1790.

Pictures of sand resemble watercolors. This bird and snake are pictured with tiny grains of sand, not paint. (Victoria and Albert Museum, London, England)

Sand pictures

The art of making pictures from sand has been referred to as a "lost art." It may be either a lost art or just ignored, because the result was barely worth the effort. Benjamin Zobel of Bavaria made sand pictures in the early 1800's. He made pictures by using colored sand that was permanently fixed to the canvas. The finished painting resembled a watercolor picture. The artist signed either his name or initials to each picture. Other artists did similar work.

The wax figure is mounted in a deep frame. The flesh is surprisingly lifelike. This rendering of "Musick" was made in 1785.

Wax portraits

Wax pictures were molded or cast, then mounted on a darker background. The art of portrait making in wax was known in the eighteenth century in England and France, and remained popular until about 1850 in America. Some of the portraits were signed. The most famous American makers include Patience Wright, Joseph Wright, Mrs. Platt, Robert Hughes, and Henry Adams.

Be careful of the wax portraits of the Presidents. Some clever fakes have been made by casting in wax from plaster models made from bronze medals originally made at the United States Mint.

Wax portraits of George Washington dated 1797 and signed G. Rouse are forgeries of the 1920's. Several of these wax portraits were "found" in New York and Philadelphia in 1925. They sold for as much as $250 to collectors and dealers who believed they were authentic.

The wax portraits were exposed as frauds in 1933. The artistic, well-worked likenesses were made in Liverpool, England, in 1924 by an artist named Grey. He modeled the wax, painted it, and placed the picture in an authentic old frame.

All of his work was signed with the same fictitious name of G. Rouse.

WAX PORTRAITS ARE IMPORTANT COLLECTORS' ITEMS. BEWARE OF FAKES THAT ARE USUALLY PORTRAITS OF PRESIDENTS.

Glass paintings

There is great confusion between paintings on glass and reverse paintings on glass. The art is not lost or difficult to paint, but the style is currently out of vogue.

Reverse paintings on glass have been made since the fourteenth century. Several types of paintings were made where the design was transferred or painted on the back of the glass with oil paints. During the eighteenth century Jean Glomi invented a method of framing prints against glass with black and gold bands painted as borders on the glass. "Églomise" is the French term for a special type of reverse painting on glass that is backed with gold or silver-leaf foil. There is great doubt that Monsieur Glomi ever made the type of glass painting that has been named for him.

The value of the picture is determined by the subject matter, the excellence of the painting, and the condition. Peeling paint will lower the value. OLD PICTURES WERE PAINTED ON GLASS THAT HAD AN UNEVEN SURFACE. THE NEWER PICTURES ARE PAINTED ON HEAVY GLASS AND APPEAR TO BE PRINTS PASTED ON AND COLORED.

AN OLD GLASS PICTURE IS ALMOST ALWAYS IN ITS ORIGINAL FRAME. The painting is so delicate that it might be destroyed if the frame is removed.

Most of the glass paintings seen today were made in England during the 1770–1800 period. The finest ones were made prior to 1825.

In the United States reverse painting became the vogue during the eighteenth and nineteenth centuries, and it was often a hobby for the housewife. *Godey's Magazine* in July of 1857 had an article that explained how to paint on glass.

Most American reverse paintings were made by using a simple five-step process. A piece of glass was first completely covered with turpentine while a paper print was being soaked in water. After the paper dried slightly, it was placed face down on the turpentine-covered glass. The print was pressed so that no bubbles remained. As the print dried, it was rolled off the glass so that the outline of the picture remained on the glass until it dried and could be painted.

The American paintings of the Pennsylvania-German areas are gay, crude portraits of heroes or religious subjects. Many examples of portraits of Washington can still be seen.

New England painters preferred the still life. Pictures or foil were often pasted to the inside of the glass to add to the glitter of the finished picture. Landscapes and sea battles were also painted. Many of these paintings were made for clock and mirror decorations.

The English method of transfer-glass pictures was developed about 1700. The pictures were usually signed, and the subject matter is named. English pictures are more formal than the American folk-art paintings.

IF THE SUBJECT MATTER IS INTERESTING, YOUR GLASS PAINTING IS WORTHWHILE. OLDER REVERSE GLASS PAINTINGS ARE MORE SOPHISTICATED THAN VICTORIAN ONES.

Tintypes, daguerreotypes

A tintype is a picture made by a photographic process that used a black enameled metal plate. It originally used a piece of japanned metal and was called a "ferrotype." The tintype was developed by Hamilton L. Smith of Kenyon College, Gambier, Ohio, in 1856. He sold the patent to Peter Neff, who continued the work.

The daguerreotype was a picture made on a copperplate coated with silver. It was developed by Louis Jacques Mandé Daguerre of France. Because the tintype was simpler and cheaper to use, it quickly replaced the daguerreotype.

EXAMPLES OF EARLY TINTYPES AND DAGUERREOTYPES ARE COLLECTED FOR THE SUBJECT MATTER OF THE PICTURE. HISTORICAL PICTURES ARE BEST.

Magic-lantern slides

Franchesco Eschinard described a magic-lantern machine in 1668. This was about the same time that a German Jesuit, Athañasius Kircher, claimed that he invented the magic lantern.

The early machines were lighted by oil lamps, and a series of hand-

Each stereopticon slide had two photographs that were almost identical. All the slides came in a standard size, 7 inches by 3½ inches, mounted on a stiff cardboard. (Facsimile here has been reduced 30 percent.)

A series of pictures were painted on this glass magic lantern slide. As the slide was pushed through the projector, the subject appeared to move.

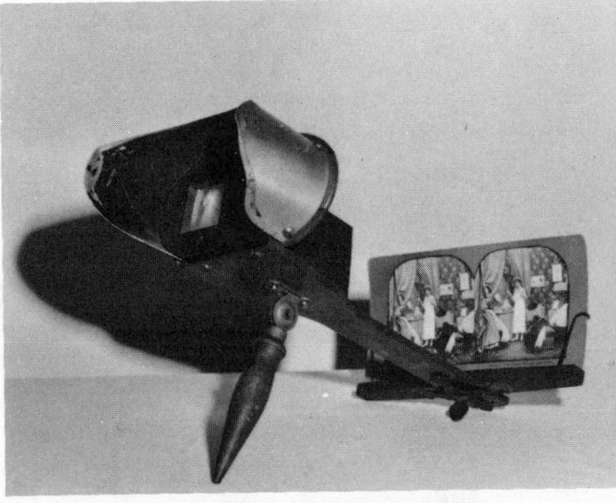

The stereopticon viewer is needed to appreciate any collection of slides. Viewers were made from 1840 to the present.

painted pictures was moved across in front of the light. The pictures appeared to be moving on the screen.

The ox-hydrogen light was developed in 1840, and it gave a brighter and clearer picture than the oil lamp. Many types of magic lanterns have been developed over the years. The Zoetrope projected drawings. The vitascope of 1896 and the Mutascope, or peepshow, were all later developments.

Fred Langenheim and his brother, of Philadelphia, patented magic-lantern slides from photographs in 1850. The photographic slides created great interest and soon replaced the earlier painted slides. Many of the slides of the late 1800's were made in Germany.

If you collect old pictures made by any type of camera, always look for the unusual subject. Civil War pictures, early views of cities, and life in the West are among the best. Just remember that there are no photographs of George and Martha Washington. They died years before the first permanent photograph was made in 1822.

Three-dimensional stereoscopic pictures are not new, as the stereoscopic viewer was a favored parlor pastime during the Victorian era, beginning about 1850. Two separate pictures were mounted on one card. They were viewed through the stereoscope viewer, and a single three-dimensional picture appeared.

Sir Charles Wheatstone developed an experimental viewer in 1838. By 1840, several different types of stereography were made by using photographs. Pictures were made by using two lenses in one camera or by taking two separate pictures two to three inches apart. The hand stereoscope that we still see today was invented in 1859 by Oliver Wendell Holmes, and his name appears on many pictures of the 1866–1869 period. By 1875, more than a hundred American photographers were selling thousands of views, and many thousands more were being made in Europe.

Collectors specialize in different types of stereographs. The views made from 1850 to 1935 are still obtainable, but the earliest ones are the most desired. If you want to start a collection, first choose a subject. There were Civil War views, Northwestern scenes, scenic pictures of many cities, pictures of industry, home interiors, natural history, comic views, and pictures of fine arts. Procure as much information as possible about each picture.

If they are not labeled, make notes about where they were found, plus any information about the date of the cards, as it is possible to trace a card through the shape, the photographer's name, and the type of picture. One word of warning: The condition of the cards is important. Do not try to clean the cards without full instructions.

Daguerreotype cases

The early daguerreotype case was made from pressed paper that was painted to imitate leather. Samuel Peck invented a composition case in 1854 that was made of shellac and sawdust and pressed into a mold. The case was velvet-lined on one side, and the picture was on the other side. The label of the daguerreotype casemaker could sometimes be found under the picture.

List of makers (date of first known cases by maker)

E. Anthony, New York (c. 1857)
A. P. Critchlow & Company, Northampton, Massachusetts (c. 1856)
Florence Manufacturing Co., Florence, Massachusetts (c. 1866)
Frederick P. Goll, Jr., New York (c. 1841)
Gordon & Stadley, Boston, Massachusetts (c. 1846)
A. Henning & Eymann, New York (c. 1860)
Holmes, Booth and Haydens, Waterbury, Connecticut (c. 1856)
Improved Union Cases—S. Peck & Co., New Haven, Connecticut (c. 1854)
Littlefield, Parsons & Co., Union Cases (c. 1856)
I. A. Martine & Co., New York (made linings) (c. 1850)
J. F. Masher, Philadelphia, Pennsylvania (c. 1853)
Anthony Schaefer, New York (c. 1859)
Scoville Mfg. Co., Superior, Waterbury, Connecticut (c. 1844)
F. Seiler, New York (c. 1849)
Seiler & Rupp, New York (c. 1850)
William Shew, Boston, Massachusetts (c. 1844)
Fred Smith, New York (c. 1850)
F. B. Smith & Hartman, New York (c. 1850)
Wadams & Company (c. 1858)

Prints, Paintings, Pictures to Hang: Bibliography

Cadfryn-Roberts, John. *British Sporting Prints.* London: Ariel Press, 1963.

A small collection of color prints of the English sporting subjects of the nineteenth century.

Chatterton, E. Keble. *Old Ship Prints.* London: Spring Books, 1965.

An extensive study, well illustrated, of prints from the fifteenth century to modern times, that show ships and the sea.

Comstock, Helen. *American Lithographs of the Nineteenth Century.* New York: Barrows, 1950.

An entertaining, tiny book with seventy-five illustrations of typical lithographs.

Conningham, F. A. *Currier and Ives.* Cleveland: World, 1950.

A tiny book that is a good introduction to the collecting of Currier and Ives prints.

———. *Currier & Ives Prints, An Illustrated Check List.* New York: Crown, 1970.

Over 6,000 Currier & Ives prints are listed by name, date and size in this check list.

Darrah, William Culp. *Stereo Views.* Gettysburg, Pennsylvania: Privately printed. (Order from author, R.D. 1, Gettysburg, Pennsylvania 17325.)

Ettlinger, L. D. and R. G. Holloway. *Compliments of the Season.* London: Penguin, 1947.

A small book with color and black-and-white photographs and an introductory text about greeting cards.

Hughes, Therle. *Prints for the Collector.* New York: Praeger, 1971.

This book tells the collector how to recognize a woodcut, engraving, etching, lithograph, mezzotint, aquatint, and other types of prints. The emphasis is on English production.

The Museum of Graphic Arts. *American Printmaking, The First 150 Years.* Washington, D.C.: The Smithsonian Institution Press, 1969.

This is a catalog of an exhibit of prints made in America before 1820. One hundred and fifteen prints are pictured.

Peters, Harry. *America on Stone.* Garden City, New York: Doubleday, Doran, 1931.

The definitive work on lithography in the United States. Pictures, makers' history, and all other important information.

———. *Currier and Ives.* Garden City, New York: Doubleday, Doran, 1927.

An important work about Currier and Ives, including many pictures and the history of the firm.

Rinhart, Floyd and Marion. *American Daguerreian Art.* New York: Clarkson N. Potter, 1967.

The collector will welcome this study of the art in daguerreian pictures. Examples of the most desirable types of pictures are shown. There is also a good chapter on daguerreotype cases.

Zigrosser, Carl, and Christa Gaehde. *A Guide to the Collecting and Care of Original Prints.* New York: Crown, 1965.

The guide for the collector of prints who wishes to take proper care of his antiques.

13

Paper Antiques

COLLECTORS are a compulsive lot, and almost every family has one relative who saves everything. The ridiculous in saving is an accumulation of huge piles of old newspapers, magazines, boxes, cans, and other debris strewn throughout the house, halls, on tables, floors, and in almost every possible cleared area. Fortunately, the "saving" mania is most often seen in its milder forms, but if any of your relatives has lived in one house for over twenty-five years, the attic will show distinct evidence of "collectivitis." Boxes and packages of unlabeled pictures, unwanted books, and assorted useful and useless junk is stored in attics for years.

It is every collector's dream to be turned loose in an attic that has been untouched for fifty years. China, glass, old furniture, jewelry, toys, and even household tools are usually sorted and saved, but many old newspapers, books, catalogs and other paper materials are often overlooked, and burned.

It is virtually impossible to save everything, but here are a few hints about some things worth studying. Now go back into your wonderful dream attic and sort the piles of debris. Study each pile carefully to see what you really own.

Newspapers

Old newspapers are not as valuable as most beginners believe. NEWSPAPERS PUBLISHED IN AMERICA FROM 1690 TO 1820 ARE IMPORTANT AND SHOULD BE KEPT OR SOLD TO A COLLECTOR. Some papers printed after 1820 are rare and desirable. ANY PAPER THAT IS VOLUME ONE, NUMBER ONE, IS IMPORTANT.

Papers were first printed in western states and territories years after many of the eastern newspapers had been started. Sometimes a late-nineteenth-century western paper is of great importance. To be sure that your old newspapers are worthy of a finer fate than the trash can, look up the information in *American Newspapers: A Union List of Files in United States and Canada,* by Winifred Gregory (1947), and *History and Bibliography of American Newspapers 1690–1820* by Clarence

Brigham (1947). Any paper listed as "no copy found" or even any paper of the early dates that are not listed in either book is of value. Sometimes early papers are especially in demand if a full year or a long run of the paper is available. Local historical societies and libraries often search for this sort of reference material.

It is frequently the content of the newspaper that makes it of value to the collector. Interesting early advertisements, announcements of important historical events, or the first publication of great literary works are always in great demand.

The Ulster County "Gazette" of January 4, 1800

The original Ulster County *Gazette* was published in Kingston, New York, and only two copies of the original paper are known to exist. One of the papers is in the Library of Congress, and the other is in the American Antiquarian Society in Worcester, Massachusetts. George Washington died on December 14, 1799. The first printed reports of his death appeared three weeks later in the Ulster County *Gazette* of January 4.

Thousands of reprints of the famous paper were made during the nineteenth century. There was a celebration in Kingston, New York, in 1846, and the paper was reprinted as part of the festivities. There have been at least 21 to perhaps 75 additional printings since that time. The original *Gazette* had a double fleur-de-lis watermark 3⅛ inches by 1$^{15}/_{16}$ inches in the paper, and the style of type used featured an "S" similar to today's "F." The book *The Ulster County Gazette and Its Illegitimate Offspring,* by R. W. G. Vail (New York: New York Public Library, 1931), tells more of this tale.

New York "Morning Post," November 7, 1783

Washington's farewell address to the army appeared in the New York *Morning Post* of November 7, 1783. It has been reprinted several times for various centennial celebrations. If you can see the closed fingers of the hand at the left of the printer's notice in the heading, you own a copy.

New York "Herald," Saturday, April 15, 1865

The death of Lincoln was reported in detail in the New York *Herald* of April 15, 1865, and the paper has been reprinted at least four times. The 1890 reprint was published with two pages of advertisements, while many of the later editions were printed without the advertising. One issue even showed Lincoln's picture, which was not in the original paper. All the forgeries are interesting, but they are not of great value. THE ORIGINAL PAPER HAD EIGHT NUMBERED PAGES; MOST COPIES HAVE TWO OR FOUR UNNUMBERED PAGES.

The "Daily Citizen," Vicksburg, Mississippi, July 2, 1863

During the Civil War, there were a few southern newspapers that were printed on any paper that was available, some of them printed on wallpaper. The "wallpaper" newspapers became such great curiosities that many facsimiles have been printed, and the above date is the most common one found on facsimiles.

OTHER PAPERS

The Library of Congress, Washington 25, D.C., has eighteen printed circulars telling about the reprints of many important newspapers. A copy of the information is sent free from the Periodicals Division of the Library of Congress.

Hints on care

Preserve paper antiques by keeping them flat or under glass whenever possible. Old prints may be bleached and ironed to remove stains and wrinkles, but it is an elaborate process that requires the touch of an expert. Never use cellophane tape to repair paper. Badly neglected paper can be mounted on a special backing that will preserve it, but its status as an antique will change. It is often the only way to save the paper, and the attempt should be made.

Copy of the original *Ulster County Gazette.*

ULSTER COUNTY GAZETTE.

Published at KINGSTON, Ulster Co., N. Y., BY SAMUEL FREER and SON.

[Vol. II.] SATURDAY, January 4, 1800. [Num. 88]

AMERICAN CONGRESS.
TUESDAY, December 10.

The hour having arrived which the President appointed, Mr. Speaker, attended by the members present, proceeded to the President's house to present him their address in answer to his speech at the opening of the present session; and having returned the President's reply thereto was read as follows:

Gentlemen of the House of Representatives

THIS very respectful address from the representatives of the people of the United States, at their first assembly, after a fresh election, under the strong impression of the public opinion and national sense, at this interesting and singular crisis of our public affairs, has excited my sensibility and receives my sincere and grateful acknowledgments.

As long as we can maintain with harmony and affection, the honor of our country, consistently with its peace, externally and internally, while that is attainable, or in war, when that becomes necessary—asserts its real independence and sovereignty, and support the constitutional energies and dignity of its government—we may be perfectly sure under the smiles of Divine Providence, that we shall effectually promote and extend our national interests and happiness.

The applause of the Senate and House of Representatives, so justly bestowed upon the volunteers and militia, for their

Knowing as we do, that the United States are sincerely anxious for a fair and liberal execution of the treaty of amity, commerce and navigation entered into with Great Britain; we learn with regret, that the progress of adjustment has been interrupted by a difference of opinion among the commissioners. We hope, however, that the justice, the moderation, and the obvious interest of both parties will lead to satisfactory explanations, and that the business will then go forward to an amicable close of all the differences and demands between the two countries. We are fully persuaded that the Legislature of the United States will cheerfully enable you to realize your insurances of performing on our part, all engagements with punctuality and the most scrupulous good faith.

When we reflect upon the late uncertainty of the result of the late mission to France; and upon the uncommon nature, extent, and aspect of the war now raging in Europe; which effects materially our relations with the powers at war, and which has changed the condition of those colonies our neighborhood; we are of opinion with you, that it would be neither wise or safe to relax our measures of defence, or to lessen any of our preparations to repel aggression.

Our enquiries and attention should be carefully directed to the various other im portant subjects which you have recommended to our consideration; and from

had his horse shot under him but himself received no injury, although exposed to the greatest personal danger under a heavy fire, being frequently in the front of the line, animating by his example the exertions of his troops, upon which on this and every other occasion where the British arms are brought into action, it is impossible to bestow too much praise.

—

The Hamburgh mail due on Sunday last arrived this morning. It bring accounts of the events which took place in Switzerland in the latter end of Sept. except only those which relate to Marshal Suwarrow of which we have no positive information. The Arch Duke, it appears, was rapidly advancing to repair the evils which had been occasioned by his absence. His force we know, by private letters, to consist of 26000 men, with which he was at Schaffhausen on the 2d. The army of Conde consisting of 6000 men was the same day at Stoach.

The forces joined to the Bavarians and to the corps of Gen. Korsakow, are it must be allowed, more than sufficient to secure that part of Germany from all danger. We rejoice at seeing the conjectures which we have from the first instance averred, respecting the probable consequences of the victory of Maffena, thus confirmed.

The Hamburgh mail which became due on Wednesday had not arrived when this paper went to press.

the right the point on which the great efforts of the enemy were directed.

At a late hour in the forenoon some reinforcements arrived on this side of the Limmat, but the enemy were already masters of some of the principal heights which command the town; and notwithstanding the bravery displayed by the Russians in their repeated attacks, the superiority in point of force and position on the side of the French rendered it impossible for them to regain that which had made themselves masters of part of Zurich Berg and nearly surrounded the town. The attack on the position of General Horze had terminated rather in favor of the Austrians; but Gen. Horze was unfortunately killed at the commencement of the action and Gen. Petracsh who succeeded to the command of the army, having resolved in consequence of the loss he had sustained, to avoid the attack which he expected the next morning, retreated in the night from Uznach. The situation of the Russian army was thus rendered still more critical, and it became absolutely necessary to abandon Zurich, and the position in that neighborhood without delay. On the 26th in the morning the retreat took place, and the whole arrived in the course of that night in the neighborhood of Englisan and Schaffhausen without experiencing any loss of consequence during their march. We have to regret the loss of between two

14

Store Stuff

THE COUNTRY STORE has become the center of a whole new area in collecting. Items that were found in the old general store, even though many of them are only twenty-five years old, have now become a part of the history of our country, and the objects are sought by a great many collectors. Some of it is really junk, not art, but it is junk with a personality loaded with humor, history, whimsy, or even mystery. As the fine antiques become more scarce, and the everyday items become more desirable, many homemakers now feature the cobbler's bench or an old kitchen cupboard in the living room, topped by painted cans from the grocery store or signs that advertise other items of an earlier era.

Saving these Victorian or twentieth-century store items is not so ridiculous as it might at first appear to the serious antique collector. Many museums now feature hatboxes covered with old wallpaper, or shaving cream jars with Pratt transfer decorations. Let us not forget that they were commercial packages made before the mid-nineteenth century.

What's good in the old store

Bottles have been described in detail, but remember that any bottle made before 1900 or any specially shaped bottle will be a collector's joy.

Boxes, tins, and cans

The painted tinwares known as toleware are collectors' items. Most types of store boxes are in demand and being collected. The early boxes of metal were painted or stenciled directly on the metal. The Somers Brothers of Brooklyn, New York, invented a method of lithographing a design onto the metal box, instead of on a paper label, in 1850. These lithographed tins are now in great demand. One of the very unusual examples pictures the Boston tea party. ANY LITHOGRAPHED CAN WITH A PICTURE IS OF MORE VALUE TO THE COLLECTOR THAN A LITHOGRAPHED CAN WITH JUST NAMES.

Cans with paper labels are among the most difficult items to find. Boxes or cans featuring elaborately designed paper labels, or even the

Can labels like these of paper are very scarce today. The Potter and Wrightington's soup was made about 1880. Notice the celery holder on the table. The Shakers of Mount Lebanon, New York, used this label for their string beans, one of many products canned by this group. Bowman Brand tomatoes used this label before the invention of the horseless carriage.

label alone, are in great demand. Labels that mentioned the Shakers, who packed stringbeans, jellies, flower seeds, and other foods, are especially desirable, or labels that feature scenes of a time long past. A label picturing a maid serving soup or a Victorian factory building can help to date the package. Canned food was first made about 1825 in America. ANY PAPER-LABELED CAN THAT CAN BE DATED BEFORE 1875 IS RARE.

The Roly Poly, made about 1900, is a special type of metal tobacco tin that is at a premium. The Roly

The cigar-store Indian of wood is almost impossible to find today at the average collector's price, but the papier-mâché cigar-store figures can still be found. This three-foot figure of William Penn offered cigars for sale before 1900. It was made by the Old King Cole Papier Mache Works, of Canton, Ohio.

Poly lithographed colored tin cans were shaped like fat human figures with round bottoms, and could be tipped from side to side like a child's toy. Sports figures, policemen, Negro mammies, clowns, and other characters were pictured on these cans, many of which held Mayo cut-plug tobacco. Another specialized type of can that is much in demand is the gunpowder can. They often had attractive hunting scenes or animals lithographed on the metal, and there are collectors who specialize in this sort of container. (See picture in Chapter 17, "Toys.")

Boxes and crates with unusual labels are in great demand by the country-store enthusiast. Some over-eager decorators remove the end of the case with the paper label and hang it as a picture in a living room. It is an entertaining bit of advertising Americana but not great art.

Signs of the times

(For more about advertising, see paper antiques, trade cards, signs, and so on.)

Many good store signs were painted directly on tin, and designed to look like a picture with a frame. They are rare and valued. The Grapenuts ad featuring a girl and her St. Bernard is one of the best examples. ANY OF THESE EARLY ADS THAT PICTURES AN AMERICAN FLAG OR A NEGRO HAS ADDED VALUE BECAUSE COLLECTORS WANT THEM. KNOWN BRAND NAMES ARE ALSO OF GREATER VALUE.

Store furniture

The store cabinet used to store thread has been refinished, repainted, rehardwared, reworked, and has found a place in many living rooms. The original cabinets had very narrow drawers with glass on the front, and were used as display pieces for thread from about 1880. Many said "Clark Company O.N.T. (Our New Thread)" or "J and P Coates Spool Cotton." We feel that they should be kept in original condition to be of value.

A new style of thread cabinet was used in stores by about 1890. It was

Old store signs were made of paper or lithographed tin or glass, and are eagerly collected today. The Grape-Nuts girl lithographed on tin with an embossed tin frame is one of the finest of the store signs. It was made about 1900. The New York City Insurance Company sign showing a street corner in New York was lithographed by the Kellogg and Bulkley Co. of Hartford, Connecticut, in 1867. "Kitty's Bath" was a paper ad for Dingman's soap, printed in 1883. The Lorillard snuff ad is printed on paper by J. O'Flyn of New York City about 1880.

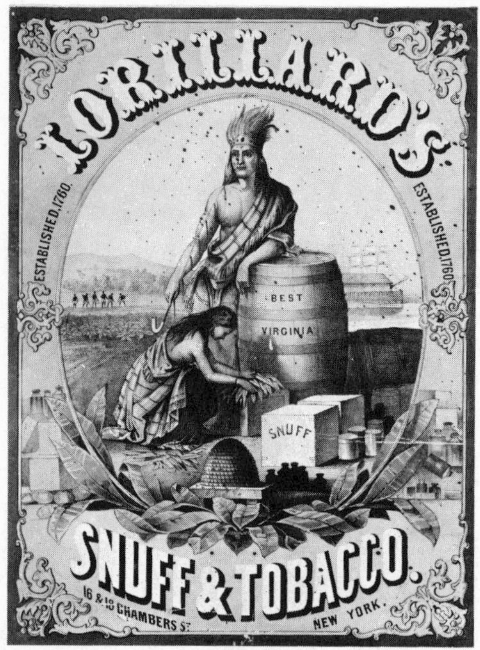

a tall four-sided chest with glass panels on two sides and louvered doors on the other two sides, with a swivel base so the thread could be seen.

Other large cabinets were used in country stores. Deep bins for food, collars, or sundries are very scarce, and because most of them are too large for the average home they are only in demand by the country-store addict. There are a surprising number of collectors (museums and villages) that have stores or store-like setups, and display numerous cans, bottles, toys, banks, and even apple peelers.

Coffee grinders

The original coffee grinder was used to grind coffee in a grocery store, but about 1950 someone decided that it would make a "cute" lamp. Thousands of reproductions have been made of the early home coffee grinders, so that thousands of lamps could be made. Coffee mills were not listed in the 1886 catalog of one large hardware firm, but by 1894 several ads began to appear. Royal and The Telephone Coffee mills were mentioned by name, and by 1912 the Lightning, Kin, Fast Grinder, Superior, Queen, Premier, and Swift's Family mills were being made. The coffee mill seems to have lost favor by the 1930's, but a few are still being made.

The large Enterprise No. 1 Store Mill was patented in 1870, and had one side wheel. The two-wheel model was made in 1873. The large floor-model store grinder or the large counter model mills or grinders date from about the same time. THE TWO-WHEEL MILLS OR GRINDERS SHOULD HAVE THE ORIGINAL PAINT AND ALL THE PARTS.

Peelers, shredders, choppers, and so on

The country store sold all sorts of gadgets for the housewife. The late-Victorian period was the time of the gadget, and therefore the cherry pitter, cabbage chopper, and the apple peeler were in great demand. Many of the "kitchen helpers" were made of iron. MOST HAVE A PATENT DATE MOLDED INTO THE HANDLE. Look for the date, as it is one of the best clues to the age of the item. Try to specialize. If you like this type of collecting, a complete collection of apple peelers or eggbeaters showing the continuous improvements and changes can be of great interest, and the study behind it can help others interested in similar fields. Once you learn about a particular invention or idea, you can continue to date it with fair certainty from its various stages of sophistication.

Country stores were filled with inventions that are no longer in demand but are historically interesting because they show a former way of life. The wooden mouse trap with a mallet that hit the mouse on the head, the flytrap maze baited with honey, the ice tongs made for fifty-pound blocks of ice, and hundreds of other things no longer needed were made.

An apple peeler, c. 1880, of cast iron.

The Gilbert flycatcher, late nineteenth century. (Index of American Design)

Iron pan for cooking over the fire in a fireplace. (Old Sturbridge Village, Sturbridge, Massachusetts)

Warming pan of iron and brass (Pilgrim Society, Plymouth, Massachusetts)

ANY OLD TOOL OR KITCHEN UTENSIL THAT IS IN ORIGINAL CONDITION AND MADE BEFORE 1900 IS OF INTEREST.

Never, never repaint, refinish, or restore an old metal or wooden piece if you want it because of its value as an antique. If the kitchenware is still for use, refinishing or restoring might add to the beauty, but it will detract from its worth to the serious collector. Rusty iron can be cleaned, and the rust removed, but *never* repaint the piece.

There are many old and odd pieces that can be considered under the chapter heading "Store Stuff." Like any other field of antiques, it takes study and perseverance to learn all you should know. The best we can offer is a list of the type of store stuff, kitchenware, and tools that are now in demand:

Blickensderfer typewriter, c. 1900. (Frederick C. Crawford Auto Aviation Museum of Western Reserve Historical Society, Cleveland, Ohio)

Popular	Interesting	Ignored
apple peelers	bone- or wood-handled table forks and knives	bathtubs
brass utensils	bootjacks	brooms
butter molds	bottle openers	candy-making tools
cake molds	clothes	early electrical equipment
candle molds	cookie boards	early typewriters
churns	copper wash boilers	egg carriers
cookie cutters	corkscrews	eggbeaters
copper utensils	farm pitchforks, other wooden implements	flour sifters
corn-stick pans	irons (sad irons)	gas mantles
cranberry scoops	lemon squeezers	glass rolling pins
crocks and jugs	mannikins	"graniteware" (or enamelware or agateware—mottled enamel-on-tin dishes)
decoys	match holders	(old) iceboxes
fireplace cooking equipment	meat grinders	ice-cream makers
gaming devices	nutcrackers	ice-cream scoops
ice-cream molds (pewter)	nutmeg graters	needle cases
iron teakettles	pastry cutters	peanut-butter pails
large wooden bowls	potato mashers	pencil sharpeners
mortars and pestles	sausage stuffers	soapstone foot warmers
scales	sewing machines on stand	turkey-feather dusters
spoons, skimmers, forks for cooking	slaw slicers	washing machines
stoves	spittoons	
stringholders	waffle irons	
trivets	washboards	
wall telephones		
woodworking tools		

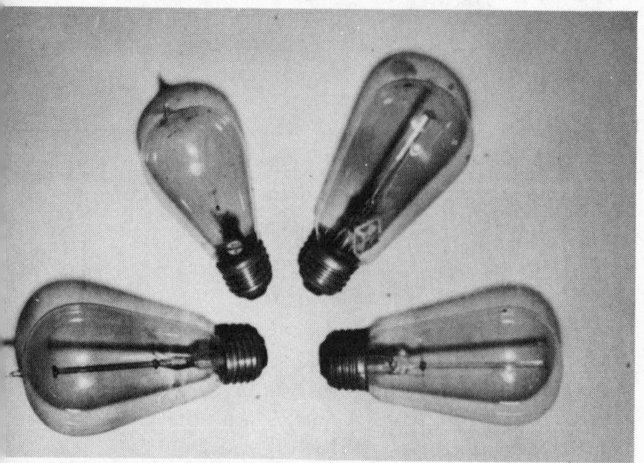

Early lightbulbs c. 1900–1920. (Lee Kovel)

Butter mold, Pennsylvania, c. 1790. (Metropolitan Museum of Art, New York City)

Turk's head mold for baking bread. (Arlene and Paul Greaser, Allentown, Pennsylvania)

Woodworking tools

It would be nice to be able to write a chapter about many of the tools that were used by our ancestors and are now being collected. Very little can be written that would be of help to a collector searching for the maker or age of a special tool. Cabinetmakers, blacksmiths, tinsmiths, and all the other tradesmen usually made their own special tools for special jobs. They were patterned after tools they had used or seen while learning their trade.

There are several books that list and picture old tools, and they should be of some aid in identifying many tools. Help might be obtained on any really confusing "what's it" by contacting the Early American Industries Association, Colonial Williamsburg, Virginia.

The best advice of a collector of tools is IF IT LOOKS LIKE AN UNUSUAL TOOL, SAVE IT. TRY TO IDENTIFY IT THROUGH BOOKS, MUSEUMS, OR OLD TIMERS. DON'T PAINT IT, REFINISH IT, OR OTHERWISE CHANGE THE CONDITION.

Barbed-wire fencing

Barbed wire is one of the unusual items collected in the West. The first patents for a wire fence with barbs or points was issued in 1867. The wire had wooden blocks strung on a wire. Each block had two sharp

Wooden tools, scoop, piggin, and soap dish from nineteenth century. (Old Sturbridge Village, Sturbridge, Massachusetts)

points projecting from it, while the later types of barbed wire had small wheel-like attachments, sharp spiral wire, or other variations.

Collectors want eighteen-inch samples made before 1890. Early types are often mounted on wooden plaques. Collectors have been able to find bits of the old wire still clinging to old fenceposts or in barns.

HINTS ON CARE OF WOODENWARE AND IRON

Wooden molding plane, late nineteenth century.

Woodenware

Never soak wood in water, but wash it quickly with a mild soap and water. Use a stiff brush, rinse with clear water, wipe dry, and let the piece air-dry at room temperature. Oil or wax wood lightly if it is necessary.

Iron

Remove the rust by soaking the piece in kerosene for twenty-four hours or use any one of several commercial preparations made for the removal of rust. Wash, dry, and coat the piece with a light oil to protect it.

The Climax washing machine of 1876, made in Ohio. (Henry Ford Museum, Dearborn, Michigan)

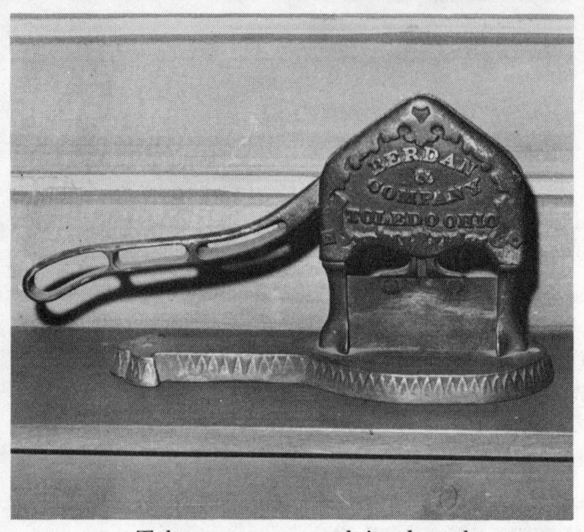

Tobacco cutter, used in the tobacco store about 1880.

Spinning wheel of the nineteenth century. (Index of American Design)

Store Stuff: Bibliography

Beitz, Les. *Treasury of Frontier Relics.* New York: Crown, 1966.

A collection of western antiques, including early gold mining equipment, tools, barbed wire, and store stuff

Carson, Gerald. *The Old Country Store.* New York: Oxford University Press, 1954.

A pleasant story of the workings of the country store, with valuable index and source-material listing.

———. *Country Stores in Early New England.* Sturbridge, Massachusetts: Old Sturbridge Village, 1955.

A pamphlet about the New England store.

Davis, Alec. *Package & Print, The Development of Container and Label Design.* New York: Clarkson N. Potter, 1967.

This English book gives the history of food packaging in both England and the United States. It has detailed history and is well illustrated.

Dolan, J. R. *The Yankee Peddlers of Early America.* New York: Clarkson N. Potter, 1964.

The story of where the peddler traveled, what he sold, and how he lived in America before 1900. Illustrated but not indexed.

Drepperd, Carl W. and Marjorie Matthews Smith. *Handbook of Tomorrow's Antiques.* New York: Crowell, 1953.

A book telling of the many types of "not yet antiques" that could be collected. Several chapters about store items, including agricultural tools, cake molds, cast iron, catalogs, clock containers, commercial, bakers', dairy, and gaming devices, inkwells, kitchen implements, matches, signs, tobacco, and woodenware. Well illustrated.

Faber, A. D. *Smokers' Segars and Stickers.* Watkins Glen, New York: Century House, 1949.

An 80-page book with illustrations, line drawings of old cigar labels.

Glissman, A. H. *The Evolution of the Sad-Iron.* Privately printed, 1970. (Order from author, P.O. Box 215, Carlsbad, California.)

Over 400 irons from all over the world are illustrated and identified. The irons date from early Chinese to the 1930s.

Goodman, W. L. *The History of Woodworking Tools.* New York: McKay, 1964.
Illustrated history of the development of different types of tools from ancient times to this century.

Gould, Mary Earle. *Antique Tin and Tole Ware.* Rutland, Vermont: Tuttle, 1958.
Two hundred and fifty photographs of small tin pieces have been included in this excellent book about the handmade tinwares of the nineteenth century. One chapter is about painted tinwares.

———. *Early American Wooden Ware.* Rutland, Vermont: Tuttle, 1962.
An excellent book picturing and describing hundreds of different pieces of early woodenware.

Hankenson, Dick. *Trivets Old and Re-Pro.* Privately printed, 1968. (Order from author, Maple Plain, Minnesota.)
A picture listing of trivets, names, and prices, but with no other history included.

Johnson, Laurence A. *Over the Counter and on the Shelf.* Rutland, Vermont: Tuttle, 1961.
The best general book about the contents of a general store and storekeeping from 1620 to 1920.

Kauffman, Harry J. *Early American Ironware.* Rutland, Vermont: Tuttle, 1966.
The history of all types of ironware, including lamps, hardware, guns, tools, locks, and tinware.

Lantz, Louise K. *Old American Kitchenware, 1725–1925.* New York: Nelson, 1970.
The utilitarian kitchen items such as egg beaters, can openers, pie crimpers, coffee grinders and just plain pots and pans are pictured from catalog reprints and photographs. Historic information is given when available.

Lewis, John. *Printed Ephemera.* New York: Dover Publications, 1962.
Several chapters in this book show early labels, letterheads, and other package information that is difficult to find.

Peirce, Josephine H. *Fire on the Hearth.* Springfield, Massachusetts: Pond-Ekberg Company, 1951.
A good book, well illustrated, with detailed history of the heating stove.

Pinto, Edward H. *Wooden Bygones of Smoking and Snuff Taking.* London, England: Hutchinson, 1962.
This book gives detailed information of early smoking accessories such as pipes, tobacco stoppers, tobacco jars, humidors, cigar cases.

Rendell, Joan. *Matchbox Labels.* New York: Praeger, 1968.
This is an English book which gives the history of matches and shows paper matchbox labels.

Smith, H. R. Bradley. *Blacksmiths' and Farriers' Tools at Shelburne Museum.* Shelburne, Vermont: The Shelburne Museum, 1966.
This is a very detailed study of the design and use of tools used by a blacksmith.

Wildung, Frank H. *Woodworking Tools at Shelburne Museum.* Shelburne, Vermont: Shelburne Museum, 1957.
A catalog of the tools at Shelburne Museum.

Many reprints of old mail-order catalogs are now available. These include selected years of Sears, Roebuck & Co., Montgomery Ward, Marshall Field, and others.

15

Books

BOOKS, like oil paintings, are a specialty that requires an expert to know the really authentic rarity. Books can be purchased, collected, and sold with a fair degree of certainty that a fortune has not been overlooked. There are just a few tips regarding the books that might be of great value; other books are usually bought and sold on a supply-and-demand basis.

Everyone has heard about the rare manuscript that has been found and then sold for millions. This is about as likely to happen to you as the first prize in the Irish Sweepstakes, but it never hurts to dream.

MOST BOOKS WANTED BY COLLECTORS ARE FIRST EDITIONS, AND THE EASIEST WAY TO IDENTIFY A FIRST EDITION IS TO COMPARE THE DATE ON THE BOOK'S TITLE PAGE WITH THE COPYRIGHT DATE PRINTED ON THE BACK OF THE TITLE PAGE. The book must be in fine condition, with all its pages intact. Some of the newer books have made things easier by marking the title page with the words "First Edition."

BOOKS WITH COLORED ILLUSTRATIONS OF FLOWERS, BIRDS, AND SO ON, ARE OF VALUE BECAUSE THE PICTURES CAN BE REMOVED AND SOLD INDIVIDUALLY. LOCAL HISTORIES OVER FIFTY YEARS OLD ARE IMPORTANT. EARLY BOOKS ABOUT INDIANS, INVENTIONS (IF WRITTEN AT THE TIME OF THE INVENTION), CATALOGS, FIRST CITY DIRECTORIES, AND EARLY DIME NOVELS AND COMIC BOOKS ARE BEING COLLECTED.

At times it is easier to tell what is not going to have a value. Old Bibles are rarely in demand unless they are printed in Europe before 1600 and in America before the 1800's. There is always an exception to every rule, and even some of these early ones have no interest or value. An unusual family genealogy written in the Bible would make it worth saving for some historical society.

Encyclopedias that are over twenty-five years old are almost valueless unless they are first editions. Old geography books, mathematics books, and other school textbooks have very little interest. THE McGUFFEY READER WAS FIRST PRINTED BY WILLIAM HOLMES MCGUFFEY IN

1836. HIS FIRST AND SECOND READERS APPEARED THAT YEAR, AND THE THIRD AND FOURTH READERS WERE PRINTED IN 1837. THEY ARE THE ONLY COPIES, OF THE MORE THAN 122,000,000 McGUFFEY READERS, THAT HAVE A VALUE TO THE COLLECTOR.

The best way to determine which books have a value is by checking magazine ads, reading lists in the library, and by doing some hard research. There are more worthless old books than there are those of great value.

Dime novels

The dime novel has been gaining new respect, and can be useful as historic background material, but not as great literature. The dime novel reflected the interest of the average man. The category "dime novel" includes adventure stories and detective stories, but never love stories. The first dime novels were issued by Irwin P. Beadle and Co. of New York about 1860, and they originally sold for ten cents each. The form was popular with the Civil War soldier who wanted a small book with a complete story. Millions were sold until the dime novel form lost favor about 1925. The stories of Horatio Alger, Ned Buntline, Frank Merriwell, Nick Carter, and Deadwood Dick are collectors' items. The thirties saw the rise of the detective magazine, Doc Savage, Nick Carter, The Shadow, Tarzan, and Captain Fury.

Big Little books were popular, since the fat small book could be read quickly, yet seemed to contain so much. Comic books and early science-fiction comics have become collectors' items. (There are several collectors' groups that specialize in these types of books.)

Other printed matter

There seems to be a collector for anything and everything. Don't throw "it" away before checking.

Old store catalogs are important to the historian and collector, and can offer hours of fun for the amateur. OF IMPORTANCE ARE OLD SEARS, ROEBUCK CATALOGS, OR ANY CATALOG PRINTED BEFORE 1850, OR A CATALOG ABOUT A NEW INVENTION IF IT WAS WRITTEN WITHIN THE FIRST FEW YEARS OF THE INVENTION.

Baseball cards

Baseball cards have been printed since the 1880's and half a million cards have been issued. Only the baseball cards over twenty-five years old are of great value.

CHRISTMAS SEALS, EASTER SEALS, TAX STAMPS, AND MATCHBOOK COVERS ARE COLLECTIBLE. The first Christmas seal was printed about 1910, and the first matchbooks in 1892.

There isn't space enough to list all the old paper items that are being collected, but it may be interesting to note that there are large, well-documented collections of Valentines, advertising cards, broadsides, railroad passes, and other memorabilia, as well as circus posters, labels for paper cans, and cigar labels. (See also Chapter 12, "Prints, . . ." and Chapter 14, "Store Stuff.")

Books: Bibliography

American Book-Prices Current 1969. New York: Columbia University Press, 1972.

Bradley, Van Allen. *The New Gold in Your Attic.* New York: Arco, 1972.

This is a paperback price list for over 2,500 books.

The Card Collectors' Company. *Baseball Card Check List.* Privately printed. (Order from author, Box 293, Franklin Square, New York.)

This paperback is a complete listing of baseball gum cards issued since 1948.

Gardner, Ralph. *Horatio Alger.* Mendota, Illinois: Wayside Press, 1964.

The Horatio Alger stories and how they were written is told in this book.

Goulart, Ron. *Cheap Thrills, An Informal History of the Pulp Magazines.* New Rochelle, N.Y.: Arlington House, 1972.

The Shadow, Doc Savage, Science Fiction Tails, and other pulp fiction magazines are discussed in this book.

Lewis, John. *The Twentieth Century Book.* New York: Reinhold, 1967.

This is a book, written for illustrators and designers, which pictures the layout of many of the fine illustrated books of the 1900s.

Mebane, John. *Books Relating to the Civil War.* New York: Yoseloff, n.d.

Pearson, Edward. *Dime Novels.* Boston, Massachusetts: Little, Brown, 1929.

Quayle, Eric. *The Collector's Book of Children's Books.* New York: Clarkson N. Potter, 1971.

This attractive well-illustrated history of children's books, although English, is a good introduction for the beginner.

Rosenbach, A. S. W. *Early American Children's Books.* New York: Dover Publications, 1971.

This is a reprint of a 1933 book which has been a standard reference in the field. Eight hundred and sixteen books are discussed in detail.

All these books will give help in identifying and pricing old books.

16

Music

"I OWN A STRADIVARIUS VIOLIN," is one of the most positive statements of an almost impossible fact that is repeated daily in this country. If you think you own a Strad, read on, but when you have finished, at least be honest enough to admit the truth to yourself.

Many farmers living in the northern part of the United States and southern Canada have carefully guarded the valued Stradivarius violin that has been passed down through the family. Question each family and you will learn the same story. From about 1880 until the first part of the twentieth century, a hungry peddler sold his treasured violin because of a desperate need for money. It was labeled "Antonius Stradivarius Cremonensis Faciebat Anno 1734," so of course it must be true—but the real, unglamorous, and often unwelcome story is that ACCORDING TO THE EXPERTS, THERE ARE NO UNLISTED STRADIVARIUS VIOLINS.

Ernest Doring, in his book *How Many Strads,* states that there is little if any chance that any new Stradivarius violins will be found. He has traced all the available records and checked all of the known violins by Stradivarius. He determined that none of them could be missing. There is always a chance that Doring made a mistake, but this is very doubtful. There is also the slim chance that several rumors about Strads being stolen during World War II are true. Supposedly, a famous German musician owned an authenticated Strad that vanished during the war. A G.I. might have picked it up.

The forged Stradivarius violins which have been found in the United States and Canada were made and sold in great numbers during the last part of the nineteenth century. Some copies were made with a label that read "Made in Germany" or some other English or German words. The original Stradivarius label was printed in Latin, with the last two digits of the date written by hand. It said, "Antonius Stradivarius Cremonensis Faciebat Anno 1714." The forged label says exactly the same thing. It has been written on aged paper and pasted inside the violin.

A true Stradivarius violin is an exceptional musical instrument. Any good violinist can tell a good violin from a poor one by inspection, and if you still believe that yours is really a Strad, take it to a violinist. He can quickly tell you about your violin.

Be of good cheer. The peddlers that sold the thousands of fake violins sold many types that were not Strads. We have seen labels listing Giovanni Paolo Maggini (1580–1640), Nicolo Amati (1596–1684),

A real Stradivarius violin is a musical instrument of beauty as well as exceptional tone. This "Strad" was made about 1709. (Henry Ford Museum Collection, Dearborn, Michigan)

the teacher of Stradivarius, Giuseppe Guarnerius (1687–1745), Carlo Bergonzi (1683–1747), and Jacob Stainer (Steiner) (1621–1683)—all on forged violin labels.

It is amusing that Guarnerius, although named Giuseppe in Italy, had his name anglicized to Joseph by one forger. We saw a Bergonzi label on a violin that was dated 1757, and this was about ten years after his death.

Forged violins were made as late as 1930 in Metten, Bavaria; Markneukirchen and Klingenthal, Saxony; Mirexoud, France; and Gaslitz and Schonback, Czechoslovakia. Thousands of violins were made in each town, with some originally selling for as little as fifty cents.

If you own a violin where the label does not say "Stradivarius," the possibilities are greater that you may own a valued musical instrument. Quick research at most public libraries can help you determine whether the violin maker named ever made any important work. A check with any qualified musician or music store will give you more of an idea of the actual value of the violin.

Music, music, music came from these early boxes. The pipes are part of a music box made by the Astor Company, London, England, about 1800. The Swiss box with the dancing doll, bellringer, and tambour-playing dolls was made about 1890. The metal disk was the source of music in the famous Regina made in New York City about 1903. (Henry Ford Museum, Dearborn, Michigan)

There is one possible use for that forged Strad that Grandma always said would be the down payment on a house: Cut a hole in it and mount an electric clock inside, or remove the front, put in notched shelves, and use it as a spoon rack.

The music box—one big Instant Expert tip

Music boxes were improved during the nineteenth century. The early music boxes had a revolving brass cylinder set with steel pins. The pins hit a metal comb that had from fifteen to twenty-five teeth. The pins and cylinder were made from a single piece of steel after 1820. Small quills that made the tone more definite were added about 1825.

A two-comb music box that could play loudly or softly was made in 1838. More combs were added, and by 1840 as many as five were used. The cylinders also became longer.

Bells and drums were added by 1850, and by 1854 interchangeable cylinders were used. Elaborate tune changes and springs improved the music box after 1875.

Large circular disk cards that looked like the phonograph records of today were made in 1885. The metal disk replaced the cylinder box by 1890.

The improvements will help to date a music box, but all of the boxes have a value.

Bells

There are many bell collectors, and many bells to be collected. A bell collector usually wants a special type of bell, such as a school bell, cowbell, or a sleigh bell. ANY BELL IS COLLECTIBLE, and most of them are worth a small amount of money. MOST BELL COLLECTORS DO NOT WANT BELLS THAT HAVE BEEN BUFFED OR REFINISHED IN SOME WAY.

Colored glass bells were most popular from 1820 to 1860 in England. Many have been made since then, but cut-glass bells are rare because of the problem of cutting a bell that would not break when struck.

One of the most available bells in America is labeled "Chiantel fondeur 1878 Saignelegier." It was cast by Chiantel, a very famous bell maker living and working in Saignelegier, Switzerland. The bell was first made in the year 1878, but there were many made and signed that were made in later years.

The gramophone was first made in America. This example was designed by Emile Berliner and made by the U.S. Gramophone Company of Washington, D.C. It was made of oak, with a tin horn and belts of rubber bands, in 1887. (Index of American Design, Washington, D.C.)

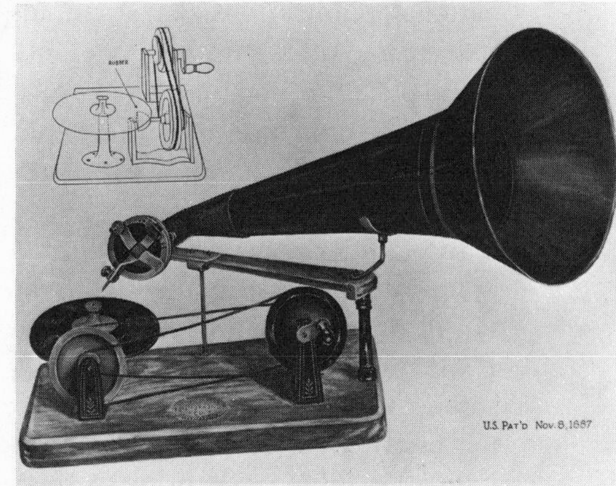

The talking machine

Edison phonographs are far from a hundred years old, but they have become a very sought-after collector's item. Any Edison with a horn, especially the type with a large "morning-glory" horn, is waiting for an eager buyer. The records are also collectible, and it still is possible to find a whole box of old records in an attic. Some of the very rare recordings have considerable worth, and there is no doubt that most of the old records will go up in value through the years.

Covers of old sheet music are often attractive pictures that are prized by collectors. "Barbara Frietchie" was a song written in 1874; "Songs of the War," written in 1864, was lithographed by Henry C. Eno of New York City. (Western Reserve Historical Society, Cleveland, Ohio)

Pianos

Player pianos, nickelodeons, and large music-making devices are most desirable. They were large and expensive when they were new, and are now found in a very limited supply. They are some of the "fun collectibles" that are loved for the joy they give, not their artistic or historic value. A simple ad in a local paper is usually enough to turn up many buyers for an antique as gay as a player piano.

The only practical use for a piano roll is to find the proper size working player piano. There are several national publications that have ads requesting and offering the old piano-player rolls.

Old pianos and organs are not nearly so loved as the less sophisticated nickelodeons and player pianos. There were many formal pianos made, and consequently the supply today is greater. Modern pianos and organs have many advantages over the old ones, so that the best market for an old piano is limited to those made prior to 1860. Melodeons or reed organs are old enough and rare enough to be of value.

It is surprisingly easy to date your piano or organ if it has a maker's name. Most libraries have a book called *Michel's Piano Atlas* or *Pierce Piano Atlas.* The date of manufacture of most American pianos and organs can be found in either book.

OTHER MUSIC MAKERS

The Instant Expert clue for other types of musical antiques is a simple rule using common sense: IF IT IS ODD ENOUGH, SOMEONE WILL WANT IT AND TREASURE IT. There are many collectors of old instruments, but they are often hard to locate. While a dulciphone can be bought, it will usually take time and patience. Hard research work at a library is one of the only ways to learn more about many instruments. Very little has been written about the many types of musical oddities developed during the late nineteenth century. It is a safe guess that if your "thing" looks like a Rube Goldberg invention and makes some sort of music, it is a product of the delightfully inventive minds of the 1850–1900 period when many unusual instruments were at the height of their popularity.

Sheet music

Piles of sheet music sometimes appear in the most unexpected places. Don't throw it all out. Sheet music of the nineteenth century has been collected for many years, but collectors have begun to take a new interest in the music that was printed before World War I. The cover of the sheet music that pictures the old car, train, or Gibson Girl intrigues many collectors. Some shops are selling framed copies of old sheet music.

The older music is important for its contents and the rarity of the song. One must use common sense in dating old sheet music, and the subject matter of the song, the type of paper, the style of printing must all be considered. For example, a car song certainly couldn't be written before the car was made. Early lithographs appear on some sheet music, so check the section on prints, and it might help you to find the age of your sheet music.

Music: Bibliography

Bowers, Q. David. *Encyclopedia of Automatic Musical Instruments.* New York: Vestal Press, 1972.

A well-illustrated encyclopedia of over 1,000 pages.

———. *Put Another Nickel In.* Vestal, New York: Vestal Press, 1966.

Read, Oliver, and Walter L. Welch. *From Tin Foil to Stereo. Evolution of the Phonograph.* Indianapolis: Howard W. Sams, 1959.

This is a rather technical discussion of phonographs and records through the 1950's.

Pierce, Bob. *Pierce Piano Atlas.* Privately printed, 1966. (Order from author, 2188 Lakewood Boulevard, Long Beach, California 90815.) (Originally called *Michel's Piano Atlas.*)

An alphabetical listing of piano makers, city or origin, and the dates they were working.

17

Toys

Any old toy has a value to the collector. Age alone will not determine value, but as a general rule the Instant Expert tip is: IF THE TOY WAS MADE BEFORE 1900, SOME COLLECTOR WILL WANT IT. The other important rule for the collector of toys is: NEVER REPAINT AN OLD METAL OR WOODEN TOY, FOR IT LOWERS THE VALUE.

The "little old toymaker" who lived a hundred or so years ago is always pictured working in a little village toyshop. This is just another one of the myths connected with antiques in America. Many "little old toymakers" did have shops, but by the early 1800's, toys made in factories were sold in quantity. Hundreds of factories began producing toys, rocking horses, doll furniture, blocks, and even board games after the Civil War.

Handmade toys were a necessity in most of the western areas of America. Houses were far from towns and stores, but some factory-made dolls, wagons, sleds, and whistles still found their way into almost every area.

Many of the factory toys were labeled, and ANY PRE-1900 TOY WITH ITS ORIGINAL LABEL IS OF INTEREST. The collector of toys is interested not only in the item but also in the history that it represents. A labeled toy can be dated and be considered in its proper historical perspective. It is part of the charm of the old toy. For example, a board game like Monopoly, which included large sums of play money, became the rage during the Depression when money was scarce. Another early game, The Grocery Store, will take on a new meaning when you realize that the prices on the cards (such as twenty-five cents for a dozen eggs) were considered authentic prices for the year 1887 when the game first appeared.

Many types of toys were invented in earlier years. The list opposite will furnish the approximate starting dates for many types of toys and games:

Games reflect the interests of a period in history. These Victorian games are collector's items because of the lithographed boxes and the complete game inside. (Collection of Kim Kovel)

Toys (Type)	Approximate Date of Commercial Manufacture
Animal-powered toys	Nineteenth century
Baseball (see Sports)	
Board games	1840
Cap guns and cap exploders	Mid-nineteenth century (most popular 1885–1915)
Card games (Authors, Old Maid, etc.)	1808
Cast-iron American toys	1825 (most popular 1880–1920)
China teasets	Imported since 1800
Clay marbles	Nineteenth century
Clockwork toys (see Windup toys)	
Clockwork track trains	1901
Dolls	
Adult dolls	to 1850, then not until 1950's
Billiken	1909
Brownie	1883
China head (European): curls on neck of head	1840
China head (European): short curls	1850
China head (European): chignon or waterfall style	1860
Composition head	1800–1850
Closing eyes in head	1800
Glass eyes in head	Beginning nineteenth century

Toys (Type)	Approximate Date of Commercial Manufacture
Kewpie	1911
Papier-mâché head, kid body	1820
Paper dolls	Eighteenth century, pantins; nineteenth century—made commercially; height of popularity 1890
Rag dolls	1840 popular
Talking	1827
Tin head	1840
Vulcanized rubber head	1850
Walking	1826
Wax head	Seventeenth century, most found today from nineteenth century
Electric trains	Early 1900's
Friction toys, metal	After 1875
Glass marbles	Nineteenth century
Horsedrawn carts and wagons	1880–1890 most popular
Ice skates—all metal with clamp (other types earlier)	1870
Jack-in-the-box	Early 1800's
Mechanical banks	Late 1870's
Playing cards	
With index number in corner	After 1877
With no index number	Probably before 1877
Rocking horse	Probably 1780
Rocking horse—spring	1845
Roller skates	1863
Rubber toys	1850
Sand toys (American-made)	After 1825
Schoenhut wooden toys with elastic joints	1903
Slot machines	1895
Sports	
Baseball	1840
Football	1870
Golf	Mid-eighteenth century
Steam-powered toys (factory-made)	1870
Steam trains	1830 (limited number)
Steel pull toys	1920 (popular)
Teddy bear	1902
Tin soldiers (style of uniform helps to date, but not too accurate)	Eighteenth century
Tin toys	1840 (most popular 1870–1900)
Whirligig	Fifteenth-century Europe
Windup toys (clockwork toys)	Most after 1860
Wooden pull toys	Eighteenth century (factory-made 1860–1900)

Wooden wagons have always been popular in America. This elaborate example holds a "roly-poly," a tin figure, sometimes a can that originally held tobacco, that tips from side to side on its round bottom. (Frederick C. Crawford Auto-Aviation Museum of Western Reserve Historical Society, Cleveland, Ohio)

A toy Conestoga wagon of wood was made about 1840 for a lucky child. (Hagley Museum Collection, Wilmington, Delaware)

WOODEN TOYS

Rocking horse

The exact date of the first rocking horse is not known. It has been assumed that it was about 1780, the time of the first rocking chair. Rockers on cradles had been known for centuries, and why it took so long for the rocker to get on the chair or the horse is still a mystery.

Wooden rocking horses in America were made at home by 1800, and were used as gifts for children.

A German rocking horse made in 1845 inspired Benjamin Potter Crandall to make a commercial rocking-horse toy. Mr. Crandall's horse "Cricket" was so popular that he made a toy stuffed horse with rockers. His son developed a rocking horse on a spring platform because many mothers complained that the wooden rockers cut carpets. The spring horse was so popular that adult-sized versions were made. The child's wooden rocking horse and the spring horse are still popular children's toys and are still being made.

Whirligig

The whirligig came from Europe in the fifteenth century. It is a figure

The whirligig was popular for hundreds of years. This painted wooden figure has arms that move. (Index of American Design)

The policeman's arms waved when touched, a metal version of the earlier whirligig-type toy. (Frederick C. Crawford Auto Aviation Museum of Western Reserve Historical Society, Cleveland, Ohio)

made of wood with the head and the long body made from a single piece. The arms were separate and placed on a rod that went through the body. When the wind blew, both arms would go around. The figure was usually painted to resemble a man, although the elongated body made the likeness very odd. It was a popular toy because it moved, unaided, on a windy day.

A tin toy of about 1900 was made that resembled the wooden whirligig.

Animal-powered toys

The wind moved the whirligig, but some toys, particularly those made in Italy during the early nineteenth century, were made to run on "bird power." A string was tied to a bird's leg, and the bird was placed inside the toy. The struggles of the frightened bird moved the toy. This cruel method of entertainment soon stopped, but some later toys, including American ones, were made to hold flies or insects. The trapped fly would wiggle the loosely joined arms, legs, or ears. This type of hand-carved wooden toy has been made in Mexico in recent years.

Metal toys

Tin, iron, lead, pewter, steel, and other metals have been used to make toys. The style and construction of many toys changed through the years, so it is possible to arrive at an approximate date for an old metal toy based on its appearance. There is one major problem in dating old toys, particularly cast-iron wheel toys such as horse-drawn fire engines. The toys have become so popular and expensive for collectors that several firms started making fine reproductions of the old toys. The new toys are not being made to fool the collector, but with a few years of aging in the hands of a normal three-year-old child, plus a sales pitch from an unscrupulous dealer, the new toy might be passed off as one of the nineteenth-century versions.

Tin toys

The earliest manufactured American toys were made of tin. Pieces of tin were cut by machine, assembled

Tin toys like these were popular in the 1870–1900 period. The painted, tinned sheet-iron toy bus (13 inches long) was probably made in New York City. The wheels are cast iron. The painted tin house was typical of the stationary tin toys. (Index of American Design)

and soldered by hand. The first "factory" for the tin toys was begun in Meriden, Connecticut, during the 1840's. Tinners began using their scrap pieces to make toys. Toymakers in Connecticut, New York, and Philadelphia, Pennsylvania, were making tin toys by the 1870's. Some of the factories had outputs of more than 50 million toys a year.

The toys that seem to have survived through the years are usually of the same general style and construction. They were made from about 1870 to 1900, although some were still made after 1900. ANY PRE-1900 TIN TOY IS OF INTEREST TO COLLECTORS TODAY IF IT IS IN GOOD CONDITION. THE LARGER THE TOY, THE MORE VALUABLE IT IS. Since millions of tin toys were made, it is only reasonable to assume that the more expensive ones were made in small quantities. The large toys required more labor, and consequently were more expensive when they were new. Now they are worth more as antiques.

Tin toys are rarely marked, and while the mark is of interest, it does not add to the value because there is so little information to help identify a marked piece.

Toy tin kitchens and kitchen utensils are common, while toy household furniture is scarce. All sorts of wagons, fire engines, stagecoaches, and buses are good; locomotives, trains, and horsecars are better; old tin boats are the rarest. Animated groups of animals or people, toys that make noise with a gong, bell, or whistle, or those that move are very desirable. Tin mechanical banks are very, very rare and very valuable.

Tin railroad trains are collected eagerly, especially those made in America. EUROPEAN-MADE TIN TRAINS, EVEN THOSE WITH AMERICAN NAMES, CAN BE RECOGNIZED BECAUSE THE CARS HAVE THE NUMERALS I, II, OR III, INDICATING THE FIRST-, SECOND-, OR THIRD-CLASS COACHES USED ON EUROPEAN RAILROADS.

Iron toys were first made in 1825, but did not become numerous until the 1880's. (Right) The Black Diamond Express is a pinewood and iron-wheeled train. (Above) Carpenter made the toy train of cast iron, painted red and black and gold, about 1880. (Index of American Design)

Iron toys

The first American cast-iron toys were made about 1825. Small irons with trivets, miniature garden tools, and a few wheel toys were also made.

Cast-iron banks, cap guns, and possibly doll furniture were made in the 1870's, but it was during the 1880's that we saw the great influx of American-made cast-iron toys. They became larger, more elaborate, had more moving parts, and were made with greater detail until the 1920's. Most of the horse-drawn iron toys that are found today date from the 1915–1930 period, but even the late examples are still of interest and value.

The early iron horse-drawn toys were made by at least six American manufacturers during the 1880–1890 period. Most of them cannot be recognized, but one maker, CARPENTER, MARKED HIS TOYS WITH THE PATENT DATE NOVEMBER 16, 1880, AND MARCH 20, 1883, ON THE ROD BETWEEN THE HORSES. The best American iron toys were made by E. R. Ives of Connecticut, who made toys from 1868 to 1932. HIS TOYS WERE NOT MARKED "IVES" UNTIL AFTER 1907. The word "Phoenix" between the horses, or the dates June 13, 1893, or July 28, 1896, suggests it may be an Ives toy.

The largest iron toys are sought after by most toy collectors. Trains of the nineteenth century are particularly rare. Any fire-fighting equipment is on the "very much wanted" list.

The fire engine has always been a popular toy for children, and this 1880 cast-iron example still retains its charm. A rear fireman was needed to steer the long engine around the corners. (Frederick C. Crawford Auto Aviation Museum of Western Reserve Historical Society, Cleveland, Ohio)

Any toy with moving parts is in demand. Some of the twentieth-century iron toys picturing comic-strip characters, and any of the many circus toys, are especially wanted by collectors. Early styles of automobiles are in demand by a special group.

ALL EARLY TOY TRAINS ARE WANTED TODAY. Tin, iron, even steel trains made more than twenty-five years ago are wanted by the toy-train collectors.

Moving toys

Clockwork toys were made in quantity in America from about 1865 to 1900. THE TOYS WERE QUITE LITERALLY MADE WITH BRASS CLOCKWORKS ON THE INSIDE to move the arms or legs of the toy. Moving toys were made from painted tin, wood, cast iron, and cloth. Dancing figures, walking figures, cigarette-smoking men, circus wagons, merry-go-rounds,

About 1880 the friction toy was invented. This boy on a sled was made of metal.

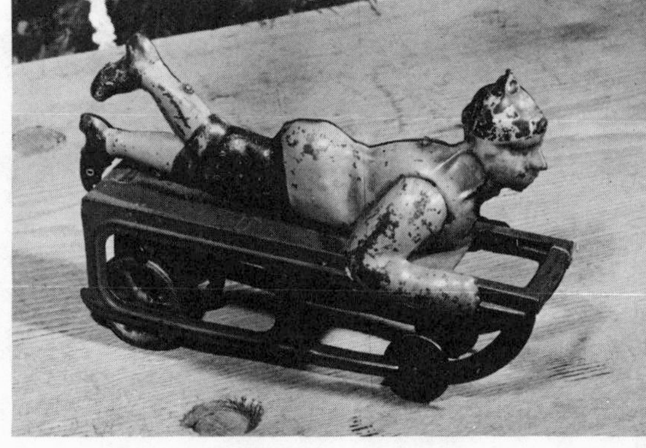

Banks have been one of the most popular toys for men to collect. (Above left) The hungry politician ate the penny in this mechanical bank called "Tammany Hall"; (Below) J. E. Stevens Co. of Cromwell, Connecticut, made this 1875 bank of cast iron that depicted a Negro eating a watermelon (Index of American Design) Salt-glazed stoneware was the material used in this nineteenth-century bank (above right). (Index of American Design)

boats, and other moving vehicles were also made.

The clockwork toys were made about 1900 with steel works, and about 1920 tin clockworks were used.

The clockwork toys were wound with a crank or with a key.

Metal friction toys were first introduced during the last quarter of the nineteenth century.

Banks

Moving metal banks have always intrigued the child or collector, as it is more fun to save pennies when the penny makes a pig jump through a hoop or if the penny is eaten by a hungry clown. Adults have been just as fascinated by the moving banks as the children.

Books have been written about these banks, and several lists of banks, furnishing the rarity and value, are to be found at the library.

There are mechanical banks, still banks, and registering banks. The "best" of the collectors' banks are the mechanical types that move when the penny is inserted. Metal banks have been made from 1868 to the present, many of the old ones being reproduced since 1950 in either iron or plastic. The value of the bank today is determined not by age alone but by rarity and condition. Some banks of the 1900's are worth more than those made during the 1800's.

Still banks became popular with collectors as the price rose on mechanical banks. Painted or lithographed tin, cast iron, white metal, pottery, wood, glass, and porcelain were used to make still banks. Many were made in the form of a bank building or a safe. Here again rarity helps to determine the value.

Registering banks were made like cash registers, and the amount of money deposited is totaled on the face of the bank. They are not so valuable as the other types, but they are still of interest to a bank collector. Registering banks are not so old as the other types. The bank you may have owned twenty-five years ago that was shaped like a cash register is worth more today than it was when purchased new at the store.

Warning

Although it has been said before, this Instant Expert tip is so important that it must be repeated: NEVER REPAINT AN OLD METAL TOY. A new paint job destroys the value of the old toy.

OTHER TOYS

Marbles

Glass marbles were made during the nineteenth century. Many of the glass factories had workers that made marbles for their own children. The Venetian swirl type, with ribbons of colored glass in a clear marble, are desirable. Sulphides, or marbles with frosted white figures of animals, flowers, or faces embedded in the clear glass, are rare and expensive.

Real stone marbles of cobalt, onyx, carnelian, jade, and jasper can still be found.

Early hand-made toy marbles were not round enough by today's machine-made standards. The clay marbles were used fifty years ago, many of them made by the famous Bennington factory. Many Ohio, Pennsylvania, and Indiana pottery firms also made these brown or blue glazed marbles.

Carpet ball

The balls are about the size of a softball, ranging from 2½ to 4 inches in diameter. They often were decorated with plaids, stripes, or with bull's-eye or flower design. Most of the carpet balls were made in England and Scotland. Carpet bowls was a popular game during the first half of the nineteenth century.

Playing cards

Early decks of playing cards, or those with unusual designs on either side of the card, are being collected. There are several national card collectors' clubs. Rare European decks of cards made before 1850 will probably not be among the antiques found by the casual American collector, but American-made decks from the past seventy-five years are often of great interest and value.

NO INDEX NUMBERS WERE USED IN THE CORNERS OF CARDS UNTIL 1877. If the deck is wrapped or boxed, save the wrapper; it may be of more interest than the card.

Playing cards have been made for centuries. The collector searches for decks with unusual aces, backs, picture cards, or histories. At top right, the 34 stars in the flag hint that the pack was made in 1871; the round card was made in 1920's; the miniature ace is from a small deck; the card with cherubs was made about 1915; at lower right is a card made in Vienna before World War II; the other cards were made about 1922. (United States Playing Card Co.)

Any deck that pictures well-known people instead of the usual kings or queens should be saved. If the faces on your deck of cards are of Shirley Temple or Marilyn Monroe, etc., they, too, are wanted by many collectors.

Slot machines

Since there are antique autos, there is no reason why you couldn't find an antique slot machine. If you were able to find one it would be very valuable.

A twenty-nine-year-old mechanic named Charles Fey made the first slot machine by hand in San Francisco, California, in 1895. The machine was an instant success in the local gambling parlors, and Fey rented his slot machine for one-half the profits. The machine was called the "Liberty Bell," and did not have a jackpot. The symbols were diamonds, spades, hearts, bells, horseshoes, and stars.

Because Fey would not let others manufacture his game, it remained in California for many years. Herbert Mills made a similar machine in Chicago in 1907, but his machine used the jackpot, bars, bells, and lemons just like today's "One-armed Bandit."

DOLLS

Many books have been written about old dolls, and several national collectors' magazines devote a section to the latest information about old dolls. Collecting dolls requires a special knowledge.

The beginner may find it hard to realize that an "old" doll is quite often the same as one she played with as a child. Shirley Temple dolls, Charlie McCarthy, and the Dionne Quintuplets are all collectors' dolls that have been made since 1930. The Brownies, the Campbell kids, Kewpie dolls, Buster Brown, and other comic figures were dolls that were made a few years earlier. They have all become collectors' items. Remember, IF IT IS A DOLL AND IT IS MORE THAN TWENTY-FIVE YEARS OLD, IT IS WORTH KEEPING.

The antique dolls prized by collectors are more than twenty-five years old. It is difficult arbitrarily to decide the exact dates that should be included in a collection of "antique" dolls, but we feel that any doll made before World War I is old enough to qualify.

The composition materials used to form the dolls made today are easy to recognize, so the Instant Expert tip is: ANY DOLL WITH A HEAD MADE OF SOME UNUSUAL MATERIAL IS OF INTEREST. These unusual materials include wood, rag, papier-mâché, tin, china, bisque, leather, rubber, wax, and celluloid heads. Dolls have been made from many strange natural materials, such as corncobs, apples, or nuts, but they were hand-made dolls and must always be considered individually on their own artistic merit.

The china-headed doll receives the most attention from the average collector. It is a doll that usually has a leather or fabric body, a shiny glazed head, and painted hair and features. The age of a china-headed doll can be determined with some degree of

Dolls of all ages fascinate girls of all ages. These three ladies sharing the picture are all dolls of the nineteenth century. The doll at the left has a painted tin head; the others have china heads and cloth and leather bodies. (Collection of Kim Kovel)

accuracy from the hair style. THE DOLL WITH CURLS ON THE NECK WAS MADE ABOUT 1840, SHORT CURLS ABOUT 1850, AND THE CHIGNON STYLE ABOUT 1860. DOLLS WITH BROWN EYES ARE MORE DESIRABLE THAN THOSE WITH BLUE EYES. COLLECTORS PREFER BLONDES, but not for the same reason the gentlemen do. Blonde dolls were less common because blondes were much less numerous than they are today.

In spite of the fact that bisque is really unglazed china, the doll collectors of this country differentiate the types of doll heads, glazed and unglazed, by calling one china and the other bisque. This may confuse the novice, but there is nothing to be gained by argument, so just learn the proper "doll word." The bisque-headed doll with a wig of composition hair was popular during the nineteenth century. According to the import laws of the United States, any doll brought into this country after 1891 had to be marked with the country of origin, so that helps to make a perfect Instant Expert tip for the doll collector. IF THE DOLL HEAD HAS THE NAME OF A COUNTRY PRINTED ON IT, IT WAS MADE AFTER 1891. Most of the bisque and china-headed dolls were made in Germany or France. A few of the European dolls were labeled with a factory name. IF YOU OWN A DOLL MARKED "BRU" (FRANCE, 1867), "GREINER" (PHILADELPHIA, 1840–1883), "JUMEAU" (FRANCE, 1843–1920), "SIMON AND HALBIG" (GERMANY, 1867–FINISHING DATE UNKNOWN), OR "STEINER" (GERMANY, FRANCE, 1855–1926), IT IS A COLLECTOR'S DOLL. Many porcelain factories made plates, bowls, and china doll heads. CHECK THE MARKS ON THE DOLL HEADS IN A BOOK OF PORCELAIN MARKS, not only in the books about dolls.

There are several other tips for the doll collector. MACHINE STITCHING OF THE DOLL'S CLOTH BODY COULD NOT HAVE BEEN DONE BEFORE ABOUT 1850 (the invention of the sewing machine). THE PORCELAIN DOLL'S HEAD WAS SEWN TO THE CLOTH BODY. HOLES WERE PUT IN THE NECK OF THE DOLL'S HEAD TO PERMIT THE SEWING. A DOLL HEAD WITH ONE HOLE IN THE BASE OF THE FRONT AND ONE HOLE IN THE BACK IS OLDER THAN THE HEAD WITH TWO HOLES IN THE FRONT AND TWO IN THE BACK.

Wax dolls

The wax doll was made in Germany during the seventeenth century, but chances are it is not the type of doll you will ever find. Most of the wax dolls that are now hiding in attics were made during the nineteenth century. Dolls with wax heads and *glass* eyes were known at the beginning of the nineteenth century. By 1826 the wax dolls had eyes that could close. Many different types of wax-headed dolls were made as late as the mid-1930's by factories in Europe. One of the best ways to determine the age of these dolls is to observe the style of the dress, plus other hints, such as (hopefully) a label.

Milliner's models

The milliner's model is a type of doll that was made in the 1820's, with papier-mâché head, kid body, and wooden arms and legs. The hair was molded in the latest style, and the doll ranged from 5 to 26 inches in height.

Each doll was dressed to model the latest styles. Most of them were manufactured in Holland or Italy.

Dolls were also used as models by many traveling salesmen of the 1800's. It was much easier to carry a miniature than the actual item of merchandise. Manufacturers made models of furniture, stoves, kitchen utensils, and other household belongings.

Frozen Charlotte

A frozen Charlotte is a stiff doll with unjointed and immovable arms and legs. They were usually made with their arms at their sides or pointing straight out. A few have been found with the arms in the folded position of prayer. Most frozen Charlotte dolls were made from china.

They were named for a girl, Charlotte. Legend says she rode five miles on a cold day in a lightweight dress, and was frozen stiff by the time she reached the end of the ride.

Mary Todd doll

The Mary Todd doll was not a portrait doll, but it was named after Mrs. Abraham Lincoln. The china-headed, apple-cheeked doll had a short Civil War type headdress, with a chignon or waterfall hairstyle molded on the doll head.

Kewpie doll

The Kewpie doll was first made in 1911, and for several years thereafter. The Kewpie was a baby with a topknot of light hair. Rose O'Neill drew pictures of the Kewpie for the *Ladies' Home Journal* and wrote many stories about her Kewpies.

A German factory made the first Kewpie doll from bisque, but within a year several American firms also made them. The dolls were made in a range of sizes and from many materials. Some were dressed; others had no clothes. The most popular Kewpie was a celluloid doll made about 1914. Most of the dolls were made without the authorization of Rose O'Neill, but at that time little could be done to stop this. Collectors not only value the Kewpie dolls but also search for the original magazine pictures and the many other pictured forms of the Kewpie. Kewpie dolls are still being made. Many similar round-faced, topknotted dolls have been made since Rose O'Neill drew her famous Kewpie.

Brownies

The brownies were invented in 1883 when the first book about their lives was written by Palmer Cox. Thirteen different brownie books were printed. Brownies had long legs and round bellies, and they did good deeds because brownies like to do good. Brownies never wanted thanks. They were so popular that they were made as dolls and were pictured on china, glass and advertising cards, and in magazines and books. The brownie fabric that was cut and stuffed to make rag dolls was reprinted in 1962.

Kate Greenaway

Kate Greenaway was an English artist who gained fame for her drawings of children in high-waisted empire dresses. She lived from 1846 to 1901. Her children's pictures were popular in the 1880's. The Kate Greenaway child was pictured as a doll on chinaware, Valentines, and glassware, in books, and on hundreds of other items, all eagerly collected.

Felix the Cat

The jointed wooden dolls made to resemble Felix the Cat were first patented in 1922. The cartoons of Felix were popular in newspapers and movie theaters. Felix still charms a new generation in newspapers, cartoon shows, and on TV.

Many other comic-strip characters have also been made into dolls.

Teddy bear

Theodore Roosevelt refused to shoot a bear cub when on a hunting trip in Smedas, Mississippi, in 1902. Clifford Berryman, a newspaper cartoonist, drew a picture of the incident and called it "Teddy Bear." The name was an instant success, and manufacturers of stuffed toy animals took immediate advantage of the news item. The first Teddy bear was made in Germany, but many others followed. A clever mechanical bank picturing Teddy Roosevelt shooting at a tree and a bear was also made.

Paper dolls

Paper dolls developed from the "pantins" of the eighteenth century. In the fashionable circles in Europe it was a clever adult game to make a new pantin each day. They were paper doll caricatures of the people of fashion. By the nineteenth century the more familiar paper dolls used by children were sold in stores. The first American paper dolls were published in Boston in 1854 by Crosby, Nichols and Company. John Greene Chandler was the artist, and he illustrated several children's books, made children's games and many types of paper dolls. His first sets of paper dolls consisted of the doll and several sets of clothing in a decorated paper envelope.

Godey's Lady's Book printed paper dolls in 1859, and was followed by most of the other women's magazines, including *Ladies' Home Journal, Pictorial Review, McCall's, Woman's Home Companion,* and *Good Housekeeping.* Paper dolls still appear in many magazines. The dolls were so popular that even the newspapers started printing them in the 1890's. Toy and book manufacturers quickly realized the profits that could be made, and started printing paper dolls in many forms. Many food-product companies, especially packers of coffees and spices, as well as the thread companies, began giving paper dolls as premiums.

The Raphael Tuck paper dolls popular in America were made in England. Raphael Tuck produced several of the very famous series of paper dolls about 1860. The firm had offices in London, Paris, and New York, and were the publishers for Queen Victoria. They also made many fine color prints, trading cards, Valentines, and other pictures.

The paper dolls were often printed on the back and the front. By the 1890's, when paper dolls were at the height of their popularity, Raphael Tuck was the leader in the field. The paper dolls made in the 1890's often had heads that were made separately and pasted on the doll. The clothes were made to fit under the chin.

Tin soldiers

The first lead figures were made in the third century B.C. Lead and tin figures were known in almost every civilization and in every century.

The tin soldier was still not a toy for the average child by the seventeenth century. Wooden or papier-mâché soldiers were often substituted. The tin soldier as we know it really started in Germany during the eighteenth century.

Frederick the Great saw his victories interpreted to the children with tin soldiers. IN THE EIGHTEENTH CENTURY, A GERMAN, ANDREAS HILPERT, DESIGNED THE FIRST SOLDIER ON A STANDING PLATE. He also designed about forty different types of soldiers. His firm continued successfully even after his death.

Ernest Heinrichsen of Germany introduced standard sizes for the tin soldiers in 1839. Through the years Germany became the leading country in the production of toy lead or tin soldiers. By 1900, there were over twenty factories in Germany making the toy soldiers.

There are adult collectors who have formed societies, museums, and have spent large sums of money for new and old tin soldiers.

Toys: Bibliography

GENERAL

Foley, Dan. *Toys Through the Ages.* New York: Chilton, 1962.
A good general book about toys through the ages. It includes a bibliography of over 100 books about toys.

Freeman, Larry, and John Meyer. *Old Penny Banks.* Watkins Glen, New York: Century House, 1960.
An illustrated listing of 242 mechanical and still banks.

Freeman, Ruth and Larry. *Cavalcade of Toys.* Watkins Glen, New York: Century House, 1942.
An excellent general book about toys.

Hertz, Louis H. *The Handbook of Old American Toys.* Wethersfield, Connecticut: Mark Haber, 1947.
A fact-filled book concerned primarily with metal toys. Illustrations from old catalogs are included.

———. *The Toy Collector.* New York: Funk & Wagnalls, 1969.
This is a good book for any toy col-

lector. It stresses identification, research, and desirability of toys. A bibliography and mark list is included.

McClintock, Marshall and Inez. *Toys in America.* Washington, D.C.: Public Affairs Press, 1961.
The best general history of the toy industry in America that has been written. Illustrated with photographs and catalog reprints. An extensive bibliography of books about all types of toys and a list of known toy manufacturers before 1900 is included.

McClinton, Katharine Morrison. *Antiques of American Childhood.* New York: Clarkson N. Potter, 1970.
An entertaining book that includes information on toys, games, dolls, clothing, furniture and other items strictly for children.

Remise, Jac and Jean Fondin. *The Golden Age of Toys.* New York: Time-Life Books, 1967.
Every serious toy collector should invest in this lavishly illustrated book of toys. Many color and black and white illustrations.

Dolls

(See all books listed for Toys, also the monthly columns about dolls that appear in most of the magazines about antiques.)

Anderton, Johana Gast. *Twentieth Century Dolls From Bisque to Vinyl.* North Kansas City, Missouri: Trojan Press, 1971.
This is a well-illustrated listing of dolls from 1900 to 1970. Unfortunately, almost no history is given.

Coleman, Dorothy S., Elizabeth A., and Evelyn J. *The Collector's Encyclopedia of Dolls.* New York: Crown, 1968.
Over 2,000 illustrations are included in this 675 page encyclopedia of dolls. It is an important research tool for the doll collector.

Jacobs, Flora Gill. *A History of Dolls' Houses.* New York: Scribner's, 1965.
The standard work in the field of doll houses, well illustrated.

White, Gwen. *European and American Dolls.* New York: Putnam's 1966.
An English oriented book, this includes marks, patent information, and photographs of many types of dolls.

Lead Soldiers

Nicollier, Jean. *Collecting Toy Soldiers.* Rutland, Vermont: Tuttle, 1967.
This is a color illustrated detailed story of the tin soldier from Europe and was originally published in Switzerland.

Playing Cards

(See *Hobbies* magazine each month for regular column about cards.)

Benham, W. Gurney. *Playing Cards.* London: Spring Books, n.d.
An interesting history of playing cards of Europe, with many line drawings of early cards.

Hargrave, Catherine Perry. *A History of Playing Cards and a Bibliography of Cards and Gaming.* New York: Dover Publications, 1966.
This paperback reprint of a 1930 book is the most complete history of early playing cards to be found.

Mann, Sylvia. *Collecting Playing Cards.* New York: Crown, 1966.
A book written for the advanced collector but of interest to the beginner because it includes the history of the design of cards, pictures, and a bibliography.

18

Other Collectible Items

EVERYONE KNOWS that money is valuable, so it should not be surprising that most old money is worth owning. At least with American money, you can be quite positive that the coin will never be worth less than the original face value. To decide the current value of a coin, you must know its condition, and then search through one of the many price guides that are available. If you are not familiar with the meaning of the numismatic terms "mint," "very fine," "fine," "good," "fair," or "poor," as referred to in all coin books, ask a coin dealer to show and explain the difference. In general, COINS IN POOR CONDITION HAVE A LOW VALUE. The price asked for a coin is determined by its condition and rarity. Age is not important. Many ancient Roman coins can be purchased for less than the price of some rare nineteenth-century American coins.

IT IS LEGAL TO SELL OR BUY GOLD COINS. It was not legal after the law of 1933 required that gold coins be redeemed. The government passed a new law in 1956, and collectors may buy and sell gold coins at more than their face value.

Elongated pennies

Remember the elongated pennies sold at the county fair a few years ago? A penny was placed in a machine and rolled out so that the proper words were impressed on the finished oval-shaped piece. The Lord's Prayer, important events, Presidents' faces, and famous men have been honored by the elongated coins. Pennies, nickels, dimes, quarters, half dollars, silver dollars, and foreign coins have been used. The date of the coin can often be seen on the finished piece. There are collectors for the coins, as well as for the machines that made them.

Coin jewelry

Silver coins have been linked together to make bracelets for years. About 1860, it was the style to engrave the back of a dime with elaborate initials or names, and join several of the coins into a bracelet. Small gold pieces are often found with holes that permitted the owner to wear them on a charm. Any type of coin jewelry would be interesting to own, and has a value as jewelry, but not as coins.

All types of political tokens are important to save. The William McKinley badge and cane are unusual campaign tokens; the other assortment shows what a collector can find in a few years. (Canehead from the Frederick C. Crawford Auto Aviation Museum of the Museum of the Western Reserve Historical Society, Cleveland, Ohio; badge from the Ohio Historical Society, Columbus, Ohio; collection is that of Lee Kovel)

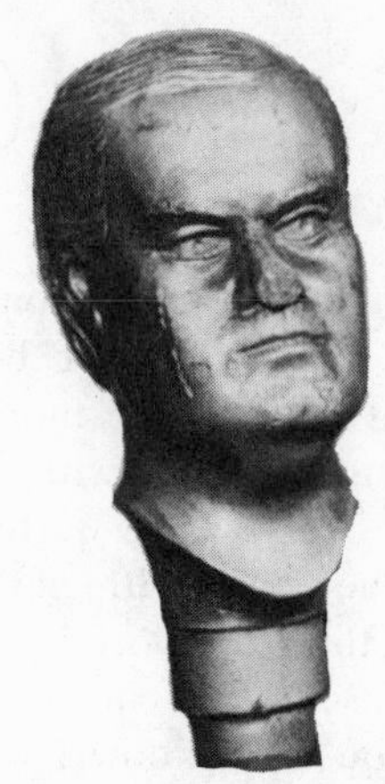

Trade dollars

It was customary to print factory money that could be used in trade at the company store in the nineteenth century. This was not a national legal tender, but it was used as money, and coin collectors want any of the many types of money that were ever put into use.

This unusual banner shows the candidate "Col. J. C. Fremont." He was nominated but did not run in the election for President in 1864. (Western Reserve Historical Society, Cleveland, Ohio)

Tokens

If you find a box of old coins, don't even throw away the box. Sometimes the things that are not real money have more value than the coins. Streetcar tokens, political tokens, medallions commemorating special events and even lodge tokens have a value to some collector. At most antique shows the dealers in coins, political badges, and tokens would be interested in any of the odd assortment you may have. One token might only be worth a small amount, but a box of these items could be of value. The political campaign items are of special interest today, and any BUTTON OR ITEM FROM A PRESIDENTIAL CAMPAIGN MORE THAN TWELVE YEARS OLD IS OF VALUE.

And the things you usually throw away

There is a time in everyone's life when you must decide what to do with an attic, basement, or even a drawer full of odd bits of small "junk." Perhaps you will find an old box full of little coins, medals, and unrelated items. There may be a box of old postcards or letters. As you are about to move, you might realize that Grandma's old trunk or wooden box has a tantalizing rattle but there's no key! What should you do with an odd assortment that finally appears? Follow our Instant Expert tip Number One: DON'T THROW ANYTHING AWAY. More good antiques have been lost because of an eager housewife than by all of the other ways combined. Open all boxes and sort the contents. Stop for a moment, and then think, study, read, and ask lots of questions. THERE IS A COLLECTOR FOR ALMOST ANYTHING. We know of individuals and organizations that want matchboxes, playing cards, coins, stamps, racetrack betting tickets, theatre-ticket stubs, theatre programs, postmarks, Christmas seals, funeral invitations, old Valentines and greeting cards, ads, trading cards, buttons, military insignia, railroad passes, coffin markers, sheet music, comic books, newspapers, magazines, almost anything—including the box it came in.

To sell or buy any of the many types of strange mementos people save, you must search through some of the antiques publications. Be patient. No item loses value with age. If, after looking around, you can find no value for the items, give them to a collector, historical society, or even a neighbor's young son. It will go into another box of "junk," to be saved for another generation of collectors. Maybe in twenty-five years it will have a value, and for the next twenty-five it will give joy to the boy who received it.

Maybe we should all become junk collectors, or pack rats!

And a little more—the things left over but still being collected: Fire-fighting equipment

Fire-fighting equipment is a field by itself, and there are numerous collectors who will buy anything that relates to a fire department. The firemark is the most popular fire antique. The plaques were originally made and placed on insured homes as an indication to the firemen that the owner of the house had paid for special fire protection. All firemen knew that if the house was marked, the insurance company paid a reward to the volunteer firemen. The firemark went out of use when firemen's salaries were paid by the community, a practice that started in most communities soon after the Civil War.

The "U. F." firemark was used by the United Firemens' Insurance Company of Philadelphia, Pennsylvania, about 1860. An old-fashioned steam engine is shown on the cast-iron mark. This mark has been copied. (Western Reserve Historical Society, Cleveland, Ohio)

Firemarks were used in the eighteenth century, and were found on many homes before the 1870's, when they were no longer used. Each company had its own symbol, and the marks were made of wood, lead, cast iron, or stamped tin.

Leather fire buckets were used in America from the seventeenth century, with the name of the firehouse, the city, or its insignia painted or stamped on the bucket. Some were decorated with elaborate paintings of arms, eagles, figures, and insignias. The leather bucket was in use in the bigger cities until the 1840's, in rural areas for many years after that time.

John Rogers

John Rogers was one of the most popular of the Victorian sculptors in America. His works were realistic, inexpensive, and attractive, and his figures were made by the thousands from bronze and painted plaster. The large Rogers figures were about

This wooden shield-shaped mark, one of several firemarks picturing a tree, was used by the "Mutual Assurance Company for Insuring Houses from Loss by Fire" in Philadelphia after 1784. This mark was issued in 1786. The tree is of cast lead. (Collection of the Home Insurance Company)

The cast-iron oval mark picturing a fire hydrant and the letters "F. A." was used by the Fire Association of Philadelphia after 1817. This style was used about 1865.

two feet high, and pictured historical or legendary heroes. The John Rogers group is now important enough in our history to be represented in the White House collection and other museums in the country.

John Rogers was a machinist, and he made clay models that were sold at various fairs. When his sight began to fail, Rogers began selling plaster casts of his work, from five to fifty dollars each. The cast figures were made of red plaster on a metal frame, and were painted gray. A special paint was sold with the figure that was used for the repair of chips and scratches. There were over

John Rogers groupings were large; this figure is two feet high. The plaster "Council of War," depicting Grant, Lincoln, and Secretary of War Stanton, was made of bronze painted plaster in 1868. (Toledo Museum of Art, Toledo, Ohio)

a hundred different statue groupings that were made, and more than 100,000 were sold. SMALL SALESMEN'S SAMPLES OF THE GROUP, ABOUT FOUR INCHES HIGH, WERE MADE, AND ARE EXTREMELY RARE.

THE VERY VALUABLE JOHN ROGERS GROUPS ARE MADE OF METAL. THE PLASTER GROUPS ARE COLLECTED BY RARITY.

Don't wash a statue of plaster, as water will harm the painted finish. Rub gently with an art-gum eraser. Don't repaint it unless the finish is completely beyond hope.

Forgery—George Washington's hatchet

A cast bronze hatchet labeled "Washington Inaugurated President of the U.S. Apr' 1789" is one of the most misunderstood antiques. It certainly isn't the hatchet used to chop the mythological cherry tree. The story of the cherry tree was started in 1808. The hatchet was distributed during the hundredth anniversary of Washington's inauguration in 1889. It is interesting but of little value.

Other Collectible Items: Bibliography

Bulau, Alwin E. *Footprints of Assurance.* New York: Macmillan, 1953. The definitive work about fire marks.

Kahler, James G. *Hail to the Chief.* New York: Scribner's, 1972.
An interesting pictorial record of 46 political campaigns which includes not only buttons, but also other types of political souvenirs.

Wallace, David H. *John Rogers, The People's Sculptor.* Middletown, Connecticut: Wesleyan University Press, 1967.
This is the story of John Rogers as a person and includes a catalog of his known works.

19

Price Guides

General

The Antique Trader Price Guide to Antiques & Collector's Items. Dubuque, Iowa: Babka Publishing Company, P.O. Box 1050.

Cohen, Hal L. *Official Guide to Paper Americana.* New York: H. C. Publishers, 1972.

———. *Official Guide to Popular Antiques Curios.* New York: H. C. Publishers, 1971.

DeVincenzo, Ralph. *Curios & Collectibles.* New York: Dafran House Publishers, 1971.

———. *Flea Market Shopper.* New York: Dafran House Publishers, 1972.

Freeman, Larry. *How to Price Antiques.* Watkins Glen, New York: Century House, 1948.

General price list, but good only for comparative values. Current prices are different.

Grotz, George. *Antiques You Can Decorate With.* Garden City, N.Y.: Doubleday, 1966.

———. *The New Antiques: Knowing and Buying Victorian Furniture.* Garden City, N.Y.: Doubleday, 1964.

Average prices for antiques of average quality that you might find. Poor line drawings for illustrations; the text is entertaining but not always accurate.

Kaduck, John M. *Sleepers That Have a Future.* New York: Crown, 1972.

Kovel, H. M. and Terry H. *The Complete Antiques Price List.* New York: Crown, 1972.

This is the most complete price last available.

———. *The Official Bottle Price List.* New York: Crown, 1971.

Over 10,000 bottles, old and new, are priced.

Rush, Richard M. *Antiques Is an Investment.* Englewood Cliffs, New Jersey: Prentice-Hall, 1968.

Unitt, Peter and Doris. *Canadian Price Guide to Antiques & Collectibles.* Peterborough, Ontario, Canada: Clock House Publications (P.O. Box 103).

Warman, Edwin. *11th Guide to Antiques and Their Current Prices.* Uniontown, Pennsylvania: Privately printed. (Order from author, 8 Frankhoover Street, Uniontown, Pennsylvania.)

General—English

The Antique Collectors' Club. The Antique Collectors' Club, Clopton, Woodbridge, Suffolk, England.

Coysh, A. W. and J. King. *Buying Antiques Reference Book 1971.* New York: Praeger, 1971.

Books

Bradley, Van Allen. *Gold in Your Attic.* New York: Fleet Publishing, 1958.

———. *More Gold in Your Attic.* New York: Fleet Publishing, 1961.

Good general information.

Lazare, Edward. *American Book Prices Current*. Privately printed. (Order from author at 509 Fifth Avenue, New York, N.Y. 10017.) A compilation of book prices from auction sales in the United States and London.

Mebane, John. *Books Relating to the Civil War: A Priced Check List*. New York: Yoseloff, 1963. Excellent coverage of a limited field.

Sterne, Edward. *Is My Old Book Valuable?* Taneytown, Maryland: Antiques Publications, 1966. Excellent guide to selling books, including a list of available price lists, but no prices are given in the book.

Warman, Edwin G. *2nd Value Guide to Old Books*. Uniontown, Pennsylvania: Warman Publishing, 1961. A listing of specific prices for specific books. Of limited value, but a list of shops that buy and sell old books is included.

Bottles

Agee, Bill. *Collecting the Cures*. Privately printed, 1969. (Order from author at 1200 Melrose, Waco, Texas 76710.)

Ballou, Hazel. *The Beginners Book: Collecting Jars and Bottles for Fun and Money*. 1966. (Order from author at 1802 Margrave, Fort Scott, Kansas.)

Blumenstein, Lynn. *Old Tyme Bottles*. Salem, Oregon: Old Time Bottle Publishing Company, 1966.

Bressie, Wes and Ruby. *Ghost Town Bottle Price Guide*. Salem, Oregon: Old Time Bottle Publishing Company, 1966.

Davis, Marvin and Helen. *Antique Bottles*. Ashland, Oregon: Old Bottle Collecting Publications, 1967.

———. *Bottles and Relics*. Ashland, Oregon: Old Bottle Collecting Publications, 1970.

Decanter Collector's Guide. Pewee Valley, Kentucky: Pewee Valley Press, n.d.

Fike, Richard E. *Guide to Old Bottles, Contents and Prices*. Privately printed, 1969. (Order from author at 1135 Maxfield Drive, Ogden, Utah.)

———. *Guide to Old Bottles, Contents and Prices,* Volume II. Privately printed (see above), 1969.

Fountain, John C. and Don Colcleaser. *Dictionary of Spirits and Whiskey Bottles*. Amador City, California: Ole Empty Bottle House Publishing Company, 1969.

Howe, John. *A Whiskeyana Guide: Antique Whiskey Bottles*. Privately printed, 1967. (Order from author at 4894 Sandy Lane, San Jose, California 95124.)

Kovel, Ralph and Terry. *The Official Bottle Price List*. New York: Crown, 1971.

Matthews, Robert T. *Antique Candy Containers*. Privately printed, 1966. (Order from author at Cloverfield, Glenelg, Maryland 21737.)

Taylor, Gordon. *Milk Bottle Manual*. Salem, Oregon: Old Time Bottle Publishing Company, 1971.

Tibbitts, John C. *1200 Bottles Priced*. Privately printed, 1970. (Order from The Little Glass Shack, 161 56th Street, Sacramento, California 95820.)

Umberger, Art and Jewel. *It's a*

Corker: Bottle Price Guide. Privately printed, 1966. (Order from author at 819 W. Wilson, Tyler, Texas 75701.)

———. *It's Sarsaparilla!* Privately printed (see above), 1968.

Yount, John T. *Bottle Collector's Handbook & Pricing Guide*. San Angelo, Texas: Educator Books, 1970.

Walter, Leo G., Jr. *Walter's Inkwells of 1885* (Book 1). Privately printed. (Order from Stagecoach Antiques, 443 West Market Street, Akron, Ohio 44303.)

AVON

Hastin, Bud. *Avon Bottle Encyclopedia*. Privately printed, 1971. (Order from author at P.O. Box 9868, Kansas City, Missouri 64134.)

Western Collector's Handbook and Price Guide to Avon Bottles. San Francisco: Western Collector Books, 1969.

BEAM

Cembura, Al, and Constance Avery. *Jim Beam Bottles, 1971–72 Identification & Price Guide*. Privately printed, 1970. (Order from Al Cembura, 139 Arlington Avenue, Berkeley, California 94707.)

BISCHOFF

Avery, Constance and Leslie, and Al Cembura. *Bischoff Bottles, Identification and Price Guide*. Privately printed, 1969. (Order from Al Cembura, 139 Arlington Avenue, Berkeley, California 94707.)

EZRA BROOKS

Western Collector's Handbook and Price Guide to Ezra Brooks Decanters. San Francisco: Western Collector Books, 1970.

GARNIER

Avery, Constance and Al Cembura. *Garnier Bottles*. Privately printed, 1970. (Order from Al Cembura, 139 Arlington Avenue, Berkeley, California 94707.)

Schwartz, Jeri and Ed. *Just Figurals, A Guide to Garnier*. Privately printed, 1969. (Order from author at 270 North Broadway, Yonkers, New York 10701.)

LUXARDO

Avery, Constance and Al Cembura. *Luxardo Bottles, Identification and Price Guide*. Privately printed, 1969. (Order from Al Cembura, 134 Arlington Avenue, Berkeley, California 94707.)

FRUIT JARS

Bird, Douglas, and Marion and Charles Corke. *A Century of Antique Canadian Glass Fruit Jars*. Privately printed, 1970. (Order from Douglas Bird, 859 Valetta Street, London 74, Ontario, Canada.)

Burris, Ronald B. *An Illustrated Guide for Collecting Fruit Jars with Price Guide*. Privately printed, 1966. (Order from author at 2941 Campus Drive, Visalia, California 93277.)

———. *Collecting Fruit Jars, Book #2, with Price Guide*. Privately printed, 1967. (see above).

———. *Collecting Fruit Jars* (3 Volumes). Privately printed, 1968. (see above).

———. *More Collectable Jars, Book 3, with Price Guide*. Privately printed, 1968. (see above).

Creswick, Alice and Arleta Rodrigues. *The Cresrod Blue Book of Fruit Jars*. Grand Rapids, Michigan: Cresrod Publishing Company, 1969.

Harvest 2nd Fruit Jar Finders Price Guide. Milwaukee, Wisconsin: Harvest Publishing Company, 1970.

Rodrigues, Arleta and Alice Creswick. *A Collection of Yesterday's Fruit Jars from Great Aunt May's Cellar*. Privately printed, 1967. (Order from Arleta Rodrigues, P.O. Box 2413, Castro Valley, California 94546.)

Schroeder, Bill. *1000 Fruit Jars Priced and Illustrated*. Privately printed, 1970. (Order from author at Route 4, Paducah, Kentucky 42001.)

MEDICINE

Bartholomew, Ed. *1001 Bitters Bottles*. Fort Davis, Texas: Bartholomew House, 1970.

———. *1200 Old Medicine Bottles with Prices Current*. Fort Davis, Texas: Frontier Book Company, 1970.

MINIATURES

Snyder, Robert E. *Bottles in Miniature*. Privately printed, 1969. (Order from author at 4235 West 13th, Amarillo, Texas 79106.)

———. *Bottles in Miniature,* Volume II. Privately printed, 1970. (see above).

———. *Bottles in Miniature,* Volume III. Privately printed, 1971. (see above).

Spaid, David. *Mini-World—1971–72 Identification & Price Guide*. Privately printed, 1972. (Order from B & K Enterprises, P. O. Box 42558, Los Angeles, California 90050.)

BUTTONS

Adkins, Gertrude D. *Price Guide to Button Parade*. Leon, Iowa: Mid-America Book Company, 1968. Price list to use in conjunction with the book *Button Parade* by Dorothy Foster Brown.

CATALOGS

Richard A. Bourne Co., Inc., Catalog of Sales, Corporation Street, Hyannis, Massachusetts 02601.

Garth's Auction Barn, Catalog of Sales, 1570 Stratford Road, Delaware, Ohio 43105.

O. Bundle Gilbert, Catalog of Sales, Garrison-on-Hudson, New York 10524.

Parke-Bernet Galleries, Inc., Catalog of Sales, 980 Madison Avenue, New York, New York 10021.

Pennypacker Auction Centre, 1540 New Holland Road, Reading, Pennsylvania 19607.

Guy & Gladys Saulsbury Antiques, Highway 23, Spicer, Minnesota 56288.

Weschler's Galleries, 905-7-9 E Street, N.W., Washington, D.C. 20004.

CLOCKS AND WATCHES

The Art and Antiques Investor. *Antique Watches as an Investment*. Privately printed, n.d. (Order from The Art and Antiques Investor, 9538 Brighton Way, Suite 330, Beverly Hills, California 90210.) Paperback listing with price ranges given.

CUMHAILL, P. W. *Investing in Clocks and Watches*. New York: Clarkson N. Potter, 1967.

Beautifully illustrated hard-cover book with English-American prices.

Dolls

Leuzzi, Marlene. *Antique Doll Price Guide,* Second Edition, 1972. Privately printed. (Order from author at 6 South Lane, Englewood, Colorado 80110.)
Well-illustrated paperback price list.

Furniture

Andrews, John. *The Price Guide to Antique Furniture.* The Antique Collectors' Club, Clopton, Woodbridge, Suffolk, England, 1969.
An English guide to moderate price furniture.

Field Guide to Early American Furniture. Boston, Massachusetts: Little, Brown, 1951.
The best general book about antique furniture pricing. A comparative range of prices is given. The descriptions are invaluable.

Ormsbee, Thomas. *Field Guide to American Victorian Furniture.* Boston, Massachusetts: Little, Brown, 1952; paperback 1964.

Glass

ART GLASS

Hotchkiss, John F. *Price Guides* to the following books: *Collectible Glass* (Volumes 1, 2, 3 & 4); *American Art Glass; Art, Colored and Cameo Glass;* and *Carder's Steuben Glass.* Privately printed, n.d. (Order from Hotchkiss House, 89 Sagamore Drive, Rochester, New York 14617.)
Each price guide is keyed to the proper color picture book.

CARNIVAL GLASS

Hartung, Marion. *Carnival Glass, A Guide to Prices 1969–70.* Privately printed, 1970. (Order from author at 718 Constitution Street, Emporia, Kansas 66801.)
Spiral-bound, unillustrated price list.

Hotchkiss, John F. and Sherman Hand. *Price Guide Number Two to Carnival Glass.* Privately printed, 1969. (Order from Hotchkiss House, 89 Sagamore Drive, Rochester, New York 14612.)
Price guide keyed to *Color in Carnival Glass,* Books 1 & 2 by Sherman Hand; *Carnival Glass in Color* by Marion Hartung; and *Carnival Glass,* Books 1 through 8 by Marion Hartung.

Presznick, Rose M. *Carnival and Iridescent Glass Price Guide.* Privately printed, 1970. (Order from author at Route 1, Box 173, Lodi, Ohio 44254.)
Spiral bound, unillustrated price list.

CUT GLASS

Daniel, Dorothy. *Price Guide to American Cut Glass.* New York: Morrow, 1967.
Hard-cover listing of 50 patterns of cut glass and black and white line drawings.

Hotchkiss, John F. *Cut Glass Handbook and Price Guide.* Privately printed, 1970. (Order from Hotchkiss House, 89 Sagamore Drive, Rochester, New York 14617.)
Illustrated paperback listing with price ranges.

DEPRESSION GLASS

Weatherman, Hazel Marie. *Price Trends IV: Spring, 1972.* Privately printed, 1972. (Order from author at 4501 Jackson Drive, Route 12, Springfield, Missouri 65804.)
A supplement to *Colored Glassware of the Depression Era.*

MILK GLASS

Warman, Edwin G. *Milk Glass Price Guide.* Privately printed, 1960. (Order from author at 8 Frankhoover Street, Uniontown, Pennsylvania 15401.)

PATTERN GLASS OR PRESSED GLASS

Lee, Ruth Webb. *Price Guide to Pattern Glass.* Privately printed, 1955. (Order from author at 105 Suffolk Road, Wellesley Hills, Massachusetts 02181.)
A listing of patterns and prices with line drawings.

———. *Current Values of Antique Glass.* Privately printed, rev. 1969. (see above).
A price list of Victorian glass, art glass, Sandwich glass, and cut plates with line drawings.

Metz, Alice Hulett. *Early American Pattern Glass* (Volumes 1 & 2). Privately printed, 1958. (Order from author at 2004 West 102nd Street, Chicago, Illinois 60643.)

———. *Much More Early American Pattern Glass.* Privately printed, 1965. (see above).
Well-illustrated paperback books with identification and prices of pressed glass, mainly goblets.

INSULATORS

Brown, Gerald. *Collectible Porcelain Insulators.* Privately printed, 1971. (Order from author at Two Buttes, Colorado 81084.)

Cranfill, Gary G. and Greg A. Kareofelas. *The Collectors' Guide for Glass Insulators with Prices Book I Revised.* Privately printed, 1969. (Order from author at 5536 Keoncrest Circle #2, Sacramento, Calif. 95841.)

———. *The Collectors' Guide for Glass Insulators with Prices Book 2.* Privately printed (see above), 1970.

Milholland, Marion C. *Glass Insulator Reference Book #2.* Privately printed, 1970. (Order from author at Rt. 2, Box 368, Sequim, Washington 98382.)

———. *Suggested Insulator Price List and Index for Book #2.* Privately printed (see above), 1970.

Stuart, Lynn R. *Stuart's Insulator Guide.* Privately printed, 1968. (Order from author at P.O. Box 862, Gilbert, Ariz. 85234.)

Terrill, Frances M. *Choice Insulators priced.* Privately printed, 1972. (Order from author at 2356 NW Quimby Street, Portland, Oregon 97210.)

———. *Hemingway Insulators Priced Book #3.* Privately printed, n.d. (see above).

———. *Insulators with Embossing Errors.* Privately printed, 1971. (see above).

———. *Rare Insulators with Prices.* Privately printed, 1971. (see above).

———. *Scarce Insulators Priced.* Privately printed, 1970. (see above).

Tibbitts, John. *A Guide for Insulator Collectors* (Volumes 1, 2, 3). Privately printed, 1968. (Order from The Little Glass Shack, 3161

56th St., Sacramento, Calif. 95820.)

Jewelry

Aston Industries. *Antique and Old Jewelry Price Guide.* Privately printed, n.d. (Order from Aston Industries, 3956 Mayfield Road, Cleveland Heights, Ohio 44121.)
Paperback catalog reprints.

Falkiner, Richard. *Investing in Antique Jewelry.* New York: Clarkson N. Potter, 1968.
Beautifully illustrated hard-cover book with English-American prices.

Kitchenware

Lantz, Louise. *Revised Price List to Old American Kitchenware.* Privately printed, 1970. (Order from author at P.O. Box 155A, Williams Road, Hydes, Maryland 21082.)
Pamphlet price list of assorted kitchenwares, illustrated by early catalog woodcuts.

Knives and Razors

Mayes, Robert. *Two in One Knife and Razor Book,* 1971 Edition. Privately printed, 1971. (Order from author at P.O. Box 475, Middlesboro, Kentucky 40965.)

Ritchie, R. B., *Kentucky Knife-Traders Manual.* Privately printed, 1971. (Order from author at Box 384, Hindman, Kentucky 41822.)

Schroeder, Bill. *1000 Razors Priced and Illustrated.* Privately printed, 1970. (Order from author at Route 4, Paducah, Kentucky 42001.)

Paper Antiques

Burdick, J. R. *The American Card Catalogue.* Franklin Square, New York: Nostalgia Press, Box 243, Franklin Square, New York 11010, 1967. A check list of advertising cards, insert cards, rewards of merit, tokens, and giveaways, etc., with out-of-date prices.

Kaduck, John M. *Mail Memories.* Privately printed, 1971. (Order from "Memories," Box 02152, Cleveland, Ohio 44102.)
Illustrated price list of picture postcards.

Kurzrock, Lawrence. *United States Playing Cards, Price Catalogue.* Privately printed, 1965. (Order from author at 9 East 96th Street, New York, New York.)
Paperback catalog of current prices paid for playing cards by a dealer and collector.

Lowe, James L. *Lincoln Postcard Catalog.* Privately printed, 1967. (Order from author at 318 Roosevelt Avenue, Folsom, Pa. 19033.)

———. *Standard Postcard Catalog.* Privately printed (see above), 1968.
Paperback listings with few illustrations.

Political

Bristow, Dick. *The Illustrated Political Button Book.* Privately printed, 1971. (Order from author at P.O. Box 1741, Santa Cruz, Calif. 95060.)
Paperback picture listing.

Hake, Ted. *The Button Book.* New York: Dafran House Publishers, 1972.
Paperback picture listing of political advertising and buttons.

Pottery and Porcelain

Altman, Vi and Si. *Price Guide to Buffalo Pottery.* Privately printed,

n.d. (Order from author at 28 Clifford Heights, Amherst, New York 14226.)
Separate price guide keyed to *The Book of Buffalo Pottery* (Crown Publishers).

Ball, A. *The Price Guide to Pot-Lids and Other Underglaze Colour Prints on Pottery*. The Antique Collectors' Club, Clopton, Woodbridge, Suffolk, England, 1970.
English picture listing with prices given by classification.

Dimsdle, June. *Steins and Prices*. Privately printed, 1970. (Order from Old World Antiques, 8009 Corona, Kansas City, Kansas 66112.)
Paperback pictured listing of glass, pewter, and ceramic steins.

Hotchkiss, John F. *Price Guide to Rookwood Pottery*. Privately printed, 1969. (Order from Hotchkiss House, 89 Sagamore Drive, Rochester, New York 14617.)
Separate price list keyed to *The Book of Rookwood Pottery* by Herbert Peck (Crown Publishers), 1968.

———. *Price Guide to the Enchantment of Hand-Painted Nippon Porcelain*. Privately printed, n.d. (see above).

Kircher, Edwin J., and Barbara and Joseph Agranoff. *Rookwood: Its Golden Era of Art Pottery 1880–1929 with Price Guide*. Privately printed, 1969. (Order from Rookwood Golden Era, P.O. Box 6501, Cincinnati, Ohio 45206.)
Spiral-bound, color picture listing of Rookwood pottery and marks.

Mohr, R. H. *Mettlach Steins and Their Prices*. Privately printed, 1963. (Order from author at 2208 Douglas Street, Rockford, Illinois 61100.)
Pamphlet reprint of old catalog, with descriptions and current prices.

Mount, Sally. *The Price Guide to 18th Century English Pottery*. The Antique Collectors' Club, Clopton, Woodbridge, Suffolk, England, 1972.

Purviance, Louise and Evan, and Norris F. Schneider. *Zanesville Art Pottery in Color with Revised Price List*. Leon, Iowa: Mid-America Book Company, 1968.
Spiral-bound book with color pictures of pottery.

Spero, Simon. *The Price Guide to 18th Century English Porcelain*. The Antique Collectors' Club, Clopton, Woodbridge, Suffolk, England, 1970.
English picture listing with prices given by classification.

Silver

Delieb, Eric. *Investing in Silver*. New York: Clarkson N. Potter, 1967.
Beautifully illustrated hard-cover book with English-American prices.

Hankenson, Dick. *Trivets: Old and Re-Pro with Supplement #1*. Privately printed, 1968. (Order from author at Maple Plain, Minnesota 55359.)
Spiral-bound, illustrated list with out-of-date prices.

Harris, Ian. *The Price Guide to Antique Silver*. The Antique Collectors' Club, Clopton, Woodbridge, Suffolk, England, 1969.
English pictorial listing of English silver priced in pounds.

La Perriere, H. Baile de. *Silver Auc-*

tion Records, 1970–71. Hilmarton Manor Press, Calne, Wiltshire, England, 1971.
Listing of English silver sold at auction with some pictures and priced in pounds and dollars.

Tin and Advertising

Cope, Jim. *Collectable Old Advertising.* Privately printed, 1973. (Order from author at P.O. Box 1417, Orange, Texas 77630.)
Paperback picture listing of tin trays.

Davis, Marvin and Helen. *Tobacco Tins.* Privately printed, 1970. (Order from author at P.O. Box 216, Ashland, Oregon 97520.)
Color picture paperback listing.

Goldstein, Sheldon. *Coca-Cola Collectibles.* 1971. (Order from author at P.O. Box 301, Woodland Hills, Calif. 91364.)
Paperback color picture listing of Coca-Cola trays and other items.

Klug, Ray. *Antique Advertising.* Privately printed, n.d. (Order from L-W Promotions, Box 69, Gas City, Indiana 46933.)
Paperback price list with signs, tins, and trays pictured and listed.

Pettit, Ernest L. *The Book of Collectible Tin Containers with Revised Price Guide for Book I.* Privately printed, 1970. (Order from author at P.O. Box 361, Wynantskill, New York 12198.)

———. *Collectible Tin Containers with Price Guide.* Privately printed, 1970. (see above).
Spiral-bound books with color pictures of tin containers.

Polansky, Tom. *Advertising Tin Containers,* Vol. II. Privately printed, 1972. (Order from author at 10720 Lilac Street, Loma Linda, California 92354.)

———. *Advertising Trays.* Privately printed, 1971. (see above).
Paperback picture listing of beer, whiskey, soda water, political change trays, and Vienna art.

Somlo, Jean and Thomas. *Pharmaceutical Antiques and Collectables with Price Guide.* New York: Crown, 1971.
Spiral-bound, color picture listing of medical bottles, mortars, funnels, etc.

Tools

Farnham, Alexander. *Tool Collectors Handbook.* Privately printed, 1972. (Order from author at P.O. Box 205, R.D. 2, Stockton, New Jersey 08559.)
Paperback picture listing.

Western Antiques

Britz, Les. *Treasury of Frontier Relics.* New York: Crown, 1966.
Excellent book about the tools, household goods, and so on of the West. Photographs with very general price ranges given.

20

Antique Publications

Magazines

Antique Collector, 16 Strutton Ground, Victoria Street, London S.W. 1, England.

Antiques, 551 Fifth Avenue, New York, N.Y. 10017.

Antiques Journal, Babka Publishing, Box 1046, Dubuque, Iowa 52001.

Antiques Today, Box 1034, Kermit, Texas 79745.

Canadian Antiques Collector, 1 Heath Street West, Toronto, Ontario, Canada.

Collector's World, Collector's World Publishing, P.O. Box 654, Conroe, Texas 77301.

Early American Life, 206 Hanover Street, Gettysburg, Pennsylvania 17325.

Explore Magazine, Box 313, Hartford, Vermont 05047.

Hobbies, Lightner Publishing, 1006 South Michigan Avenue, Chicago, Illinois 60605.

National Antiques Review, P.O. Box 619, Portland, Maine 04104.

Old Stuff, Johnson Hill's Press, 1233 Janesville Avenue, Fort Atkinson, Wisconsin 53538.

Relics, P.O. Box 3338, Austin, Texas 78764.

Spinning Wheel, Hanover, Pennsylvania 17331.

Yankee, Yankee, Inc., Dublin, New Hampshire 03444.

Newspapers

The American Collector, 3717 Mt. Diablo Blvd., Lafayette, California 94549.

Antique Monthly, P.O. Drawer 2, Tuscaloosa, Alabama 35401.

The Antique Trader Weekly, Babka Publishing, P.O. Box 1050, Dubuque, Iowa 52001.

Antiques News, Box B, Marietta, Pennsylvania 17547.

The Antiquity, Mt. Hermon Road, Hope, New Jersey 07844.

Collector's News, P.O. Box 156, Grundy Center, Iowa 50638.

Collector's Weekly, Box 1119, Kermit, Texas 79745.

Depression Glass Daze, Box 57, Utisville, Michigan 48463

The Indian Trader, P.O. Box 404, La Mesa, California 92041.

The Mid-America Reporter, Leon, Iowa 50144.

The Plate Collector, 209 North Oak Street, Kermit, Texas 79745.

Pottery Collectors' Newsletter, P.O. Box 446, Asheville, North Carolina 28802.

Tin Type, 1496 S. Macon Street, Aurora, Colorado 80010.

Tri-State Trader, P.O. Box 90-DM, Knightstown, Indiana 46148.

West Coast Peddler, P.O. Box 4489, Downey, California 90241.

Specialized Catalogs

Antiques Growth Corporation (musical instruments), 52 First Street, Hackensack, New Jersey 07601.

Barden & Clark, 22 Rutland Square, Boston, Massachusetts 02118.

The Compass, Kenneth Nebenzahl, 333 North Michigan Avenue, Chicago, Illinois 60601.

N. Flayderman & Company (military catalogs), Squash Hollow, R.F.D.

2, New Milford, Connecticut 06776.

The Kennedy Quarterly, Kennedy Galleries, 20 E. 56th Street, New York, New York 10022.

G. W. MacKinnon (music catalogs), 453 Atardo Avenue, Charlotte, North Carolina 28206.

The Print Collector, Kenneth Nebenzahl, 333 North Michigan Avenue, Chicago, Illinois 60601.

Karl F. Wede (catalogs about books, ship models, marine antiques & curios), R.F.D. 3, Box 344, Saugerties, New York 12477.

Specialized Magazines

The Antique Toy World, 3941 Belle Plaine, Chicago, Illinois 60618.

Bulletin of the Musical Box Society, Mrs. Clarence W. Fabel, Secretary-Treasurer, 1765 East Sudan Circle, Greenville, Mississippi.

Bulletin of the National Association of Watch & Clock Collectors, American Bank Building, 401 Locust Street, Columbia, Pennsylvania 17512.

Button World Magazine (for political collectors), Gary Lundquist, R.D. 4, Young Street, Easton, Pennsylvania 18042.

The Check List (check collecting), Robert Flaig, P.O. Box 27112, Cincinnati, Ohio 45227.

The China Decorator, P.O. Box 45375, Los Angeles, California 90045.

The China Painter, 3111 N.W. 19th, Oklahoma City, Oklahoma 73107.

The Chronicle (early American tools and mechanical devices), Early American Industries Association, Old Economy, Ambridge, Pennsylvania 15003.

Graphic Antiquarian, P.O. Box 3471, Wilmington, Noth Carolina 28401.

Insulators, Crown Jewels of the Wire, Route 1, Box 475, Chico, California 95926.

Just Buttons, Box 576, Southington, Connecticut 06489.

The Magazine Silver (formerly *Silver-rama*), P.O. Box 1208, Vancouver, Washington 98660.

Paperweight Collectors' Association Newsletter, 47 Windsor Road, Scarsdale, New York.

Bottle Magazines

Bottles & Relics, P.O. Box 654, Conroe, Texas 77301.

Bottle News, Box 1000, Kermit, Texas 79745.

The Bottle Trader, P.O. Box 69, Gas City, Indiana 46933.

The Lionstone Legend, P.O. Box 75924, Los Angeles, California 90075.

Milkbottles Only Organization, Fred Rawlinson, Box 5456, Newport News, Virginia 23605.

Miniature Bottle Mart, 24 Gertrude Lane, West Haven, Connecticut 06516.

The National Bottle Gazette, P.O. Box 1011, Kermit, Texas 79745.

Old Bottle Magazine, The Old Bottle Exchange, 525 E. Revere, Bend, Oregon 97701.

Pictorial Bottle Review, B & K Enterprises, P.O. Box 42558, Los Angeles, California 90050.

English Publications

Art & Antiques Weekly, 40 Craven Street, London WC2, England.

Collectors Guide, 167 Fleet Street, London EC4, England.

21

Bibliography of General Books About Antiques

Christensen, Erwin O. *The Index of American Design.* New York: Macmillan, 1950.
A beautiful book of color pictures of many types of American antiques, including sections about Western art, lighting, costume, furniture, tools, and wooden carved signs and figureheads.

Cole, Ann Kilborn. *Antiques.* New York: McKay, 1957.

———. *The Beginning Antique Collector's Handbook.* New York: McKay, 1959.

———. *How to Collect the New Antiques.* New York: McKay, 1966.
A group of three very general books about antiques, with many lists but not much specific information. The material about "new" antiques is of value.

Comstock, Helen. *The Concise Encyclopedia of American Antiques.* New York: Hawthorn Books, 1958.
An authoritative encyclopedia, with sections about furniture, Shakers, mirrors, silver, pewter, iron, copper, brass, tin, stoves, export porcelain and other pottery and porcelain, glass, bottles, needlework, cotton printing, coverlets, rugs, lighting devices, buttons, trade cards, playing cards, quillwork, treen, chalkware, swords, firearms, clocks, paintings, engravings, toys, folk art, coins, books, maps, ship models, stamps, wallpaper, greeting cards, autographs, dime novels, tools, and southwestern art.

Connoisseur. *The Concise Encyclopedia of Antiques* (5 vols.). New York: Hawthorn Books, 1955.
These five volumes are valuable research tools, and should be used at a library. Most of the material is about European antiques.

———. *Connoisseur Period Guides* (6 vols.). New York: Reynal, 1954.
Beautiful, scholarly research books about English periods of antiques.

Drepperd, Carl W. *First Reader for Antique Collectors.* New York: Garden City Books, 1954.

———. *The Primer of American Antiques.* Garden City, New York: Doubleday, 1952.

Drepperd, Carl W., and Marjorie Smith. *Handbook of Tomorrow's Antiques.* New York: Crowell, 1953.
All of the books written by Carl Drepperd (there are several others) are important to the beginning collector. He has used old catalogs to produce research materials that have never been equaled.

Hertz, Louis H. *Antique Collecting for Men.* New York: Hawthorn, 1969.
Detailed history of offbeat subjects

such as typewriters, electrical antiques, tools, amusement park devices, military miscellania, etc.

Hughes, G. Bernard. *Horse Brasses and Other Small Items for the Collector.* London: Country Life, 1956.
Contents tell about horse brasses, sugar tongs, snuffboxes, tiles, beadwork, pewter measures, earthenware loving cups, music boxes, and flower-encrusted china, all English antiques.

Hughes, Therle. *Cottage Antiques.* New York: Praeger, 1967.

———. *More Small Decorative Antiques.* New York: Macmillan, 1963.

———. *Small Antiques for the Collector.* New York: Macmillan, 1965.

———. *Small Decorative Antiques.* New York: Macmillan, 1963.
All four of these excellent books tell about small English antiques, many types of pottery, silver, boxes, glass, and so on.

Jenkins, Dorothy. *Fortune in the Junkpile.* New York: Crown, 1965.
A very general book about antiques in America, with a bibliography and some photographs of value.

Lord, Priscilla Sawyer, and Daniel J. Foley. *The Folk Arts and Crafts of New England.* New York: Chilton Books, 1965.
A very good book about the antiques of a limited section of the United States, with 500 pictures and much valuable information.

McClinton, Katharine Morrison. *Antique Collecting for Everyone.* New York: Bonanza Books, 1951.

———. *Antiques Past and Present.* New York: Clarkson N. Potter, 1971.

———. *The Complete Book of American Country Antiques.* New York: Coward, McCann & Geoghegan, 1967.

———. *The Complete Book of Small Antiques Collecting.* New York: Coward-McCann, 1965.

———. *A Handbook of Popular Antiques.* New York: Bonanza Books, 1946.
Five very good books about antiques, with special chapters devoted to each of many kinds of pottery, metal, furniture, and so on.

Mebane, John. *The Coming Collecting Boom.* Cranbury, New Jersey: Barnes, 1968.

———. *New Horizons in Collecting.* New York: Barnes, 1966.

———. *The Poor Man's Guide to Antique Collecting.* Garden City, New York: Doubleday, 1969.

———. *Treasure at Home.* New York: Barnes, 1964.
Four good books about small antiques, with approximate prices given.

Michael, George. *The Treasury of New England Antiques.* New York: Hawthorn, 1969.
Hodgepodge of general information about antiques found in New England.

Ormsbee, Thomas H. *Collecting Antiques in America.* New York: Deerfield Books, 1940, 1962.

———. *Know Your Heirlooms.* New York: McBride, 1956.
Of all of the many books by Ormsbee, these are but two, but they are informative and interesting, although some of the material is now out of date.

Savage, George. *The Antique Collector's Handbook*. London: Barrie and Rockliff, 1959.

An interesting book for the collector who is interested in the small antiques available in England.

Scott, Amoret and Christopher. *Collecting Bygones*. New York: Mckay, 1964.

Unusual small antiques are mentioned briefly in this dictionary type of book. Mousetraps, flycatchers, moustache cups, and handwarmers are just a few of these oddities.

Stevens, Gerald. *In a Canadian Attic*. Toronto: Ryerson, 1963.

This is a general book about the everyday antiques of Canada, including documents, books, stamps, coins, woodenwares, furniture, textiles, silver and pewter, china, glass, lamps, copper, and other items.

Towne, Morgan. *Treasures in Truck and Trash*. Garden City, New York: Doubleday, 1950.

A book of short hints about many types of antiques not usually collected.

Winchester, Alice. *The Antiques Treasury*. New York: Dutton, 1959.

A picture-filled book about the antique collections at the seven "working" museums of American antiques.

———. *How to Know American Antiques*. New York: Mentor, 1951.

A good paperback book about American antiques before 1840.

Victorian

Butler, Joseph. *American Antiques 1800–1900*. New York: Odyssey Press, 1965.

Drepperd, Carl. *Victorian, the Cinderella of Antiques*. Garden City, New York: Doubleday, 1950.

Lichten, Frances, *Decorative Arts of Victoria's Era*. New York: Scribner's, 1950.

Shull, Thelma. *Victorian Antiques*. Rutland, Vermont: Tuttle, 1963.

Yates, Raymond F. and Marguerite W. *A Guide to Victorian Antiques*. New York: Harper, 1949.

All these books about Victorian antiques discuss furniture, silver, pottery, and other decorative arts. There are also many books that specialize in one part of the decoration of the Victorian period.

22

Collectors Groups

ABRAHAM LINCOLN
APPRECIATION SOCIETY

Mrs. A. M. Pate, Jr. (Temporary Secretary)
48 Valley Ridge Road
Fort Worth, Texas 76107

ADIRONDACK DOLL CLUB

Mrs. Hugh Herron
Cadyville, New Jersey 12918

ADVENTURERS CLUB
OF NEW YORK

54 West 40th Street
New York, New York 10018

AERONAUTICAL HISTORICAL
ASSOCIATION

Box 44
Hebron, Connecticut 06248

AGRICULTURAL HISTORY
SOCIETY

Economic Research Services
U.S. Department of Agriculture
Washington, D.C. 20250

AMERICAN ARMS
COLLECTORS'
ASSOCIATION, INC.

John H. Wetzelberger
1101 Hampton Garth
Towson, Maryland

AMERICAN BELL
ASSOCIATION

Louise Collins
Box 286, R.D. #1
Natrona Heights, Pennsylvania 15065

AMERICAN BRANCH,
FIREMARK CORDE

Max Klein
Crestwood Insurance Association
13047 Ventura Boulevard
Studio City, California 91604

AMERICAN CARNIVAL
GLASS ASSOCIATION

Charlotte Ormsbee, General Secretary
730 24th Street, N.W.
Washington, D.C.
($3 a year. An educational organization formed to assist collectors of, and promote interest in, carnival glass.)

AMERICAN CUSTARD
GLASS COLLECTORS

O. Joe Olson, Editor
4129 Virginia Avenue
Kansas City, Missouri 64110

AMERICAN GRAMOPHONE
SOCIETY

1226 Montgomery Avenue
Narbeth, Pennsylvania
(For preservation of Master Records.)

AMERICAN NUMISMATIC
ASSOCIATION

Jack R. Koch, Executive Director
P.O. Box 2366

Colorado Springs, Colorado 80901
($11 admission, $6 a year thereafter. Members collect and study coins and promote the science of numismatics.)

AMERICAN NUMISMATIC SOCIETY

Raymond E. Main, Assistant Secretary
Broadway between 155th and 156th Streets
New York, N.Y. 10032
($20 a year for Fellow, $10 a year for Associate. Founded in 1858 "to advance numismatic knowledge as relates to history, art, archeology. . . .")

AMERICAN PHONOGRAPH COLLECTING SOCIETY

P.O. Box 5046
Berkeley, California 94705

AMERICAN SOCIETY OF MILITARY INSIGNIA COLLECTORS

Ira L. Duncan
744 Warfield Avenue
Oakland, California 94610
($6 a year. Members collect military insignia in an effort to understand military heraldry and gain historical knowledge.)

AMERICAN TAX TOKEN SOCIETY

Charles L. Carter
721 Glencoe Street
Denver, Colorado 80220

ANTIQUARIAN SOCIETY

185 Salisbury Street
Worcester, Massachusetts 01609

ANTIQUE AIRPLANE ASSOCIATION

Route #5—Industrial Airport
Ottumwa, Iowa
($12.50 a year. Members preserve, restore, and fly airplanes made before 1936, but you do not need to own an airplane to belong.)

ANTIQUE AUTOMOBILE CLUB OF AMERICA, INC.

William E. Bomgardner, Manager
West Derry Road
Hershey, Pennsylvania
($6.50 a year. Members restore and maintain automobiles made before 1930. Applicants do not need to own an antique car, but must be recommended by a member.)

ANTIQUE TELEPHONE COLLECTORS ASSOCIATION

P.O. Box 536
La Crosse, Kansas

ANTIQUE TOY COLLECTORS OF AMERICA

William Holland
1621 Monk Road
Gladwyne, Pennsylvania 19035

THE ANTIQUE WIRELESS ASSOCIATION

Holcomb, New York

AUTO ENTHUSIASTS INTERNATIONAL

Box 451
Mount Clemens, Michigan 48044
($6.00 a year. Members swap automobile literature and catalogs.)

AUTOMOBILE LICENSE PLATE

COLLECTOR'S ASSOCIATION, INC.

Mr. Vance A. Crilly
771 Martha Drive
Franklin, Ohio 45005
($5 a year, includes bi-monthly newsletter.)

AUTOMOTIVE OLD TIMERS, INC.

National Headquarters
P.O. Box 62
Warrenton, Virginia 22186
($12 to $20 a year. Members must have been associated with the automobile industry at least twenty years to be active; sustaining members may have spent less time in the industry. The group perpetuates the memory of automotive pioneers.)

THE BEECHER DOLL CLUB

Mrs. Mary K. Margraff
660 Park Place
Elmira, New York 14901

BEER CAN COLLECTORS OF AMERICA

Box 9104
St. Louis, Missouri 63117
($5 a year.)

BELLEEK SOCIETY INTERNATIONAL

P.O. Box 2661
Houston, Texas 77001

BETTER POSTCARD COLLECTORS' CLUB

James L. Lowe
318 Roosevelt Avenue
Folsom, Pennsylvania 19033
($2.50 a year, $6 for three years. Collectors learn about older, more valuable cards.)

BOY SCOUT MEMORABILIA

1000 Golfview Road
Glenview, Illinois 60025

BROOME COUNTY DOLL CLUB

Mrs. Warren McGregor
Maine Road
Maine, New Jersey 13802

BUTTON SOCIETY OF AMERICA

353 Stockton Street
Hightstown, New Jersey 08520

CALIFORNIA BARBED WIRE COLLECTORS ASSOCIATION

Ellwyn M. Carlson
1046 N. San Carlos Street
Porterville, California 93257

CELEBRITY DOLL CLUB

Loraine Burdick
5 Cojurt Place
Puyallup, Washington 98371

CHECK COLLECTORS

Robert Q. Flaig
P.O. Box 27112
Cincinnati, Ohio 45227

CHICAGO PLAYING CARD COLLECTORS, INC.

Mrs. Dorothy Powills, Director
9645 South Leavitt Street
Chicago, Illinois 60643
($3 a year, $1.75 junior membership. The group promotes the hobby of collecting trade cards with members the world over.)

THE CHINESE SNUFF BOTTLE SOCIETY OF AMERICA, INC.

2601 North Charles Street
Baltimore, Maryland 21218

CHRISTMAS SEAL AND CHARITY STAMP SOCIETY

Miss Jocile Maret
1906 Murphy Avenue
Joplin, Missouri 64803

CIRCUS FANS ASSOCIATION OF AMERICA

P.O. Box 605
Aurora, Illinois 60507

THE CIVIL WAR ROUND TABLE

Army and Navy Club
1627 Eye Street N.W.
Washington, D.C.

CIVIL WAR TOKEN SOCIETY

Box 112
Iola, Wisconsin
($4 a year. Above address is for their *Journal.*)

COLLECTORS ASSOCIATION
5011 Ewing Avenue
South Minneapolis, Minnesota 55410

COLONIAL COVERLET GUILD

825 South Fairfield Avenue
Lombard, Illinois

CONNECTICUT TOOL COLLECTOR'S SOCIETY

Robert H. Carlson
Box 121
Deep River, Connecticut 06417

DATE NAIL COLLECTORS ASSOCIATION OF TEXAS

405 North Daugherty
Eastland, Texas 76448

DELTIOLOGISTS OF AMERICA

318 Roosevelt Avenue
Folsom, Pennsylvania 19033

THE DIME NOVEL CLUB

1525 West Twelfth Street
Brooklyn 4, New York
($10 introductory, $20 a year thereafter to receive one dime novel a month: photo-offset facsimiles.)

DOLL STUDY CLUB OF BOSTON

Mrs. Ronald E. Thomas
Box 328, Old Main Road
North Falmouth, Massachusetts

EARLY AMERICAN INDUSTRIES ASSOCIATION

John P. Fox, Jr., Membership Chairman
Corning Glass Cente:
Corning, New York
(Collect, preserve, and study early tools and crafts.)

EARLY AMERICAN INDUSTRIES ASSOCIATION—WEST

Arnold Gordon, President
6668 W. 80th Place
Los Angeles, California 90045

EARLY TOOL COLLECTORS

Elliot Sayward
60 Harvest Lane
Levittown, New York 11756

GENESEE VALLEY DOLL CLUB

Mrs. James Davis
117 Pine Ridge Drive
Newark, New York 14513

GRANITE STATE DOLL CLUB

Mrs. Arrin E. Murrill
Gossville, New Hampshire 03239

GREEN MOUNTAIN DOLL CLUB

Mrs. Ralph Paturroff
R.D. 1
Shelburne, Vermont

HARRISBURG DOLL CLUB

Peg Steele
237 Hamilton Street
Harrisburg, Pennsylvania 17102

HEART OF AMERICA CARNIVAL GLASS ASSOCIATION

Dorothy Taylor, Secretary
7806 Arlington
Raytown, Missouri 64138
($3 a year, single, and $5 a year, couple.)

HEISEY COLLECTORS OF AMERICA

Louise Ream, President
P.O. Box 27
Newark, Ohio 43055
($25 initiation fee for active member with voting rights. $6 a year thereafter. $6 a year associate member, plus $1 per person for each additional household member. All privileges of the club, except voting.)

HORATIO ALGER SOCIETY

Mrs. Blanche Lloyd, Secretary-Treasurer
471½ North Grant
W. Lafayette, Indiana
($5.00 a year. Members swap duplicates of Alger books, present yearly awards to deserving boys, and in other ways try to keep alive the memory of Horatio Alger.)

INSULATOR SOCIETY OF AMERICA

P.O. Box 622
Manasquan, New Jersey 08736

INTERNATIONAL AVON COLLECTORS CLUB

P.O. Box 1406
Mesa, Arizona 85201
($6 a year, including monthly newsletter.)

INTERNATIONAL DEPRESSION GLASS CLUB

Helen Burk
4850 Broadway
Live Oak, California 95953
($3 a year, single, and $5 a year, couple.)

INTERNATIONAL MUSIC BOX SOCIETY

Mrs. Clarence W. Eabel
4301 Forest Manor Avenue
Indianapolis, Indiana

INTERNATIONAL SEAL LABEL & CIGAR BAND SOCIETY

Harry Copleston, Secretary
4371 Meadowcraft Road
Kettering, Ohio 45429

JENNY LIND DOLL CLUB

Mrs. John J. Grossman
1708 Huntington Turnpike
Trumbull, Connecticut 06611

KATE GREENAWAY SOCIETY

James L. Lowe
Folsom, Pennsylvania 19033

THE MANUSCRIPT SOCIETY

K. W. Duckett, Executive Secretary
Morris Library
Southern Illinois University
Carbondale, Illinois 62903
($7.50 a year. Members are interested in original autographs in various forms as mementos of the great and near-great.)

MARTHA'S VINEYARD DOLL CLUB

Mrs. Isabel Corliss
Union Street
Vineyard Haven, Massachusetts 02568

MECHANICAL BANK COLLECTORS CLUB OF AMERICA

E. T. Richards, Jr.
28 Fairway Drive
Barrington, Rhode Island 02806
($10 a year, $5 junior membership. An educational and social organization for bank collectors, but you must own a minimum of five banks to join.)

THE METROPOLITAN POST CARD COLLECTORS CLUB

Joseph J. Nardone, Corresponding Secretary
436 E. 9th Street
New York, New York 10009
($3 a year, including monthly bulletin.)

MID-WEST TOOL COLLECTORS' ASSOCIATION

William H. Holden, President
1113 Duncan Avenue
Elgin, Illinois 60120

MID YORK DOLL CLUB

Miss Mescal Amadon
2465 Falls Road
Marcellus, New York 13108

MUSICAL BOX SOCIETY

Mrs. Clarence W. Fabel, Secretary-Treasurer
1765 East Sudan Circle
Greenville, Mississippi
($10 the first year, $5 thereafter. Members study and preserve musical boxes and their history.)

THE NATIONAL ASSOCIATION OF TIMETABLE COLLECTORS

William L. Wagner, Membership Director
Box 842
Richmond, Indiana 47374
($4 a year.)

NATIONAL ASSOCIATION OF WATCH AND CLOCK COLLECTORS

E. H. Parkhurst, Jr., President
93 Conestoga Blvd.
Lancaster, Pennsylvania 17602

NATIONAL BUTTON SOCIETY

Mrs. James C. Booth, Secretary
4273 River Street
Willoughby, Ohio 44094
($3.50 a year. Founded in Chicago in 1938, an organization of 2,000 button collectors, libraries, museums, members of the button trade, and others.)

NATIONAL DOLL AND TOY COLLECTORS' CLUB

Mrs. Lloyd Steiker
1127 Neilson Street
Far Rockaway, New York 11691

NATIONAL EARLY AMERICAN GLASS CLUB

Dr. Edward W. Linney, President
47 Sycamore Road
South Braintree, Massachusetts 02185

NATIONAL TRUST FOR HISTORIC PRESERVATION

IN THE UNITED STATES

815 17th Street, N.W.
Washington, D.C. 20006

NEW LONDON DOLL CLUB

Mrs. Howard Stanton
29 High Rock Terrace
Groton, Connecticut 06340

NUMISMATIC SOCIETY OF AMERICA

Broadway at 155th Street
New York, New York 10032

NUTMEG DOLL CLUB
Mrs. William Swift
Grassy Hill Road
Old Lyme, Connecticut 06371

OLD LACERS
Mrs. Louise Leonberger
88 Juanita Way
San Francisco, California

PAPERWEIGHT COLLECTORS ASSOCIATION

Paul Jokelson
47 Windsor Road
Scarsdale, New York
(No dues. Formed to exchange information and "stimulate interest in the collection of crystal paperweights which contribute to the sum total of man's creative effort.")

PEWTER COLLECTORS' CLUB OF AMERICA

Thomas D. Williams, President
Litchfield, Connecticut
(The club is interested in furthering the study of American pewter.)

PHILATELIC AMERICANS SOCIETY

Box 266
Cincinnati, Ohio 45201

PHOTOGRAPHIC SOCIETY OF AMERICA

2005 Walnut Street
Philadelphia, Pennsylvania 19103

PLAYING CARD COLLECTORS ASSOCIATION, INC.

Mrs. Walter Boeyer
3869 North 84th Street
Milwaukee, Wisconsin

THE POSTMARK COLLECTORS CLUB

Robert K. Francis, Director
11 Jeralds Avenue
Yalesville, Connecticut 06492
($3 a year. Members collect postmarks and related items, especially the first day of issue marks, military and commemorative marks. Prospective members need recommendations and an official membership blank.)

THE QUESTERS

Mrs. John R. Pear
National President
707 Trombley Road
Grosse Pointe Park, Michigan 48230

(Non-profit group organized for research and study of antiques and to preserve historical buildings and landmarks. Personal contact is made to interested groups by the state or national organization chairman. No dues or requirements are published.)

RATION TOKEN COLLECTORS SOCIETY

Mrs. Viola Thomas, Secretary
5751 63rd Street

Sacramento, California 95824
($2 a year, including quarterly publication.)

ROGERS GROUP

John Rogers Studio and Museum
13 Oenoke Ridge
New Canaan, Connecticut

THE RUSHLIGHT CLUB

Mrs. Harry W. Rapp, Jr., Corresponding Secretary
21 Clair Road
R.F.D. #4
Vernon, Connecticut 06086

SHAKER DOLL CLUB

Mrs. Eunice Thomen
R.D. 2
Winsted, Connecticut 06098

SOCIETY OF CARNIVAL GLASS COLLECTORS

O. Joe Olson, Secretary-Editor
4129 Virginia Avenue
Kansas City, Missouri 64110
($3 a year. Information and exchange of ideas on collecting carnival glass.)

SOCIETY FOR THE PRESERVATION OF OLD MILLS

P.O. Box 435
Wiscasset, Maine 04578

THE SOCIETY OF MEDALISTS

F. Kimmerle, Secretary
P.O. Box 3022
Grand Central P.O.
New York, New York 10017
($12.50 a year brings membership and two medals a year. The society develops and encourages appreciation of medallic sculpture.)

SOUTHERN CALIFORNIA POSTCARD CLUB

W. von Boltenstern, Program Director
2649 San Marino Street
Los Angeles, California 90006
($2 a year. Comprises 500 members devoted to collecting postcards.)

SPRINGFIELD DOLL CLUB

Mrs. Edward F. Kozut
14 Bucknell Street
Ludlow, Massachusetts 01056

STANDARD GAUGE ASSOCIATION, INC.
(Toy Trains)
107 Park Avenue
Harrison, New York

STEIN COLLECTORS GUILD

206 Watterson City West
Louisville, Kentucky 40218

STEIN COLLECTORS INTERNATIONAL

15 Haven Court
Sacramento, California 95831
($20 a year for special membership includes eight-page quarterly, *Prosit*, membership card, special calendar, a special hardbound yearbook, and extra printed materials year round. $4 a year for subscription to *Prosit* only. Both run only January through December.)

STEVENGRAPH COLLECTORS' ASSOCIATION

Lewis Smith, President
Irvington-on-the-Hudson, New York 10533
(No dues. Members exchange information on origin, history, and ac-

quisition of silk pictures made by Thomas Stevens, Ltd.)

SUBURBAN SPRINGFIELD DOLL CLUB

Mrs. Marjorie Carlson
1547 Allen Street
Springfield, Massachusetts 01118

TEXAS ANTIQUE & CLASSIC MOTORCYCLE ASSOCIATION

H. J. Norman
P.O. Box 568
Weatherford, Texas 76086

TEXAS DATE NAIL COLLECTOR'S ASSOCIATION

405 N. Daughtery Street
Eastland, Texas 76448
($5 a year, including monthly *Nailer News*.)

TIN CONTAINER COLLECTORS ASSOCIATION

Clark & Mary Beth Secrest
1496 S. Macon Street
Aurora, Colorado 80010
($5 a year, including newsletter.)

TOKEN & MEDAL SOCIETY

Journal
Box 194
Iola, Wisconsin
(Are also regional exonumist clubs: California, Arizona, New England and Lake Erie Exonumist Society.)

TOPICAL ASSOCIATION (Stamps)

3306 North 50th Street
Milwaukee, Wisconsin 53216

UNITED FEDERATION OF DOLL CLUBS

Mrs. Rudolf Seibert
109 Sandringham Street
Rochester, New York

THE VETERAN MOTOR CAR CLUB OF AMERICA

J. Byron Hull, Secretary
15 Newton Street
Brookline, Massachusetts 01246
($10 a year. Members exhibit "veteran" cars at meets, arrange tours and shows.)

VICTORIAN SOCIETY IN AMERICA

The Athenaeum
East Washington Square
Philadelphia, Pennsylvania 19106

THE WEDGWOOD SOCIETY

Harry N. Buten
The Buten Museum of Wedgwood
246 N. Bowman Avenue
Merion, Pennsylvania
($10 a year. Members collect Wedgwood, exchange information, and hold frequent get-togethers.)

WESTERN NEW YORK DOLL CLUB

Mrs. Robert W. Zimmerman
45 Louis Avenue
West Seneca, New York 14224

WORLD'S FAIR COLLECTOR SOCIETY

Edward J. Orth
1436 Killarney Avenue
Los Angeles, California 90065

Index

"A," one-inch mark on silverplate, 164
A. H. Heisey and Company, mark, 82
Abraham & Straus, Inc., 86
Actress Glass, 77, 78
Adam brothers, 122
Adams, 20, 28
Adams, Harvey, and Company, 45
Adams, Henry, 270
adventure stories, 291
advertisements, 240
advertising, 281
  cards, 291
"African silver," 187
agata, 67, 68
agate, 236
age of furniture, 135
age of ownership, 140, 141
Alcock, Samuel, and Company, 32
alcohol, 147
Alford, C. G. & Company, 86
Alger, Horatio, 291
Alpha factory, 8, 9
alphabet design on samplers, 222
alphabet plates (children's), 42
Amati, Nicolo, 293
amber, 236
amberina, 63, 64, 65, 67
  painted, 65
  pressed, 65
Amelung factory, 83
American
  flag, 281
  newspapers, 276
  pottery and porcelain, bibliography, 53
American Antiquarian Society, 277
American Wholesale Corporation, 86
animal
  fat tallow, 150
  prints, 240
  powered toys, 302
animals, 281
  animated, 303
antique
  dealer, ix
  publications, ix–x, 324
Antonius Stradivarius Cremonensis Faciebat Anno 1734, 293
Apostle spoon, 168, 169
apple peeler, 283, 284
applied glass decorations, 61
appliquéd quilt, 208, 210
appraisal, x
Appraisers Association of America, x
Argand, Aimé, 152
Argand lamps, 147, 152
"armorial" china, 19
Armstrong Glass Company, mark, 81
art pottery, American, 32–36
Art Prices Current, 240
artware, 36
asphaltum, 197
Astor Company, 294
Atlantic and Pacific Tea Company, 55
Atterbury and Company, 69
Atterbury Glass Company, 73
auctions, ix
Audubon prints, 265, 266
Aurene glass, 58, 59
Austria, bisque, 42
Austria, glass, 59
automobiles, 305
Aynsely, Chelsea-grape pattern, 17

Babbitt and Crossman Company, 194
baby feeding bottle, 111
Bach, Martin, Sr., 58
Bache silhouettes, 267
bail handle with escutcheon, 120
Bakewell, Pears and Company, 69
ball-and-claw foot, 122
balloon ascension print, 265
Baltimore assay mark, 163, 164
bamboo, 141
banana stand, 95
banded creamware. *See* mocha ware
banjo clocks, 204
banks, 283, 306, 307
  cast iron, 304
  mechanical, 303
banquet lamps, 153
"Barbara Frietchie" (songs), 296
barbed wire, 286
  fencing, 286
Barberini vase, 83
basalt, black, 7, 21
baseball cards, 291
batch (materials for glass), 56
Battenburg work, 228
Baxter print, 265
bayberry, 150
Beadle, Irwin P. and Co., 291
bed
  brass, 142
  rope, 142
beeswax, 150
Belleek, 36, 37
  Irish, 37
Belleek-Fermanagh, 37
bells, 295, 303
Belter, John, 129
Bennett, Edwin and William, 32
Bennington pottery, 32, 33, 41
  bibliography, 53
Bergen, J. D., 86
Bergonzi, Carlo, 294
besser, 149

"Better Homes Bureau," 86
Betty lamp, 147, 148, 149
betyng, 149
bibles, 290
bibliography, general, 325–327
Big Little books, 291
Bing and Grondahl, 43
Bininger bottles, 107
bird illustrations, 290
Birks (of Minton), 46
biscuit porcelain, 44
biscuit ware, 41, 42
bisque, 41, 42
bisque-headed doll, 310
bitters bottles, 108–110
black basalt, 7, 21
black milk glass, 73
"bleeding blue," 12
bleeding bowl, 180
Blickensderfer typewriter, 285
blocked tin, 197
blocks, 298
blown glass, 73
blown molded glass, 56
blown three mold glass, 56
blue milk glass, 73
blue-printed earthenware, 7
blue slag, 74
Blue and White Society of Deerfield, 227
board games, 299
boards, wide (cabinetmaking), 135, 136
"boar's head" platter, 191, 192
Boch, Jean François, 26
Bohemia, 61, 70
Bohemian glass, 83, 94
bone china, 4, 21, 36, 42
bone dishes, 42
"bonnet" highboy, 120
books, 290–292
  bibliography, 292
  price guide bibliography, 321, 322
Booz bottles, 108
Borden, George L., 87
border designs, on china, 9–11
Borgfeldt, George, and Company, 87
Boston and Sandwich glass, 67
Boston and Sandwich Glass Company, 69, 70, 72, 73, 75, 76, 78, 95
Boston and Sandwich Glass Works, 65
Bostwick and Burgess Manufacturing Company, 205
bottle tickets, 181
bottles, 100–116, 279, 283
  age, 106
  bibliography, 115–116
  bitters, 108–110
  colors, 105, 106
  household, 110–112
  labels, viii, 106
  lips and tops, 101, 102, 103, 104
  manufacture, 100–101
  name in glass, 109
  shapes, 106, 114
  value, 105, 106
bottoms and bases, bottles, 104
Bouillotte lamp, 156
Bourgoing, Baron de, 45
boxes, 279, 281
braided rugs, 230
brass beds, 142
brass candlesticks, 151
brass chandelier, 159
brasses, big, 122
brazier, 179
"Brazil silver," 187
bread mold, 286
bread trays, pressed glass, 79
breadboard top, 142
Brewster chair, 118
Brianchon china, 37
bride's basket, 94
Brigham, Clarence, 276
"brilliant cut" diamond, 237
Brilliant period cut glass, 83, 84, 85
Briscoe, Thomas, 198
Britannia, 194
Britannia metal, 164
broadsides, 291
broché (brochet) shawls and fabric, 226
Bromley, William, 37
Brown silhouettes, 267
brown ware, 32
Brownie dolls, 309, 312
Bru French doll, 310
Bryan, William Jennings, 73
bubble pink luster, 17
bubbles, in glass, 83
bubbles, in pressed glass, 75
Buckley, Oliver, 198
Buffalo, N.Y., willow pattern, 20
Buffalo Cut Glass Company, 87
Buffalo pottery, 35
bull's-eye glass, 94
Buntline, Ned, 291
burglar's horror, 156
Burlington Glass Works, 80
Burmese glass, 62
burned wood picture, 270
Burslem Staffordshire, 8
buses, toy, 303
Buster Brown, 309
Butler, Aaron, 198
Butler, Ann, 198
Butler, B. Minerva, 198
butter dish, 186
butter knife, 186
butter mold, 286
butter pats, 42
"buttermilk" glass, 72
button rugs, 230
buying antiques, ix–x

C. Dorflinger & Sons, Inc., 87
C. F. Monroe Company, 70
C. G. Alford & Company, 86
cabbage chopper, 283
cabinets, store, 281, 283
cabriole leg, 120
Cadogan pot, 47
calendar plates, 42

calligraphy, 269
Cambridge Glass Company, mark, 81
cameo, 236
cameo glass, 61, 68, 69, 83
  American, 69
campaign tokens, x, 316, 317
Campbell kids, 309
camphene, 147, 152
camphor glass, 73
can labels, 280, 291
Canadian pressed glass, 80
Canadian silver marks, 163
"canary" (Vaseline) glass, 72
candle chandelier, 160
candleholder, 154, 156
candleholder clamps, 149
candleholder clips, 149
candlepower, 150
candles, 147, 150, 154, 157, 159
candlestand, 154
candlesticks, 147, 150, 154, 155, 171, 172, 173
candlewood, 147, 149
caneware, 21
Canfield & Brothers, 150
canned food, 280
canning jar, 73
cans, 279, 281, 283
Canton ware, 19
canvas sampler, 222
Capo di Monte mark, 49
Captain Fury, 291
caramel glass, 74
caramel slag, 74
card table, 120
carder, 74
Carder, Frederick, 58
Carder glass, 58, 59
cards, playing, 308, 309
carnelian, 236
Carner, Captain John, 149
carnival colors, 59
carnival glass, 55, 56
carpet ball, 308
carpets, 232, 233
Carter, Nick, 291
Carver chair, 118
cased, cut glass, 84
cased glass, 67
cast iron apple peeler, 284
cast iron toys, 302, 304, 305
casters, furniture, 142
castle mark, 26, 27
castor sets, 183, 184
catalogs, 290, 291
cathedral castor, 183
Caughley willow pattern, 20
cauliflower ware, 21
Centennial, Philadelphia, 229
Centennial Exhibition, 84
center seam, coverlet, 213
Central Glass Company, 77
ceramic art pottery, 37
chafing dish, 179
chair, Pennsylvania painted, characteristics, 132
chairs, styles pictured, 133, 134
Challinor Taylor Company, 74
chamberstick, 150, 154
chandelier, 147, 159, 160
  tin, 199
Chandler, John Greene, 312
Chauncey, Jerome, shelf clock, 204
Chelsea mark, 49
Chelsea-grape pattern, 17
Chelsea Keramic Art Works, 34
Chelsea Pottery, U.S., 34
Cheney, Benjamin, 203
cherry pitter, 283
chest-on-chest, 122
Chiantel Fondeur 1878 Saignelegier bell, 295
children's alphabet plates, 42
china. *See* pottery, porcelain
china-headed doll, 309–310
China trade, gray body, 19
  porcelain, 18–19
  porcelain designs, 18–19
Chinese export, 13, 18, 19. *See also* China trade
  porcelain, bibliography, 51, 52
chintz, 209
Chippendale, 123
  chair, 134
  chair, characteristics, 122
  furniture, 121, 122
Chippendale, Thomas, 121
chocolate milk glass, 73
chocolate pot, 173
choker necklace, 238
chopper, 283
Christmas plates, 43
Christmas seals, 291
Christopher Columbus clock, 205
chromolith ware, 27
cigar labels, 291
cigar-store Indian, 281
cigarette-smoking men, 305
Cincinnati Britannia Company, 193
circular disk cards, music box, 295
circus
  posters, 291
  toys, 305
  wagons, 305
city directories, 290
Civil War prints, 240
clambroth, 72, 73
Clark, T. B., and Co., Inc., 87
"Clark Company O.N.T.," 281
Clarke Company, England, 155
clay marbles, 307–308
Climax washing machine, 287
clock-shaped bottle, 108
clocks, 202–207
  bibliography, 207
  dials, 202
clockwork toys, 305, 307
cloth toys, 305
clowns, 281
coal oil, 153
coal-scuttle mugs, 43

Coalport, willow pattern, 17, 20
coat of arms, 19
cobalt, 12, 13
coffee
  can, 43
  cups, giant size, 4
  grinders, 283
  mills, 283
coffeepot, 173, 174, 193
"coffeepot" era, 191
coin
  jewelry, 315
  pattern, 76, 77
  silver, 163–164
"coin" mark on silver, 164
coins, bibliography, 320
collectors' groups, 327–330
Colorado Springs, Colorado, 36
colored glass, 56, 71–74, 84
"Columbia Shield" pressed glass, 79
"Columbian" coin glass, 77
comb, 295
"comfort" chair, 131
comforter, 9
comic books, 290, 291
comic strip toys, 305
company names, viii
condiment box, 96
Conestoga wagon, 301
Connecticut tin, 198
copper wheel engraving, 84
copyright law, 241
coral, 236
coralene, 60, 61, 62
corner chair, 120
Corning, New York, glass, 86
Corona Cut Glass Company, 87
coronation cup, 43
cotton cloth, 209
cottonseeds in quilt, 208
country furniture, 117, 126, 130
country name on silver, 164
country of origin, 1
country store, 279, 281, 283
coverlet
  makers, 214–221
  woolen, 210
  woven, 211–221
cow creamer, 32
cowbell, 295
crackle glass, 70
cranberry glass, 72
Crandall, Benjamin Potter, 301
crates, 281
craze, in old glazes, 9
crazy quilt, 209
cream pitchers, 176–177
creamware, 23
cresoline lamp, 157, 158
crewel, 229
Cricket, rocking horse, 301
"Cries of London," 265
crimping, 57
Critalleries de Baccarat, 65
crocheted rugs, 232
Crosby, Nichols and Company, 312
Crosley mosaic, 228
cross-hatch decoration, glass, 84
crossed sword, 49
crossed swords mark, 25–26
crown glass, 94
Crown Milano glass, 62
crown top, 102, 105
crowned circle, 49
cruet, 72, 95, 96
Cruikshank, George, 17
crystal chandelier, 160
Crystolene Cut Glass Company, 87
cuckoo clocks, 205
cup shapes, 4
Currier and Ives, 241–243
  reprints, 243
Curtis, Lemuel, 204
custard glass, 72–73, 74
cut glass, 57, 83–91
  basket, 94
  bells, 295
  bibliography, 99
  care, 86
  difference from pressed glass, 83
  marks, 86–91
  patterns, 83–84
cutout paper, 267
cylinder box, 295

Daguerre, Louis Jacques Mandé, 272
daguerreotype cases, 274
daguerreotypes, 272–273
Daily Citizen, 278
"Daisy" pressed glass, 76
"Daisy and Button" pressed glass, 76–78
Dalzell, Gilmore and Leighton Company, 71
dancing figures, 305
date letter hallmark, 162–163
Daum, Auguste and Antonin, 69
Daum, Nancy, 69
Davenport factory, 20
Day silhouettes, 267
daybed, 120
Deadwood Dick, 291
dealers, antique, ix–x
"dearest" jewelry, 157
"dearest" lamp, 157
decals, 4
decanter labels, 181
decoration, glass, 57
  pottery and porcelain, 4
Dedham pottery, 34
Deerfield blue embroidery, 226–227
deerskin rugs, 230
Deidrick Glass Company, 87
Deldare ware, 35
Delft, 5
  bibliography, 50
Denmark, 45
detective magazines, 291
  stories, 291
Detroit, 36
Dewey, Admiral, 73

"Diamond Finish" mark on glass, 90
Diamond Glass Company mark, 81
diamond-shaped mark. *See* registry mark
diamonds, 236, 237
"DiamonKut" mark on glass, 89
dime novels, 290, 291
Dionne quintuplet doll, 309
directories, 290
dishwasher, 49
doll head, 309
  furniture, 298
dolls, viii, 298–299, 309–313
  bibliography, 314
Dorflinger, C., & Sons, Inc., 87
Doring, Ernest, 293
double cloth weave coverlet, 211, 212
double-woven geometric coverlet, 212–213
dovetailing, 135, 139, 140
Drake, Colonel Edwin L., 153
dredging box, 96
Dresden (Meissen), 25
drums, 295
Dugan Glass Company, mark, 81
Dulciphone, 297
Duncan Phyfe. *See* Phyfe, Duncan
Durand, Victor, 58
Durand glass, 58
duster, 96
Dutch majolica, 6
dye, 212

E. Woods and Sons, 30
"EPNS" mark on silver, 164
"EPWM" mark on silver, 164
early period cut glass, 83, 84
earring backs, 238
East Liverpool, Ohio, lotus ware, 36
Easter seals, 291
Eastlake, 130
Edison phonographs, 296
Édouart, Auguste, 266–267
egg frame, 186
eggbeaters, ix, 283
Egginton, O. F., Company, 87
"églomisé," 271
Egyptian scene on glass, 62
Eichholtz, Jacob, 198
"800" mark on silver, 165
1847 Rogers Brothers Company, 194–195
electricity, 147
electroplate, 164
Elgin watch, 206
elongated coins, 315
embossed letters on bottles, 105
embroidered rugs, 230, 231, 232
embroidered shawls, 225
Empire Cut Glass Company, 87
Empire furniture, 126–128
enamel on glass, 61
encyclopedias, 290
End of Day glass, 67
England, 5, 9, 12, 18, 45, 61, 70, 83
English majolica, 6
  registry mark, 2, 3
  wares for the American market, 27–31
engraved
  decorations, 84
  glass, 57
engraving, 240
Enoch Wood and Sons, 7
Enterprise No. 1 Store Mill, 283
epergne, 182
Eschinard, Franchesco, 273
etching, 240
  glass, 57
Etruscan majolica, 6
Excelsior Glass Company, 80
extension table, 123

"F" mark on glass, 82
"fairings," 44
Fairmont Glass Works, mark, 82
fairs, 27
fairy candle, 155
fairy lamp, 147, 155
Fast Grinder coffee mill, 283
fat lamp, 155
"Favrile," 58
Federal period, 125
  furniture, 127–129
Felix the cat, 312
Fenton, England, pot lids, 46
Fenton Art Glass Company, 59
ferrotype, 272
figural bottles, 112
figure, wooden, 301
filigree, 235
Filley, Harvey, 198
Findlay, Ohio, glass, 71, 79
fire
  buckets, 318
  engine, 302, 303, 305
  fighting equipment, 318
firemark, 318–319
  bibliography, 320
first editions, 290
fish plates, 44
fish slice, 170–171
"flame" mark, 33
flashed
  cut glass, 84
  glass, 72
  glassware, 65
flat wick burner, 151
"flatbacks," 9
flow blue, 12, 14
flower illustrations, 290
flower prints, 240
flute cutting, 84
flycatcher, 284
flytrap, 283
foil, glass painting, 272
food-named glasswares, 72–74
foot, unglazed, 3
foot rim, 3
forks, 158, 165
"Four Petal" glass, 55
France, 45, 61, 70, 75
Franklin, Benjamin, 8
free blowing (of glassware), 75

freeblown glass, 56, 100
Frost, Edward, 230
frozen Charlotte doll, 311
"Fry" glass mark, 88
fuel, lamp, 146
furniture, 117–146
  bibliography, 144–146
  care, 143
  construction, 135–140
  doll, 298, 304
  price guide, 322
  wear, 136

"GSH," 6
Gallé, Emile, 68–69
Gallowy, Elijah, 233
game plates, 44
games, 298, 299
  board, 298
garnet, 237
gas (coal), 147
gateleg table, 118, 120
Gates pottery, 36
gather, 56
"Gaudy Dutch," 14, 30–31
"Gaudy ironstone," 14
"Gaudy Welsh," 14, 30, 31
Gazette, 277
geography books, 290
George Borgfeldt & Company, 87
George Washington's hatchet, 320
German flint glass, 83
"German silver," 187
Germany, 5, 70
Gibson Girl, 297
Gilbert flycatcher, 284
gill (measure), 192
Gillinder and Sons, 78
Girandole clock, 204
"Give us this day our daily bread" on pressed glass, 79
glass, 55–99
  bells, 295
  bibliography, 97
  care, 96
  chimney, 152
  decoration, 75
  definitions, 56, 57
  painting, 271, 272
  price guide, 322–323
  reproduced, 56
  signs, 282
Glomi, Jean, 271
"glorification" of furniture, 140
"glorified" silver, 162
Godey print, 265
Godey's Lady's Book, 312
Godey's Magazine, 271
gold anchor, 49
gold cans, 315
gold glass, 71
gold leaf on glass, 61
Golden Agate glass, 80
Golden Glow glass, 86
goldstone, 237
"Gone with the Wind" lamp, 153
gong, 303
Good Housekeeping, 313
Gorham Manufacturing Company, 168
Gothic panel bottle, 111
gramophone, 295
grandfather clock, 202
Grandmother Chelsea-grape pattern, 17
grandmother's clock, 203
"granite ware," 13, 32
"grape" pressed glass, 76
Grapenuts, 281, 282
"gravure découpée," 268
gravy ladle, 186
gray earthenware, 34
grease, 147
grease lamp, 148, 149
Greek revival, 128
Greenaway, Kate, 312
Gregory, Mary. *See* Mary Gregory
Gregory, Winifred, 276
Greiner doll, 310
Griffin, Smith and Hill majolica, 6
grinder, 283
grocery store, 298
Grueby Faience Company, 36
Guarnerius, Giuseppe, 294
Guarnerius, Joseph, 294
Gunderson-Pairpoint Works, 63
Gunderson peachblow, 63–64
gunpowder can, 281
guns, cap, 304

"H," glass mark, 88
hair receiver, 71
hair work, 268, 269
hallmarks, 162, 163, 164, 165
Hamilton, Ontario, 80
Hamilton watch, 206
"hand dressing," 136
hand painted, 20
hand-painted plates, 4
Handel, Philip, 158
Handel lamp, 158
handleless cups, 4
handles, 138, 139
Hanley, 8
hardware styles, 138, 139
Harker Pottery Company, 36
Harvey, Isaac A., 36
Harvey Adams and Company, 45
hatchet, George Washington's, 320
hats, glass, 79
Haviland, 37–41, 53, 54
Haviland, David and Daniel, 37
Haviland marks, 38, 39
Hawkes, 88
"Hawley Penna" mark on glass, 89
heavy dish, 3
heavy oils, 147
Heisey and Company, A. H., mark, 82
Hepplewhite, 122–124, 129
Hepplewhite, George and Ann, 122
Hepplewhite chair, 123, 134
Hickory Dickory Dock clock, 205

Higbee, J. B., mark, 82
highboy, 120
Hilpert, Andreas, 313
hinges, 138
Hinsberger Cut Glass Company, 88
historic blue, 14
historic flask, 107
historic Staffordshire, 9
historical societies, viii
history and bibliography of American newspapers, 276
Hitchcock chair, 142
Hitchcock-type furniture, 132
Hoare, J. and Company, 88
Hobbs, Brockunier and Company, 63, 65, 78
Hobbs Glass companies, 77
hobnail, 72, 76
Hoechst, mark, 49
holes, teapot, 4
Holland, 5, 18, 45
Hollins (of Minton), 46
hollow-stem candlestick, 150
hollow ware, 191
Holly Amber, 80
Holmes, Oliver Wendell, 273
Homan and Company, 193
hooked rugs, 230, 231
Hope Glass Works, 88
Horn, phonograph, 295, 296
horse brasses, viii
horsecars, 303
horse-drawn fire engine, 302
horse-drawn iron toys, 304
hot-water dish, 44
hound handle pitcher, 32
house sale, ix
Hughes, Robert, 270
Humphrey Glass Works, 80
hunting scenes, 281
hydrofluoric acid vapor treatment, 60

"I G" mark on glass, 81, 82
ice tongs, 283
imari, 14, 30, 31
Imperial Glass Company, 59, 60, 81, 88
impressed numbers, 3
Indian shawl, 224, 226
Indiana Tumbler Company, 80, 81
Indiana Tumbler and Goblet Company, 74
Indians, books about, 290
initial, hallmark, 163
ink bottle, 112
Ink Stand Company, 92
inlay, 120
insurance, x
inventions, 290
iridescent glass, 57–60
iron, 287
iron candlestick, 150
iron pan, 284
iron toys, 302, 304
iron trains, 305
irons, 304
ironstone, 4, 12, 13, 14, 15
ironstone (*Cont.*)
  American, 14
  bibliography, 51
  dating, 14
  patterns, 14
  white, 15
"Irving," mark on glass, 88
Irwin P. Beadle and Co., 291

J. B. Higbee, mark, 82
"J and P Coates Spool Cotton," 281
jack-in-the-pulpit vase, 94
Jacob Stainer (Steiner), 294
Jacquard coverlet, 213
Japanese willow pattern, 20
japanned ware (*See also* tin), 197
jasper, German copies, 21
jasper ware, 7, 21, 23, 81
Jefferson Glass Company mark, 82
Jerome, Chauncey, 206
"Jersey turtle" paperweight, 92
jet, 237, 238
jewelry, 235–239
  appraisal, 235
  bibliography, 239
  made from coins, 315
  marks, 235
Jumeau doll, 310

KPF mark, 26
KPM mark, 26
KTK lotus ware, 36
Kamm, Minnie Watson, 76
Kashmir, 225
Kellogg and Bulkley Co., 282
Kelva glassware, 70, 71
kerosene, 147, 153
kerosene lamp, 153, 155
kettle lamp, 146
Kew Blas, 58
Kewpie doll, 311, 312
Kier, Samuel M., 153
Kin coffee mills, 283
king's head hallmark, 162, 163
Kingston, New York, *Gazette*, 277
Kinnear patent lamp, 146
Kircher, Athanasius, 273
kitchen utensil, 284, 303
kitchens, 303
"Koh-I-Noor" mark on glass, 89
knife rest, 84, 186
knives, 165, 168
knotty pine, 136
Knowles, Homer, 36
Knowles, Isaac W., 36
Knowles, Taylor, and Knowles, 36, 37
"Krystal Krafters," 87
"Krys-Tol," 82
kyal, 156

L.C.T., 158
LTD, 1
La Belle Glass Works, 72
label, 279, 280, 291, 298
labels on bottles, 106
lacemaker's lamp, 157

lacquered furniture, 142
lacy pressed glass, 75, 76
ladderback chair, 141
Ladies' Home Journal, 312
lamp, 72
Langenheim, Fred, 273
Lansburgh & Bro., 88
lard oil, 147, 152
lazy Susan table, 142
lead glass, 83
lead poisoning, 196
lead soldiers. *See* tin soldiers
  bibliography, 314
lead toys, 302
leaded glass shade, 147
leaf carved handle, 130
leather fire buckets, 318
Lee, Ruth Webb, 76
Leeds, 16, 17, 19, 28, 44
Lenox, Walter Scott, 37
leopard's head hallmark, 162, 163
Libbey, 85
Libbey mark on glass, 89
"Liberty Bell" pressed glass, 79
lid, teapot, 4
light bulbs, 147, 286
lighthouse coffeepot, 198
lighting, bibliography, 161
lighting devices, 147–161
Lightning coffee mill, 283
lilypad, 57
Limoges, France, 37–41
Limoges marks, 38–41
Lincoln, Abraham, 277
linoleum, 233
linsey-woolsey, 210
lion, hallmark, 162, 163
"Lion" pressed glass, 76, 77
lion and unicorn, 15
lips, bottles, 101, 102, 103, 104
lithograph, ix, 240, 297
lithographed
  boxes, 299
  signs, 282
  tin, 279
lithopane, 44
Locke, Joseph, 64, 67
locket, 238, 239
locomotives, 303
Loetz glass, 59
Lonhuda, 36
loopings, 57
Lord's Supper bread tray, 79
"Lotus" mark on glass, 89
Lotus ware, 36, 37
Louwelsa, 35, 36
love stories, 291
loving cups, xiii
Lowestoft, 18, 19. *See also* china trade porcelain
Lowestoft, England, 18, 19
luster, 14, 15, 16, 17
  bibliography, 51
  care, 17
  colors, 15, 16
luster (*Cont.*)
  dating, 16
  pearly, 15, 16
  pink, 16
lusters, 154
lusterware, 21
Lyman and Fenton, 32
"Lyons" mark on glass, 89
lyre-shaped pedestal, 125, 126

M P M mark, 26
McCall's, 313
McGuffey, William Holmes, 290
McGuffey Reader, 290, 291
McKanna Cut Glass Company, 89
McKee Glass Company, 82
McKee-Jeannette Glass Works, 89
machine sewing, 212
machine stitching, 310
"made in England," 1
magazine, 291
Maggini, Giovanni Paolo, 293
magic lantern slides, 273
magnet to detect brass, 135
mail-order antiques, ix, x
majolica, 4, 5, 6, 21
  bibliography, 50
  Victorian, 6
Mallett's Index of Artists, 240
mantel clocks, 204
manuscript, 290
Maple City Glass Company, 87
marble glass, 74
marble tops, 130
marbles, 307, 308
marine print, 265
marked china, vii
  glass, vii
  pewter, vii
  silver, vii
marks, vii, viii, 49
  carnival glass, 60
  forged, 49
  majolica, 6
  Mason's, 13
  Meissen, 25
  Mettlach, 49
  peacock on blue slag glass, 74
  pewter, 190, 191, 196
  pottery and porcelain, 1, 3
  pottery and porcelain, bibliography, 50
  pressed glass "I G," 81
  Rookwood, 33, 34
  silver, 162–165
  Spode, 49
  Tiffany glass, 57, 58
marquetry, 120
"married" furniture, 136
Martin's Ferry, Ohio, 59, 60
Mary Gregory, 69, 70
Mary Todd doll, 311
Maryland, 30, 75
Mason
  Charles James, 13
  John, 96
  Miles, 13, 14

Mason jar, 110
match dishes, glass, xii
matchbook covers, 291
mathematics books, 290
Mayo cut-plug tobacco, 281
Mead, John, 194
mechanical banks, 307
Meissen, 5, 25, 26, 49
  bibliography, 52
  colors, 25
  copies, 25
  dating, 25
  factory, 25
  Germany, 18, 45
Mellor (of Minton), 46
melodeons, 297
memorabilia, 291
mercury glass, 71
Meriden Britannia Company, 195
Meriden Cut Glass Company, 89
Merrimac Ceramic Company, 36
Merriwell, Frank, 291
merry-go-round, 305
metal
  boxes, 279
  clock works, 203
  disk, 295
  glass term, 56
  toy, repaint, 307
  toys, 298, 302
Mettlach, 3, 26, 27
  mark, 27
  steins, 26, 27
Middle period cut glass, 83, 84
Midwest glass, 76
milk bottles, 110
milk glass, 73, 74
  jars, 112
mill lamp, 156
millefiori, 91, 92
milliner's model, 311
Millville Rose, 92
miniatures, 182
Minton, 20, 46
Mission furniture, 130
mocha ware, 27, 28
  marks, 28
Model Flint Glass Company, 79
mold, 286
mold-blown bottles, 100
mold-blown glass, 73
mold seams, 100
money, 298, 315
Monopoly, 298
Monroe Company, C. F., 70
Monteith bowl, 178, 179
moonstone, 238
Moravian Pottery and Tile Works, 36
Morgan (of Minton), 46
morning glory horn (phonograph), 296
Morris, William, 130
mosaic ware, 27
Moss Rose china, 45
mote spoon, 169, 170
mother-of-pearl, 60, 61, 62
moulding plane, 287
Moulton, Ebenezer, 180
"Mt. W. G. Co." mark on glass, 89
Mt. Washington Glass Company, 60, 61, 62, 64, 65, 69
mourning jewelry, 238
mouse trap, 283
moustache cup, 45
moving toys, 305
Murr, Richard, 89
mushroom-turned wooden knobs, 130
music, 293–297
  bibliography, 297
  box, 294
  sheet, 297
mustard pot, 180
Mutascope, 273

"N" and crown, 49
"N" mark on glass, 73, 82
"Nacre," 37
nails, 137
Nailsea, 57
Nakara glassware, 70, 71
Nanking china, 19
Napanee Glass House, 80
napkin ring, 184, 185
Nash, J., 265
Neale and Company, 8
"Near-Cut" mark on glass, 81
neck shapes, 112, 113
needle painting, 227
needlework, 208–235
  bibliography, 234
  quality, 208
Negro, 281, 306
Negro mammies, 281
Netherlands, 12
New England Glass Company, 63, 65, 66, 69, 75, 84, 95
New York *Herald,* 277
New York *Morning Post,* 277
Newcastle pink luster, 16
Newcomb Art Pottery, 36
newspapers, 276–278
nickelodeon, 296
Nippon, mark, 49
Noritake ware, 49
Northwood, cameo glass, 69
Northwood Company, 74
Northwood Glass Company, 59, 60
Norton, 32
Nova Scotia Glass Company, 80
novel, 291
novelties, glass, 79
"Nucut" mark on glass, 82, 88
numismatic terms, 315
nutbowl, 186
nutmeg grater, viii
nutmeg lamp, 153
Nutting prints, 265

O. F. Egginton Company, 87
O.N.T., 281
O'Connor, J. S., 89

O'Donnell bottle, 111
offhand blown glass, 56
O'Flyn, J., 282
Ohio Flint Glass Company, mark, 82
oil lamps, 153
Old King Cole Papier Mache Works, 281
"old mine" diamond, 237
one wick candle, 155
O'Neill, Rose, 311
onion pattern Meissen, 26
opal glass, 73
"opaque porcelain," 13
opaque pottery, 5
open salts, 95, 96
orange spoon, 169
"Oregon silver," 187
organs, 296, 297
  reed, 297
Oriental rug, 232
Ott and Brewer, 37
oval brasses, 124, 126
overlay, 72
  glass, 93
overshot weave, coverlet, 211, 212
oxblood, 34

padfoot, 120
painted
  boxes, 279
  clock dials, 202
  floor, 232, 233
  furniture, 132
  metal toys, 307
  tin, 197–201
  tin, colors, 197
  tin, history, 197–199
  tin toys, 305
  tinware, 279
  wood toys, 305
paintings and pictures, 240–275
Pairpoint Manufacturing Company, 71
Paisley, Scotland, 225
paisley design, history, 224–225
paisley design, meaning, 225
paisley shawl, 222–226
paisley shawl, dating, 226
Palissy, Bernard, majolica, 6
paper, 276, 297
  antiques, 276–278
papers, bibliography, 278
  can labels, 291
  care, 278
  clock dial, 202
  doll, 312
  filigree work, 268
  labels, 279, 280, 281
  pictures, 267, 268
  signs, 282
paperweight decoration, 57
paperweights, 91–93
  bibliography, 99
papier-mâché
  cigar store figures, 281
  clock case, 204
Parian, 32, 36, 46
"Parisian granite," 13
pastor's lamp, 156
patchwork quilt, 208–209
pâté sur pâté, 46
patent, viii
pattern molded, 56
Pattison, William and Edward, 198
Pauline Pottery, 36
peachblow, 63–64, 70
Peale, Charles Willson, 266
"Peale Museum," 266
pearl satin glass, 60, 61
peeler, 283
peg lamp, 155
Penn, William, 281
pennies, elongated, 315
Pennsylvania Dutch ware, 29
Pennsylvania tinware, 198
perfume bottle lamp, 156
perfume lamp, 156
Persian shawl, 226
Peter Cooper rocker, 134
Peterson print, 265
Pewabic pottery, 36
pewter, 190–196
  bibliography, 196
  care, 190
  maker, viii
  mark, 194
  quality, 190
  shape, 192
  toys, 302
Philadelphia Centennial, 78
Philadelphia "peanut," 122
Phoebe lamp, 147, 149, 150
Phoenix, 304
phonograph, 296
phonograph records, 295
photographs, 273
Phyfe, Duncan, 126, 127
piano, 296–297
pickle castor, 184
Pictorial Review, 313
pictures, 240–275
pieced quilt, 208, 209, 210
piecrust table, 122
pierced tin, 199–201
  how to tell age, 200
piggin, 287
"Pilgrim century," 118
pillar-and-scroll case clock, 204
pinchbeck, 235, 236
pine splint, 147
pink slag, 74
pinprick pictures, 268, 269
pitcher, water, silver, 149, 180
plane, 287
plaster statue, 318–320
plate, 165
"plate" mark on silverplate, 164
plate shape for dating, 14
plated amberina, 65, 66
platinum, 236
Platt, Mrs., 270
play, 298

player piano, 296
playing cards, ix, 308, 309
  bibliography, 314
  price guide, 323
Plymouth rock paperweight, 92
pocket sundial, 206, 207
Poillon pottery, 36
poison bottle, 112
policemen, 281, 302
Polo, Marco, 18
"polychrome" delft, 5
Pomona, 66, 67
pontil, 56
pontil mark, 56, 104
  paperweights, 93
Pontypool ware (*See* also tin), 197
poodles, Staffordshire, 9
Pope Cut Glass Company, 89
porcelain, 1–54
  discovery of, 18
  -lined silver pot, 165
  stopper, 105
porringer, 180, 192, 193, 194
Portland vase, 83
Portneuf, 29, 30
portrait figures, 9
  Staffordshire, 8
portraits, 240
postcards, price guide, 323
pot lids, 46
pottery, 1–54
  and porcelain, bibliography, 50–54
  and porcelain, care, 49
  and porcelain, differences, 4, 5
Pratt, F. and R., Company, 46
Pratt, Felix, 46
Premier coffee mill, 283
"premium" mark on silver, 164
"Prescut" mark on glass, 82, 89
pressed glass, ix, 57, 73, 75–82
  Canadian, 80
  carnival, 59, 60
  designs, 75–77
  factories, 76
  molds, 75
  pattern cycle, 76
  price guide, bibliography, 321–323
  reproduction, 77–79
  salts, 95, 96
pricket candleholder, 151, 159, 160
Prince Albert, 8
printed Staffordshire, 9–12
printmakers' names, 240, 241, 244–264, 265
prints
  color, 313
  paintings, bibliography, 275
  pictures, paintings, 240–275
  price guide, 323
prunts, 57
punch bowl, 178
punched tin, 199
punty rod, 56, 100
purple glass from exposure to sun, 93
purple slag, 74
puzzle jug, 47
"quadruple" mark on silverplate, 164
"Quaker City" glass mark, 90
"quality" mark on silver, 164
Queen Anne chair, characteristics, 120, 121
Queen Anne furniture, 120
Queen coffee mill, 283
queensware, 21, 23
Quezal glass, 58
quillwork, 268
quilts, 208–212
  all white, 208, 210
  crazy, 209, 210
  design, 208, 209, 210
  friendship, 210
  red and green, 210
  size, 210
Quintal, 47

rabbi's lamp, 156, 157
"radiant crystal" mark on glass, 91
rainbow satin glass, 61
railroad passes, 291
railroad train, 303
Raphael Tuck paper dolls, 313
rattail spoon, 165
rattle, 181
Reader's Guide, viii
"Rebecca at the Well," 32
records, 295
rectangular panel construction, 117, 118
red bisque, 34
red slag, 74, 75
redbud onion, 26
redware, 21
Reed and Barton Company, 194
reed organs, 297
reeded leg, 126
Regina music box, 294
registry marks, 2, 3
  English, 24
registry Patent Office design, 3
"Rekston," mark, 36
religious prints, 240
Rembrandt tankard, 192
repainted chair, 132
replating silver, 187
reservoir (fuel), 151
resinous wood, 149
resonance, glass, 83
restrike, 243
Revere, Paul, 162, 170, 172, 265
reverse painting, 271, 272
Rhead (of Minton), 46
Rice (of Minton), 46
Ridout, George, 172
Riley, Gaudy Dutch, 30
rim, plate, 3
Robertson and Sons, 34
rock crystal, 238
rocker, spring type, 143
rocking chair, 301
rocking horses, 298, 301
Rogers, Gaudy Dutch, 30
Rogers, John, 318, 319, 320
Rogers, William, 194

Roly Poly, 280, 281, 301
rookwood, 3, 33, 34, 35
rope beds, 142
rose amber, 64, 65
rose bowls, 64
"rose cut" diamond, 237
"Rose in Snow" pressed glass, 76
Roseville Pottery Company, 36
round ball, 133
"round ball" on furniture, 119, 120
round clock dials, 202
Rouse, G., wax portraits, 270
"Royal Bayreuth," 48
Royal
  coffee mills, 283
  Copenhagen, 41, 43
  Doulton, 49
  Flemish, 62, 63
rubena crystal, 65
rubena verde, 65
ruby amber, 65
ruby glass, 72
rugs, 229–232
rung, chair, 141
rush mats, 230
rushlight, 149
rushlight holder, 150

"S" mark on glass, 90
sadware, 191
Salt, Ralph, 8
saltglaze, 47, 48
St. Johns, Quebec, 80
Saint-Louis, France, 91
salt shaker, 95, 96
sampler, 221–222
  dated, 221, 222
  designs, 222
  fabric, 222
  shape, 222
Samuel Alcock and Company, 32
sand pictures, 270
Sanders (of Minton), 46
Sandwich. *See* Boston and Sandwich
satin glass, 60–62
sauceboat, 178
"saucering," 4
Savage, Doc, 291
saw marks, 136
Saxe Meissen, 25
Schlick, Benjamin, 155
school bell, 295
school textbooks, 290
scoop, 287
Scotch stone jewelry, 239
screws, 135, 136, 137
scroddle, 32
seal of Great Britain, 15
seal of United States, 15
seals, Christmas and Easter, 291
Sears, Roebuck catalogue, 291
secret drawers, 120
selling antiques, ix
"semi-china," 13
"semi-porcelain," 13
Seneca Glass Company, mark, 82
Sèvres, 46
sewing machines, vii
sewing table, 123, 124
Shadow, The, 291
Shakers, 280
Shakespearean figures, 8
shaving mug, 48
sheet music, 296, 297
Sheffield silver, 164
shelf clock, 204
Sheraton, 129
  furniture, 124–126
  and Hepplewhite compared, 125, 126
  Thomas, 124
Shirley, Frederick, 62
shoe buckles, 238
shoemaker's lamp, 157
shoes, glass, 79
shredder, 283
"Siberian silver," 187
Sicard, 36
"sick" glass, 86
sideboard, 124, 125
sifter, 96
signs, 281
silhouettes, 265–267
"Silvart," 87
silver, 162–189
  bibliography, 188–189
  candlesticks, 151
  care, 187
  forms, 165
  jewelry, 238–239
  locket, 238–239
  marks, 162–165
  plate, x, 164
  "Siberian," 187
silvered glass, 71
silversmith, viii
Simon and Halbig, 310
"Sinclaire" mark on glass, 90
slag, 74, 75
slant-top desk, 120
sleds, 298, 305
sleigh bell, 295
slot machine, 309
slut, 154
Smith, Hamilton L., 272
Smith, Nathan, 233
Smith, Sampson, 9
Smith Fife and Company, 31
Smith and Stonesifer patent lamp, 146
"snow" paperweight, 93
soap dish, 287
sofa, 122
Solon, Marc Louis, 46
Somers Brothers, 279
Somerville, Massachusetts, 58
Sommerville Glass Works, 86
"Songs of the War," 296
soup tureen, 178
souvenir spoons, 187
Sowerby's Ellison Glass Works, Ltd., 65
Sowerly Glass Works of England, 74

Spain, 5, 15
spangled glass, 67
"Spanish foot," 120
spark lamp, 155
spattered glass, 67
spatterware, 28, 29
  bibliography, 52
  dating, 29
sperm oil, 151, 152
spermaceti, 150
spice box, 96
spike candleholder, 151
spindles on Windsor chair, 130, 131
splint lights, 149
splints, 149
Spode, 19, 42, 46
sponged ware, 28, 29
spool furniture, 130, 131, 132
  age, 132
spoon, handle, 168
spoon, shape of bowl, 165–167
spoons, 165–170
sporting prints, 265
sports figures, 281
Sprague, W. S., 232
spring candlestick, 150
spring horse, 301
spur marks, 3
square-headed nails, 137
Staffordshire, 7–12, 44
  bibliography, 51
  district, 16
  potteries, 29
  potters, 30
  pottery, 46
  printed, bibliography, 51
  -type ware, 32
stagecoaches, 303
stained dishes, 49
Stainer, Jacob, 294
stamps, 291
Standard Cut Glass Company, 90
"standard" mark on silver, 164
Star Holly, 81
steel
  chair, 134
  toys, 302
  trains, 305
Steiner, Jacob, 294
Steiner dolls, 310
stenciled boxes, 279
stencils on tin, 197
stereopticon, 272–274
"sterling" mark on silver, 165
sterling silver quality, 165
Steuben, 58
  glass mark, 90
  Glass Works, 74
Stevengraph, 228, 229
Stevens, J. E., Company, 306
Stevens, Zachariah, 198
Stiegel, Baron, 83, 95
still banks, 307
stilts, on dishes, 3
Stockton Art Pottery Company, 36
Stockton Terra Cotta Company, 36
"stone china," 13
stoneware, 4, 32, 36
  inlaid, 27
stoppers and closures, bottles, 103
stopwatch, 206
store
  boxes, 279
  cabinet, 281
  catalog, 291
  country, 279
  furniture, 281
  signs, 281, 282
  stuff, 279–289
    bibliography, 288–289
Stradivarius, 293, 294
"Straus Cut Glass," mark, 90
stretcher, chair, 121, 122, 124, 141
Stuart period furniture, 117–118
stump work, 227, 228
sucket fork, 168
sugar bowl, 177, 178
sugar shaker, 72
sugar tongs, 171, 173
sulfide paperweight, 92
summer and winter weave, coverlet, 212, 213
sun coloring glass, 93, 94
Sunderland, 16, 17
Sunderland pottery, 68
sundials, 206, 207
sunglow glass, 93, 94
Superior coffee mill, 283
Swift's family coffee mill, 283
swirls, 56, 57
Swiss music box, 294
Switzerland, 70
Sydenham Glass Company, Ltd., 80
Syrian temple shrine glassware, 95

table, lazy Susan, 142
talking machine, 295
tall case clock, 202, 203
Tallis factory, 8, 9
tallow, 150
tambour desk, 123
"Tammany Hall" bank, 306
tan slag, 74
tankard, 181
tapestry china, 48
Tarzan, 291
tax stamps, 291
Taylor, Goodwin and Company, 14
Taylor, John, 36
"Taylor" mark on glass, 90
T. B. Clark & Co., Inc., 87
tea caddy, 173
tea caddy spoon, 170
tea scoop, 173
  service, 172–178
  strainer, 173
  urn, 173, 176
tea-leaf decorations, 14, 15, 17
teapot, 173, 175, 176
  holes, 4

teapot (*Cont.*)
  lid, 4
  shape, 4
  small, 4
teardrop handles, 120
Teddy bear, 312
Teichert, C., 25
Telephone coffee mills, 283
Temple, Shirley, playing cards, 309
  dolls, 309
Terry, Eli, 206
textbooks, 290
Thatcher Brothers, 90
thimble, 239
Thistle pressed glass, 76
Thomas, Seth, 206
thread cabinet, 281, 283
threading, 57, 61
Three Face pressed glass, 76
three-piece mold, 100, 101
Tiffany
  lamp, 158
  red glass, 74
Tiffany, Louis Comfort, 57, 58, 158
Tiffany and Company, 158
tiles, 48
tilt-top table, 120
tin
  bibliography, 201
  boats, 303
  cans, 281
  care, 200
  -glazed pottery, 5
  horn, 295
  railroad train, 303
  signs, 281, 282
  soldiers, 313
  toys, 302, 303
  trains, 305
tins, 279
tinsel picture, 268
tintype, 272, 273
tinware, 197–201
"Tithe Pig, The," 7
tobacco
  tin, 280, 301
Toby jug, 7, 48
toe candlestick, 154
Toft (of Minton), 46
tokens, 317
toleware, 197–201, 279
tongue rugs, 230
tools, 284, 286, 287
  garden, 304
toothpick holder, 186
tops, bottles, 101–104
tortoiseshell glass, 67
toy furniture, 303
toy silver spoon, 169, 170
toymaker, 298
toys, 281, 283, 298–314
  bibliography, 313–314
  dating, 299–300
  metal, 298
  wooden, 298, 301
trade cards, 281, 313
trade dollars, 317
"trademark," 1
trains, 297, 303, 304, 305
transfer designs, 4, 9–11, 20
transfer patterns, black, 17
transfer prints, 14
  with luster, 17
translucent porcelain, 5
trestle table, 118
"triple" mark on silverplate, 164
trivets, 304
Tuck, Raphael, 313
Tucker, Thomas Ellis, 31
turkey work, 227
Turk's head mold, 286
Turner, Thomas, 20
turpentine, 147
Tuthill mark on glass, 90
"22 carat," 4
twin beds, 126
twisted rag wick, 149
two-comb music box, 295
two-wick candle, 155
types of glass, 57–99
typewriter, 285

Ulster County Gazette, 277
umbrella, 239
"Unger Brothers" mark on glass, 90
Union Glass Company, 58
U.S.A.-made pottery and porcelain, 31–37
United States Glass Company mark, 82
U.S. Gramophone Company, 295
United States Pottery Company, 32
upholstered easy chair, 120
upright wick tube, 151
uranium in glass, 72

Vail, R. W. G., 277
valentines, 291
Van Briggle Pottery, 36
"Van Heusen, Charles, Company" mark, 90
"Van Houten" cut glass mark, 91
variants of pressed glass design, 76, 78
Vasa Murrhina, 67
vase-shaped pedestal, 125
vaseline glass, 72
veneer, 120, 141
Venetian glass, 70
"Vicar and Moses, The," 7
Vickers, James, 194
Victoria, Queen, 226
Victorian
  antiques, bibliography, 327
  chair, 134
  furniture, 129, 130
  Staffordshire, 8
Villeroy, Nicholas, 26
Villeroy and Boch, 26
violin, 293
vitascope, 273

wag-on-the-wall clock, 205
wagons, 298, 301, 303
"Waldo" tableware, 187
walking figures, 305
Wall, Dr., viii
wall clocks, 204
wallpaper, 278
walnut, 120
Waltham watch, 206
Walton, Frederick, 233
Walton, John, 8
warming pan, 284
washing machine, 287
"Washington," 8
Washington, George, 277
watch paper, 206
watches, 206
water pitcher, double wall, 182, 183
Waterford, 75
Waterford glass, 83
"watermelon glass," 65
Watson, Lumen, 203
Wavecrest glassware, 70, 71
wax doll, 310, 311
wax portrait, 270, 271
wear, dishes, 4
Webb, Thomas and Sons, 68, 69
Wedgwood, 3, 6, 19, 20, 21–24, 81, 83
  bibliography, 52
  Josiah, 21, 22
  marks, 21–23
Weller, Samuel, 36
Weller pottery, 35, 36
"Westward Ho" pressed glass, 76–78
whale oil, 147, 151, 152
  lamp, 150, 151–152
  peg lamp, 150
whale spermaceti candles, 150
wheat pattern, ironstone, 15
Wheatley, Francis, 265
Wheatstone, Sir Charles, 273
wheel toys, 302, 304
Wheelock, C. E., and Company, 91
Wheildon factory, 6
Wheldon, Thomas, 21
whirligig, 301, 302
whiskey bottles, 107, 108
whistles, 298, 303
whistles and bells, 181
"white granite," 13
whittle marks, 101
Who's Who in American Art, 240
wick, 149
wick pick, 148
wicker furniture, 142, 143
wild rose, 63, 67
Willard, Simon, 204, 206
Willard banjo clocks, 204
Willett's Manufacturing Company, 37
William and Mary furniture, 118, 119, 120
willow pattern, 19–21
  legend, 20, 21
Windsor chair, 130, 131, 141
wire, 286, 287
wire fence, 286
witch ball, 94, 95
wolfhound, 37
Woman's Home Companion, 313
Wood, Aaron, 7
Wood, Enoch, 7
Wood, Ralph, 7
Wood and Caldwell, 7
wood shrinkage, 135
Woodall, cameo glass, 69
woodcut, 240
wooden chandelier, 161
  clockworks, 203
  figure, 301
  moulding plane, 287
  tools, 287
  toys, 298, 301
  wagons, 301
  ware, 287
woods in furniture, 118
woodworking tools, 286
Worcester pottery, viii, 19, 46, 48, 49
Wright, Joseph, 270
Wright, Patience, 270
Wyllie, John, 14

yellow ware, 32
Yusuf, Khwaja, 225

Zobel, Benjamin, 270
Zoetrope, 273